DANTE AND THE GRAMMAR OF THE NURSING BODY

The William and Katherine Devers Series in Dante Studies

Theodore J. Cachey, Jr., and Christian Moevs, editors
Simone Marchesi, associate editor
Ilaria Marchesi, assistant editor

DANTE AND THE

GRAMMAR OF THE

NURSING BODY

Gary P. Cestaro

University of Notre Dame Press
Notre Dame, Indiana

Published by the University of Notre Dame Press
Notre Dame, Indiana 46556
www.undpress.nd.edu

Book design by Nancy Berliner
Set in type by Berliner, Inc., New York, New York
Printed and manufactured in the United States of America by Edwards Brothers

Library of Congress Cataloging-in-Publication Data
Cestaro, Gary P.
Dante and the grammar of the nursing body / Gary P. Cestaro.
p. cm. — (The William and Katherine Devers series in Dante studies)
Includes bibliographical references and index.
ISBN 0-268-02553-3 (cloth : alk. paper)
ISBN 0-268-02554-1 (pbk. : alk. paper)
1. Dante Alighieri, 1265–1321—Views on language and languages.
2. Dante Alighieri, 1265–1321—Views on identity. 3. Wet-nurses in
literature. 4. Breast feeding in literature. 5. Language acquisition.
6. Identity (Psychology) in literature. I. Title. II. Series.
PQ4429.A2 C47 2003
851'.1-dc21

2003009025

Chapter 3 is a revised and expanded version of an essay in *Dante Studies* 109 (1991):
15–27, published under the title ". . . 'quanquam Sarnum biberimus ante dentes':
The Primal Scene of Suckling in Dante's *De vulgari eloquentia.*"

⊗ This book is printed on acid-free paper.

for Ma and Pa

Contents

ABOUT THE WILLIAM AND KATHERINE DEVERS SERIES IN DANTE STUDIES

The William and Katherine Devers Program in Dante Studies at the University of Notre Dame supports rare book acquisitions in the university's John A. Zahm Dante collections, funds an annual visiting professorship in Dante studies, and supports electronic and print publication of scholarly research in the field. In collaboration with the Medieval Institute at the university, the Devers program has initiated a series dedicated to the publication of the most significant current scholarship in the field of Dante Studies.

In keeping with the spirit that inspired the creation of the Devers program, the series takes Dante as a focal point that draws together the many disciplines and lines of inquiry that constitute a cultural tradition without fixed boundaries. Accordingly, the series hopes to illuminate Dante's position at the center of contemporary critical debates in the humanities by reflecting both the highest quality of scholarly achievement and the greatest diversity of critical perspectives.

The series publishes works on Dante from a wide variety of disciplinary viewpoints and in diverse scholarly genres, including critical studies, commentaries, editions, translations, and conference proceedings of exceptional importance. The series is supervised by an international advisory board composed of distinguished Dante scholars and is published regularly by the University of Notre Dame Press. The Dolphin and Anchor device that appears on publications of the Devers series was used by the great humanist, grammarian, editor, and typographer Aldus Manutius (1449–1515), in whose 1502 edition of Dante (second issue) and all subsequent editions it appeared. The device illustrates the ancient proverb *Festina lente,* "Hurry up slowly."

Theodore J. Cachey, Jr., and Christian Moevs, editors
Simone Marchesi, associate editor
Ilaria Marchesi, assistant editor

DANTE

AL · DVS

LIST OF ILLUSTRATIONS

IMAGE 1. Grammar as rite of passage involving transfer to punitive masters of the art. Benozzo Gozzoli, *Saint Augustine Given to the Grammar Master* (1465), first panel of fresco on the life of the saint.

IMAGE 2. Lady Grammar on her throne, rod in her right hand as with her left hand she invites a group of students. Early tenth-century manuscript illustration.

IMAGE 3. Lady Grammar with scourge in her right hand over the head of "bad boy" and open book in her left hand over the head of "good boy." Chartres Cathedral, West façade (Royal Portal).

IMAGE 4. Lady Grammar opens a door with her right hand and with her left hand squeezes a round object, at breast level. Andrea di Bonaiuto (14th century), *Triumph of Saint Thomas Aquinas,* detail of fresco.

IMAGE 5. Lady Grammar suckles child with her right breast and covers her left breast with a whip. Illustration in manuscript of Bartolomeo di Bartoli da Bologna, *Song of the Seven Virtues and Seven Liberal Arts.*

IMAGE 6. Lady Grammar as nurse-with-whip. Manuscript illumination showing the seven virtues and the seven arts.

IMAGE 7. Lady Grammar as nurse-with-whip. Manuscript illumination used alongside Augustinian definitions of the arts.

ACKNOWLEDGMENTS

I'd like to express my gratitude to the many individuals who read drafts of all or parts of this book at various stages during its long evolution and provided generous advice and encouragement: Albert Ascoli, Zyg Barański, Ted Cachey, Paul Gehl, Rachel Jacoff, Keala Jewell, Christian Moevs, Michael Naas, Wayne Rebhorn, Brenda Schildgen, Mario Trovato, Eugene Vance, and Jan Ziolkowski. I'd like to thank my colleagues at DePaul University, particularly my friends in the Department of Modern Languages for giving me an academic home and the members of the Ancient and Medieval Studies Colloquium for useful discussion of an early draft of chapter 3. I am also grateful to the university for granting me a research leave during the winter and spring quarters of 1997 and a Faculty Research and Development Grant in summer 1998. Finally, my love and thanks to friends in the U.S. and Europe for invaluable material and moral support along the way, especially Giorgio Ciotti, Rich DeNatale, Arthur Little, and Peter Nesset; and to Rob Garofalo in particular for helping see this through to the end. Many thanks are due to the assistant editor of the Devers series, Ilaria Marchesi (Hofstra University), and to the series' associate editor, Simone Marchesi (Princeton University), for their expert assistance in revising *Dante and the Grammar of the Nursing Body*.

Introduction

Ben distese in garrire alquanto l'alia,
contro a' suo cittadin, che per consilio
gli avevan tolto la poppa e la balia

Antonio Pucci (1310–88)[1]

Today's visitor to Florence can still see the remnants of the early Christian basilica of Santa Reparata below the famous Duomo of Santa Maria del Fiore. A short stairway leads through the floor and down into the dark earth where fragments of the primitive church's foundations yet reside. The much smaller Santa Reparata had stood on that site for centuries. Only in 1296, as Florence came to know ever-increasing economic and social power, was the ancient structure at last demolished in order to erect a larger, more magnificent church worthy of the *comune*'s mighty status. What remained of her foundations was conveniently buried in darkness under the new symbol of civic pride.

By way of introduction, I offer the image of Santa Reparata undone and buried beneath the Duomo. The third-century female martyr Saint Reparata suffered death at the hands of Roman soldiers via a particularly gruesome bodily mutilation that bears directly on the argument of this study. Like her more celebrated colleague Saint Agatha, Saint Reparata had her breasts torn from her body. Indeed, some scholars discern in the peculiar torture and martyrdom of Saint Reparata a reactionary violence against the pagan cult of female beauty represented by the idealized body of Aphrodite or Venus.[2] Thus the early Florentine church dedicated to Reparata's memory, now largely demolished and buried, aptly represents a horror of the nurturing female body that underlies culture and that we will uncover in various ancient and medieval discourses, some of which demand the nurse's sacrificial death and burial. That Santa Reparata saw the light of day but was destroyed and buried to make room for a less ambiguous symbol of civic power[3] during Dante's life in Florence may indeed bespeak nothing more than an utterly fortuitous bit of historical coincidence. Nonetheless, the image of her remains embedded in the soil beneath Florence's proud, towering dome captures in visual terms the basic cultural configuration that informs and unites the chapters that follow.

This book investigates the function of the nursing body in Dante. Drawing on a number of resources, ancient, medieval, and modern, I argue that the nursing body is a figure central to Dante's thinking about language and selfhood. Specifically, I locate in Dante's texts a horror of nurturing corporeality general to culture: a broadly relevant paradigm that dictates the rejection of the nursing body as prerequisite to rational language and selfhood. I explore the evolving role of this paradigm from the minor works *De vulgari eloquentia* and *Convivio* through *Inferno, Purgatorio,* and *Paradiso.* I also delineate how the texts of Christian salvation, *Purgatorio* and *Paradiso,* appropriate and rewrite this paradigm.

Historically, this notion that the reasoned constructs of language, selfhood, and society necessitate a rejection of the nurse was widely available to an early fourteenth-century intellectual such as Dante. Principally and most immediately, Dante had access to the idea in verbal and visual texts on first-language acquisition and, most crucially, grammar. We will look closely at some of these texts in chapter 1 and in chapter 2 argue that fear of nurturing corporeality motivates, structures, and ultimately puts an end to the grammatical aspirations of the *De vulgari.* Neoplatonism in its various forms provides another major source for Dante's thinking about the body in general and the nursing body in particular. Plato's mind/body dualism was gendered male/female virtually from its inception; thus, in the Neoplatonism Dante knew, the nursing body becomes the perfect emblem for the fluid, process-ridden "body" *tout court.* Chapter 3 explains the metaphorical trajectory of the nurse from *Inferno* to *Paradiso* by considering her metaphorical burial and resurrection in largely Neoplatonic (but ultimately Christian) medieval allegorical readings of Virgil. Chapter 4 posits the relevance of Plato's *Timaeus* (in Chalcidius's translation and commentary), with its representation of primal chaos as a wet nurse, to Dante's deconstruction of temporal personhood in antepurgatory. The final chapter traces Dante's reconstruction of a new Christian selfhood in *Purgatorio* and *Paradiso,* which reflects and transforms all of these discourses: grammar, epic, Neoplatonic moral allegory, and Neoplatonic cosmology.

My study is grounded in relatively traditional methods of close reading and intellectual history. Nonetheless, I must convey at the start that, on a broader conceptual level, this book has been shaped by ideas found in contemporary, mostly French, psychoanalytic and feminist theory. In particular, my reading of nursing corporeality in medieval literature and in Dante owes its primary debt to Julia Kristeva's theory of the semiotic *(le sémiotique)* in the wake of Lacanian psychoanalysis. While direct engagement with Kristeva's texts in the pages that follow is only occasional, her ideas about language, the body, and selfhood inform the whole. Appropriately, we should take a moment to introduce, however briefly, Kristeva's theory.[4]

By *semiotic,* Kristeva intends something more specific than that word's general definition relating to the science of signs, though that general meaning is surely implicated. For Kristeva, *semiotic* defines a kind of spatial and temporal realm wherein the individual human subject—one with language—begins to emerge. Kristeva associates the semiotic with the nursing body. Symbiotic union between infant and maternal body defines early mental life and anticipates the binary logic of self/other, symbolic exchange, and language proper. She borrows from Platonic cosmology to label this space of maternal authority *chora,*[5] wherein the infant-not-yet-subject begins to attach a kind of precocious meaning to bodily drives at a time when it has no firm sense of the mother's body as discrete object. Always, already moving toward separation into subject and object, and thus the birth of desire proper in language, this infant-mother continuum is marked by the flow and stases of bodily functions, and the beginnings of desire in, and eventually for, the nursing body. Coterminous with infant vocalizations, Kristeva characterizes *chora* as a musical and rhythmic motility that precedes and underlies language as a clearcut system of symbolic exchange, a motility where the developing subject enacts in intimate corporeal terms the processes of absorption and repulsion, displacement and condensation eventually necessary for language acquisition. Thus while implicating a corporeal signifying practice, *chora* predates the full-blown linguistic signifier that substitutes bodily drives with a sign. Not yet symbolic, *chora* is nonetheless semiotic.[6] That is to say, while not properly symbolic or grammatical, the nursing body possesses a curious sort of grammar all its own. Where better to seek this corporeal grammar than in Dante, would-be vernacular grammarian, pioneer poet in the mother tongue?

For Kristeva, semiotic *chora* endures as a constant of adult mental life. Necessary to language and subjectivity as buttressing other, the semiotic simultaneously threatens these symbolic constructs by recalling that early pseudo-space where binary distinctions (subject/object, signifier/signified) collapse in bodily drives.[7] In *Powers of Horror*, she explains cultural notions of the horrific and the monstrous[8] as rituals of defilement through which the subject defines its clean and proper body *(le corps propre)* by attempting to distance itself from what threatens the subject/object binary: the non-object or ab-ject. The horrific or ab-ject is inextricably bound to early maternal authority and the semiotic body. What is more, it constantly threatens, and occasionally erupts into, symbolic, patriarchal discourse and thus constitutes a potentially powerful theoretical construct for feminism.[9]

Kristeva enlists the aid of structuralist anthropology and in particular the work of Mary Douglas, for whom the threat of pollution resides not in a given object but rather only in relation to a symbolic boundary: filth is the other side of a border.[10] And the first border is defined by the body. Anything that violates this primal border—and in particular corporeal humors—threatens pollution.[11] Already in this most literal sense, the image of the nurse and infant suckling milk bespeaks the horrific. Douglas assimilates other borders—social, political, linguistic—to this primal bodily limit.[12] I will employ this classic structuralist gesture of assimilation to read Dante's *De vulgari,* a text that tries to define, unsuccessfully, a great many borders: historical, political, and linguistic, but ultimately—I will argue—corporeal.

In the pages that follow, we will discover a basic—what I call *classical*—image for the development of discrete, individual human speech and selfhood as weaning, a turning away from the nursing body, in a number of ancient and medieval texts. The image is present in Dante's own texts as a crucial symbolic structure. This picture of a primal border between nursing and weaning takes on profoundly personal significance in Dante and helps shape his writing on grammar and vernacular, society and exile, Babel, Eden, and human salvation. Dante's texts comprehend an implicit (and sometimes not so implicit) theory of the speaking subject, a theory whose full explanation requires more than pointing to the grammarians, to Virgil and his allegorists, to Plato and the Neoplatonists, though exploration of these traditions remains fundamental to my endeavor. Dante's texts conjoin ideas about the human body, human language, and human selfhood with a psychological force that at times lends itself to articulation in a contemporary critical register. Hence my debt to Kristeva.

There is a certain historical logic to my use of Kristeva in particular. Kristeva has studied a great many texts—ancient, medieval, and modern—for evidence of the "nurturing horror" she discerns in culture. She appropriates Plato's *chora*—mysterious third term between mind and body, Being and Becoming—to describe the semiotic, where bodily drives intermingle with the beginnings of symbolic language. Medieval discussions of first-language acquisition and grammar attempt to negotiate this same, culturally perilous, in-between space. Chapter 1 shows that, in its very defining gesture, *grammatica* draws a line between body and mind, desire and reason; grammar founds and sustains itself on this primary opposition. But as certain grammatical intellectuals, such as Augustine in the opening books of the *Confessions,* John of Salisbury in the *Metalogicon,* and Dante in the *De vulgari,* attempt to think through the origins of the first art, they arrive inevitably at the scene of language learning in the nursing body, where the strict binaries body/reason or nursing/discipline come undone. Traditionally the harbinger of patriarchal law, grammar undergoes a gradual process of maternalization at the hands of Christian humanists. Alongside the better-known portrayals of the nursing Virgin and the nursing body of Christ, a nursing Lady Grammar will come to light in the twelfth century. Unable to ignore Lady Grammar's traditional association with corporeal discipline as transmitted to the Middle Ages by Martianus Capella's frightful personification, John of Salisbury will nonetheless attempt to rewrite Martianus's description in a way that promotes Grammatica as nursing mother.

Chapter 1 examines this process of maternalization while providing background on the first art and its important social function—unique among the *artes*—as gateway to, and thus guardian of, culture. Most significantly, chapter 1 calls attention to a colorful tradition of personification allegory relevant to Dante's understanding of *grammatica*. While a few intellectuals pondered the origins of language and self in philosophical texts, a more immediate, visual, quasi-popular image of Grammar permeated fourteenth-century Italy in allegorical poetry and iconography. Most significant for Dante are portraits that originate in twelfth-century Chartres: here we find a Lady Grammar who offers her pupils one breast for suckle while blocking access to the other with rod or whip. These portraits provide striking testimony of grammar's founding movement away from the nursing body. They offer a snapshot in time of a long-standing and widely diffused discursive practice according to which grammatical learning recalled and re-enacted the primal separation of the *infans* from the nursing body. Such an image evoked for a medieval linguist of Dante's insight the original intermingling of desire and language, body and selfhood. These portraits offer a clear medieval inscription of Kristeva's semiotic. While providing some historical background, then, chapter 1 develops an appreciation for *grammatica* at once historical and theoretical.

Chapter 2 argues that a primal scene of nursing motivates Dante's discussions of language in the roughly contemporaneous, postexilic minor works *Convivio* and *De vulgari eloquentia.* The image of the nursing body in its relation to language and grammar structures the Latin treatise in particular. The metaphorical figure of exile is central to the *De vulgari,* a text written hard upon Dante's political exile from Florence. The metaphorical logic of the *De vulgari* conflates political exile with the individual's linguistic exile from the mother tongue in grammar and humanity's universal exile from linguistic Eden after Babel. At base lies the primal corporeal exile of the infant from the nursing body. This persistent, troubling scene of language in the nursing body brings Dante's grammatical project to its precocious end in midsentence.

Chapters 1 and 2 thus discover in Dante's minor works a classical grammar of linguistic selfhood that turns against the nursing body. Chapters 3–5 trace this grammar through the *Comedy.* The transformation we discover there (already announced by the incompleteness of the Latin treatise) may come as a surprise to few: the image of nursing corporeality present only obliquely in the repressed subtext of the *De vulgari* comes to full light as a central, perhaps the central, metaphor of *Paradiso,* where joyous nurses and nurslings populate virtually every canto. But we will examine more closely the contours of this reversal and discover the influence of the classical model of weaning as a continuous, and sometimes conscious, point of reference. Chapters 3–5 articulate the progressive evolution of the metaphorical nursing body through *Inferno, Purgatorio,* and *Paradiso.* In this analysis, *Purgatorio* will prove most significant as the text in-between: the text that, at its beginning, deconstructs classical selfhood in order, at its end, to reconstruct a new Christian selfhood upon entry into paradise.

As we explore the increasingly visible role of the nursing body in the *Comedy,* we must also expand our historical critical focus beyond grammar to other philosophical and poetic traditions where the nursing body is key. We will consider the difficult case of *Inferno* with reference to the virtuous nurse in classical epic, for Dante, Aeneas's Gaeta. The brief and apparently trivial mention of Gaeta in Virgil takes on enormous symbolic significance for Virgil's medieval allegorists, for whom the *Aeneid* was a hidden tale about

human moral (and linguistic) growth. Virgil's story about Aeneas's founding
of empire told another story about everyman's founding of self. We discover
here the same paradigm for subjectivity as a turning against the nursing body
toward whole language that we culled from grammatical discourse. Virgil's
allegorists, however, construct a somewhat more dramatic image of burial
and containment of the nursing body within the linguistic act of naming.
Aeneas must bury and name his nurse in order to construct an empire, just
as everyman must bury his nurse in grammatical memory to achieve adult
selfhood. Thus grammatical discourse and epic discourse merge upon the
nursing body as Gaeta becomes a kind of Lady Grammar.

The importance that even the pre-Christian allegorists bestow upon the
figure of burial in discussing Gaeta sets the metaphorical stage for Christian
resurrection. Once again, John of Salisbury, this time in the *Policraticus,* provides a crucial text. John writes from within the tradition of Virgilian allegory
to unbury and exalt the nursing body as a site of Christian truth. I locate a parallel movement in Dante's *Comedy.* John's metaphorical celebration of the nursing body of Christ is of course absent from *Inferno,* a text that can only allude
to maternal nursing in sly, parodic terms. And yet, *Inferno* does find space in
canto 26—the classical canto that opens a vertical series on human language
and selfhood—to pay homage to the sacrificial role of the classical nurse in
order to resurrect and glorify her body two canticles later in *Paradiso* 27.

Having located a clear trace of the classical grammar of selfhood in a key
canto of *Inferno,* the book shifts its focus in the final two chapters to Dante ·
as character and model subject in *Purgatorio.* Chapter 4 reviews the lessons
learned by the pilgrim in antepurgatory about the limitations of the classical
paradigm of selfhood. Through a close *lectura* of *Purgatorio* 5 in particular,
chapter 4 argues that Dante's text stages the deconstruction of individual
human selfhood in body and time by calling our attention to the eternal fact
of corporeal dissolution and flow as visible in the text of the created universe.
We acknoweldge here one final intellectual tradition that was undoubtedly
critical to Dante's thinking on the nursing body: the representation in Plato,
Chalcidius, and the Chartrian Neoplatonists of universal primal chaos—*chora,
hyle, silva*—as the "wet nurse of creation." The Neoplatonists teach that the
perpetual transformations of invisible *silva* can be read in the text of the visible universe, on the macrocosmic body of Mother Earth and on the microcosmic body of the nurse.

Thus the trace of the nursing body can be read everywhere in the text of
Purgatorio 5. In this canto, pilgrim and reader are forced to acknowledge her

primal truth: that all bodies are in perpetual flux, that apparent corporeal borders are illusory. Most importantly, Dante's text deliberately employs this scientific truth to dissect the classical notion of language and selfhood in opposition to the fluid body. That Kristeva's psychoanalytic *chora* has something to tell us about Dante's psychologically intuitive text finds solid historical ground. Within a poetic context inspired by Neoplatonic science, the astonished testimonies of Jacopo del Cassero and Bonconte da Montefeltro on the hour of their violent demise poignantly illustrate these characters' fatal blindness to the fragility of corporeal borders so evident in the natural world. But Dante's verses fuse Neoplatonic insights on the body of the natural world with psychological insights on the bodies of the human individual and human language. The characters of canto 5 demonstrate a naive and misplaced faith in the stability of temporal names and things, of language and corporeal self. These souls are overly invested in a classical ego that promotes the myth of a cleanly defined, self-sustaining body over and against ceaseless corporeal flow. Chapter 4 argues that *Purgatorio 5* invites pilgrim and reader to turn back toward the nursing body as we prepare to replay the drama of selfhood atop Mount Purgatory according to a revised Christian script.

In chapter 5, we follow the pilgrim up the mountain of Purgatory into paradise regained and demonstrate how Dante's text strategically reconstructs the classical paradigm for selfhood that *Purgatorio 5* had undone. We see the pilgrim returned to a state of linguistic and poetic *infantia,* the very scene of suckling that so troubled the *De vulgari* grammarian. Near the top of the mountain on the terraces of gluttony and lust, Dante's text evokes the classical subject as the pilgrim enacts a new Christian subjectivity that forever embraces nursing corporeality. We note the metaphorical triumph of this new nursing selfhood throughout *Paradiso,* beyond the resurrection of Gaeta in canto 27 to the final verses and uppermost reaches of the poem. I conclude that Dante's generous deployment of the nursing body in the poetics of *Paradiso* is intended to anticipate the resurrection body that will come at the end of time, Christianity's simple response to the classical fear of corporeal process. Tellingly, Dante's text projects the resurrection body not as the cleanly delimited unit we might expect of the guarantor of eternal selfhood, but rather as the nutritive body of permeable boundaries. Dante's text thus appropriates and redeems the very site of physical, linguistic, and subjective instability that horrified classical grammar. The nurse's body becomes the emblem of a primal and eternal truth.

Lady Grammar between Nurturing and Discipline

The territorialization of the infant's body provides the means whereby the outpouring of libido can be directed and contained. By indicating the channels through which that libido can move, the mother or nurse performs a social service, assists in the conversion of incoherent energy into coherent drives which can be culturally regulated. Indeed, by organizing the infant's body in relation to its reproductive potential, the mother or nurse already indicates the form which that cultural regulation will take: the orchestration of the drives around sexual difference.

Kaja Silverman, *The Subject of Semiotics,* 155

Defining *grammatica*

This chapter begins by taking a broad look at *grammatica* in an attempt to define some of the many things this ancient word might have suggested to an early fourteenth-century Italian intellectual. I move quickly, however, to the core of my argument, which is to show that grammatical discourse from earliest times evoked the primal scene of language learning in the nursing body. We will consider some of the ways in which this fundamental association between nursing and speaking, between the body and language, developed through the Middle Ages into a popular poetic and iconographical personification allegory, Lady Grammar, bearer of painful whip and nurturing milk, who was given her most conspicuous and elaborate expression in twelfth-century Chartres. The provocative image of Grammatica as both punishing and nurturing is present in grammatical and iconographical texts from Dante's Italy. This larger cultural definition of *grammatica* as a metaphorical discourse that posited the emergence of a rational, self-sufficient linguistic subject over and against nursing corporeality is crucial to Dante's understanding of *grammatica* and significantly shapes his writing about human language and human selfhood. We will then be in a position to uncover the primal scene of suckling in the *De vulgari eloquentia* in chapter 2.

Dante's texts give us only one formal academic definition of the word *grammatica* in book 1, chapter 9, of the *De vulgari,* which says that grammar is "a certain immutable identity of language in different times and places."[1] This supremely rational definition of grammar as an abstract pattern that unifies the Babelic differences of concrete, historical tongues may have come into Dante's intellectual lexicon from many sources, including the speculative grammar that was in vogue at the University of Paris at the time, which some recent critics have argued is central to Dante's linguistics.[2] But if we step back from this single definition to consider its immediate context, other occurrences of the word *grammatica* in Dante's texts, and the many more places where grammatical discourse is implicated, we will soon appreciate the futility of attempting to limit Dante's understanding to any one definition. We will begin this consideration in chapter 2.

First, we must note that *grammatica* was a word charged with, not to say plagued by, a plurality of meaning virtually from the inception of the discipline. It is not my intention here to recount, even in brief, the long, complex history of grammar; many excellent studies already exist.[3] Most notably, in his 1994 *The Making of Textual Culture: "Grammatica" and Literary Theory, 350–1100,* Martin Irvine provides a comprehensive, richly documented history of the discipline through the beginning of the twelfth century.[4] Nevertheless, in our effort to discover what *grammatica* might have meant to Dante, we should review some of the most significant issues at stake in defining the role and content of the first art. This will entail some highly selective delving into the history of grammar.

One of the first and most enduring questions asked about *grammatica* regards the precise content of its teachings: Was it the study of language or of literature? The simple and, in the end, correct answer is of course both. Nonetheless, this was a significant point of discussion throughout the medieval period. Coined on the Greek word for line or letters *(gramma, grammata),* the word has always indicated some activity having to do with "letters," the Latin *litterae,* in both the common and sophisticated sense that the word retains in English to this day: both the elementary ABCs and the study of what we today call literature.[5] The place of literary interpretation in the grammatical curriculum was unclear from the start. The earliest *grammatikós* was simply one who had attained basic competence in reading and writing, or perhaps one who speculated on the nature of language, such as Plato in the *Cratylus*. These primarily linguistic conceptions, however, soon evolved to embrace the study of poetic literature from a critical perspective.[6] This twofold conception of *grammatica* passed directly into the Roman world.[7] Thus while Varro (166–27 B.C.) formulated an almost exclusively literary definition, Seneca (4 B.C.–A.D. 65) acknowledged *grammatica*'s elementary and advanced meanings.[8] Quintilian (c. A.D. 35–c. A.D. 100) dealt plainly with the potential for confusion between grammar and rhetoric, specifically the encroachment of the former upon the literary provinces of the latter; he hoped to limit *grammatica* to basic instruction and the passive description of linguistic structures.[9]

In this way, the postclassical encyclopedists inherited a not entirely focused conception of *grammatica* for the Middle Ages. In the *De nuptiis Philologiae et Mercurii,* Martianus Capella (fl. 410–29) codified and allegorized the seven disciplines that became the liberal arts.[10] Although Martianus largely confined his allegorical treatment of Grammar to basic language pedagogy, at the end of book 3 he began to define barbarisms, metaplasms, and the importance of figurative language to literary texts.[11] Cassiodorus (480–575) confirmed grammar's status as the source and foundation of the liberal arts ("origo et fundamentum liberalium litterarum") and rhetorical creation.[12] Isidore of Seville (?560–636) set down the standard medieval definition, which reflected the first art's elementary and advanced possibilities: "Grammar is the science of speaking correctly, and the origin and foundation of liberal letters."[13] Some two centuries later, the bishop Rabanus Maurus (776–856), in his defense of the utility and, indeed, necessity of grammar for reading Scripture, synthesized previous definitions and pointed explicitly to grammar's two roles.[14]

The blurring of the boundary between grammar and rhetoric continued into the later Middle Ages with the creation of several relatively distinct verbal disciplines that drew on grammatical and rhetorical knowledge. Largely the result of renewed interest in linguistic standards and the nature of language per se, this atomization of *grammatica* is, for Murphy, the natural fate of a discipline that had simply outgrown its bounds.[15] The thirteenth century saw the development of several contemplative and pragmatic fields, any of which might consider itself a part of *grammatica:* the analysis of the *ars rithmica,*[16] the codification of the art of letter writing or *ars dictaminis,*[17] the proliferation of manuals on the *ars praedicandi,*[18] the composition of several arts of poetry,[19] the continuation of the pedagogical tradition in basic textbooks on syntax and phonology,[20] and, finally, the rise of a radical Aristotelian or speculative grammar at the University of Paris.[21]

For the speculatives or *modistae, grammatica* became the science of language per se, a purely logical category detached from the study of classical texts and ultimately uninterested in actual usage.[22] The speculatives recognized *grammatica* as a universal structure that could obtain for any language but which lay above and beyond them all. Thus, in Aristotelian terms, concrete linguistic difference was merely accidental; *grammatica* was one in essence, as Roger Bacon explained: "Grammar is one and the same in substance for all languages, though it vary accidentally."[23] Thus we must note another basic tension in *grammatica* between the humanist study of the *auctores* of the sort carried out in twelfth-century Chartres and Orléans, and a purely scientific Aristotelian linguistics.[24] While I will argue for a basic cultural definition of *grammatica* in Dante as elementary language learning, we will see some of these more advanced possibilities reflected in his uses of the word.

As the first and founding science of classical education, *grammatica* lay at the heart of another fundamental conflict for medieval thinkers between pagan *artes* and Christian faith.[25] Beginning with the earliest Church fathers, Christian intellectuals agonized over the appropriateness of pagan schemes of learning for a Christian education. Irvine has demonstrated the essential continuity of grammatical methodologies from classical to Christian texts in third-century Alexandria,[26] and, of course, Augustine forged a new grammatical *doctrina christiana* that affirmed the basic utility of grammar for Christian culture.[27] The medieval cleric could hardly do without some basic sense of grammar to read and teach Scripture, and this reality was generally accepted by the seventh century.[28] Thus one common Christian attitude was to accept the necessity of Latin language pedagogy ("recte scribendi loquendique") while rejecting study of the *auctores.*[29] But twelfth-century Chartres accepted, indeed promoted, *grammatica* in its broadest humanist acceptation as zealous study of the *auctores* and their language. We will see that John of Salisbury's texts in particular attempt a difficult reconciliation between classical and Christian through their strategic deployment of the metaphorical nursing body. Fundamentally, Dante's texts reflect the dichotomy of classical/Christian evoked by *grammatica* in their conflicting configurations of nursing corporeality.

Dante critics and commentators have looked to all of these grammatical traditions for background to his grammatical-rhetorical education and to *De vulgari eloquentia*. In the prodigious apparatus to his critical edition, Mengaldo moves freely from John of Garland to Boncompagno da Signa, Raimond Vidal to Donatus, Priscian, and Eberhard of Béthune in search of verbal reflections to Dante's prose.[30] Critics such as Maria Corti and Marianne Shapiro have worked hard to tie Dante's *grammatica* to speculative theory.[31] More recently, Zygmunt Barański has argued that Dante ultimately rejects any one definition of grammar as an attempt to impose strict linguistic boundaries or limits.[32] Barański suggests that Dante's most profound understanding of *grammatica* tends toward linguistic openness and fluidity, a plurilingualism in the comic mode that Barański associates with the *sermo humilis* of Scripture. In the pages that follow, we will have occasion to refer more specifically to Barański's views, which I feel largely support my argument here.

I propose that the image of the nursing body, associated with *grammatica* most conspicuously in twelfth-century representations, emblematizes Dante's most nuanced ideas about language between grammatical regularity and openness. Most immediately reflecting *grammatica*'s basic function as elementary language instruction ("la prim'arte," as Bonaventure calls it in *Paradiso*),[33] this image nonetheless resonates on many levels. Grammar was the first *disciplina*,[34] mental and corporeal, that snatched young boys from the realm of maternal affection and initiated them into the patriarchal social order.[35] Irvine has established that, from its very origins and throughout its long history, grammar created and regulated textual culture; grammar was the founder and careful guardian of a patriarchal law that reached far beyond mere linguistic norms.[36] In an important study of reading texts, Paul Gehl has recently confirmed that grammar in Dante's Florence specifically performed an important social function by inculcating the moral attitudes required of an adult citizen.[37] Grammar's ancient popular association with corporeal punishment is a clear sign of the discipline's basic legislative function. Despite the undoubted variety of his grammatical experience in later life, Dante too had his first encounter with the discipline of grammar and textual culture at the hands of a *doctor puerorum*.[38] But grammar's traditional alliance with strict discipline was countered from early on by pleas for a more humane, maternal approach to language education. We will see that this discourse drew significantly on an original metaphorical link between language learning and nursing. Of all the many conflicts that may inform Dante's *grammatica,* this opposition between nurturing and discipline is, I argue, the most significant.

nutrix as *magistra*

That grammar came to be represented as wet nurse reflects on one level the complementary historical reality that the wet nurse was often considered a kind of first grammar teacher. This was particularly true in the classical and early patristic period, when the distance between mother tongue and grammar was, to say the least, less dramatic.[39] Several thinkers recognized a quasi-biological, cause-and-effect link between the nurse's and the infant's characters and, more specifically, between the nurse's milk and the child's eventual speech.[40] For Quintilian (c. 35–c. 100), it was as though the very phonemes of language were imbibed with those first nourishing draughts. Quintilian devotes serious attention to the infant's early linguistic education in book 1 of the *Institutiones oratoriae*. Here the metaphorical association between language acquisition and suckling looms large as the nurse takes center stage. Not only should she be of good moral character; more importantly, she should speak correctly. These are the first linguistic sounds the child will experience and try to imitate, and these first impressions are the most tenacious. For Quintilian, the ingestion of breast milk serves as figure for the immediacy and thus endurance of all early experience. Just as virgin white wool soaks up indelible color, so the infant drinks in language.[41]

Quintilian's attitude toward language skill as a combination of natural talent and gradual, nurturing education remains unchanged through the several stages of language acquisition, from wet nurse (1.1.4–5) and parents (1.1.6–7), to *paedagogus* (1.1.8), *praeceptor* (1.2–3),[42] and finally *grammaticus* (1.4ff.) and *rhetor* proper (2). Rhetorical skill unfolds along a continuum that begins with the wet nurse.[43] Indeed, for Quintilian there is a natural, uninterrupted progression from the fairy tales of the nursery to Aesop's fables, the first school text: "Aesop's fables, the natural successors of the fairy stories of the nursery."[44] Metaphorically, Quintilian thus tends to feminize the entire province of verbal ability. He recognizes the origins of adult eloquence in infant suckling.[45] Traditionally identified with male political power, oratory also boasts female exponents. Cornelia, the mother of the Gracchi, and the daughters of Laelius and Hortentius were themselves accomplished speakers.[46] Far from being a rejection of the feminine and infantile, eloquence is founded and developed under the aegis of the female body. While careful discipline and study can be useful for the perfection of natural ability, art can accomplish nothing without nature.[47]

Quintilian's vision of grammar as a natural and graduated outgrowth of first language education repudiates institutionalized thinking about grammar as an artificial mental gymnastic reinforced through brutal physical discipline. He rejects the strict binary, nature/culture, that will characterize grammar for many medieval thinkers.[48] His long diatribe against corporal punishment (1.3.13–18) relies on a belief in natural disposition and merely adds testimony to the already well-documented reality of the grammar classroom as a place of frequent and abusive punishment.[49] His spirited condemnation of flogging reflects the link between nurturing and language education developed earlier in the book, and both *loci* implicity underwrite an ideology that refuses to detach language in any form from its origins in bodily desire.

inter blandimenta nutricum

Quintilian's gesture toward reconciliation of the maternal and the grammatical anticipates certain Christian responses to grammar. Saint Jerome (340?–420) borrows liberally from Quintilian in his epistle *Ad Laetem, de institutione filiae*.[50] He too insists upon the eradicable influence of early language experience and focuses on the wet nurse: "The nurse herself should not be flighty, nor lewd, nor a chatterbox."[51] Jerome rehearses Quintilian's examples of female eloquence (Cornelia, mother of the Gracchi, the daughter of Quintus Hortentius) while suggesting metaphorically that even the father's instruction is a kind of nursing: "Hortensia's speech grew strong at her father's breast."[52] Nevertheless, within the discourse of language acquisition and education, Saint Augustine (354–430)—despite the complexity of his attitudes toward grammar—offers the most dramatic testimony of the metaphorical coalescence of the Christian and the maternal that will become so prevalent in the twelfth century.

The early books of the *Confessions* develop a veritable theory of subjectivity in their discussion of first language acquisition and grammatical education.[53] Augustine holds out the possibility of language learning as nurturing while denouncing institutionalized grammar as secular error. His bitter repudiation of grammar follows immediately upon recollections of harsh physical discipline but soon takes on a greater existential tenor. Metaphorically, Augustine aligns grammar with male puberty, initiation into the adult male social and economic system, and loss of childhood proximity to primal desire, which is for him no less than a rejection of Monica's breast, the very temple of Christ. However indirectly, Augustine's memoir of his early experiences with Latin point to a notion of natural or maternal grammar not unlike what we have witnessed in Quintilian. In this way, the suckling imagery that had characterized language education since antiquity merges with the Christian discourse of suckling as an expression of childhood humility and *caritas.*

The primacy of suckling as a crucial stage in Augustinian infant psychology—and thus an important and recurring image throughout his meditations on selfhood—cannot be overstated.[54] Straining his memory to recover the first glimmer of individual consciousness, Augustine understands that he knows not whence he came: he knows only that his desire was allayed by the comforts of human milk ("consolationis lactis humani") and that this temporary satisfaction derived, ultimately, from God.[55] Given his unwavering commitment to the principle of original sin, Augustine refuses to indulge in romantic notions of infant innocence. Although he briefly suggests that the picture of the *infans* at the breast represents a perfect match of appetite and nourishment,[56] he quickly clarifies that desire, and the potential for unsatisfied desire, is always already there.[57] Tellingly, the signs of infant sin can be discerned in the primal moment of suckling: in crying when denied the sensual pleasures of the breast ("an quia uberibus inhiabam plorans?"), and in experiencing envy and even hatred for a competing suckler ("conlactaneum").[58]

This is a crucial moment for Augustine precisely because it marks the opening of the gap of desire and thus the potential, at once, for speech and sin. Here language is born. But the first outward signs of the infant suckling's will are hardly discrete words and language proper, rather corporeal vocal and visual gestures: what we might call, with Kristeva, the semiotic: "And so I used to jerk my limbs about and make various noises by way of indicating what I wanted, using the limited forms of communication which were within my capacity and which, indeed, were not very like the real thing."[59] This early semiotic universe of suckling and corporeal gesture develops gradually into discrete words and symbolic language proper, as *in-fantia* (speechlessness)[60] becomes *pueritia.*[61] The breast represents the first in that long chain of earthly desired objects that can only partially and temporarily supplant the true object of desire, reunion with the Creator. For Augustine, sin fails to recognize the partial and temporary nature of these objects. Augustine's unwillingness to grant even the tiniest nursling immunity from the common human plight, however, will not prevent him from suffusing his earliest experience of the Latin language at the breasts of his nurses with the golden light of a nostalgia that, by contrast, indicts the horrors of institutional grammar.

Book 1, chapter 9, of the *Confessions* dramatizes Augustine's first encounter with the world of grammar. He conveys only suffering and humiliation from the very opening ("O God, my God, what misery did I experience in my boyhood, and how foolish I was made to look!").[62] Fear of physical beatings, which were condoned and even encouraged by his elders, becomes a recurrent motif in this and the following chapters. Augustine imparts existential weight to grammatical suffering by identifying it with the inevitable sorrow of all the children of Adam.[63] Still, he cannot dismiss this childhood anguish as trivial. He is particularly bothered by his parents' complicity and the ultimately futile purposes of the grammatical training that such beatings allegedly promoted. With a touch of vindictive irony, he notes that fear of being beaten for failing in grammatical study led him to prayer and thus a kind of counterdiscourse.[64] Paradoxically, Augustine's earliest eloquence was in prayer born of fear for grammatical discipline; fear of beatings gave rise to a personal, spontaneous, antigrammatical discourse. Paragraph 15 explicitly links grammatical studies to adult society and commercial exchange *(negotia)*. Augustine espies a logical absurdity in the alleged aim of grammatical discipline by arguing that the very adult affairs *(nugae)* for which a formal grammatical education aimed to prepare young boys were of no greater moral value than the idle play that kept them from their studies and for which they were beaten. Indeed, as forms of play, the adult version had even less to recommend it.[65]

We must read Augustine's well-known preference for Latin over Greek as expressed in chapters 13 and 14 in light of this preoccupation with the discipline of grammar (in both senses of that phrase). While the monotonous rehearsal of basic rules bored him in either language,[66] his affection for Latin letters over and against Greek reflects an inborn attraction to, and affinity for, the mother tongue.[67] Despite its grammatical and rhetorical sophistication, Latin literature, for Augustine, still smacked of mother's milk. As with Quintilian, the linguistic reality of the early fourth century allowed Augustine to perceive the path from mother tongue to Latin grammar as a gradual continuum and thus at least to envision the possibility of a natural, painless *grammatica* (in stark contrast to his own scholastic experience).[68]

Augustine plots fear against nurturing, the whip against the breast. The terms of his discourse become dramatically clear when he compares his attitudes toward Greek and Latin. In Greek, he confronted the obstacle of a truly foreign tongue, an experience that recalls for the retrospective adult the inherently alienating quality of all human language as sign of postlapsarian desire.[69] "But why, then, did I hate Greek literature?" he muses while recognizing that Homer was as worthy a fabulist as Virgil and that Greek schoolboys must surely struggle with the *Aeneid*.[70] Augustine allows that his problems with Greek stemmed, on one level, from the inherent difficulty of mastering a foreign language. But his difficulties were compounded by the constant terrifying threats of his grammar masters.[71] In dramatic contrast, Latin came without coercion, with the ease of suckling, among the tender caresses of his nurses.[72] At the end of the chapter Augustine acknowledges once again that his early anguish at the hands of the grammar masters perhaps served a purpose (although clearly not the purpose intended by the *grammatici*). All suffering draws attention away from vanity and toward the fallen human condition. In this sense, the masters' cane ("magistrorum ferulis"), much as the martyrs' pain ("temptationes martyrum"), embodies a kind of healthful bitterness ("salubres amaritudines"). Such generous wisdom does little to mitigate the personal poignancy of the previous lines. As represented by institutional grammar and Greek letters, foreign language acquisition runs counter to human nature: it is coercion, terror, "a bitter gall." By contrast, the mother tongue rises immediately out of desire in the mother's body. For Augustine, the infant striving to formulate his first words becomes himself a substitute mother by rehearsing the birth process ("cum me urgeret cor meum ad parienda concepta sua . . . in quorum et ego auribus parturiebam quidquid sentiebam"). But it is an easy labor ("sine ullo metu atque cruciatu . . . sine poenali onere"): all laughter, gaiety, and the affections of the nurse ("blandimenta nutricum").

The discourse of language acquisition we have analyzed thus far has consistently focused on the wet nurse over the actual mother. This of course reflects a historical and social reality.[73] But this focus also tends to belie the expression "mother tongue," or reduce *mamma* to a literal, biological function.[74] Although maternal attention may govern the infant's general progress in language skills, the intimate desire that initiates language is contained in the act of suckling. For Augustine, language fills the space of postlapsarian desire. The image of an infant at the breast of the wet nurse, in particular, conveys the always partial, supplemental nature of the comforts language has to offer. Mother/not mother, the wet nurse steps in to take the mother's place and thus to represent the object of a desire whose only true perfection remains shrouded in a radically inaccessible, original unity. In Augustine's Christian Neoplatonism, all earthly objects are mere substitutions. Lest we be lulled by the mother-infant scene into a false sense of satisfaction, the wet nurse is there to remind us that all objects from this point forward are provisional. She is in this sense the primal signifier, representation itself.[75]

Augustine expresses genuine affection for early language learning that extends to Latin grammar. Like Quintilian (albeit indirectly), Augustine champions a maternal approach to grammar through his recurrent use of the nurturing metaphor, the very same metaphor that will come to characterize Christ himself. From a Christian perspective, the alternative to this new maternal grammar appears bleak: the adolescent's painful, quasi-ritualistic initiation into an adult male social economy unworthy of human desire.[76] On the scale of human development, Augustine aligns institutional grammar with the moment of puberty: a turning away from the maternal breast toward patriarchal law. If only metaphorically, such a movement grates on his maternal sensibilities. Nowhere are these gendered polarities more explicit than in Augustine's adolescent encounter with his father at the public baths (*Confessions* 2.3.6). Patricius's vain, earthy joy upon witnessing his son's pubescence distresses the autobiographer, who takes metaphorical refuge in Monica's breast:

> In fact when my father saw me at the baths and noticed that I was growing toward manhood and showing the signs of the burgeoning of youth he told my mother of it with great pleasure, as though he were already confident of having grandchildren; but his pleasure proceeded from that kind of drunkenness in which the world forgets you, its creator, and falls in love with your creature instead of with you; so drugged it is with the invisible wine of a perverse self-will, bent upon the lowest objects. But in my mother's breast you had already begun to build your temple and had laid the foundation for your holy dwelling place.[77]

We hardly need recall the importance of Monica to Augustine's spiritual reawakening. In this passage, the maternal breast, set in diametrical opposition to the phallus as locus of patrilinear succession, becomes the very temple of God made man.[78]

Later books of the *Confessions* will confirm and amplify the figurative conflation of breast milk, language, and Christian truth. In 3.4, Augustine expresses chagrin at finding the name of Christ missing from Cicero's *Hortensius,* an otherwise useful work, for he has always known that name— ingested with Monica's milk—as the true sign of goodness: "For this name, Lord, this name of my Saviour, your son, had been with my mother's milk drunk in devoutly by my tender heart, where it remained deeply treasured."[79] In the following book, God becomes the nursing mother: "Or what am I, even at the best, except an infant sucking the milk you give and feeding upon you, the food that is imperishable?"[80] As Margaret Miles has noted, the moment of conversion in book 8 describes a return to psychic infancy, similar to the metaphorical regression of the pilgrim atop Mount Purgatory which

I will discuss in chapter 5.[81] Finally, Augustine's metaphorical choices condemn institutional grammar as perversely and uselessly harsh while promoting an ideal language learning that reflects human desire in the maternal body as a site of Christian truth. We thus see Quintilian's humanist plea for a nurturing grammar merge with the maternal vocabulary of Christian charity in Augustine. But Quintilian and Augustine represent voices of dissent from a popular notion of grammatical study as monstrous discipline.

Augustine's characterization of grammar school suggests a kind of puberty ritual imposed on boys by a largely sinister secular society.[82] His discussion provides crucial background for thinking about grammatical discipline through the Middle Ages and beyond. It will help us understand *grammatica* in the *De vulgari*. A full century and a half after Dante, Augustine's account sparked the imagination of at least one Tuscan painter of the Renaissance. Benozzo Gozzoli created the fresco cycle on the life of Augustine in the Church of Sant'Agostino in San Gimignano in 1465 (Image 1, p. 31). In the very first panel, Monica and Patricius deliver the young saint into the hands (literally) of the grammar masters in Tagaste. That this pictorial narrative means to convey grammar as rite of passage is at once apparent. A menacing, heavily bearded *magister* steps forth to accept the little boy from his parents; notably, he strokes the prepubescent hairless cheeks of the stoic young saint. Behind him, two older boys fix on the newcomer and whisper to one another in mischievous conspiracy. Farther behind still, an older boy hoists a younger student on his shoulders so that the young boy may receive upon his naked, upturned buttocks the master's whip. Proverbially known as "mounting the horse," this punishment boasts a long tradition in representations of grammar[83] and will figure at a crucial moment in the *De vulgari*.[84]

Lady Grammar's Whip

We are fortunate to possess a clear expression of grammar as torment from the end of Augustine's lifetime. For a portrait of Augustine's nemesis, we need look no further than Martianus Capella's *De nuptiis Philologiae et Mercurii*. Flourishing in the second and third decades of the fifth century, Martianus codified the liberal arts for the Middle Ages and, perhaps even more instructive for our present purposes, allegorized the seven sisters in a series of intricate portraits that would exercise huge influence for centuries over both verbal and visual depictions.[85] Although condemned by modern readers for his stylistic eccentricity and dubious literary taste,

Martianus's allegories distill ancient and early medieval cultural common-
places about the arts.[86]

With Martianus, Lady Grammar is born, "an old woman indeed, but one
of great charm." In no sense a nurturing mother, Martianus's Grammar relates
the widespread image of the first discipline as punishing, initiatory, and fright-
eningly mysterious. If she is a charming old woman, her charm is that of the
wizard or necromancer. Martianus provides her an alternate identity as the
enigmatic "Genethliaca"; some four centuries later, John Scotus Eriugena will
gloss this line as defining "the art of the progenitors of mankind which is called
magic."[87]

Cloaked in Roman robes (penulata, as Augustine's magistri), Grammar
cuts an imposing figure:

> She carried in her hands a polished [teres][88] box, a fine piece of cabi-
> netmaking, which shone on the outside with light ivory, from which
> like a skilled physician the woman took out the emblems of wounds that
> need to be healed. Out of this box she took first a pruning knife with a
> shining point, with which she said she could prune the faults of pro-
> nunciation in children; then they could be restored to health with a cer-
> tain black powder carried through reeds, a powder which was thought
> to be made of ash or the ink of cuttlefish.[89]

Circumcisor of infant tongues, Martianus's Grammar initiates young boys in
a painful discipline. Martianus sets up a clever and subtly ironic series of double entendres, whereby the portrait of Grammar as surgeon and healer is
everywhere undercut by simultaneous references to the real pain (physical,
linguistic, psychological) of grammatical experience as conceived by the fifth-
century mind. Grammar's scalpel conveys the surgical invasion inherent in
regulating and controlling the mother tongue, sign of spontaneous and as yet
relatively unruled desire. The mysterious black healing powder carried
through reeds recalls the ink pen. Martianus's strategy becomes even more
apparent in what follows: "Then she took out a very sharp medicine which
she had made of fennelflower and the clippings from a goat's back, a medicine of purest red color, which she said should be applied to the throat when
it was suffering from bucolic ignorance and was blowing out the vile breaths
of a corrupt pronunciation."[90] This strange and most bitter new medicine—
applied to students' throats to correct regional pronunciations, cobbled
together with reed stalks and straps of goat hide—can only refer to the magister's whip, as the red color suggests the bloodied welts of its victims.[91]

The remainder of Martianus's portrait is hardly more pleasant. Grammar displays a salve, the product of much labor and many sleepless nights, which renders harsh voices more pleasing. She cleans out students' windpipes with a weird amalgam of wax smeared on beechwood, gallnuts, gum, and papyrus rolls ("the Nilotic plant," a clear reference to Grammar's alleged birthplace in Egypt).[92] The waxed wood recalls the schoolboys' writing tablets. While this poultice indeed heightens powers of attention and memory, it also keeps one awake at night. Grammar may offer a kind of medicine, but what a bitter pill it is: scalpel, whip, late night vigils, and lost sleep. Finally, she wields a file: artfully divided into eight sections (the already hallowed eight parts of speech from Donatus), the file cleans dirty teeth and impurities of the tongue "picked up in the town of Soloe" (solecisms). Here Martianus alludes to Lady Grammar's altra ego by suggesting a relationship between teeth and language skills, an implicit reminder of the cultural notion of grammar as a kind of teething or weaning (loss of the maternal breast) and a metaphorical element that will reappear in later discussions.[93]

Between them, Augustine and Martianus nicely capture the dualistic significance of Grammar for late antiquity and the early Middle Ages: her ability to reflect simultaneously classical humanist and Christian values of education as nurturing and their precise opposite in a nefarious secular discipline. Both authors thus set the metaphorical stage for the twelfth-century representations of *grammatica* that I think most directly influenced Dante. Before arriving in the twelfth century, however, let us briefly consider the birth of an iconographical tradition for the liberal arts and the endurance of the themes of discipline and nurturing in representations of grammar through the Carolingian period.

Sapientia nutrix and *Grammatica nutrix*

For Cassiodorus (480–575), Grammar at once presents a picture of imposing authority and maternal fertility: "Glorious mother of fecundity . . . mistress of words."[94] Similarly, Gregory the Great (pope 590–604) prefers a maternal Grammar in open defiance of Donatus. Gregory writes that the language of his commentary should reflect the language of Scripture, for it is only proper that "the newborn babe take on the looks of her mother."[95]

For Smaragdus of St. Mihiel, author of an early ninth-century commentary on Donatus and champion of Christian grammar, Lady Grammar is both father and mother but in either case nurturing: "She longs to hold all of her newborns at her bosom;/she nourishes in the manner of a father and caresses with the love of a mother."[96] Here we find little trace of grammar's monstrous discipline. Grammar may be both mother and father for Smaragdus, but this is a nourishing father. Smaragdus's conspicuous assignment of *nutrio* to the father, when he could simply have exchanged the two verbs for less dramatic effect, underscores his commitment to a maternal conception of grammar. Smaragdus casts grammar in an even gentler light by emphasizing the gradual progression of her instructional nourishment: "She gives out sweets and promises magnificent powers/she will provide cups of milk with bits of solid bread."[97] The strategic interlacing of adjectives and substantives in this phrase lends visual reality to the idea of maternal liquid giving way to bits of bread. Beyond the metaphorical register, Smaragdus makes clear that the pages of Scripture themselves function as the real facilitator of grammatical learning, the sugar coating to a potentially bitter pill. Heir to Quintilian's nurse and Augustine's own Monica, Scripture's inherent sweetness and wisdom will mitigate any linguistic challenge, "so that he can with greater ease and sweetness gulp down the harshness of grammar along with the sweetness of the celestial mead."[98]

In an important essay on representations of Wisdom and the liberal arts, d'Alverny studies the image of Lady Philosophy nursing her seven daughters (the liberal arts), which appears to have been in vogue in the area of the Rhine during the eleventh and twelfth centuries.[99] Indeed, Carolingian culture and its heirs through the eleventh century tend to focus imaginative representations on the entire group of arts as constituent of Philosophy or Wisdom; Philosophy thus becomes the central focus. We can attribute the beginning of this trend to Alcuin (735–804), who in the *De grammatica* reads Proverbs 9.1 ("Wisdom has built herself a house, she has hewn out seven pillars") as an allegory of the liberal arts.[100] Grammar becomes—in a rather abstract and, given her history, colorless fashion—merely one of the seven pillars of the house of Wisdom.

The ninth century experienced a resurgence of interest in Martianus's text and grammatical culture in general.[101] John Scotus Eriugena depicts the seven arts as seven streams converging on wisdom, which is Christ.[102] Théodulph of Orléans (bishop c. 798–821) opts for a tree-and-branch motif to portray the relationship among philosophy and the arts. His poem "De septem liberalibus artibus in quadam pictura depictis" appears to describe figural depictions of the Arts, possibly wall frescoes at Charlemagne's Palace Chapel at Aix-la-Chapelle.[103] Here Grammar holds pride of place as foundation and queen of the arts. She also bears the marks of Martianus's discipline: she holds a whip in her left hand, a sword in her right, "the former to goad lazy boys, the latter to cut down vices":

> *There was a disk formed in the polished image of the world,*
> *which was adorned by the depiction of a unique tree.*
> *Among whose roots was seated mighty Grammar,*
> *deliberating over whether to generate and multiply herself or hold herself in.*
>
> *Every tree is thus seen to proceed from her,*
> *For no art is strong enough to advance without her.*
> *In her left hand she holds a whip, while in the right a sword,*
> *the former to inspire lazy boys, the latter to cut down vices.*
> *And because she carries the prize in wisdom in all places,*
> *a diadem adorned her head for that reason.*
> *And because good judgment or common opinion generate you, lofty Sophia,*
> *both of her hands here attend to you.*[104]

Lady Wisdom or Philosophy takes on the role of nursing mother in the work of the anonymous ninth-century Irish monk Hibernicus the Exile: "The words of Philosophy to her followers: 'Whosoever among you wish to know the various causes of things as my students, cherish me in your heart as your affectionate nursemaid.'"[105] In the anonymous eleventh-century French poem published in an appendix to d'Alverny's essay, Lady Philosophy's lacteal power overflows as the Christian motif of the virgin mother is introduced.[106] Here we witness a curious conflation of the imagistic repertoires of grammar and the Virgin, as again in a poem of Baudri de Bourgueil (1046–1130), which purportedly describes figurettes on the bed of the Countess Adèle, daughter of William the Conqueror.[107] In the *Rhetorimachia* (c. 1049–56) of Anselm of Besate (also known as Anselm the Peripatetic), the role of nurturing virgin mother is shared by all three sisters of the trivium as representatives of the language arts. These three ravishing maidens ("tres virgines formosissimas") must battle the Muses for control of the young adult Anselm, whom they had suckled at their breasts in infancy and nourished through adolescence.[108]

Only in the Carolingian age do we begin to have evidence of a signifi-cant iconographical tradition for grammar,[109] although earlier iconography can be culled from verbal descriptions.[110] While some representations throughout the tradition convey the specific attributes of Martianus's Grammar (*ferculum*, scalpel, file),[111] most others offer a more generic Lady

Grammar, a draped female figure usually with rod or whip in one hand and an open book in the other, often accompanied by one or more *pueri*.[112] Throughout most of the Middle Ages, then, Lady Grammar reflected a popular notion of the first art as physical and mental discipline. We have already had occasion to cite Théodulph's song of the arts, which corresponds to frescoes in Charlemagne's Palace Chapel in Aix-la-Chapelle. There Grammar sits at the base of the Tree of Wisdom with whip and sword in hand.[113] An early tenth-century manuscript illustration (Paris, Bibliothèque Nationale, MS lat. 7900A, 127v) shows Lady Grammar seated high on her throne with rod prominently foregrounded in her right hand; with her left she invites response from a homogeneous group of *pueri,* who clutch their writing tablets (Image 2, p. 32).[114]

Meanwhile, the Carolingian image of a nursing Sapientia with seven nursling arts remains current through the twelfth century in northern European depictions. In the *Hortus deliciarum* of Harrade of Landesburg, prioress of Hohenbourg monastery (Alsace, 1167–96), Philosophy is the central focus of a miniature with the streams of wisdom flowing from her breasts. The arts are located in an arcade around the central circle. Grammar is situated directly above Philosophy. She holds the traditional whip in her right hand and a book in her left. It is perhaps significant that, of all the seven sisters, only Grammar and Rhetoric (the language arts) are portrayed with breasts delineated beneath their flowing robes.[115] Likewise, Sapientia nourishes the arts by means of seven streams that flow from her breast in a twelfth-century School of Salzburg miniature (Basel, Hirsch Collection; formerly in the Collection Forrer, Strasbourg).[116] Scholars have identified Grammatica as the first figure on her right, who offers a round cup (Martianus's *ferculum*?) and a key.[117]

But only twelfth-century Chartres was in a position to construct a Lady Grammar who is at once bearer of milk and discipline: an image that recuperates late-antique discussions of *grammatica* while drawing on the intervening iconography of Grammar and Wisdom. This fantastic Chartrian invention will survive in fourteenth-century Italy. Central to the configuration of the nursing body at Chartres is John of Salisbury's writing about grammar.

Grammatica in the Metalogicon

In book 1 of the *Metalogicon,* the celebrated Chartrian master John of Salisbury (1115?–80) forges a thorough, comprehensive statement on grammatical education of the sort not seen since Quintilian or Augustine. Indeed, all the metaphorical elements of the tradition—elements that had made only fragmented and disparate appearances since the fifth century—come together once again in John's lengthy treatment. John's subjects are grammar and eloquence, and his themes are by now familiar to us: nature and art in grammar, early language acquisition, pedagogical methods, the role of discipline. Not surprisingly, John makes frequent use of the suckling image.

What is perhaps most notable in John's exposition from our perspective is his ardent, but not altogether successful, attempt to synthesize nature and art in language learning. John wants to have it both ways. He wants grammar to be an enriching, healthy experience for all, as it was for him in Bernard of Chartres's classroom; and yet he is forced to admit that grammatical knowledge is not wholly natural, cannot simply be absorbed with the ease and pleasure of the suckling babe—whence his discourse on the relationship of nature to art. John sets out to attenuate the border between the two in hopes of deflating the threat posed by grammatical learning.[118]

His struggle with this dilemma has much in common with those of Quintilian and Augustine, though on the surface he appears to take an opposite view. Still, all three favor a humane approach to grammar, just as all three must come to terms with the inherent difficulty of foreign language learning. In this regard, it must be recognized that John's sincere efforts to disregard the increasingly alien quality of the Latin language are even less plausible than those of his predecessors; grammatical Latin of the twelfth century was simply that much more foreign and distant with respect to the mother tongue.[119]

John manipulates the metaphorical tradition with great cunning and skill. His strategy is subtle but effective. While forced to concede in argument that grammar cannot be natural, his imagery supports a different view. John begins his diatribe against "natural eloquence" by arguing the other side. In *Metalogicon* 1.6 he takes on the role of his alleged nemesis, Cornificius, and argues the position of natural grammar. In terms strongly reminiscent of Augustine in the *De doctrina christiana,* John masked as Cornificius claims that only practice in speech with fellow speakers will bring eloquence while study of rules is of little or no benefit. All the peoples of the world have attained to eloquence through practice and imitation in their respective tongues: Greeks, Latins, Gauls, Britons, Scythians, and Arabs. Harkening back to Quintilian, John as Cornificius quips that the grammar master is virtually powerless to mold speech when compared with the wet nurse:

> The Greeks and Hebrews use their languages to advantage without bothering about rules; and the peoples of Gaul and Britain, as well as oth-

ers, learn how to talk at their nurses' breasts long before they receive instruction from doctors who occupy official chairs. The way one talks in manhood often smacks of the manner of speech of one's nurse. Sometimes the [most] strenuous efforts of teachers cannot extricate one from habits imbibed at a tender age.[120]

John exaggerates the case for natural grammar in order to prepare his own view. Significantly, his final position is by no means opposed to the idea of natural grammar. He defines what might be considered merely a modified version of it. His parodic rehearsal of Cornificius's arguments betrays yearning for a pre-Babelian universe where grammar would indeed be natural, which is to say unnecessary.[121] This conflicted nostalgia for an Edenic ideal foreshadows Dante's attitude in the *De vulgari*.[122]

In his rebuttal to Cornificius, "Quod natura usu iuvanda est, et exercitio," John distinguishes between *prima natura*—prelapsarian unity of divine will—and *natura creata*—the secondary, derivative nature that exists in the world since the Fall. From his perspective, the Cornificians' insistence on natural eloquence necessarily rings false, for nothing can be truly natural (in the sense of *prima natura*) since the Fall, which in this context is Babel. Thus nature *(natura creata)* can and must be assisted by extranatural means. In this way John legitimates the role of the arts: "Although the gifts of nature are definitely helpful, they are never or rarely so effective that they are fully realized without study."[123] Thus, much like Dante in the *De vulgari,* John mournfully admits that the Fall has rendered natural eloquence impossible. Just as in the *De vulgari,* humanity's primal Fall from grace (Eden) and linguistic Fall from grace (Babel) tend to merge as both John and Dante define the world in linguistic terms.[124]

Like Dante, John adheres to the majority patristic opinion regarding the history of language. Hebrew was the language of all humanity up until Babel; humanity was linguistically one in Hebrew at some primal moment when *prima natura* remained intact.[125] John recalls this history in order to taunt the Cornificians:

> Why, therefore, oh most learned Cornificians, do you not understand all languages? Why do you not at least know Hebrew, which, as we are told, *mother nature* gave to our first parents and preserved for mankind until human unity was rent by impiety, and the pride which presumed to mount to heaven by physical strength and the construction of a tower, rather than by virtue, was leveled in a babbling chaos of tongues? Why do not the Cornificians speak this language, which is more natural than the others, having been, so to speak, taught by nature herself?[126]

Although a prelapsarian, intact Mother Nature *(natura parens)* nursed her human children on an ideal, unchanging natural language in a world before grammar, she no longer exists. Slain by human presumption and impiety, our primary Mother Nature has disappeared, and someone must step in, however imperfectly, to take her place. In their naive insistence on natural grammar, the Cornificians have overlooked this basic fact. Were it not that Nature had been lost in our fallen universe, we would all still speak that original sacred idiom.[127] In a postlapsarian world, the arts are our only hope.

Grammar cannot be known naturally simply because it is no longer the same among all peoples, which is to say, in speculative terms, it is not universal: "Although some of the arts pertaining to and imparting the power of eloquence approach Nature, still that art [of grammar], which is in essence arbitrary and *subject to individual will,* cannot be known by nature since it is not natural. *For it is not the same among all [peoples]."*[128] John's phrasing challenges the speculative grammar that was coming into vogue at this time.[129] The confusion of tongues has barred humanity from linguistic wholeness once and for all. Only through rational toil (the arts) might we ever even approximate that original linguistic unity.

But John's frank pessimism ends here. The remainder of this book is devoted not to insisting upon the gaping chasm that lies between nature and grammar, but to bringing the terms together. His use of metaphor is significant. Were John's purpose to communicate the irreconcilability of nature and art, we might expect a Capellian Grammar: harsh, prone to discipline, patriarchal. Nature, on the other hand, would be maternal, gentle, and nurturing. Instead, in chapter 11, John takes pains to cast both nature and art as mothers:

> Art is a system that reason has devised in order to expedite, by its own short cut, our ability to do things within our natural capabilities. Reason neither provides nor professes to provide the accomplishment of the impossible. Rather, it substitutes for the spendthrift and roundabout ways of nature a concise, direct method of doing things that are possible. It further *gives birth (so to speak)* to a faculty of accomplishing what is difficult. Wherefore the Greeks also call it *methodon,* that is, so to speak, an efficient plan, which avoids nature's wastefulness, and straightens out her circuitous wanderings, so that we may more correctly and easily accomplish what we are to do.[130]

The parenthetical "so to speak" ("ut ita dixerim"), a phrase that will recur in connection with John's metaphorical choices, verifies that his use of "gives birth" *(parit)* is both self-conscious and significant. Reason too gives birth. John then goes on to confirm nature's traditional role as mother, which places him in a bit of a quandary. Two mothers? His solution is notable: "However vigorous it may be, nature cannot attain the facility of an art unless it be trained. At the same time, nature is a parent to all of the arts, and as the parent (by means of whom they progress and attain perfection) gives to them *reason as a nursemaid*."[131] That nature is our true mother John confirms at the end of the chapter: "The mother of the arts is nature, to despise whose progeny amounts to insulting their parent."[132] As though in imitation of nature, however, the rational arts become our wet nurse, our substitute mother.

John thus sets the stage, conceptually and metaphorically, for his treatment of grammar in chapter 13.

> Grammar . . . is "the science of speaking and writing correctly—the starting point of all liberal studies" [Isidore, *Etymologiarum* 1, 5, 1]. Grammar is the *cradle* of all philosophy, and *in a manner of speaking, the first nurse of the whole study of letters. It takes all of us as tender babes, newly born from nature's bosom. It nurses us in our infancy,* and guides our every forward step in philosophy. *With motherly care,* it fosters and protects the philosopher from the start to the finish [of his pursuits].[133]

Thus nature may give birth, but grammar must give suck, for we humans are lost to the breast of nature *(prima natura) ab origine.* Almost fortuitously, the wet nurse metaphor is there for John to provide him with precisely the image he needs to illustrate the difficult idea of natural/not natural that is grammar. The wet nurse is that queer anomaly that he has been laboring to define since the beginning of the *Metalogicon.* She functions as mother, but, like grammar, can only pretend. She is an imitation, marked by lack. She is presence signifying absence, always already fallen away.

John explains her mimetic status in the following chapter, "Quod ipsa, etsi naturalis non sit, naturam imitatur,"[134] while reaffirming nature's role as the true (but unattainably distant) mother: "Since grammar is arbitrary and subject to man's discretion, it is evidently not a handiwork of nature. Although natural things are everywhere the same, grammar varies from people to people. However, we have already seen that nature is the mother of the arts."[135] We once again note John's apparent challenge to the pre-*modistae.*[136]

John thus performs a delicate highwire act. While to some extent embracing the view of grammar as a difficult and at times painful achievement, he nonetheless makes metaphorical use of images from the opposite camp. One might say that he is attempting to synthesize Augustine and Martianus, a view borne out with dramatic clarity by his reading of the *De nuptiis* in chapter 21. All of John's efforts go to reducing the monstrousness of Martianus's portrait:

> In similar vein, Martianus, in *The Marriage of Mercury and Philology,* represents grammar as provided with a knife, a rod, and the ointment case carried by physicians. She uses the knife to prune away grammatical errors, and to cleanse the tongues of infants as she instructs them. *Nursing and feeding her charges,* she conducts them on to the art of philosophy, thoroughly training them beforehand so that they will not babble in barbarisms or solecisms. Grammar employs her rod to punish offenders; *while with the ointment of the propriety and utility which derive from her services, she mitigates the sufferings of her patients.*[137]

As with Isidore, John has introduced the nurturing image into Martianus's description. What is more, there is nothing in Martianus (or, for that matter, in his ninth-century glossators) about Grammar's ointments representing "propriety and utility," and there is certainly nothing about their easing pain. Quite to the contrary, we have seen that Grammar's ointments in Martianus seem rather the concoctions of a necromancer. In fact, in Martianus the ointments metaphorically represent the very instruments of grammatical torture so abhorrent to John, Augustine, and Quintilian. John thus transforms Martianus's one-sided portrait into a more nuanced figure. In his zeal to counteract the negative, however, he errs on the side of generosity. John's rereading produces a personification more charitable than anything ever dreamt of by Martianus and his kin. His obvious affection for Grammar is that of a child for his mother. Indeed, it is not long before he forgets his earlier designations and, in the same chapter, declares Grammar "mother and arbiter of all speech" ("totius sermonis mater et arbitra").[138]

Against this background of filial affection (of a child for his mother) we must read John's poignant account of Bernard of Chartres at the end of book 1. Bernard's methods embody the abstract principles discussed thus far in the chapter, providing a real-life summation and exemplar. The same tensions that informed John's philosophical discussion reappear here. John's nostalgic description in many ways reflects his own preoccupations more than the actions of a historical man. John continues to struggle with Grammar's ambivalence: nature or artifice, nurturing mother or punishing father? In many ways, Bernard's teaching demonstrated natural, or maternal, grammar in action. He trained memory through gentle exhortations and imitation exer-

IMAGE 1. Grammar as rite of passage involving transfer to punitive masters of the art. At left, the grammar master in Tagaste accepts the boy Augustine from his parents Monica and Patricius; at right, another *magister* whips a small boy. Benozzo Gozzoli, *Saint Augustine Given to the Grammar Master* (1465), first panel of fresco on the life of the saint (San Gimignano, Church of Saint Augustine). *Courtesy of Art Resource, New York, New York, for Fratelli Alinari* © 1993.

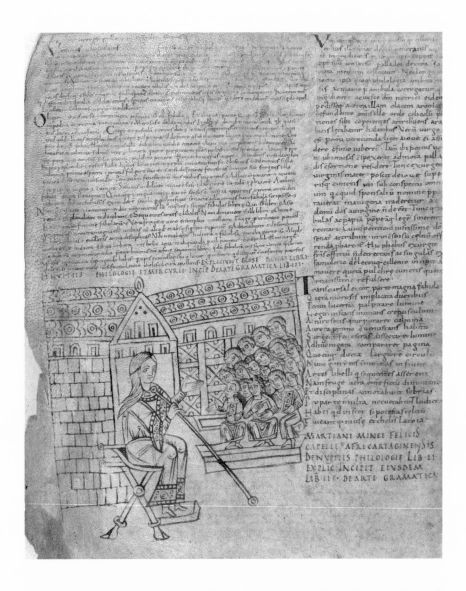

IMAGE 2. Lady Grammar on her throne, rod in her right hand as with her left hand she invites a group of students. Early tenth-century manuscript illustration. Paris, Bibliothèque Nationale, manuscript Lat. 7900A, folio 127 verso. *Courtesy of Bibliothèque Nationale, Paris.*

IMAGE 3. Lady Grammar (top, right) with scourge in her right hand over the head of "bad boy" and open book in her left hand over the head of "good boy." Chartres Cathedral, West façade (Royal Portal), relief with personifications of the arts. *Courtesy of Art Resource, New York, New York, for Foto Marburg.*

IMAGE 4. Lady Grammar (far right) opens a door with her right hand and with her left hand squeezes a round object, at breast level. Andrea di Bonaiuto (14th century), *Triumph of Saint Thomas Aquinas*, detail of fresco, with the seven arts and seven sciences ranged below Thomas (far left, top). Florence, Church of Santa Maria Novella (c. 1365), Spanish Chapel. *Courtesy of Art Resource, New York, for Scala.*

IMAGE 5. Lady Grammar suckles child with her right breast and covers her left breast with a whip. Illustration in manuscript of Bartolomeo di Bartoli da Bologna, *Song of the Seven Virtues and Seven Liberal Arts.* Chantilly, Musée Condé, manuscript 599, folio 7 recto. *Courtesy of Art Resource, New York, New York, for Réunion des Musées Nationaux (photograph by R. G. Ojeda).*

IMAGE 6. Lady Grammar (bottom row, far left) as nurse-with-whip, in pose similar to Image 5. Manuscript illumination (1354) showing the seven virtues and the seven arts, from Giovanni d'Andrea, *Novella in libros decretalium*. Milan, Biblioteca Ambrosiana, manuscript Lat. 42 INF., folio 1 recto. *Courtesy of Biblioteca Ambrosiana, Milan (all rights reserved).*

IMAGE 7. Lady Grammar as nurse-with-whip, in pose similar to Image 5. Manuscript illumination used alongside Augustinian definitions of the arts, with Bartolomeo di Bartoli da Bologna's poetry replaced by bits of moral and historical prose. Florence, Biblioteca Nazionale Centrale, manuscript Banco Rari 38, folio 32 verso. *Courtesy of Ministero per i Beni e le Attività Culturali, Italy.*

IMAGE 8. Lady Grammar (without whip) squeezes both her breasts toward students. Manuscript illumination of northern Italian origin from the second half of the fourteenth century. Paris, Bibliothèque Nationale, manuscript Paris Lat. 8500. *Courtesy of Bibliothèque Nationale, Paris.*

cise but also, when necessary, with the whip.[139] For all his aspirations to construct Bernard's instruction as an ideal nurse's grammar, John cannot ignore the difficulty and discipline of grammar, even in Bernard's classroom. But as with Martianus's text, all John's efforts go to minimizing discipline and thus maternalizing grammar. If Bernard caught a student plagiarizing, he would reprimand him, but often, John adds eagerly, he would not beat him.[140] John feels compelled to focus on Bernard's sense of discretion in wielding the rod, his quasi-"natural" use of discipline to encourage memory. Appropriately, Bernard's grammar bespeaks nature and artifice, nurturing and discipline, mother and father, as we find ourselves once again in that shady region in-between, realm of the wet nurse.

That John mentions the whip at all demonstrates the extent to which grammar was associated with physical punishment, even in his mind.[141] Still, Bernard's classroom seemed in many ways a veritable nursery. His unfailing diligence, coupled with a graduated method of reading that moved from grammar to rhetoric to dialectic, always kept the individual student's personal abilities in mind.[142] All this is a far cry from the monstrous *magistri* who angered Quintilian, terrorized the young Augustine, and animated Martianus's allegory.[143] For all his protestations against the Cornificians, John posits Bernard's "natural" methods as ideal pedagogy. Bernard's strategies were so intuitively human that he virtually restored grammar to its prelapsarian universality. This is particularly apparent in John's reference to the *declinatio,* or evening exercise: "The evening exercise, known as the 'declination,' was so replete with grammatical instruction that if anyone were to take part in it for an entire year, provided he were not a dullard, he would possess a ready mastery of correct speaking and writing and could not possibly fail to grasp the meaning of words in common use."[144] By means of this year-long course, Bernard literally made the universal speech once again natural for all. Anyone who sat in this course could not fail to master grammar by the year's end. Bernard's grammar thus functioned in relation to Babel much as Christian baptism functioned in relation to lost Eden; it removed the original stain for anyone who thus willed (anyone, that is, who was not a complete dullard, who did not lack the basic capabilities expected of the average human).

Like the *De vulgari,* then, book 1 of the *Metalogicon* is characterized by an overwhelming desire for linguistic unity, tempered by an awareness of its impossibility. For John, grammar is almost natural, it can almost put an end to desire: the picture of a babe at the nurse's breast. John's treatment of grammar in many ways encompasses and interrogates tensions regarding the first

art that have been building since antiquity. What is more, John's uneasy resolution of nature and art in characterizing grammar as quasi-mother, at once
nurturing and disciplinary, explicates the many allegories we find in the twelfth
century and beyond.

Lady Grammar in the Twelfth and Thirteenth Centuries

In his portrait of Lady Grammar, John's teacher Thierry of Chartres (d. c.
1150) had already taken a step away from Martianus's frightening severity. In
the *Heptateuchon,* Lady Grammar is an authoritative matron, austere in dress
and demeanor, *in loco materno* perhaps but not really maternal.

> In this assembly of the seven liberal arts, brought together for the cul-
> tivation of humanity, grammar advances first amidst all the rest, a matron
> severe in look and demeanor. She calls together the boys, dictates the
> doctrines of writing and speaking correctly; she translates fittingly the
> idioms of their tongues, professes that the exposition of all authors is
> her responsibility; whatever is spoken is entrusted to her authority.[145]

But while Grammar may lack the nurturing warmth of many of her predecessors, as well as the youth and beauty of Anselm's maidens, she is not sinister; she wields neither sword nor whip. Most significantly, she has recovered
the leadership role temporarily usurped by Sapientia in the Carolingian age.
For Thierry and many of his Chartrian colleagues and disciples, grammar is
again the central humanist discipline, the bedrock and ultimate authority for
human knowledge.[146]

A host of other twelfth-century allegorical poems reflect the renewed
interest in *grammatica*'s positioning between nurturing and discipline which
was recovered and developed by John. Somewhat less intellectual than John,
these writers are titillated by the notion of a body at once nurturing and
penal, bearing breast and rod, milk and blood. Undoubtedly influenced by
contemporary images of the *virgo lactans,* they are furthermore enticed by
the Christian paradox of a virgin mother, an image we earlier encountered
in eleventh-century depictions of Sapientia.[147] Thus in the *Fons philosophiae,*
Godfrey of St. Victor (= Godfrey de Breteuil, c. 1130–c. 1194) represents the
arts as seven streams in imagery reminiscent of Carolingian allegory. Donatus,
surrounded by boisterous schoolboys, presides over the first riverbank. He
both fills their desirous mouths with milk and beats them with his rod.[148] In
the *De eodem et diverso,* Adelard of Bath portrays the arts as seven virgins.

Grammar gives milk to those just commencing study. She holds a book with many marks of corrections in her left hand, a rod in her right hand.[149]

For the most imaginative portrait of Grammar in the twelfth century, however, Alan of Lille takes the prize. Alan appears incapable of mentioning grammar without evoking breast milk. There is a moment in the *De planctu naturae* remarkably similar to *Metalogicon* 1.25, wherein Alan scorns the intellectual pretense of those still in need of basic grammatical skills who fancy themselves dialecticians and philosophers. Whereas John favors the rod in his passage, Alan employs the nursing image: "Others, while still wailing in the cradles of the Art of Grammar and being nursed at her breasts, affect the topmost height of Aristotelian subtlety."[150]

For a full-fledged Lady Grammar, however, we must turn to book 2 of the *Anticlaudianus.* Here Grammar attends to the production of the pole that will lead the cart of Prudence to God:

> Since the bloom of virginity is not deflowered in her nor does the cleft of Venus ruin her chastity. Her breasts, however, float in a deep flood of milk and give the appearance of the ravages that come from lost nulliparity. While the child still sighs at the breasts of his nursing mother, this food feeds him and the one who cannot yet take solids is nourished by liquid. While at this milk-white age, he enjoys draughts of milk and, in one and the same draught, there are food and drink coming from milk alone. She increases the severity of one of her hands with a whip with which she punishes the faults which youth in its way absorbs. Thus by blows she makes the milk more bitter, by the milk she makes the blows more mild. In one and the same action she is father and mother. By the blows she makes up for a father, by the milk she fills the role of mother.[151]

Alan delights in Grammar's various paradoxes to create the most comprehensive image to date. Overflowing with milk but showing no signs of lost virginity, Grammar nourishes her charges with milky knowledge while punishing faults with a whip. Alan's metrical symmetries balance the breast against the whip, an idea that will be rendered visible by the iconographical tradition. As in Smaragdus, Grammar is thus both mother and father.[152] But unlike Smaragdus, Alan revels in the apparent contradiction of nurturing and pain existing side by side in the same body. As poetic image of our argument, then, we will have none more complete or more compelling.[153]

While French poets were creating this new nursing Grammatica, however, twelfth-century visual artists still tended to fall back on more traditional themes. The iconographical programs of many twelfth- and thirteenth-century French cathedrals included the liberal arts: Notre Dame in Déols, Sens, Laon, Notre Dame de Paris, Auxerre, Rouen, Clermont, St.-Omer, Soissons. Sadly, few of these monuments exist today in a condition that allows study. From what we can discern, however, it seems that most adhered to the basic book-and-rod motif.[154]

Interestingly, however, the cathedral at Chartres, while promoting the standard image of Lady Grammar as whip-bearing mistress, reflects a new interest in grammar's relationship to the body (Image 3, p. 33). Grammar forms part of a cycle of the arts on the west façade (the Royal Portal) in the archivolt of the right door; she sits at lower right at the beginning of the cycle. She raises a scourge in her right hand and holds an open book in her left; two boys below her hold open books. As far as I can tell, Chartres gives us one of the first examples we have in grammatical iconography of what I will call the good boy/bad boy motif:

> The representation of Grammar shows only too clearly the troubles of this discipline. She teaches two boys. (This may refer to her double function: to instruct in the right kinds of writing and of speaking.) The boys are strongly contrasted. One is shown semi-nude; the other wears a monk's cowl. This in itself implies a definite contrast of moral values. But more, the semi-nude boy, obviously not very eager to learn, is naughty and impetuous. He pulls the hair of his companion and prevents him from studying. The victim is unable to offer resistance. By their attitudes the boys embody conflicting concepts about the study of grammar. When John of Salisbury describes the teaching methods of Bernard of Chartres, he points out that thorough study requires loving care and humility. One cannot serve at the same time letters and carnal vices. In the relief the boy in the cowl is intent on serving letters. The nakedness of the little aggressor alludes to the idea that he is serving vices. He represents the impetuosity of the stupid crowd, as John of Salisbury calls it.[155]

Clearly, Katzenellenbogen here has sensed Grammar's duality, but Viollet-le-Duc's reading seems more to the point: the bad (naked) boy raises his hand not to pull his mate's hair, rather to receive a "correction" from Lady Grammar's poised scourge.[156] Some two centuries after Chartres, the portico sculptures of the cathedral at Freiburg im Breisgau display much the same motif: "Grammar is just about to flog one of her students, who has removed his robe, for he has not been as diligent as the other student, who sits at her right foot and busies himself with reading a book."[157]

A northern French manuscript from the same period now in the Laurenziana in Florence[158] combines details from Martianus with the good boy/bad boy motif: "At the feet of the schoolmistress sit the clamorous troop of students holding up their writing tablets and rolls; outside on the right and left a lazy student, whose naked upper body significantly displays the lashes suffered by the rod (while the first boy is hard at work) writes on his tablet the words 'Amara radix, dulcis fructus.'"[159] That the bad boy is naked from the waist up makes of him a representative of the flesh. The welts he has suffered pose Grammatica in opposition to carnal pleasure. Lest the pictorial treatment seem too severe, the moral inscribed on the student's writing tablet recalls for viewers the purpose and sweet reward of such chastisement. But the distant intellectual reward held out by *dulcis fructus* is of an entirely different order from the innate bodily pleasures whose renunciation Grammar demands. Here Grammatica has been constructed as a rejection of the body.

French and other northern European literature of the following century will inherit the nursing Grammatica of twelfth-century French allegory, though none will be as concise as Alan regarding Grammar's dual nature. In the *Bataille des septs arts* (c. 1250), Henri d'Andeli reproaches the Aristotelians for attacking Grammar, their own mother.[160] Henri's near contemporary, Jean Le Teinturier, casts the arts as lily-white virgin sisters and Grammar, the eldest, as their mother.[161] Rhetorical texts paint a similar picture. In the *Morale scholarium,* John of Garland (first half of the thirteenth century) heaps scorn upon the grammars of Alexander of Villedieu and Eberhard of Béthune by claiming that they "offer poison instead of milk."[162] Gervase of Melkley (c. 1185–after 1213), whose very name says "milky meadow" ("Gervasius de saltu lacteo"), sings the praises of his teacher, the rhetorician and fruitful *inventor* Jean de Hauvilla, "whose breasts have nourished him on discipline since he was an uncultured infant."[163]

In an amusingly ironic moment of the *Laborintus,* Eberhard the German (fl. before 1280) laments the plight of the *magister,* who will spend his life unappreciated, underpaid, teaching the alphabet. Eberhard recounts the birth of the grammarian. While all newborn baby boys cry "ah!," which derives from "Adam" (and thus recalls original sin and the sorrowful condition of exiled humanity), the nascent grammarian cries "alpha!" which foreshadows hours of drudgery in the classroom with intransigent schoolboys. Like John

and Augustine, Eberhard thus associates grammar (presumably only necessary after Babel) with the suffering of postlapsarian existence:

> He is born crying. Although this is a general phenomenon, he will nev-
> ertheless have a special cry. For he will often see his cheeks flooded with
> tears without becoming any more devoted as a result. Now every little
> boy screams "Ah!" as he comes forth to light: he derives this from the
> root of our first parent Adam: But this little boy belches forth an extraor-
> dinary "alpha!," which he will rehearse while reciting syllables to his
> unlearned pupils.[164]

As one glossator explains, the very title of Eberhard's handbook signals inherent pain *(Labor habens intus).*[165]

And yet, although perhaps not overly affectionate, Eberhard's Lady
Grammar nurses her charge. Thus Philosophy summons the arts: "Among
your hierarchies at the threshold is the first sister, who carries her breasts
filled with milk."[166] Philosophy later bids the *grammaticus* to drink from
Grammar's breasts, but with moderation lest he overcome his pupils:

> Thus let your herald, who is called by the law of providence, drink with
> sobriety the breasts of grammar. If he is filled with milk, he will chal-
> lenge his students and will not be feeding the unlearned on an empty
> stomach.[167]

Sensing in grammar both nourishment and a vague threat, Eberhard's text
bespeaks the same duality we saw in Alan of Lille. We should note that the
metaphorical association between studying and suckling, student and suckler, is implicit in the very word *alumnus,* at once "student" and "object of nourishing care" from *alo, alere.*[168]

France and Germany did not hold a monopoly on these images, although,
admittedly, twelfth-century France provided many of the most coherent allegorical statements. A nursing Lady Grammar is also found in Italian literature of the twelfth and thirteenth centuries. In the *Elegia* (an uninspired imitation of Boethius's *De consolatione philosophiae*), Arrigo da Settimello (fl. c.
1194) portrays Lady Philosophy in the company of seven young maidens, the
arts, and casts Grammar in her new standard maternal role: "The first maiden
cares for and caresses the children, the second constructs syllogisms
[Dialectic], the third leads in discourse [Rhetoric]."[169] In the prologue to his
Magnae derivationes, Uguccione da Pisa (d. 1210) characterizes his very text

as a nursing mother: "For here the young boy will be nursed with milk, here the adult man will be fed with greater nutrition."[170] With clear reference to Alan of Lille's virgin nurse, Bonvesin de la Riva in the following century paints Grammar as a radiant virgin queen pregnant with wisdom.[171]

The self-promoting Boncompagno da Signa (1165–1240) deserves special attention for his manipulation of grammar's milky metaphorical tradition.[172] Proud rhetorician at Bologna in the first quarter of the thirteenth century, Boncompagno uses grammar's long-standing association with infancy and nurturing to ridicule the first art as simpleminded while affirming the sophisticated glories of rhetoric. He repeatedly compares the *grammaticus* to the nursing and teething infant. Book 9, chapter 3, of the *Rhetorica novissima* compares the seven arts to a series of large and small wheels. Naturally, grammar is the first wheel: "The first wheel was driven by a difficult and tiring force, yet it proceeded from that milk which was given to those whose teeth were just coming in."[173] Boncompagno thus recalls grammar as both difficult and nurturing.

Two chapters later, he elaborates his conception of grammar while belittling grammarians for their elementary concern with mere sentence construction to the exclusion of more advanced matters such as meaning: "Nevertheless I liken all grammarians to the infant whose teeth have just come in, who sucks milk, who recites like the schoolboy, and when he says *a, e, i, o, u* looks just like a crying little baby. Moreover, he can only judge physical sounds, for he maintains that it is fine and in line with the rules to say, 'the fly gives birth to the lion' and 'an angel is a fire-breathing monster.'"[174] In many ways evocative of Eberhard's nascent grammarian, Boncompagno's *grammaticus* will pass a lifetime on the edge of primal chaos, bawling like a newborn infant *(vagire)*, desiring milk, and barely negotiating that separation from the mother's body foreshadowed by budding teeth. All his efforts must go to organizing the phonic chain into discrete, identifiable units.

Within the visual arts, however, we owe the movement away from Martianus's disciplinarian toward a humanist maternal Grammatica to the extraordinary father and son team of Nicola (1220?–78?) and Giovanni Pisano (c. 1245–c. 1314), the latter a near contemporary of Dante. Nicola rejects the stylized excesses of his predecessors to pioneer a new sculpture deeply indebted to the classical sense of balance and human dimension. His rendering of Grammatica on the pulpit pedestal of the cathedral in Siena (1265–68) embodies these new values. Neither nurse nor monster, mother or father, Grammar is calm, noble, and majestic in her folds of classical drapery. She places her arm around a young boy as they consult the open book on her lap. Her gender is conspicuously underplayed in a way that anticipates the paternal gentility of Luca Della Robbia's Grammar on the Campanile in Florence almost two centuries later.[175]

Both father and son worked on the fountain in the main square at Perugia (1278), but the bas-reliefs of the arts around the lower pool are probably the work of Giovanni.[176] They have not fared well; chalk replicas made in the late nineteenth century provide the most accurate depiction of the originals. Grammar here seems the loving mother figure with arm affectionately draped around her student as they consult an open book. Both teacher and student bow their heads in humility to signal the humble nature of their discipline.[177]

Lady Grammar in Fourteenth-Century Italy

Giovanni's maternal designs for Grammar will blossom fully only with his own pulpit pedestal in the cathedral at Pisa (1302–10),[178] completed in the very years Dante was composing *De vulgari eloquentia*. In one of the panels at the base of the central supporting column, Lady Grammar gazes fondly upon the two suckling infants in her arms, one at either breast. This is the first explicit nursing image of Grammar in sculpture to date. There appears to be no trace of discipline in Giovanni's wholly maternal rendering. It is interesting to note that Giovanni uses the very same nursing motif (an infant at each breast) for Mater Ecclesia on one of the outer supporting columns.[179] Thus the potential for overlap and conflict between secular and spiritual authority translates into iconographical ambiguity.

Nicola and Giovanni's movement toward a humanist or maternal Grammar by no means expunges the harsher elements of the tradition. The bas-reliefs of the arts created for Giotto's Campanile in Florence by the school of Andrea Pisano (fl. first half of the fourteenth century) take a step backward into more traditional themes.[180] Grammar is a large, matronly figure with scourge prominently displayed. She lords it over three cowering schoolboys who are squeezed into the frame of the diamond-shaped tableau. Thus Italian sculpture of the due- and trecento reveals a contest between old and new, Grammar as discipline and Grammar as mother.

But the terms of this conflict come head to head in a dramatically explicit manner only in Italian painting and manuscript illuminations of around the same period. A wall mural at the Castello Roncolo, near Bolzano, depicts Grammar holding a child to suckle with one hand while grasping Martianus's wicked scalpel in the other.[181] Closer to Dante's personal milieu is Andrea Bonaiuti's (= da Firenze) fresco, "The Triumph of St. Thomas," in the Spanish Chapel of Santa Maria Novella (c. 1365) (Image 4, p. ooo). The seven sciences and seven arts form an arcaded row below the triumphant Thomas. Grammar is on the far right. She gazes imperiously upon the exemplar (Donatus or Priscian?) crouched at her feet, hard at work. She is austere but does not hold a whip or rod. Three boys kneel at her left in reverence, almost as if in prayer. With her right hand she opens a small door (the door to learning, a motif we will see again in Della Robbia); with her left she squeezes an unidentified round object at breast level, indeed, precisely where her left breast should be. D'Ancona describes it as "un oggetto rotondo, forse un pomo."[182] But surely, Andrea is having fun with the suckling imagery that had begun to permeate the figural tradition. He was perhaps unwilling to render the scene explicitly, but it was clearly in his design. Grammar directs her gaze and gestures at the upturned faces of the three boys.[183]

Giusto Fiorentino's (= da Padova) paintings in the Augustinian Church of the Eremitani in Padua (second half of the fourteenth century, destroyed by a seventeenth-century restoration) probably showed Lady Grammar as wet nurse and whip-bearer. Judging from fifteenth-century descriptions, both Venturi[184] and Dorez[185] conclude that Giusto must have been inspired by one of a closely related group of manuscripts of Bartolomeo di Bartoli da Bologna's *Canzone delle virtù e delle scienze* (1355). Bartolomeo's vernacular text consists of a definition and poem for each of the seven liberal arts (here called "sciences") and seven virtues. "Each page devoted to one of the Sciences or Virtues is divided into three parts: at the top is the definition of the Science or Virtue transcribed from the works of St. Augustine; in the middle is a color depiction of the Virtue or Science; finally, at the bottom we read the stanza dedicated to that Virtue or Science."[186] Here is Bartolomeo's rendition of Lady Grammar:

> *Beautiful, gentle, and graceful is Grammar.*
> *She is the young maiden who with her breast*
> *To the little boy distills*
> *The knowledge of letters, so that he can know*
> *More on account of that milk and can*
> *Attain perfection in deed and possess wisdom.*[187]

Like the figure on Giovanni Pisano's pulpit pedestal at Pisa, Bartolomeo's Lady Grammar is fully maternal, a nursing mother with no hint of discipline.

But the illustration tells another story: all of these manuscripts depict Lady Grammar as nurse-with-whip (Image 5, p. 35). In every case, the illustrator has taken pains to expose Grammar's full breast and nipple, thus rendering the act of suckling in anatomically graphic detail. Her other breast, however, is covered by the scourge she holds in her raised hand. The duality of Grammar's character is thus illustrated by a kind of symmetrical balancing of elements linked to her anatomy. She offers pleasure with one breast, pain via the whip and blocked access to the other. Several other manuscripts from this period offer similar illustrations (Images 6–8, p. 36, 37, and 38).[188] Thus fourteenth-century Italy produces the most perfect illustration of Alan of Lille's Lady Grammar between nurturing and discipline. What is more, these illustrations were inspired by Augustinian definitions in a specifically Augustinian intellectual milieu.[189] Although produced some years after Dante composed the *De vulgari,* these illustrations capture a broad cultural definition of grammar between nurturing and discipline which had been building since antiquity and which was certainly current in Dante's Italy.

As the first of the seven liberal arts, Grammatica was the pre-eminent site of social law, the first science of border inscription, a drawer of lines at once linguistic, social, and corporeal. Lady Grammar took young boys from the breast of their mothers and nurses and set them on the road to adult society. This road was often fraught with the perils of discipline in every sense: the mental and linguistic discipline that censored spontaneous self-expression in the mother tongue, and the very real physical discipline of the rod so commonly associated with the grammar classroom. Grammar checked primal desire in the mother's body and thus inhabited an important psycholinguistic border. In her most revealing late medieval incarnations, Grammar did not simply represent discipline and the strictures of the social order, rather she supervised the transition from immediate in-fant (i.e., speechless) desire to the symbolic obligations of adulthood and speech. Representations of grammar lent visual reality to the basic cultural opposition between the fluid body (female) and the acorporeal rational ego (male), while conjuring up for the most sensitive thinkers their primal interdependence. I will use this primal cultural definition of *grammatica* to read Dante's *De vulgari eloquentia* in the following chapter.

TWO

The Primal Scene of Suckling in *De vulgari Eloquentia*

Est-ce le calme rivage d'une contemplation que je me réserve en mettant à nu, sous les surfaces sournoises et policées des civilisations, l'horreur nourricière qu'elles s'occupent à écarter en purifiant, en systématisant, en pensant: l'horreur qu'elles se donnent pour se construire et fonctionner?

Julia Kristeva, *Pouvoirs de l'horreur,* 248[1]

a la tetta de la madre s'apprende

The image of the infant suckling at his nurse-mother's breast lodged deeply in Dante's metaphorical psyche as in the larger collective imagination of his day. As conveyed by a long tradition of verbal and visual allegory, the nurse's milk purveyed both physical nourishment and the beginnings of symbolic language. The nurse thus harbored a potential conflict by confusing the corporeal and the mental, two realms held in strict opposition by the Neoplatonists. Specifically in fourteenth-century Italian versions, Lady Grammar embodied a compelling paradigm for human development toward rational self-realization and, most markedly, adult language as an eventual rejection of the nurse's body. As we will see in subsequent chapters, this paradigm was available to Dante in several philosophical and allegorical figures beyond the confines of Grammar. But Lady Grammar most forcefully described the link between milk and speech and thus casts the most immediate reflection in a grammatical and rhetorical text like the *De vulgari eloquentia.*

Grammatical discipline on the one hand and the figure of the wet nurse on the other were vivid human realities in Dante's Florence. Paul Gehl's recent study of reading texts confirms the conservative moral agenda of grammar in trecento Florence.[2] Grammar aimed to inculcate the virtues of obedience and respect for the *magister* as model of authority by whatever means necessary. The classroom setting reduplicated in miniature the larger social arena, where violence was the order of the day. "It is clear that Florentines tolerated violence among schoolboys and even encouraged it. Physical punishment of students was considered a normal and necessary part of teaching and learning throughout the period."[3] As we have seen in the pervasive "mounting the horse" penalty, this institutionalized discipline commonly enlisted the aid of one's fellow students.

Moreover, the moral socialization of young boys into the adult economy was conceived of by fourteenth-century Florentines as a strict gender dichotomy. Grammar school provided the real and symbolic break with domestic maternal affection and the in any case suspect moral education that women might provide.

> Women were notorious among male Latinists for exactly the kind of flightiness and inconstancy that moral-grammatical education was designed to counteract. It was all very well to entrust very small children to the care of a child-woman, but the factual break with maternal care represented by sending boys out to the grammar school was also a symbolic break with the tutelage of women.[4]

We see that social reality precisely mirrored grammatical allegory. And yet, the pictures of Lady Grammar Dante knew allowed that the nurse's body was also an important source of learning.

At the same time, the institution—not to say enterprise—of wet nursing was flourishing in Florence, where it was common practice among middle- and upper-class families to give infants out to nurse. One of very few "careers" available to women of the time, the business of wet nursing was nonetheless dominated by males in ways that underscore the oppressively patriarchal character of that society. Although contracts were drawn up between the infant's family and the nurse, the terms therein were always dictated by the father and the *balio,* the wet nurse's husband. According to Christiane Klapisch-Zuber, the nurse's milk, particularly in its cultural association with menses and the pregnant body, harbored a constant threat of contamination at once moral and economic, and thus necessitated strict control by the male order:

The father took responsibility, both material and spiritual, for assuring the development of his seed. This was how Florentines proclaimed the superiority of the paternal "blood," transmitted in the act of generation, over the blood and the milk with which the mother, then the nurse, would nourish the child. Lastly, a "pregnant" milk was considered the final move in a feminine plot, widely denounced at the time, to destroy or dilapidate the wealth created or transmitted by men.[5]

It requires no hermeneutic finesse nor any great leap of psychoanalytic imagination to understand that grammar in Dante's Florence represented a symbolic rejection of maternal nurturing.

Indeed, Dante tells us so in no uncertain terms in *Convivio* 4. *Convivio* 4.24 does not discuss grammar per se. We find Dante instead in the middle of a lengthy explication of book 4's canzone, "Le dolci rime d'amor ch'i' solia," a verse of which necessitates clarification of the human life stages. Dante identifies *adolescentia* (through age twenty-five) as the first real life phase, generally ignoring the traditional earlier divisions of infancy, teething, and boyhood.[6] Nobility manifests itself differently at different periods of life. One noble quality appropriate to *adolescentia,* he tells us, is obedience: obedience, that is to say, of one's father, one's grammar teachers and elders ("maestri e maggiori"), and whoever else might symbolically reside in the father's place ("che loco paterno tiene"). The adolescent must obey his fathers in order not to stray in the dangerous wood that is adult life.

To illustrate his point, Dante hearkens back to the scene of nurturing. The adolescent must leave behind childhood desires and submit to paternal discipline, just as earlier the infant had first seized upon, but then turned away from, the breast, as soon as the first glimmer of reason appeared: "Onde, sì come, nato, tosto lo figlio a la tetta de la madre s'apprende, così tosto, come alcuno lume d'animo in esso appare, si dee volgere a la correzione del padre, e lo padre lui ammaestrare" (So as a child clings to the mother's breast as soon as he is born, likewise as soon as some light appears in his mind he ought to turn to the correction of his father, and his father should give him instruction).[7] The symbolic father-*magister* stands at the opposite pole from the mother's body, whose lacteal flow spells peril, as the very verb *apprendersi* conjures physicality and danger. For the stilnovists (poets of the *dolce stil nuovo*), it connotes passion, a violent grabbing hold of, a catching fire.[8] At the same time, *apprendere,*[9] along with the Latin *apprehendere,*[10] is used commonly in Dante and elsewhere to denote a principle of intellect: to seize or lay hold of a concept, to learn. Reason and desire thus intermingle in the historical semantics of that verb just as upon the allegorical body of Lady Grammar. *Apprendersi* was also used in Dante's day as a literal reflexive: to lay hold or grab hold of oneself.[11] Though such an understanding may do violence to Dante's intent in this context, we would do well to keep it in mind. Ultimately, Dante will come to imagine the scene of suckling as a site of profound subjective truth.

But this is not the case in Dante the grammarian-philosopher of *Convivio* and the contemporaneous *De vulgari eloquentia*.[12] In particular, the *De vulgari eloquentia* (c. 1304) encodes the mother's body in a complex metaphorical dialectic of concealment and revelation.[13] As the unfinished Latin treatise signals Dante's first significant attempt to sort out the vastness of human linguistic difference, so it is simultaneously the textual ground upon which the recent exile works through his relationship to the maternal body. While a voice of grammatical rationalism—fully committed to constructing a fourteenth-century Italian *koine*—turns dutifully away from maternal desire, a more poetic voice asserts its textual presence obliquely by recalling the nurturing moment's fundamental allure.[14]

The image of a babe suckling at his mother's breast constitutes the primal scene of the *De vulgari*. By this I mean simply that the several linguistic and historical propositions put forward in the treatise can all be shown to point to the powerful presence of this original vignette in the poet's mind. My use of the phrase *primal scene,* while not in strict accordance with the Freudian *Urszene* (the child's repressed witnessing of his parents in sexual intercourse), nonetheless conforms to Freud's eventual understanding of that structure as a therapeutically useful, narrative reconstruction of some original event. Somewhere between history and invention, the primal scene allows for the organization of disparate realities around a single unifying narrative whose ontological status is forever undecided and undecidable. As Ned Lukacher has shown, the primal scene can thus serve as an important critical discursive term, "a trope for reading and understanding."[15] It is precisely in this sense that the primal scene of suckling informs the difficult logic and troubled paragraphs of the *De vulgari*. Between them, *Convivio* and *De vulgari* homologize a number of what we might call "exile events" both universal and individual: Babel, the Flood, the Fall from grace, political exile, and grammar as loss of linguistic innocence. Motivating such homologies and underlying both texts is the generalized cultural notion of a scene of exile in the mother's body, a scene to which Dante had immediate access through Lady Grammar.

nutricem imitantes

Critics' attempts to understand Dante's problematic conception of *grammatica* in the treatise have focused exclusively on traditional academic definitions.[16] These fall into four specific categories: (1) grammar as the study of Latin language and letters, the first of the seven liberal arts;[17] (2) grammar as a synonym for the Latin language;[18] (3) grammar as an attribute of any of an elite group of sacred languages (Latin, Greek, Hebrew), which somehow participate in the divine *Ursprache;*[19] (4) grammar as linguistic science in general, and specifically as a universal structural principle underlying all historical tongues. This last highly technical definition was current among the speculative grammarians or *modistae* in the thirteenth century. Much has been made in recent criticism about Dante's possible indebtedness to these thinkers.[20]

Unfortunately, no one of these definitions can account for Dante's several uses of *gramatica* in the *De vulgari* and in the contemporaneous *Convivio*.[21] Dante recognizes *gramatica* in its most traditional acceptation as the first of the seven liberal arts in three instances in the *Convivio*.[22] The most common meaning of *gramatica* in Dante's works is as synonym for the Latin language, category two of my typology.[23] The remaining instances (with one conspicuous exception to be discussed below) conceive *gramatica* as a theoretically constructed language that few select societies in history have possessed. Struggling against the inexorable flow of individual linguistic will ("propter variationem sermonis arbitrio singularium fluitantis") through space and time, the mythical founding fathers of grammar *(inventores)* set down lines, inscribed borders, articulated rules.[24] Whence the only formal definition of the word in the *De vulgari* at 1.9.11: "Gramatica nichil aliud est quam quedam inalterabilis locutionis ydemptitas diversibus temporibus atque locis" (*Gramatica* is nothing less than a certain immutable identity of language in different times and places).

Dante's description of personal speech as a liquid flow ("sermonis fluitantis") participates, as we will see, in a larger metaphorical motif in the treatise which figures universal linguistic history through space and time as river flow. In subsequent chapters, we will have occasion to note the many times Dante matches speech production to fluviality, as well as the specific Neoplatonic connection between corporeal humors (including mother's milk) and the various nourishing flows in the body of Mother Earth. We will also soon see that at a crucial moment in the *De vulgari,* the recent exile recalls the Arno as a nurturing breast. But Dante prefaces his entire project by defining grammar as a rational discipline emphatically distinguished by its opposition to the nursing body, which is where the vernacular—the mother tongue—resides:

> Vulgarem locutionem appellamus eam qua infantes assuefiunt ab assistentibus cum primitus distinguere voces incipiunt; vel, quod brevius dici potest, vulgarem locutionem asserimus quam sine omni regula nutricem imitantes accipimus. Est et inde alia locutio secundaria nobis, quam Romani gramaticam vocaverunt. Hanc quidem secundariam Greci habent et alii, sed non omnes: ad habitum vero huius pauci perveniunt, quia non nisi per spatium temporis et studii assiduitatem regulamur et doctrinamur in illa. (*De vulgari* 1.1.2–3)

> I call "vernacular language" that which infants acquire from those around them when they first begin to distinguish sounds; or, to put it more succinctly, I declare that vernacular language is that which we learn without any formal instruction, by imitating our nurses. There also exists another kind of language, at one remove from us, which the Romans called *gramatica*. The Greeks and some—but not all—other peoples have this secondary kind of language. Few, however, achieve complete fluency in it, since knowledge of its rules and theory can only be developed through dedication to a lengthy course of study.[25]

The natural primacy and relative immediacy of the vernacular ("naturalis est nobis") will lead Dante in the following paragraph to his problematic declaration of its superiority over *gramatica* ("nobilior est vulgaris") in apparent contradiction to his views in *Convivio* 1.6.10.[26]

   While apparently less personal, Dante's characterization of vernacular and grammar here recalls Augustine's discussion of Latin and Greek in book 1 of the *Confessions*. His suggestion of a critical union between biology and language, the nurse's body and early speech, reflects the long allegorical tale of Lady Grammar that we sketched in the previous chapter. It is to this visual, poetic, and, if you will, more popular understanding of the first art that we must turn to comprehend the function of *gramatica* in the *De vulgari*. The very body of Lady Grammar furnished a kind of cultural primer by warning would-be speaking subjects away from the seductive perils of nurturing female corporeality, while at the same time affirming her presence as the basis of all life and learning. The nurturing body carried no small amount of associational freight for Dante: it was melded in his metaphorical imagination with an intimate affection for the vernacular, a nostalgic desire for an idyllic childhood in Florence before exile, a sincere hope for a unified Italian tongue, and a larger intellectual drive for a space and time before Babel.

As the simultaneous site of mysterious wisdom and dark cultural terror, Lady Grammar embodies the fundamental contradiction at work in the treatise. Two voices were mentioned earlier, the grammatical and the poetic. Although reductive and dualistic, this simple binary—grammarian/poet—precisely reflects the kind of dualistic thinking promoted by personifications of Grammar and thus provides a historically accurate structural tool that can help us gain access to the complex reality of Dante's thinking about language and self. There is an important sense in which all poetry (and most dramatically vernacular poetry) allies with the musical and rhythmic (semiotic) resources of the mother tongue over and against grammar. I draw a distinction between Dante the prescriptive grammarian and rational dogmatist, and Dante the observer of nature and human realities, in many ways the "poet" of the *Comedy*. For as Kristeva shows in her theory of the semiotic body,[27] poetry is precisely what challenges and upends linguistic rules, normative syntax, and rational categorizing—in a word, grammar.

The poet's choice of the wet nurse image in connection with the vernacular must be read in the context of the imposing history we have just traced. From a Christian perspective, there is a sense in which Dante, like Augustine and John of Salisbury before him, evokes the inevitably inadequate nature of all human constructs in his metaphorical choice. The vernacular's *naturalis* is secondary nature (John's *natura creata*), not the *prima natura* to which the grammarian will on some level aspire. Thus while the grammarian argues for the greater nobility of the vernacular over *gramatica* because of the former's natural primacy, the poet's metaphor is already working to undercut that privilege. Even the image of a babe suckling at the breast is marked by postlapsarian desire: always, already fallen, the imitation of an imitation ("nutricem imitantes").[28]

But the grammarian turns right around to forget this disturbing fact. With unwavering structuralist fervor, he aims to bestow grammatical status on the new vernacular by fixing rules, drawing boundaries, and thus excluding words, structures, accents, dialects, and whole worlds of language. Much of the remainder of the treatise consists of his attempt. The grammarian's project of exclusion constitutes nothing less than a betrayal of the treatise's initial inspiration. And the poet alerts us to this fact throughout by providing the grammarian with treacherous metaphors. For we soon discover that the grammarian's intent to draw a line and somehow step beyond history entails nothing less than a metaphorical rejection of the nurturing female body. The grammarian would turn his back on the wet nurse, the very figure that engendered his project. Fortunately, the poet is there to ensure that he will not succeed.

Dante, then, is of at least two minds regarding *gramatica*. Momentarily attracted to the rationalist project of grammar as historical recuperation, his larger poetic sense cannot ignore the inexorable flow of all human material through time and space. This dispersive force is gendered female. As we will see, this force subtly invades his grammatical endeavors in the *De vulgari;* in the contemporaneous *Convivio,* it makes a dramatic appearance precisely where Dante makes his most elaborate attempt to define the first art.

His explication of "Voi ch'intendendo il terzo ciel movete" occasions a general discussion of cosmology and eventually, in *Convivio* 2.13, a conceptual linking of the heavens to the sciences and of the seven liberal arts to the first seven heavens. Dante then addresses each heaven-science pair to elaborate upon his analogies. He begins with Grammar and the moon:

> *Dico che 'l cielo de la Luna con la Gramatica si somiglia [per due proprietadi], per che ad esso si può comparare. Che se la Luna si guarda bene, due cose si veggiono in essa proprie, che non si veggiono ne l'altre stelle: l'una si è l'ombra che è in essa, la quale non è altro che raritade del suo corpo, a la quale non possono terminare li raggi del sole e ripercuotersi così come ne l'altre parti; l'altra si è la variazione de la sua luminositade, che ora luce da uno lato, e ora luce da un altro, secondo che lo sole la vede. E queste due proprietadi hae la Grammatica: chè, per la sua infinitade, li raggi de la ragione in essa non si terminano, in parte spezialmente de li vocabuli; e luce or di qua or di là in tanto quanto certi vocabuli, certe declinazioni, certe construzioni sono in uso che già non saranno: sì come dice Orazio nel principio de la Poetria quando dice: "Molti vocabuli rinasceranno che già caddero." (Conv. 2.13.9–10)*

> I say that the heaven of the Moon resembles Grammar because it may be compared to it; for if the Moon is closely examined, two things will be seen peculiar to it which are not seen in the other stars: one is the shadow in it, which is nothing but the rarity of its substance in which the rays of the Sun cannot terminate and be reflected back as in its other parts; the other is the variation of its luminosity, which shines now on one side, now on the other, according as the Sun looks upon it. These two properties Grammar possesses; for because of its infinitude the rays of reason are not terminated, especially in the particular of words; and it shines now on this side, now on that, insofar as certain words, certain declensions, and certain constructions are

now in use which formerly were not, and many were formerly in use which will yet be in use again, as Horace says at the beginning of his *Poetics,* when he says: "Many words shall be born which have long since fallen out of use."[29]

The poet's inventions are fantastic. The moon exhibits two major characteristics: (1) shadows, which are due to variations in its material density and the consequent inability of the sun's rays to reach its surface equally in all parts,[30] and (2) varying luminosity (waxing and waning), which is the direct result of its positioning in relation to the sun ("che ora luce da uno lato, ora da un altro, secondo che lo sole la vede"). Just so Grammar: (1) shadows, because the "rays of reason" cannot reach all parts of it evenly (particularly when it comes to vocabulary), and (2) varying luminosity, inasmuch as words, declensions, and constructions that are now in use were once unheard, and many that were once current will pass back into usage at some future date, as Horace teaches.

What can *gramatica* mean here? The poet's imagination exceeds anything ever dreamt of even by the *modistae.* Far from a supremely rational construct, grammar is in some ways beyond reason; hardly an instrument of stability, it is the *locus* of mutability; no longer the domain of an elite few, grammar here reaches out to embrace the whole of human linguistic experience. It is at once bound (like the lunar body) and limitless (like the innumerable particles that compose it). The poet conjures up an image of Darwinian selection on an infinite linguistic gene pool.

Gramatica as Luna represents a primal female presence who at once holds out hope for an original unity of language and experience while forever foreclosing to humans complete access. The waxing and waning moon evoked for Dante the unending variability of the temporal, sublunar world. At the same time, that bulbous, milky presence in the night sky harbored associations via Diana with an alluring female corporeality both pure and unattainable. Thus in *Paradiso* 3 and 4, it is in the heaven of the changing moon that Piccarda and Costanza speak of vows of chastity honored and violated. There too *gramatica* lurks in the shadows, as Mazzotta has recently argued. Just as grammar posits a sacrifice of individual linguistic will by arbitrarily fixing the link between signifier and signified in hopes of fending off the violence of time, so the vow of chastity aims to pre-empt and disarm history's violence by arbitrarily positing a constant will. Grammatical in its sacrifice of individual desire to rational force, the vow of chastity would stem the flow of time.[31]

But the image of the changing moon that Dante presents in *Convivio* 2 surrenders grammar's rationalist pretensions and acknowledges the ultimate futility of human attempts to counter time. In the strictest allegorical interpretations, as we have seen, grammar must turn away from variability and the female body; in *Convivio* 2, the picture of variability and female corporeality becomes *gramatica*'s emblem. Dante's final reference to Horace merely underscores the point that even the allegedly privileged grammatical tongues are caught up in the same historical cycles of change that influence the myriad vernaculars. Not coincidentally, this allusion will play a central role in *Paradiso* 26, where Adam will finally refute the notion of an original linguistic unity in human history, even prior to Babel.[32]

vir sine matre, vir sine lacte

While it is true that the *De vulgari* eventually becomes a somewhat technical rhetorical manual for a specific poetic idiom, we cannot deny that at least initially Dante conceived his project in more ambitious terms. Several scholars, using widely divergent critical approaches, have concluded that on some level Dante hoped to recapture the Edenic idiom with his new illustrious vernacular.[33] This drive is particularly apparent in book 1, where the grammarian feels compelled to trace the entire linguistic history of the world as preface to his search for the new illustrious vernacular. In a great flood of linguistic dispersion, this history takes us from Eden to Babel to Europe before arriving at long last on the Italian peninsula.[34]

The point of origin is Eden, where the grammarian lays the groundwork for his history.[35] Above all, which language did Adam speak? Strikingly, this yearning for origins is not innocent in terms of gender. As Dante the grammarian seeks the purity of a unified origin, he would recapture the Edenic, purely male idiom of the first father. He would establish his grammatical authority by locating himself and subsequently his new language in a space outside of, or prior to, history—a space, that is, not contaminated by the maternal body.[36] The original idiom that he seeks belonged not simply to Adam, rather in circumlocution to that man who not only existed outside of time, but who—in what might otherwise seem a gratuitous qualifier—knew neither mother nor milk: "Quoniam permultis ac diversis ydiomatibus negotium exercitatur humanum, ita quod multi multis non aliter intelligantur verbis quam sine verbis, de ydiomate illo venari nos decet quo *vir sine matre, vir sine lacte, qui nec pupillarem etatem nec vidit adultam,* creditur usus" (Since human affairs are now carried

on in so many different languages, so that many people are no better understood by others when they use words than when they do not, it behooves us
to hunt for the language believed to have been used by *the man who never had
a mother nor drank her milk, the man who never saw either childhood or maturity*).[37] The grammarian is drawn to Adam as the emblem of a singular, radical detachment from the maternal body.[38]

Already we begin to appreciate the fundamental contradiction in Dante's
project. Just a few paragraphs before, the poet upheld the vernacular as *nobilior* because it was *naturalis,* because it was the idiom of women and children
("ad eam non tantum viri sed etiam mulieres et parvuli nitantur") and of the
nurse's milk ("nutricem imitantes"). To the extent that the grammarian would
now forge a new motherless, milkless tongue, he is in direct violation of the
poet's initial lacteal enthusiasm.

quanquam Sarnum biberimus ante dentes

Dante's text posits a figural relationship between the stages of an ideal universal history drawn from Scripture—Eden, Babel, Confusion—and his personal life itinerary—childhood in Florence, exile, wandering. Paradoxically,
the grammarian's pragmatic urge to recover origins gives rise to the poet's
insistent focus on personal experience, its fragmentary nature, and, above
all, its dispersive origins in the maternal body. The poet will not allow the
grammarian to ignore the vast discrepancy between his unified mythical ideal
and the reality of experience.

It is no coincidence that what is perhaps Dante's most substantial reference to his recent exile appears just as he is completing his treatment of the
language of Adam (1.4–6) and is about to recount the catastrophe of Babel
(1.7): on the brink, that is, of the Fall. At 1.6.2–3, the grammarian first casts
scorn upon the villagers of proverbial Pietramala, who in their provincial
naïveté assume that Adam spoke Pietramalese. He then proclaims his own
rational detachment from such parochialism: "Nos autem, cui mundus est
patria velut piscibus equor, quanquam Sarnum biberimus ante dentes et
Florentiam adeo diligamus ut, quia dileximus, exilium patiamur iniuste, rationi
magis quam sensui spatulas nostri iudicii podiamus" (To me, however, the
whole world is a homeland, like the sea to fish—though I drank from the Arno
before cutting my teeth, and love Florence so much that, because I loved her,
I suffer exile unjustly—and I will weigh the balance of my judgment more
with reason than with sentiment).[39] Exile and its consequent experience of

linguistic difference has led to grammatical enlightenment; only now can the grammarian accept that the language of Adam was other than Florentine. By evoking this critical division in his own life at the moment of that larger divid-ing line in the narrative of human history, Dante's text brings together indi-vidual and universal structures. Not fortuitously, the suckling image reappears at this moment ("ante dentes"), and we will attend to it shortly. But first, we must clarify the text's structural dynamics.

Symbolically, the two levels of narrative (individual and universal) cen-ter on a linguistic event. Universally, this is Babel; individually, it is exile. Both signal the advent of linguistic difference.[40] Fundamentally at issue is the symbolic border, the line separating unity from dispersion. In the universal narrative, the text tends to meld together the three great human cataclysms (the original Fall from grace, the Flood, Babel) and to privilege Babel as the moment of critical lapse. For a grammarian, Babel naturally bears special sig-nificance.[41] As any reader of *Paradiso* 26 can attest, Dante will eventually find it impossible to admit of a larger ontological Fall that was not necessarily also a linguistic Fall.[42]

This conceptual reduction of discrete historical events to a crucial, sym-bolic juncture can be felt in the *De vulgari* as well. The text rehearses the shame of Babel in chapter 7. Here again, the three great sins of humanity are compared to the infractions of a mischievous grammar school boy, who—either forgetful or scornful of his previous two whippings—challenges the authority of the father-*magister* yet again. This third presumption proves criti-cal, for at this point the student must mount the proverbial flogging horse. Dante discerns the antics of schoolboys in the local grammar classroom pro-jected upon the text of universal history:

> Num fuerat satis ad tui correptionem quod, per primam prevaricationem eluminata, delitiarum exulabas a patria? Num satis quod, per univer-salem familie tue luxuriem et trucitatem, unica reservata domo, quic-quid tui iuris erat cataclismo perierat, et <que> commiseras tu animalia celi terreque iam luerant? Quippe satis extiterat. Sed, sicut proverbialiter dici solet, "Non ante tertium equitabis," misera miserum venire maluisti ad equum. Ecce, lector, quod vel oblitus homo vel vilipendens disciplinas priores, et avertens oculos a vibicibus que remanserant, tertio insurrexit ad verbera, per superbam stultitiam presumendo. (*De vulgari* 1.7.2)

> Was it not enough to correct you that, banished from the light for the first transgression, you should live in exile from the delights of your

homeland? Was it not enough that, because of the all-pervading lust and cruelty of your race, everything that was yours should have perished in a cataclysm, one family alone being spared, and that the creatures of earth and sky should have had to pay for the wrongs that you had committed? It should indeed have been enough. But, as we often say in the form of a proverb, "not before the third time will you ride"; and you, wretched humanity, chose to mount a fractious steed. And so, reader, the human race, either forgetful or disdainful of earlier punishments, and averting its eyes from the bruises that remained, came for a third time to deserve a beating, putting its trust in its own foolish pride.

Dante's thoughts are never far from the dynamics of the grammar classroom. Although the earlier crimes involved whippings ("avertens oculos a vibicibus que remanserant"), only the third is marked with the special importance bestowed by the ritualistic flogging horse ("non ante tertium equitabis"). Dante ties the suffering of the local grammar school boy (exile from maternal nurturing and mother tongue) to the universal human condition in exile,[43] at once a figure for individual political exile. In our above analysis of *De vulgari* 1.6.3, we saw that the poet conceived of his pre-exilic childhood in Florence as a kind of nursing at the Arno-breast, exile as a kind of forced weaning. Thus on a profound level, the text of the *De vulgari* assimilates the experience of *grammatica* (regulated language), political and universal exile, to the loss of the nursing breast. To be sure, Dante never says this explicitly, and I presume to make no definite claims for conscious authorial intent. Nonetheless, evidence for this primal metaphorical logic is there in the treatise.

The clearest textual nexus between grammar and exile will appear in book 2 (2.6.4), where the grammarian explicates the four registers of style: (1) flavorless *(insipidus)*, (2) flavorful *(sapidus)*, (3) flavorful and graceful *(sapidus et venustus)*, and (4) flavorful, graceful, and exalted *(sapidus et venustus etiam et excelsus)*. He describes the progression from one level of sophistication to the next in terms of the educational program of his day: (1) unregulated language, (2) grammar, (3) rhetoric, (4) poetry and the exalted style. He then illustrates each stylistic level with a sentence. I have schematized the passage in Table 1. Of course, the higher we ascend in linguistic art, the deeper we descend into personal political sarcasm. The four example sentences stage Dante's political history, from innocence to exile to ever-widening realms of political reality: from the more local aggressions of Azzo VIII ("marchionis Estensis") to the international movements of Charles of Valois ("Totila secundus"), archvillain and key player in the grammarian's own exile.[44]

TABLE 1. Dante's Four Registers of Rhetorical Style, with Sample Sentences

REGISTERS OF RHETORICAL STYLE	SAMPLE SENTENCES
1. *insipidus, qui est rudium*	"Petrus amat multum dominam Bertham."
2. *sapidus, qui est rigidorum scolarium vel magistrorum*	"Piget me cunctis pietate maiorem, quicunque in exilio tabescentes patriam tantum sompniando revisunt."
3. *sapidus et venustus, qui est quorundam supeficietenus rhetoricam aurientium*	"Laudabilis discretio marchionis Estensis, et sua magnificentia preparata, cunctis illum facit esse dilectum."
4. *sapidus et venustus etiam et excelsus, qui est dictatorum illustrium*	"Eiecta maxima parte florum de sinu tuo, Florentia, nequicquam Trinacriam Totila secundus adivit."
***	***
1. *flavorless, typical of the uncultured* (unregulated language)	"Peter loves Miss Bertha a lot."
2. *flavored and no more, typical of pedantic students and teachers* (grammar)	"I am stricken with sorrow more than most, for whomever drags out his life in exile, revisiting his native land only in dreams."
3. *graceful as well as flavored, found among those who have made a superficial study of rhetoric* (rhetoric)	"The laudable discretion of the Marquis of Este, and his widely displayed generosity, make him beloved of all."
4. *flavored and graceful and also striking, typical of illustrious writers* (poetry and the exalted style)	"The greater part of your flowers, o Florence, having been snatched from your breast, the second Totila advanced in vain towards Trinacria."

We saw earlier that Dante's text links the cataclysms of universal history to his personal life trajectory. Here the *De vulgari* links moments in Dante's political biography to stages of linguistic education and sophistication. Thus a profound logic—according to which personal history signifies in terms of both individual linguistic development and universal history—begins to emerge. Table 2 (Biography, Language, History) clarifies these structures. The three rows in Table 2 define the master narratives that in many ways structure the treatise. The columns demonstrate chronological moments within each narrative that are structurally assimilable: column one represents a primal moment of perfection, column two the moment of lapse or loss of innocence, columns three and four the continuing vicissitudes of corruption and dispersion. Linguistic experience brings individual and universal history together: grammar remains the central organizing principle.[45] The passage from flavorless *(insipidus, qui est rudium)* to flavorful *(sapidus, qui est rigidorum scolarium vel magistrorum)* unmistakably evokes the individual's first encounter with linguistic regulation, grammar school. *Rudes* is commonplace in grammatical and rhetorical texts throughout the Middle Ages to describe schoolboys at the very beginning of their studies; the *magister* of course represents the grammar school master.[46] The radically personal resonance of these categories, however, becomes evident only when we consider the example sentences that the poet provides for each. While all three of the advanced examples evoke exile to some degree, the transition from *insipidus* to *sapidus,* from vernacular innocence to grammar, registers a deeply personal lament as the illustrations progress from "Peter loves Miss Bertha a lot" to "I am stricken with sorrow more than most, for whomever drags out his life in exile, revisiting his native land only in dreams"

TABLE 2. Structural Master Narratives of the *De vulgari eloquentia*

	PRIMAL MOMENT OF PERFECTION	MOMENT OF LAPSE / LOSS OF INNOCENCE	CORRUPTION	DISPERSION
BIOGRAPHY	Florence	exile	Italian politics	international politics
LANGUAGE	mother tongue	grammar	rhetoric	illustrious poetry
HISTORY	Eden	Babel	Confusion	—

(see Table 1). Clearly, the *De vulgari* situates *gramatica* in the space of an exile at once personal and universal.

Dante's text thus imagines the first encounter with linguistic legislation, *gramatica,* as a kind of protoexile, a figure of future events. But it does not stop here. The grammarian's hankering for a pure and single origin reaches further back to uncover the maternal body, the moment of weaning or teething, as the truly primal scene of exile. Dante's text is no less explicit on this point. We need only recall the crucial, nostalgic passage cited earlier: "Nos autem, cui mundus est patria velut piscibus equor, *quanquam Sarnum biberimus ante dentes.*" In a mythical, pre-exilic Florence, the infant Dante suckled at the breast of mother Arno; exile, the moment of *gramatica,* is also the moment of teething.

What we might call the figural subtext of the *De vulgari* features an Edenic primal vignette—the babe at his mother's breast—followed by a Fall from grace: teeth, grammar, exile, conflated into a single symbolic reality. The more or less contemporaneous *Convivio* offers specific support for such a reading. From its title, *Convivio* is dominated throughout by a nutritional metaphor: as he explains in the opening chapter, the *Convivio* author will act as a kind of nurse/teacher, much like Lady Grammar, who will make palatable and help digest with his bread/commentary the hard food of true philosophy.[47] He thus describes himself in terms reminiscent of the medieval wet nurse: "She first chews the food, and by chewing prepares it for the toothless lad, so that he may more easily swallow it."[48] Of course, readers of *Convivio* must already possess strong teeth and a whole palate.[49] Still, Dante's self-designation as nutritional intermediary and facilitator evokes the wet nurse, just as in book 4, as we have seen, his discussion of obedience in *adolescentia* returns to the primal scene of suckling.

No sooner does the *Convivio* author cast himself in these nurturing terms than he claims for his text—in contradistinction to the youthful, impassioned *Vita nuova*—an adult, "virile" privilege,[50] as he anticipates the discussion of life stages in book 4.[51] As we know, much of book 1 works to justify his choice of the mother tongue in the face of Latin. Thus we see that the *Convivio* narrator, philosopher in the mother tongue, is poised uneasily between maternal nurturing and patriarchal reason, much like the *De vulgari* grammarian. For all that he would claim rational manhood for his vernacular text, he is drawn to the site of original desire in the mother tongue.

In no uncertain terms, he locates the mother tongue at the very origin of his being, the Aristotelian efficient cause that brought his parents together in sexual union to effect his generation: "Questo mio volgare fu congiugnitore de li miei generanti, che con esso parlavano, sì come 'l fuoco è disponitore del ferro al fabbro che fa lo coltello; per che manifesto è lui essere concorso a la mia generazione, e così essere alcuna cagione del mio essere" (This vernacular of mine was what brought my parents together, for they conversed in it, just as it is the fire that prepares the iron for the smith who makes the knife; and so it is evident that it has contributed to my generation, and so was one cause of my being).[52] At the same time, the mother tongue brought him to Latin and higher learning: "Ancora, questo mio volgare fu introduttor di me ne la via di scienza, che è ultima perfezione, in quanto con esso io entrai ne lo latino e con esso mi fu mostrato: lo quale latino poi mi fu via a più innanzi andare" (Moreover, this vernacular of mine was what led me into the path of knowledge which is our ultimate perfection, since through it I entered upon Latin and through its agency Latin was taught to me, which then became my path to further progress).[53] I have shown that traditional grammatical culture demanded that a line be drawn between the body and reason, between the wet nurse and adult discourse. Here the *Convivio* narrator violates that cultural border even as he calls attention to it. He grants the desiring body access to Latin, traditionally a space of acorporeal male privilege. Lodged deep within, at the very origin and core of Latin learning, lies corporeal desire. Commonly represented in grammatical texts by the suckling infant, as we have scene, this desire in the mother tongue here evokes the Freudian primal scene in its most literal reading: the very desire that brought together the bodies of Dante's parents to create him.

As in the *De vulgari,* the nurse's body is there in the first book of *Convivio* too as Dante laments his exile in revealing personal terms.

> *Poi che fu piacere de li cittadini de la bellissima e famosissima figlia di Roma, Fiorenza,* di gittarmi fuori del suo dolce seno—nel quale nato e nutrito fui in fino al colmo de la vita mia, *e nel quale, con buona pace di quella, desidero con tutto lo cuore di riposare l'animo stancato e terminare lo tempo che m'è dato—per le parti quasi tutte a le quali questa lingua si stende, peregrino, quasi mendicando, sono andato.* (*Conv.* 1.3.3–4; my emphases)

> Since it was the pleasure of the citizens of the most beautiful and famous daughter of Rome, Florence, *to cast me out of her sweet bosom—where I was born and bred [nourished] up to the pinnacle of my life,* and where, with her good will, I desire with all my heart to rest my weary mind and to complete the span of time that is given to me—I have wandered like a pilgrim, almost like a beggar, through virtually all the regions to which this tongue of ours extends.

Thus, for Dante, to be exiled from Florence is to be cast from the "sweet breast," at which he had been "born and nourished"[54] right up to the apogee of his life arc, into a kind of linguistic drift. Again, the text metaphorically collapses various life episodes that played out over the course of many years onto the primal scene of nurturing and weaning.

Now we know from Dante's discussion of the stages of human life in book 4 of the *Convivio* that the "colmo de la nostra vita" (these are his exact words; see 4.24.3) falls at the mathematical center of the life triptych, the period of *gioventute* (see Table 3). Dante ignores the traditional early stages of *infantia* and *pueritia,* just as he hastily defines *senio* as some vague space beyond *senettute* ("perhaps ten years"; see 4.24.5). These other periods would seem to upset the poet's perfect triune symmetry. The mathematical center of *gioventute* (age thirty-five), in turn, nearly represents the historical date of exile and certainly represents the ideal poetic date of exile, "nel mezzo del cammin." Pre-exilic Florence is a nurturing mother.[55]

Klapisch-Zuber has situated Dante's categories within traditional definitions of the life stages:

> At the beginning of the fourteenth century, Dante gave expression to a traditional conception of the place of childhood in the system of the universe and in the uniquely human system of the "ages of life." In his *Convivio* and following Avicenna, he defines the first age, "adolescentia," which reaches from birth to 25 full years of age, as the age of growth. Previous tradition, however, particularly that of Isidore of Seville, transmitted in the thirteenth century by Vincent of Beauvais, distinguished three seven-year sub-ages within this vast segment of the lifespan: "infantia," from birth to 7 years; "pueritia," from 7 to 14; and "adolescentia," strictly speaking, from 15 to 28 years. Dante totally disregards "infantia": he states that adolescence really begins at the age of 8, but he gives no particular name to the childhood years immediately following infancy ("pueritia").[56]

We might note that, just as *De vulgari* tends to fuse the three great human tragedies around Babel, so *Convivio* here marks the first significant life stage as adolescence.

Of course, we cannot agree that Dante "totally disregards" *infantia,* for precisely in this section of the *Convivio* he recalls the primal scene of suckling that we cited at the beginning of the chapter in order to characterize the movement away from *adolescentia* toward *gioventute* ("Onde, sì come nato, tosto lo figlio a la tetta de la madre s'apprende, così tosto, come alcuno lume d'animo in esso appare, si dee volgere a la correzione del padre").[57] This rejec-

TABLE 3. The Human Life Stages in *Convivio* 4.24

STAGE	*adolescentia* (adolescence)	*gioventute* (adulthood)	*senettute* (old age)
AGE	to age 25	25–45	45–70

tion of the maternal breast motivates the grammarian's rationalist vision in the *De vulgari*.

The *De vulgari* grammarian shuns female corporeality even as he constructs the subtext elucidated above. For as he vies to recover a pure, male origin by assimilating personal experience to universal history, the poet's insistent empiricism undermines his efforts. At the origin of individual human experience, the poet discovers not the "motherless, milkless man," rather the flow of the nurse's milk, emblem of the fallen nature of human language and existence.

Dante's grammatical discourse is thus invested with a profound subjective logic. Symbolically caught up in both his individual political plight (exile) and universal human history, his construction of a new grammatical vernacular leads him to ponder the bases of selfhood. But if in the *Convivio,* through Aristotelian logic and imaginative reconstruction of the scene of his parents' coitus, Dante makes of the mother tongue the unifying origin of self, in the more empirical *De vulgari* he fails to grasp this original unity in history despite his exhaustive search through the linguistic *silva* of the Italian idiom. In the final paragraphs of book 1 of the *De vulgari,* the exile's personal investment in the invention of vernacular unity is no less explicit. Surely, we are meant to discern the reflection of the fragmented subject in the poignant phrases he employs to articulate his pseudodiscovery: the new vernacular, "whose scent is left everywhere but which is nowhere to be seen," "which has left its scent in every city but made its home in none," "wanders around like a homeless stranger."[58] Both language and subject exist in a kind of poststructuralist drift. As absent presence, the ideal vernacular's trace is everywhere, its essence nowhere. Finally, the *De vulgari* grammarian must abandon empiricism and return, as in *Convivio,* to purely rational, Aristotelian reconstruction:

> Sed dicere quod in excellentissima Ytalorum curia sit libratum, videtur nugatio, cum curia careamus. Ad quod facile respondetur. Nam licet curia, secundum quod unita accipitur, ut curia regis Alamannie, in Ytalia non sit, membra tamen eius non desunt; et sicut membra illius uno

> Principe uniuntur, sic membra huius gratioso lumine rationis unita sunt.
> Quare falsum esset dicere curia carere Ytalos, quanquam Principe carea-
> mus, quoniam curiam habemus, licet corporaliter sit dispersa. (*De vul-
> gari* 1.18.5)

> Yet is seems contradictory to say that it has been assessed in the most
> excellent tribunal in Italy, since we have no such tribunal. The answer
> to this is simple. For although it is true that there is no such tribunal in
> Italy—in the sense of a single institution, like that of the king of
> Germany—yet its constituent elements are not lacking. And just as the
> elements of the German tribunal are united under a single monarch, so
> those of the Italian have been brought together by the gracious light of
> reason. So it would not be true to say that the Italians lack a tribunal
> altogether, even though we lack a monarch, because we do have one,
> but its physical components are scattered.

Like the Italian court manqué that serves as its historical figure, the *volgare
illustre* can be apprehended only as a rational construct, in the "pure light of
reason" ("gratioso lumine rationis"). As body, it is fragmented, dispersed ("licet
corporaliter sit dispersa").

Dante thus oscillates between grammarian and poet, rational idealist and
skeptical empiricist. The *De vulgari*'s insistent, if oblique, references to the
primal scene of suckling in the nurse's body succeed, ultimately, in undermining the grammarian's project and bringing it to an untimely end. After
Augustine, Dante simply cannot ignore the original commingling of language
and selfhood. As such, the nurse's body threatens to undo any idealist notion
of language and self as a cleanly delimited, self-sufficient whole. The image
of the nurse's body threatens to unveil the grammarian/subject's constructs
as arbitrary, neither primary nor universal, always already dependent on
maternal desire.

What we find in the *De vulgari* in the wake of grammatical personification allegory, I submit, is a medieval inscription of Kristeva's semiotic *chora*.
For Kristeva, the presubjective infant experiences meaning as rhythm and
pulsations, a musical *chora*. The infant's eventual construction of an ego coin-
cides with a movement toward symbolic logic, language, and patriarchal order
("a la correzione del padre")[59] and away from the maternal body. Nonetheless,
the semiotic will live on in uneasy coexistence as the underside of the symbolic, the condition of its being. While the *De vulgari* grammarian would pretend to have overcome this maternal realm, the poet all along senses its primal importance. Kristeva teaches that the maternal body threatens the

borderline subject, and Dante in the *De vulgari* is nothing if not borderline: on the border, as we have seen, between vernacular and grammar, Florence and exile, Eden and Babel. In terms that describe our grammarian, Kristeva has charted these frontier regions outside of, or prior to, the subject/object binary, in the banished realm of the abject or deject.

> A deviser of territories, languages, works, the *deject* never stops demar-
> cating his universe whose fluid confines—for they are constituted of a
> non-object, the abject—constantly question his solidity and impel him
> to start afresh.[60] A tireless builder, the deject is in short a *stray*. He is
> on a journey, during the night, the end of which keeps receding. He has
> a sense of the danger, of the loss that the pseudo-object attracting him
> represents for him, but he cannot help taking the risk at the very moment
> he sets himself apart.[61]

The abject becomes the artist: producer of culture, fetishist of language, poet. On the edge of the subject/object binary, abjection focuses on the symbolic process itself. "Its symptom is the rejection and reconstruction of languages."[62]

Repressed maternal authority threatens the borderline subject, whose very existence *qua* subject is predicated upon this original corporeal map-ping. On the threshold of language and culture, *gramatica* evokes the anxi-eties attendant upon that primal border. The primal scene of nourishment threatens to reveal the constructed nature of the grammarian/subject's bor-ders. By violating the socially imposed separation of body from body, the image of the wet nurse recalls that time prior to the inviolate subject, thus placing subjectivity itself in crisis.[63]

In the *De vulgari*, this crisis is at once personal and universal. Dante's cryp-tic references to the Arno as maternal breast must be read in the context of his general fascination with river geography throughout book 1. Rivers pro-vide a metaphor for human dispersion, both geographic and linguistic. They depict human history as an unrelenting flow of mysterious origin. Immediately after the Confusion, human stock initiated its ramiform dispersion across the globe and into Europe, where for the first time rational gullets ("rationalia guctura") tasted at least some of her rivers ("vel totius Europe flumina, vel saltim quedam").[64]

Locally, the grammarian describes the great Apennine ridge as the peak of a slanted roof that disperses streams to one side and the other through its many gutters: "Dicimus ergo primo Latium bipartitum esse in dextrum et sinistrum. Si quis autem querat de linea dividente, breviter respondemus esse iugum Apenini, quod, ceu fistule culmen hinc inde ad diversa stillicidia grundat aquas, ad alterna hinc inde litora per ymbricia longa distillat" (First of all, then, I state that Italy is divided in two, a left-hand and a right-hand side. If anyone should ask where the dividing-line is drawn, I reply briefly that it is the range of the Apennines; for just as from the topmost rain-gutter water is carried to the ground, dripping down through pipes on each side, these likewise irrigate the whole country through long conduits, on one side and the other, as far as the two opposite shores).[65] The more personal "quanquam Sarnum biberimus ante dentes" thus evokes a complex psychological dynamic operant in the treatise, whereby personal history imitates universal history, just as distinct narrative episodes in either register are structurally assimilated one to the other. The great maternal flow of history envelops all of humanity. The *De vulgari* grammarian hopes to stem this flow, while the poet recognizes its mystical power.

ut "femina," "corpo"

To what extent can we justifiably identify the grammarian's new illustrious vernacular with the Adamic tongue described early in book 1? The first book offers no tangible definition of the new idiom, which in the final paragraphs becomes a purely rational ideal, the Aristotelian *unum semplicissimum*. The rhetorical details of book 2 would appear to signal the grammarian's renunciation of those grandiose ideals as he now aims merely to describe a concrete poetic idiom.[66] Still, there are metaphorical clues well into the second book that betray the grammarian's utopian desires. They let us know that on some level he still envisions the ahistorical tongue of the motherless, milkless man.

The grammarian's scathing review and rejection of the peninsula dialects in 1.11–15 makes exception for a small handful of poets who have somehow managed to capture the illustrious ideal. Appropriately, the sole trait that these poets share is a turning away in some degree from the idiom of their childhood, which is to say a turning away from their own, selfsame, or mother tongue. Dante couples the prepositional phrase *a proprio [vulgare]* or *a materno* with various forms of the verb *diverto* no fewer than five times in 1.12–15.[67] By repeatedly insisting on this phrase in such a highly formulaic manner, the grammarian emphasizes a primarily negative definition of the new language. Above all, the illustrious vernacular can be identified by a gesture of rejection: rejection of one's original self *(a proprio),* which is simultaneously a rejection of the mother *(a materno)*. Not surprisingly, we learn in 1.18.1 that, in relation to the myriad dialects of the peninsula, the illustrious vernacular is none other than the *paterfamilias*.[68]

Only in book 2, however, does the grammarian's conception of the new idiom as a radical detachment from female corporeality find specific textual expression. I refer to Dante's construction of word classes at 2.7. In chapters 1 through 6 of book 2, the grammarian treats the proper subject matter, poetic form, meter, and verse for writers in the new vernacular. His increasingly narrow focus thus comes to rest in chapter 7 upon vocabulary. In chapter 7 the grammarian will pick and choose specific word classes and words as worthy of inclusion in the new language while rejecting others. Chapter 7 thus represents the grammarian at his most exclusionary. He moves through a strict hierarchy of word classes to zero in on those appropriate to the illustrious vernacular. Table 4 will recall Dante's well-known categories. Dante knew of such colorful rhetorical terminology in any number of sources ranging from Aristotle to Geoffrey of Vinsauf.[69] Nevertheless, his specific adjectival choices merit consideration. The grammarian's primary exclusion of women *(muliebria)* and children *(puerilia)* seems in direct opposition to the poet's initial enthusiasm for the vernacular because of its inclusion of these marginalized groups ("For not only men, but also women and children strive to acquire it, as far as nature allows").[70] The grammarian is intent upon repressing his feminine origins and the dispersivity of nature *(silvestria)*[71] to enter into the adult male *(virilia)* social economy *(urbana)*. He eschews that which threatens chaotic slippage *(lubrica, reburra)* in order to embrace controlled, linear presence *(pexa)*.

TABLE 4. Word Classes in *De vulgari eloquentia* 2.7

Word classes referring to women *(muliebria),* children *(puerilia),* dispersivity *(silvestria),* and chaotic slippage *(lubrica* and *reburra)* are shown in regular type. Word classes referring to adult males *(virilia, yrsuta),* their social economy *(urbana),* and their controlled linear presence *(pexa)* are shown in bold.

INITIAL WORD CLASSES	*muliebria*	*puerilia*	**virilia**			
SUBCLASSES OF *VIRILIA*			**urbana**	*silvestria*		
SUBCLASSES OF *URBANA*			*lubrica*	**pexa**	**yrsuta**	*reburra*

The examples in the following paragraph support my reading. Only the noblest words are to remain in the sieve wherein the grammarian separates the wheat from the chaff. He provides representative words for each of the rejected groups, as illustrated by table 5. But his final exclusion, based upon the finest gradations, is the most revealing. For even within the social organization of the city *(urbana)* there still exists the threat of the slippery *(lubrica)* and unrefined *(reburra)*. What specific words can be offered as examples of these qualities? There was a certain inherent logic to representing the puerile idiom with *mamma* and *babbo,* the soft feminine idiom with *dolciada* and *placevole,* and the idiom of the pastoral countryside with *greggia* and *cetra.* No such logic would seem to obtain for *urbana lubrica et reburra.* Here the situation allows the poet free rein, and he takes full advantage of the moment: "Nec urbana lubrica et reburra, ut 'femina' et 'corpo.'" The female body. The dispersion that threatens the constructs of the grammarian-subject—that carries inside the walls of the city, as it were, the threat of primal confusion—resides in the female body.[72]

The grammarian hopes somehow to expunge his origins in female corporeality by assimilating his individual history to a mythical universal history predicated upon an originary male purity. His inability to effect convincingly this figural gesture gives the treatise its difficult, dialectical shape and brings it to an early finish. But Dante is troubled not only by the critical dissonance between his life story and the ideal myth. He is also plagued from the very start by serious doubts over the legitimacy of an original male purity (of the motherless, milkless man) even on the universal level. And it is none other than an image from Scripture that instills in him this doubt.

os ex ossibus meis et caro de carne mea

Later chapters will demonstrate the unabashed triumph of the nursing body in Dante's *Commedia,* a celebration of the mother tongue as Christian *sermo*

TABLE 5. Representative Words in Rejected Word Classes in
De vulgari eloquentia 2.7

REJECTED WORD CLASS	REPRESENTATIVE WORDS
puerilia	*mamma, babbo; mate, pate*
muliebria	*dolciada, placevole*
silvestria	*greggia, cetra*

humilis. By contrast, we have seen that the postexilic minor works hew closely—at least on the surface—to a classical paradigm of gender and development. As *Convivio* 4.24.14 baldly declares, adult reason demands a rejection of the nurturing body ("la tetta de la madre") in exchange for the logic of patriarchal discipline ("la correzione del padre"). Perhaps nowhere do classical and Christian values clash more dramatically. As we will see, for Dante, Christ is a nursing mother. In this context, it is instructive to investigate Dante's deployment of Christian Scripture to support his classical logic on this point in the minor works.

In fact, in the passage we have cited from Dante's discussion of obedience in *Convivio* 4.24.14, he cites Paul's Letter to the Colossians and Proverbs to support his contention that adolescent reason must follow the law of the father away from the mother's body. In both instances, Dante translates freely, and somewhat deceptively, from the Vulgate Latin.[73] The first instance immediately precedes Dante's evocation of the nursing body:

> *E però dice Salomone, quando intende correggere suo figlio (e questo è lo primo suo comandamento): "Audi, figlio mio,* l'ammaestramento del tuo padre." *E poi lo rimuove incontanente da l'altrui reo consiglio e ammaestramento, dicendo: "Non ti possano quello fare di lusinghe né di diletto li peccatori, che tu vadi con loro." Onde, sì come, nato, tosto lo figlio a la tetta de la madre s'apprende, così tosto, come alcuno lume d'animo in esso appare, si dee volgere a la correzione del padre, e lo padre lui ammaestrare.* (Conv. 4.24.14; my emphases)

> Therefore Solomon says, in seeking to correct his son (and this is his first command): "Hear, my son, *the teaching of your father.*" At once he shields him from the bad advice and teaching of others, saying: "*Do not let sinners have the power to beguile you with flatteries or delights so that you will go with them.*" So as a child clings to the mother's breast as soon as he is born, likewise as soon as some light appears in his mind he ought to turn to the correction of his father, and his father should give him instruction.

A close comparison here with the Vulgate Latin uncovers Dante's selective editing: "My son, hear the instruction of thy father, *and forsake not the law of thy mother:* / That grace may be added to thy head, and a chain of gold to thy neck. / My son, *if sinners will entice thee,* consent not to them. / If they will say: Come with us, let us lie in wait for blood . . . / My son, walk not thou with them."[74] Dante simply cuts the offending phrase that asserts an equally valid "law of the mother." As the larger context aims to impose the pure supremacy of the symbolic father, there is no room here for gendered complexity. Furthermore, the classical specter of the nurse's body looms in the scriptural Latin. Jerome's choice of the verb *lacto* here to convey luxurious enticement and seduction (Dante's *lusinghe* and *diletto*) provides spectacular semantic testimony of the nurturing horror inherent in classical language.[75] Thus it is as though Dante's textual authority offered conflicting messages: on the one hand an imperative to obey the mother, on the other a semantic evocation of the original commingling of sin and the mother's milk. The determined rationalist does away with any reference to maternal authority.

The same tendency is evident as the passage goes on to explain that obedience to the father should be understood as symbolic acquiescence to male cultural authority, equated to the law and reason, not simply and literally the biological father.[76] Dante provides a gloss on his earlier repeated translation of paternal discipline as *ammaestramento* to elucidate that by *father* he means all male elders and teachers ("deono essere obediti maestri e maggiori"). Thus the grammar master *(magister)* makes an oblique appearance *in loco paterno.*

Here he again enlists scriptural authority, for Paul had spoken of obedience to a plurality of fathers: "E se alcuno calunniasse: 'Ciò che detto è, è pur del padre e non d'altri,' dico che al padre si dee riducere ogni altra obedienza. Onde dice l'Apostolo a li Colossensi: 'Figliuoli, obedite *a li vostri padri* per tutte cose, per ciò che questo vuole Iddio'" (If someone should protest that "what is said is said only of the father and not of others," I reply that all other obedience must redound to the father. Thus the Apostle says to the Colossians: "Children, obey *your fathers* in all things, for this is the will of God").[77] Again Dante has rendered gender specific Jerome's more inclusive Latin: "Children, obey *your parents* in all things, for that is pleasing in the Lord."[78]

In conclusion, let us return to the *De vulgari* to uncover this same gendered editing of Scripture in a passage that has long vexed critics. At 1.4.2–3, Dante offers his response to the question of who first used language:

> Secundum quidem quod in principio Genesis loquitur, ubi de primordio mundi Sacratissima Scriptura pertractat, mulierem invenitur ante omnes fuisse locutam, scilicet presumptuosissimam Evam, cum dyabolo sciscitanti respondit: "De fructu lignorum que sunt in paradiso vescimur; de fructu vero ligni quod est in medio paradisi precepit nobis Deus ne comederemus nec tangeremus, ne forte moriamur." Sed quanquam mulier in scriptis prius inveniatur locuta, rationabilius tamen est ut

hominem prius locutum fuisse credamus, et inconvenienter putatur tam egregium humani generis actum non prius a viro quam a femina profluxisse. Rationabiliter ergo credimus ipsi Ade prius datum fuisse loqui ab Eo qui statim ipsum plasmaverat. (*De vulgari* 1.4.2–3)

According to what it says at the beginning of Genesis, where sacred Scripture describes the origin of the world, we find that a woman spoke before anyone else, when the most presumptuous Eve responded thus to the blandishments of the Devil: "We may eat of the fruit of the trees that are in Paradise: but God has forbidden us to eat or to touch the fruit of the tree which is in the middle of Paradise, lest we die." But although we find in Scripture that a woman spoke first, I still think it more reasonable that a man should have done so; and it may be thought unseemly that so distinguished an action of the human race should first have been performed by a woman rather than a man. Therefore it is reasonable to believe that the power of speech was given first to Adam, by Him who had just created him.

In a moment of blatant misogyny, the grammarian—apparently defying Holy Scripture itself—decides to indulge the privilege of male reason and bestow the honor of first speech upon man.[79]

But in point of fact, the scriptural account of Genesis, contrary to what the grammarian claims, does indeed support male first speech. Adam spoke first. As several critics have noted, the grammarian should have found support for his assertion at Genesis 2:20: "And Adam called all the beasts by their names, and all the fowls of the air, and all the cattle of the field"[80] (Eve's speech to the serpent is at Genesis 3:2–3).

Explanations for this oddity have varied. Could Dante simply have nodded? This seems highly unlikely given the importance and familiarity of the text in question. Critics such as Marigo and Pézard have suggested that Dante did not regard Adam's naming of the animals—a string of words in isolation—as true speech.[81] Technically, it is unclear that naming necessarily implies speaking. Moreover, Adam's naming is only indirectly referred to, whereas Eve plays the role of speaker at Genesis 3:2–3. This seems a reasonable explanation.

Dante may have ignored the oblique reference to Adam's naming of the animals in his search for the first speaker. But the question does not end here. For there is another passage in which Adam truly speaks (the verb is *dixit*)—this time in full, declarative sentences—before Eve's speech at Genesis 3:2–3. This passage has met with near complete blindness on the part of critics.[82]

The verse I refer to is at Genesis 2:23. The Lord has created woman from Adam's rib and brought her to him: "And Adam said: This now is bone of my bones, and flesh of my flesh: she will be called woman, because she was taken out of man."[83] The following verse reads: "Wherefore a man will leave father and mother, and will cleave to his wife: and they will be two in one flesh."[84]

The passage elided by Dante's text describes nothing less than the moment of sexual difference. It is a moment of division within Eden—within, that is, what Dante the grammarian presumes to be a perfect unity and, specifically, a pure acorporeal male space ("vir sine matre, vir sine lacte"). This scriptural passage reveals male corporeality in all its flesh and bones as inextricably linked to, indeed the source of, the female corporeality from which the *De vulgari* grammarian would dissociate Adam, his language, and himself. Adam literally gives birth to the woman and is shown to be caught up in the same differential complex as the dispersive female. Indeed, it is only at this point of difference that gender comes into being. The passage suggests that, even at the origin of universal history, the primal scene depicts not a motherless, milkless man, but rather an original commingling of male and female in one flesh ("in carne una").[85] The scene thus frustrates the grammarian's desire to recover an original demarcation between male purity and female dispersion. At the origin, female corporeality marks even Adam. The wet nurse is there from the very start.

By eliding this passage, Dante's text succeeds not only in casting Eve's later collusion with the serpent into the misogynic spotlight. More crucially, it banishes a scene suggestive of an originary hermaphroditic union into the nether realms of the subtext. To preface the entire project with this primal vignette of gender conflation would have been to undermine the linear, binary terms that sustain grammatical discourse. It would have negated from the start the possibility of recovering a pure origin through rational means. As we have seen, however, the poet will not allow this enabling repression.[86] The poet's gentle reminders of the primacy of female corporeality throughout the treatise prove critical in the end. The grammarian finally renounces his rationalist pretensions, turns back toward the wet nurse, and thus clears the way for the poet's ultimate triumph in the mother tongue.

THREE

The Body of Gaeta: Burying and Unburying the Wet Nurse in *Inferno*

From Lady Grammar to the Neoplatonic Nurse and Beyond

What becomes of the nurse's body in the *Comedy?* The previous chapters demonstrated that Dante had assimilated a grammatical paradigm that dictated the rejection of the nurse's body as prerequisite to rational, linguistic selfhood. At the same time, the Christian poet recognized the fundamental importance of the nurse's body to human speech and selfhood. I have argued that the incompleteness of the *De vulgari* attests to Dante's inability to reconcile these conflicting notions.

The *Comedy* offers a resolution to this conflict, a resolution that opposes the strict, and strictly gendered, dichotomy between body and mind apparent in classical developmental schemes. We will see that the *Paradiso* in particular embraces nursing corporeality as a central—perhaps the central— metaphor of divine knowledge. The nurse's body follows a carefully plotted metaphorical itinerary in the *Comedy*. In its most general outlines, this itinerary features *Inferno* as the realm of the poisonous anti-nurse, Circe, and *Paradiso* as the textual celebration of a new Christian poetics of suckling. In between—and most revealing for our analysis—*Purgatorio* dramatizes first the deconstruction of the classical subject in his inimical relation to nurturing corporeality, and, finally, at the top of the mountain as terrestrial paradise is regained, the reconstruction of a new Christian selfhood, with a new speech and poetics, whose principal distinction will be identity with the nursing body.

The vertical series of cantos 26 and 27 defines the textual poles of this development; these cantos reach across the entire poem to give questions of semiosis—language, poetics, speech, and selfhood—prominence of place. In particular, Dante's text pays nearly tacit homage to the death and burial of the nurse's body within the classical confines of *Inferno* 26 in order to resurrect and celebrate that same body as site of divine good in *Paradiso* 27. At the same time, *Inferno* 26 evokes through Virgil and his commentators the Neoplatonic poetics of microcosm and macrocosm that consider the fluid body as the open sea of moral peril and cast reasoned selfhood as the stable shore, a commonplace that *Paradiso* 27 dramatically rewrites.

The figure of burying and naming/speaking the nurse's body as alluded to in the Ulysses canto harbors deep cultural significance. Although Gaeta makes only a brief appearance on the surface of Dante's text, her name functions appropriately as a kind of textual grave marker, beneath which lies a cultural narrative important to our understanding of Ulysses. Beneath Gaeta, we will exhume a body of text that defines the value-laden relationship between Trojans and Greeks, Aeneas and Ulysses, and most significantly Gaeta and Circe—both of them nursing bodies that threaten the patriarchal projects of ego and empire.

In Virgil's commentators, an important parallel exists between Aeneas's foundational journey and the moral and grammatical education of the human individual. In particular, the Neoplatonic poetics of macrocosm and microcosm provide the larger intellectual background for the personifications of Lady Grammar that we discussed in previous chapters. The commentary tradition characterizes the fluid body as a necessary but morally perilous first phase of education, closely associated with beatings and grammatical discipline. The tradition upholds adult selfhood as a kind of triumph over the period of nursing/education, whose bitter lessons must be "buried" in memory. But John of Salisbury's commentary in the final chapters of the *Policraticus* will provide the key Christian *translatio* of the classical posture toward nursing corporeality and thus enable the metaphorical logic of *Paradiso,* which will announce the unearthing of the nurse's body and turn Aeneas's ships away from empire and back toward Gaeta.

là presso a Gaeta, prima che sì Enëa la nomasse

The opening words of Ulysses' discourse in *Inferno* 26 are well known:

Quando
mi diparti' da Circe, che sottrasse
me piu' d'un anno là presso a Gaeta,
prima che sì 'Enëa la nomasse,
né dolcezza di figlio, né la pieta
del vecchio padre, né 'l debito amore
lo qual dovea 'Penelopè far lieta,
vincer potero dentro a me l'ardore
ch'i' ebbi a divenir del mondo esperto
e de li vizi umani e del valore.

(Inf. 26.90–99)

      When I departed from Circe, who had detained me
more than a year there near Gaeta, before Aeneas had so named it,
neither fondness for my son, nor reverence for my aged father, nor
the due love which would have made Penelope glad, could conquer in
me the longing that I had to gain experience of the world, and of
human vice and worth.[1]

In particular, verses 90–93 call upon the reader to recall Ulysses' yearlong
entanglement with seductive Circe and at the same time Aeneas's burial—
very near, as Dante takes pains to underscore—of his wet nurse, Gaeta, and
the Roman hero's subsequent naming of that city as part of his foundational
itinerary. The brief allusion to Gaeta has passed largely unobserved by the
Dante commentary tradition, ancient and modern, which has generally been
content to explain that Gaeta was Aeneas's nurse, who is mentioned only
once, at the opening of *Aeneid* book 7, where she is buried and thus honored
by having a city named after her. Indeed, as we will see, *Aeneid* critics have
found the reference to her in Virgil's poem curiously brief and out of place.

    To us, however, Aeneas, in burying his nurse literally on the verge of his
arrival in and foundation of Rome, is merely rehearsing a cultural script that
mandates the death of the nurse as prerequisite to civilization. To be sure,
with Gaeta we are no longer dealing with the individual's entrance into symbolic order through the grammar of rational speech, but rather a society's
larger movement into social order through the foundation and construction
of a city and empire. Even this latter event, however, is enabled by an individual speech act, the primal speech act of naming. We will return to this
point later.

What is more, Dante manipulates his text in such a way as to remind us simultaneously of Ulysses' lustful dalliance in Circe's dominion and, by glaring contrast, Aeneas's dutiful interment of Gaeta on the way to historical triumph. Dante's text here assimilates Circe and Gaeta as instances of nurturing female corporeality: a threat to which Ulysses falls prey and thus perishes, and over which Aeneas triumphs to found Rome and enable, as we know, the sanctioned narrative of salvation history.

But Aeneas's burial/naming of Gaeta—correction to Ulysses' failure—represents positive moral development only locally within the classical confines of *Inferno* 26. The text of *Inferno* 26 reflects classical educational theory, according to which the nurse's body must be rejected and contained, replaced by whole speech and adult selfhood. The larger narrative of Christian salvation will resurrect and embrace the nursing body in defiance of human symbolic structures (grammatical speech, social regulation). In this light, it is appropriate that Gaeta, the classical nurse *par excellence,* is only briefly named in the text of *Inferno* 26. The very scarcity of her textual visibility reflects the near total invisibility of her dark, and yet crucial, role in the classical story of ego and empire building. Unearthing and bringing to light the body buried beneath that scant linguistic trace will anticipate critically Beatrice's denunciation of maternal burial in *Paradiso* 27. Let us first look briefly at this canto near the poem's end.

Ex ore infantium et lactentium

The opening of *Paradiso* 27 finds Dante and Beatrice in the heaven of the fixed stars. The pilgrim has just completed his examination on the three theological virtues (in cantos 24, 25, and 26), as well as his encounter with Adam (in the second half of 26), who has held forth at length on the origins and dispersion of human language. Peter again takes center stage at the beginning of 27 to denounce the corruption of the papacy. No sooner does Peter disappear upward than the pilgrim, at Beatrice's behest, glances downward once again (compare *Paradiso* 22.127–54) to Earth, "sì ch'io vedea di là da Gade il varco/folle d'Ulisse" (so that, on the one hand, beyond Cadiz, I saw the mad track of Ulysses).[2] Several critics have noted that these cantos form a vertical series stronger than most, developing as they do a systematic meditation on language, rhetoric, and semiosis.[3] Franco Fido has uncovered a stylistic symmetry that obtains for the cantos 26 and 27 as a pair.[4] These critics focus on the figure of Ulysses, his journey and his rhetoric. The imagery at the end of *Paradiso* 27, however, is also intended to recall the Gaeta allusion in *Inferno* 26.

The pilgrim's delight in Beatrice lifts him to the Primum Mobile in verse 99. Beatrice explains the function of this most rapidly revolving sphere in verses 106–20, and then rather abruptly opens a diatribe against human greed in verse 121 which occupies the remainder of the canto. She draws a parallel between the maturation and degeneration of fruit and human beings, which begin life as innocent, faithful buds only to be corrupted all too soon by the acid rain of human society: "Ben fiorisce ne li uomini il volere;/ma la pioggia continüa converte/in bozzachioni le sosine vere" (The will blossoms well in men, but the continual rain turns the sound plums into blighted fruit).[5] With strong biblical precedent,[6] Beatrice extends the nutritional metaphor as she exalts childhood, indeed in-fancy (speechlessness), as the site of a pure and faithful wisdom: "Fede e innocenza son reperte/solo ne' parvoletti; poi ciascuna/pria fugge che le guance sian coperte" (Faith and innocence are found only in little children; then each flies away before the cheeks are covered).[7] Bearded adolescence brings corruption. Having thus evoked the life stages, Beatrice then focuses on the development of the individual speaking subject in terms strongly reminiscent of the grammatical logic of the minor works:

> *Tale, balbuzïendo ancor, digiuna,*
> *che poi divora, con la lingua sciolta,*
> *qualunque cibo per qualunque luna;*
> *e tal, balbuzïendo, ama e ascolta*
> *la madre sua, che, con loquela intera,*
> disïa poi di vederla sepolta.
>
> (*Par.* 27.130–35; my emphases)

> One, so long as he lisps [stammers], keeps the fasts,
> who afterward, when his tongue is free, devours any food through
> any month; and one, while he lisps [stammers], loves his mother and
> listens to her, who afterward, when his speech is full, *longs to see her
> buried.*[8]

In an astonishing turn of events, what was for the *De vulgari* and *Convivio* theorist essential to the advent of reason has here become no less than sin. Dante the poet allows Beatrice to denounce, in no uncertain terms, the development of whole speech, tantamount to a violation of dietary taboos and the

murderous desire to bury the mother. Here Dante, poet of Christian paradox, could not be more opposed to the earlier theorist. Still, the underlying
conception of human development remains constant: sinful culture is predicated upon a rejection of the nurturing mother's body. Although the nurturing anxiety is, as it were, displaced in these verses, the metaphor of burial emerges fully articulated.

The conclusion of Beatrice's speech here is hardly less interesting or per-
tinent to our reading of Gaeta in *Inferno* 26. For the moment, however, we
must return to *Inferno* to acquaint ourselves more fully with Aeneas's nurse.

Aeneia nutrix

Caieta (Virgil's original Latin spelling) is mentioned only twice in the *Aeneid*,
once as a port already named at the very end of book 6, and then again at the
very opening of book 7, where Virgil celebrates Caieta as Aeneas's nurse,
who in death has bestowed eternal honor, through an eternal name, to Italian
shores:

> Aeneas made his way
> Straight to the ships to see his crews again,
> Then sailed directly to Caieta's port.
> Bow anchors out, the sterns rest on the beach.
>
> Nurse Caieta of Aeneas, in death you too
> Conferred your fame through ages on our coast,
> Still honored in your last bed, as you are,
> And if this glory matters in the end
> Your name tells of your grave in great Hesperia.
> When he had seen Caieta's funeral
> Performed, her mound of tomb heaped up, Aeneas
> Waited until the sea went down, then cleared
> Her harbor under sail.[9]

Virgil has placed the Caieta interlude directly after Aeneas's return from the
underworld in book 6 and directly before his short sail up the coast to the
Tiber and Rome in book 7.

Caieta makes her brief appearance at a moment that bears extraordinary
structural weight in the poem. She is not the first to have given her name to
the Italian shore in death, as readers since Servius have noted. Virgil's *Tu*

quoque (you too) is meant to recall the earlier honorific burials of Misenus (6.234) and Palinurus (5.857–71; 6.381).[10] Thus the deaths of Palinurus and Caieta in particular appropriately frame Virgil's central book of the dead.[11] But Caieta marks an even more imposing structural highpoint in Virgil. Book 7 opens the second half of Virgil's epic. From the end of book 6 to the beginning of book 7—the textual territory covered precisely by Caieta—the poem moves from its *Odyssey*-like first hexad to its *Iliad*-like second hexad.[12]

Given Virgil's concern for structural details of every sort, one might logically expect a fresh invocation at the opening of book 7, the second half of the poem. This new invocation will come only in verse 45 ("Nunc age, qui reges, Erato . . ."), for at the close of book 6, as we have seen, Aeneas and his men had left the Cumaean Sibyl and set sail up the coast, but had made it only as far as the port of Caieta. As book 7 begins, they still have a stretch of coast to cover from Caieta, past the lands of Circe, to the Tiber, where the *Aeneid* will begin again in earnest. The presence of Caieta in the crucial opening verses of book 7 and the consequent "displacement" of the poem's second beginning have given more than one reader pause and even occasioned elaborate textual revisions.[13] Barchiesi, in particular, reads this moment as underscoring the importance of naming as a colonizing gesture in the *Aeneid*. He highlights the contrast between the, at least initially, anonymous destiny of Palinurus at 5.871 ("nudus in ignota, Palinure, iacebis harena") and the national pride implicit in Virgil's celebration of a well-known place name at 7.1–4: the two deaths mark the transition from wandering in unknown lands to a kind of return home.[14]

For the moment, the extraordinary fact must be emphasized that Virgil chose to distinguish an important (perhaps the most important) turning point in his narrative—from desultory wandering to the foundation of civilization and culture—by describing the death and burial of a wet nurse. What is more, Virgil himself invites Dante to recognize the geographical proximity of Caieta to Circe[15] and to recall Ulysses' less successful navigation of these same waters. For directly following Caieta's interment, the poet sets down his enchanting description of moonlit waters and Circe's shore:

> Into the night
> The soft south wind blew on, the white full moon
> Left no sea-reach or path unbrightened for them,
> Shimmering on the open sea. They passed
> The isle of Circe close inshore: that isle

> *Where, in the grove men shun, the Sun's rich daughter*
> *Sings the hours away. She lights her hall*
> *By night with fires of fragrant cedar wood,*
> *Making her shuttle hum across the warp.*[16]

Aeneas's near encounter with Circe here amounts to a metaphorical close shave ("proxima Circaeae raduntur litora terrae"), which he escapes by a hair's breadth and only through divine intervention. A siren of sorts ("adsiduo resonat cantu"), Circe sits at her loom, the archetypal picture of feminine allure and peril.

But Virgil is not satisfied merely to dramatize Aeneas's close call. He must evoke the events of book 10 of the *Odyssey* and Circe's specific powers to turn men to beasts.

> *Out of this island now they could hear lions*
> *Growling low in anger at their chains,*
> *Then roaring in the deep night; bristling boars*
> *And fenced-in bears, foaming in rage, and shapes*
> *Of huge wolves howling. Men they once had been,*
> *But with her magic herbs the cruel goddess*
> *Dressed them in the form and pelt of brutes.*[17]

Virgil's text then suggests that the Trojans' essential goodness ("pii Troes") affords them narrow escape from the Greeks' monstrous fate. Neptune intervenes with favorable winds:

> *That night, to spare good Trojans foul enchantment—*
> *Should they put in, or near the dangerous beach—*
> *Neptune puffed out their sails with wind astern,*
> *Giving clear passage, carrying them onward*
> *Past the boiling surf.*[18]

Although Virgil stops short of mentioning the Greeks by name, the implicit contrast is clear, as at least one early commentator remarks.[19]

Virgil's exposition continues to emphasize the Trojans' intimate brush with Circean peril as they graze her shore through seething shallows ("vada fervida"). Virgil's structure and vocabulary begin, ever so subtly, to suggest parallels between Caieta and Circe: two encounters with death, two females, two names, two bodies separate but near, stranded together, as it were, upon a curious textual high ground. Like Caieta ("tu quoque litoribus nostris"), Circe too is a shore ("litora dira subirent"); like Caieta ("se ad Caietae recto fert litore portum . . . portumque relinquit"), she too is a harbor, into whose seductive fold the Trojans are nearly borne ("ne monstra pii paterentur talia Troes delati in portus").

Circe of course embodies a specifically female and corporeal threat to male reason. Ulysses' yearlong dalliance in book 10 of the *Odyssey* is primarily sexual. A warning signal of trangression, Circe steals human form and the pre-eminently human power of speech and thus carries her victims into the monstrous realms beyond human reason.[20] A weaver and seductress, Circe is also a sorceress, queen of magic potions and poisonous nourishment. Homer's Circe constantly mixes some liquid brew to offer her unwitting guests.[21] Homer's Circe provides a kind of foul milk, a liquid nourishment that—far from making men of unformed infants—turns men to speechless beasts. She is an anti-nurse.

Circe, the Anti-nurse

Dante did not know Homer, and Virgil barely alludes to Circe's nourishing role ("potentibus herbis induerat Circe in voltus ac terga ferarum"). But Ovid—Dante's other major source of information on Circe, Caieta, and (as we will see) their intimate interrelation—focuses and strengthens Homer's characterization of Circe as anti-nurse.[22] In book 14 of the *Metamorphoses,* Circe conceals her personal juices in sweetened wine and curdled milk. Ingestion of this sinister blend, which she offers to slake parched Greek throats, leads immediately to loss of human form and bestial nonspeech.[23] If we recall the several classical descriptions available to Ovid of the importance of the nurse and her milk to the formation of the young speaker, we may discern here in Circe a venomous parody. Ovid's Circe is forever with her magic rod in one hand ("tetigit summos virga dea dira capillos") as she dispenses her baleful juices (*sucos,* from *sugo, sugere,* "to suck") with the other; as again in the embedded narrative of Picus and his companions' transformation to birds ("Thrice she touched the youth with her wand . . . she sprinkled upon them her baleful drugs and poisonous juices . . . she touched the frightened, wondering faces with her magic wand");[24] and again as she provides the antidote to Ulysses' men: "We were sprinkled with the more wholesome juices of some mysterious herb, our heads received the stroke of her reversed rod, and words were uttered over us which counteracted the words said before."[25] In this last instance, Circe momentarily plays the reverse role of the wholesome nurse as she restores babbling men to whole speech (but, lest we forget, she does so only anomalously in exchange for Ulysses' sexual favors). Indeed, Ovid's alliterational play on *verber, verbum,* and *virga* will reappear in at least one medieval portrait of Lady Grammar.[26]

In any event, it is clear that Ovid's account of Aeneas's adventures in *Metamorphoses* 14 was Dante's source for Ulysses' distinctive locution in *Inferno* 26.90–93: "Quando mi diparti' da Circe, che sottrasse me più d'un anno là presso a Gaeta, prima che sì Enea la nomasse." *Metamorphoses* 14.308 communicates the length of Ulysses' stay—"we tarried in that country for a year"[27]—and, most strikingly, *Metamorphoses* 14.157 evokes that prehistorical time when Trojans had not yet begun to write upon Italian shores: "[Aeneas] next landed on a shore which did not yet bear his nurse's name."[28] Interestingly, Dante exaggerates the duration of Circe's power over Ulysses ("più d'un anno")[29] and casts Aeneas as naming agent upon Ovid's passive anonymous shores.[30]

Aside from these important *riscontri,* however, *Metamorphoses* 14 is crucial to our understanding of *Inferno* 26 because of the way Ovid's narrative interweaves the stories of Greeks and Trojans, Circe and Caieta. Through the characters of Achaemenides and Macareus, former Greeks and companions of Ulysses, Ovid's text brings together the two narratives, *Odyssey* and *Aeneid.*[31] Geographically, this fusion occurs at Caieta. Two Greeks thus meet again as the Trojan ship, with Achaemenides aboard, drops anchor at Caieta, where Macareus now resides. Macareus is astonished to see his old companion aboard Aeneas's ship, for he had been with Ulysses when they abandoned Achaemenides to Polyphemus near Aetna. Achaemenides recounts the horrors of the Cyclops and his eventual rescue by Aeneas, for which he will be eternally grateful and loyal to the Trojan captain.[32] It is then Macareus's turn to explain his presence on these shores near Caieta. He had fallen victim to Circe along with Ulysses and the other men. It is Macareus who speaks at length of the sorceress and her charms, her magic rod and adulterated milk, and of Picus and his companions, they too victims of Circe. At the end of the Greeks' yearlong stay, Macareus was weary and wary of further sea journeys; so he opted to stay behind in the protection of nearby Caieta.[33] Macareus's narrative evokes at once the necessary distance and perilous proximity between the Circean promontory and Caieta. Feeling relatively secure in the nurse's harbor, he nonetheless espies Circe's shore in the near distance and shudders in terror. He warns Aeneas away.[34] From the perspective of what is soon to become Caieta, Macareus beholds and bemoans the horror of Circe. Ovid's text thus sets up a subtle relationship between the two figures, suggesting on the one hand their geographical identity—they are, after all, both on the same short stretch of coast—and positing on the other Caieta—or, more precisely, the burning and entombment of Caieta—as a kind of protection against Circe.

Since the departure of Ulysses and his men from Circe, then, Macareus has stayed in the neighborhood, eeking out an existence on an adjoining strand. He finishes his tale, and the narrator's voice returns to describe Caieta's cremation and epitaph:

> Macareus had finished his story; and Aeneas's nurse, buried in a marble urn, had a brief epitaph carved on her tomb: HERE ME, CAIETA, SNATCHED FROM GRECIAN FLAMES, MY PIOUS SON CONSUMED WITH FITTING FIRE.[35]

Aeneas is then sure to steer well clear of Circe on departure: "Loosing their cables from the grass-grown shore [*aggere herboso* refers specifically to the funeral mound], they kept far out from the treacherous island."[36] In the very next verse, the Tiber, at long last, appears.

The life of Caieta in Ovid's poem, which began anonymously way back at 14.157 ("litora adit nondum nutricis habentia nomen"), ends finally at 14.441–44 with a solemn epitaph that conspicuously, and ritualistically, names the nurse. The long digression that has come between relates the monstrousness of Circe. Just as the living, unnamed nurse provided narrative entrée to Circe, so the burned and buried Caieta puts an end to her. Narratively, Caieta buried and named contains Circe.

What is more, Ovid's epitaph represents a significant development of Virgil's burial and naming. To be sure, both texts allow that the nurse's body must be destroyed and symbolized in a place name as a prerequisite to culture and, in this instance, the founding of Rome. But Ovid's invented epitaph is particularly poignant in this respect, for it actually gives Caieta a voice, albeit the bizarre, disembodied voice of the gates of Hell. Only after she has lost her body and become a mere place name is it safe to let Caieta speak. Now lacking body and soul, she can only praise Aeneas for his essential goodness ("NOTAE _ PIETATIS _ ALUMNUS"),[37] which allowed her to escape ignominious death by punishing Greek fire at Troy ("ARGOLICO _ IGNE") for a proper, symbolized death by purgative fire in the new Troy ("QUO _ DEBUIT _ IGNE").

Absent from Virgil and Dante, Ovid's mention of fire in connection with Caieta relies on an etymological tradition that perceived in the name "Caieta" an echo of the Greek verb "to burn" *(apo tu chaiein)*. This alternate tradition posited that the Trojan ships were burned here instead of in Sicily.[38] Although the dominant narrative tradition honors Caieta (while insisting, nevertheless, on her burial), this alternate tradition makes plain her implicit destructive potential. Like Circe, she represents an impediment to the Trojan's civilizing mission, an obstacle in the sanctioned course of history.

These texts bespeak a deeply rooted cultural horror of nurturing female corporeality that slips from Circe to Caieta. Both Virgil and Ovid allude to *pietas*[39] as the characteristic that separates Trojans from Greeks. That is to say, Trojan *pietas* produces a foundational gesture absent from the Greek narrative: the burial and naming of the nursing female body, a gesture that enables—and is symbolically coterminous with—escape from the monstrous body of Circe.

Bones and a Name

Thus Dante's text in *Inferno* 26 reflects an ancient association between Circe and Caieta through the culturally charged figure of the nursing female body. Indeed, it is via these nursing bodies that Dante imports into *Inferno* 26 the complex narrative interweaving of Greek and Trojan voyages from Virgil and Ovid. Within the context of proto-Roman *pietas,* the horror of Circe is transformed into the virtue of Caieta dead and buried.

What is more, Dante's text calls particular attention to Aeneas's naming of Caieta at burial. The figure of ritualistic burial and naming, already present in Virgil and Ovid, gains prominence for its symbolic significance in Virgil's commentators through the Middle Ages and into the twelfth century. Particularly in the Neoplatonizing commentaries, the universal narrative of Aeneas's historical journey from wandering on the open sea to the fateful shore of Italy encodes an individual moral narrative from the wanderings of youth to the duty and wholeness of adult selfhood. As in the highly personal structure of the *De vulgari,* the two narrative levels—universal and individual—cohere around a linguistic act. We thus begin to discern in medieval readings of the *Aeneid* a cultural configuration homologous to the one provided by the personifications of Lady Grammar. A profound and ancient metaphorical logic assimilates the founding of empire to the construction of linguistic and moral maturity as a symbolic victory over the nursing body. We will see that both medieval allegory and contemporary psychoanalytic theory single out naming as a crucial symbolic act, primal mark of victory over the body.

Taken together, medieval moralizations of the *Aeneid* describe a program of human growth and education parallel to those found in descriptions of language learning and grammar that we discussed in previous chapters.[40] Already in late antiquity, Tiberius Claudius Donatus had penned a lengthy meditation on the significance of burial and naming in his commentary on Caieta.[41] Donatus focuses on the unnatural power of naming as a way to cheat corporeal death, a means to eternal life in memory. In exchange for the unfailing material support Caieta had provided him in life, Aeneas plants her bones in the earth and preserves them with a name ("ossa cum nomine reservaret") that will live eternally.[42] Donatus's discussion suggests the nurse's quasi-sacrificial role in the origins of empire. If Aeneas stands as head of an illustrious Roman bloodline, Caieta lurks in the shadows of a prefoundational history: celebrated only in death, virtual matriarch of a parallel, obverse milkline.[43] Donatus further points out that the ritualistic naming and burial of Caieta leads directly to smooth sailing on calm seas past Circe.[44]

But it is in later Virgilian allegorists—Fulgentius, Bernardus Sylvestris, and John of Salisbury—where the curious figure of burying the nurse's body as a link to eternal life becomes most relevant to our understanding of *Inferno* 26 and *Paradiso* 27. Indeed, the metaphorical transformation effected between *Inferno* 26, where the cremation and naming of Caieta represent Roman virtue against Circean peril, and *Paradiso* 27, where Beatrice denounces adolescent burial of the maternal body, may best be understood by tracing the itinerary of the nursing body in Virgil commentary from Donatus to John. These commentaries tell us no less than the story of resurrection: resurrection of the unstable, fluid body—prototypically and emblematically the nurse's body, the body that had been buried as a threat to reason by a largely Neoplatonic educational theory. They show how the buried body of Caieta rises again as the generalized maternal body of *Paradiso* 27.

Both Fulgentius[45] in the sixth century and the author of a famous twelfth-century Chartrian commentary, who may be Bernardus Sylvestris,[46] read the *Aeneid* as an allegory of human physical and moral development through the traditional life stages. In terms exactly parallel to grammatical allegory, Fulgentius detects the movement from *infantia* to *pueritia,* from, that is, speechlessness to speech, in the progression from *Aeneid* 1 to *Aeneid* 2–3.[47] Appropriately, *Aeneid* 4–6 represent the disciplining of nature through grammatical learning, a transitional phase consummated in the discovery of the philosophical secrets of book 6. Just as the movement from infancy to boyhood and speech had been characterized as a movement from nursing to discipline, so the latter transition from grammatical discipline to perfect adult wisdom turns on the burial of the nurse, Caieta:

> In the seventh book Caieta the nurse is buried [7.2]—that is, the heavy burden of fear of one's teachers. Caieta means "forcer of youth." Among the ancients *caiatio* meant "the yielding of children" . . . And I made it very plain that Caieta symbolizes discipline when I said, "Dying you gave eternal fame, O Caieta [7.2]." Although the discipline of learning is eventually removed, it passes on the eternal seed of memory. Therefore, having buried school matters, Aeneas arrives at his much-desired Ausonia.[48]

Thus Caieta and Lady Grammar merge. Broadly construed as emblem of progression through the various life stages *(coactrix aetatis),* Caieta more specifically represents the mental and physical discipline of formal study and the fear of teachers commonly associated with grammar *(caiatio).*

And her burial symbolizes the end of grammatical learning. Although the unpleasantness and physical danger of grammar school is now dead and buried, the knowledge gained there lives on, safely stored away, as Caieta, in memory. Bones and a name. Fulgentius makes clear that this necessary burial of the nurse's body, this setting aside of things childish and grammatical, leads directly to Italy: the perfection of grammar, the consummation of Aeneas's growth into wisdom, manly struggle, the founding of Rome.[49]

While writing in a largely classical frame, Bernardus ultimately develops in a distinctly Christian direction these links among study of grammar, its burial in memory, and a kind of personal immortality. Like Fulgentius, Bernardus is interested only in reading a tale of human moral growth in the *Aeneid.* He imposes a stricter scheme upon the poem's structure so that each book corresponds to one of the traditional life stages: 1 = *infantia;* 2 = *pueritia;* 3 = *adulescentia;* 4 = *iuventus.* Thus Bernardus arrives at full adulthood already in book 5, and he treats book 6 at extraordinary length as a kind of summation of all that has come before.

Like his twelfth-century allegorical comrade John of Salisbury, Bernardus ends his commentary with book 6. As such, neither Bernardus nor John confronts directly the death and burial of Caieta at the opening of 7. Still, the larger figure of the wet nurse as purveyor of first speech and then grammatical discipline remains. Thus, discussions of the nursing body, burial, and naming in the Virgil commentary tradition move from the strictly classical Caieta to a generic nurse, just as in Dante's poem, which moves from Caieta in *Inferno* 26 to a generic *madre* in *Paradiso* 27. Particularly in the commentaries of the twelfth century, this genericizing trend reflects a Christian re-evaluation of the nursing body and new freedom from classical definitions. The discussion of corporeal death, burial, naming, and eternal life first occasioned by Caieta in Donatus, then tied to the study of grammar by Fulgentius, brings these later commentators to an articulation of eternal salvation in the resurrected nursing body of Christ.

As in the *Cosmographia,* Bernardus exploits the Neoplatonic commonplace that assimilates macrocosmic universe to microcosmic body. In this context, liquid flow and above all the open sea *(mare* or *pelagus)* represent the physical instability and moral peril of the fluid body opposed to the stable shore of reason. Microcosmically, the wet nurse and her nourishing flows translate the body of mother Earth with her rivers and seas.[50] Already we may begin to suspect the centrality of the nurse and her body to Ulysses' fate in *Inferno* 26. Similar to Fulgentius, Bernardus espies in the shipwreck of *Aeneid* 1 the storm-tossed commotion of *infantia,* as Juno is again *dea partus* and nurse.[51] Aeneas is again a speechless infant who knows only the sign language of pictures, Iopas a nurse-tutor just this side of whole speech.[52] Indeed, book 2 simply underscores the transition from speechlessness to the beginnings of speech and discipline ("initium et possibilitas loquendi").[53] Mention of Circe in book 3 evokes the perils of female corporeality as generating matrix of earthy pleasures and purveyor of venemous liquids that steal men's reason.[54]

With the death of Aeneas's father in book 4, Bernardus begins his exposition of burial. This burial is a kind of forgetfulness *(oblivio),* the unwise result of puerile anger.[55] Thus in the rainstorm, Aeneas succumbs to the storm of bodily humors and embraces Dido. Mercury, wise eloquence, restores him to reason.[56] With Dido dead, Aeneas leaves the lustful body behind and enters manhood *(virilis etas)* in 5. Manly contests commemorate his father (for Bernardus, the Christian Father), whom Aeneas had wrongly sent into oblivion, and Anchises' image reappears to beckon his son to the underworld and Elysium (for Bernardus, heaven).[57] Bernardus links this corrective vision of the father— a kind of resurrection—to the proper death and burial of Palinurus, "errant vision" for Bernardus as for Fulgentius.[58] Likewise, the death and burial of Misenus, misguided preoccupation with human glory, signals Aeneas's entry into full manhood.[59]

Palinurus and Misenus represent the proper burials of errant, childish notions and correct the earlier, improper burial of Anchises. Here Bernardus has begun to contemplate the complexity of the burial figure in ways that become apparent only in book 6. In book 6, Aeneas directs his ships, which is to say his will, toward Cuma and the Sibyl, which is to say the three verbal arts of eloquence. For the Sibyl, conveniently, inhabits a wood called Trivia.[60] At the book's opening in a passage of direct relevance to our reading of *Inferno* 26, Aeneas turns his ships seaward to face the *pelago* and then anchors them to the shore, a picture of firm will confronting the fluid body. Only now can he apply himself to the study of the arts and in particular the *trivium,* which Bernardus pictures here grammatically—a point of transition from sea to shore, flesh to reason, aimless flux to direction.[61] After Macrobius, Bernardus identifies this phase with the wet nurse:

> Since he had said that Aeneas entered the woods of Trivia, he demon-strates how that comes about. But this happens by means of instruction in the *auctores.* For the poets introduce us to philosophy, which is why Macrobius calls them "the cradles of wet nurses."[62]

Later in book 6, Bernardus will enlarge this discussion to comprehend the mortification of the flesh as a means to eternal salvation. On the shores of Cocytus where Aeneas witnesses the throngs falling to their destiny as leaves at first frost,[63] Virgil's description of fathers, mothers, sons, and daughters reminds Bernardus of teachers and students[64] and brings about a philosophical summary of burial:

> Philosophy discerns two lives and two deaths and two burials in alle-gorical disguise. According to the Stoics, one life is the liberty of the soul that persists in virtue and study, which is called philosophy by the Stoics themselves. The other life, in the way of the Epicureans, is servi-tude in the sensual pleasures of the body, which the Epicureans think is the only life. So the first is the life of the soul, the second the life of the flesh. The first death is the end of the first life (of the soul), the violent triumph of vice, which is true death. The second death is the mortifi-cation of vices, something philosophers should strive for, according to Plato. And he who commanded "mortify your members" [*Colossians* 3:5] was urging this kind of death. The first burial is that secret treasure of wisemen in solid memory where the virtues and arts are to be buried. The second burial is the tomb in which Misenus and Palinurus are to be buried, enshrouded in eternal oblivion.[65]

Here the corporeal death and burial of Misenus and Palinurus connote rejec-tion of misguided Epicurean pleasure. But there is another kind of death and burial identified with the Stoic pursuit of knowledge: the mortification of the flesh urged by Plato and, most strikingly, Paul in his letter to the Colossians.

Bernardus's description of this other kind of death and burial precisely reflects the discussions of eternal life in memory occasioned by Caieta in earlier commentators. Thus while not mentioned by name here, Caieta nonetheless asserts her subtle presence in formulaic juxtaposition to Misenus and Palinurus. Bernardus gives the discourse a small but significant push in the direction of Christian values with his final quotation from Paul. While earlier commentators could only redeem Caieta through secular notions of human glory and everlasting memory, Bernardus evokes the Christian possibility of individual immortality. Still, Bernardus elicits Christian discourse in support of a very classical paradigm, the obligatory burial of the body as emblematic of Stoic study of the liberal arts, virtual knowledge, and eventual immortality. Only John of Salisbury, at the end of the *Policraticus,* will affirmatively embrace the nursing body as path to knowledge and salvation. Quite simply, the metaphorically minded John takes advantage of the dual discourses of nursing available to him in the twelfth century—Grammar as nursing mother and Christ as nursing mother—in order to place the arts in the service of a Christian wisdom that revalorizes the fluid body in resurrection.

in misericordia uberi

We have seen that John of Salisbury emphasized the potential reward of grammatical labor—linguistic Paradise regained—over its inherent pain in the *Metalogicon.* Martianus's sadistic Lady Grammar became John's tender nurse. The allegorization of the *Aeneid* in the final two chapters of the *Policraticus* dramatically confirms his metaphorical devotion to the nurse's milk. John appropriates the classical discourse of education in the arts as path to virtuous knowledge and a kind of immortality. At the same time, he rejects the strict dualism that demanded the sacrifice and burial of the body. With the new Christian weapon of the resurrected body in his metaphorical arsenal, John boldly fuses the nurturing (but for the Platonists ultimately threatening) milk of Caieta with the milk of Christian mercy and salvation. Caieta's pagan body is here disinterred, transfigured, and glorified.

Echoing Bernardus, these climactic final books of the *Policraticus* would refute the false wisdom of the Epicureans. That their wisdom is false should be clear, for they never really attain their professed goal of pleasure on earth.[66]

John returns us to the scene of original sin in order to clarify. Man inhabited the place of earthly pleasure, but was unable to enjoy its peace as his will was corrupted by gluttonous lust. Thus he was expelled into an existence of labor, sign of this corrupted will and inherent condition of postlapsarian existence. What folly, then, to believe with the Epicureans that mortal nature can regain some measure of joy without labor.[67] For the temporary sweat in toil and pain in childbirth of Genesis can lead to virtue and eternal joy; whereas the superficial pleasures offered by the Epicureans here and now will lead only to the true pain of eternal sorrow.[68] Thus John equates Epicureanism to original sin, the desire to eat of the tree of knowledge, the desire to be like God.

He then shifts to allegorical mode to draw a parallel between this universal history of degeneration and the life of the individual human. Significantly unlike the Neoplatonic Bernardus and Dante of the *De vulgari* (not to mention Augustine), John allows preverbal, suckling *infantia* a primal innocence akin to prelapsarian man in Eden. For even though human nature is sinful, prone to evil, and corrupt ("natura namque peccatrix ad malum prona est et corrupta"), it is so for John only from adolescence forward ("ab adolescentia sua"). He could hardly be more plain. In-fancy is innocent; speech corrupts:

> Consequently the nature of man is prone to evil whose infancy of innocence, so to speak, continued as long as he abstained from communication perverted and perverting. Man spoke not and remained innocent. A deep sleep was cast upon him and he fell asleep in innocence. He awoke, and recognizing a helpmate like unto himself which God had fashioned for him, he spoke the wonderful works of God. But from the day that he was given speech and led out through the door of curiosity, he had converse with the tempter.[69]

"Man spoke not and remained innocent." Still, John also envisions a primal, innocent mode of speech (at once the language of Adam and Babel undone, a speaking in tongues): "he spoke the wonderful works of God."[70] Vaguely echoing the scientism of his Neoplatonic counterpart, John will again stress that the excess heat and subsequent tumescence of adolescence spoiled infancy and Eden, and corrupted the heretofore perfect union of body and spirit.[71]

All this John offers by way of preface to the *Aeneid* allegory. For while it is true that degeneration of the universe and the child generally follows the progression from silence to speech, language is not necessarily all evil. The by-product of a fallen world, language can contain truth where care is taken to discern the good and avoid error. Even pagan words like those of Virgil can speak the *magnalia Dei*.[72] John sees the *Aeneid* as a repository of hidden wisdom about the stage-by-stage development of a life, its hero an archetypal human soul-in-body, *corporis habitator*.[73] But his Christian appreciation for an age of milky innocence effects some significant revisions in the standard allegorical plot.

John halfheartedly alludes to the common interpretation of the book 1 shipwreck as the wind-whipped sea of infant libido. With great originality, he prefers to showcase the joyous banquet that closes book 1 as the appropriate emblem of *infantia,* a period of abundant food and drink thanks to the wet nurse's nourishing flow.[74] At this point, John fudges the standard categories, for already in book 2 he detects the beginnings of verbal commerce and corruption *(multiloquio)* that he has just associated with *adolescentia*.[75] He thus opts to pass over *pueritia* in silence,[76] and associate book 2 with *adolescentia,* book 3 with *iuventus.* He quotes liberally from Horace's *Ars poetica* on the folly of youth through manhood,[77] and recapitulates by doing away with the traditional labels altogether.[78] Book 4 brings *illicitos amores;* as in Bernardus but with a Christian addition, Mercury as reason and persuasive rhetoric draws the soul toward adult good.[79]

As Aeneas and his men pull away from the shore of Carthage and Dido's funeral pyre, John reverses the Neoplatonic navigational metaphor to cast the shore (previously the anchored will) as the site of wrongheaded and childish desire; by implication, the fluid open sea (previously the libidinous and nourishing body) becomes the path to salvation.[80] Unlike any of his predecessors, John links books 5 and 6 to the end of human life, the periods of *senectus* and *senium,* respectively.[81] In book 5, Aeneas honors his father's memory and recognizes his status as wretched exile.[82] In book 6, his life powers begin to wane, he buries Palinurus and Misenus, and he recognizes the errors of his past in the underworld.[83] He learns of his promising future in the sweet embraces of Lavinia and in Italy, the stronghold of Christian blessedness *(arcem beatitudinis).*[84] In conclusion, John reiterates that human nature is corrupt and prone to evil *ab adolescentia*[85] and, in a very Dantean touch, that the path of the Epicureans is wide and inviting but leads only to the eternal tortures of Hell.[86]

The climactic final chapter of the *Policraticus* forms a pair with the one that precedes it. If the path of the Epicureans does not lead to their professed goal, which path can be trusted to lead to true pleasure?[87] John makes no mention of specific liberal arts, preferring instead to emphasize the generic *scientia* as part of love for God. It will not suffice for salvation simply to know the path of virtue; one must actively follow it through good works.[88] Nevertheless, *scientia* is necessary. John reasons that if man fell from grace in an Epicurean attempt to ascend the tree of knowledge *(ligno scientiae)*, he can hope to return to grace only via the instrument of his demise. For *scientia* can help us discern good from evil.[89]

Thus the inborn *labor* of postlapsarian existence, so commonly linked to the discipline of grammar and the path to knowledge, is sweetened by hope of future joy.[90] We need not fear repeating original sin, however, for a Christian bough of virtue *(virtutis ramus)* has sprung forth from the ancient tree to demonstrate the way of truth.[91] Virgil taught this in the shadowy allegory of *Aeneid* 6 and the golden bough.[92]

John trains his rhetorical lens on the word *via* much as Bernardus had in his explication of *Trivia*.[93] How is one to find this path to the bough of virtue amidst the bewildering array of paths in the wood of mortal life? John reminds his reader that Ovid pointed to it in the *Metamorphoses:* "'There is a way on high, quite plain when sky/Is clear; they call it Milky Way [*Met.* 1.168–69]'; Make thy sky clear that it be not clouded to the eyes of thy soul through displeasure and thou shalt easily recognize this milky way."[94] The Milky Way. And for John, the Milky Way is nothing more than the nurturing flow of the wet nurse writ large in the heavens. In the white purity of the nurse's milk, John locates the perfect emblem of innocent *infantia* and Christian grace, the path to knowledge, virtue, and truth: "It is the Milky Way manifest in the brightness of innocence, and in its zeal to provide nutriment it performs the function of a nurse, and alone prepares for progress because without it no one can press forward."[95] Through Christ, the tree of good and evil, in which the treasure of all knowledge of the discplines and all wisdom is contained ("in quo sunt omnes sapientiae et scientiae thesauri absconditi"), has been transplanted from the garden of eternal delight to the temporal realm of human exile ("terram peregrinationis nostrae"), and taken root within the Church ("in medio Ecclesiae"), so that grace be illuminated by knowledge *(scientia),* strengthened through virtue: so that, finally, grace may spring forth in the rich milk of Christian mercy, "ut exultet in misericordia uberi."[96] From Ovid's Milky Way through Lady Grammar to the milk of Christian mercy, John has here invented a veritable *translatio uberis.*[97]

The classical wet nurse has been supplanted by Christ. The new law of Christian humility would disinter and embrace the nurse's body in an effort to reverse the path of degeneration, which is, as we have seen, the path of rhetorical development ("factus verbosior per ostium curiositatis") away from primal bliss. We have seen that, like Christ, noble Caieta exemplified a kind of eternal spiritual life in corporeal death. We may still detect the faintest echo of her honorific burial in *Aeneid* 7.1–4 in the catechism that closes the *Policraticus:* "Do you seek perpetuity for your works? The just will be in everlasting remembrance . . . Do you aim at grace of tongue? The lips of the just distill grace; likewise: The memory of the just is with praise; the name of the impious will rot . . . And the just will live for ever and they are in peace, though in the sight of the world they seem to die."[98]

Ulysses as Circe

We can now return to *Inferno* 26 and *Paradiso* 27. We should first recall, however, that Dante constructs his own moralized *Aeneid* in *Convivio* 4.24.8–15. More to the point, it is within this context that Dante articulates, in his own vernacular words, the primal model of life transition from suckling to speech so central to our investigation. The first obedience is the one that turns the infant from the mother's breast ("la tetta della madre") to the father's correction ("la correzione del padre").[99] In *Convivio* 4, Dante points to several of Aeneas's actions (in *Aeneid* 4, 5, and 6) as illustrative of qualities befitting the life stage *gioventute (iuventus)*.[100] We should not expect that Dante would mention Gaeta here where *infantia* and *pueritia,* on the one hand, and book 7 of the *Aeneid,* on the other, fall outside the focus of his discourse. It is remarkable that he nevertheless manages to include in his description of *adolescenza* a pointed reference to that early scene of maternal rejection. This clearly suggests that Dante at least took note of the symbolic significance of the nurse and her burial in moralizations of Virgil's poem. In Virgilian allegory, he discovered a paradigm for human development already familiar to him from linguistic theory and grammatical discourse.

When Gaeta does finally get mentioned in *Inferno* 26, we can be confident that she has arrived in Dante's thinking via a long and culturally charged textual journey. Several critics have noted that Dante means to cast Ulysses in *Inferno* 26 as an anti-Aeneas. Allusions in Ulysses' speech to Aeneas's subsequent, successful voyage underscore the deficiencies of the Greek hero.[101] To be sure, Dante's version of Ulysses' fate flies in the face of centuries of Neoplatonic allegorical readings of the *Odyssey* (echoed by some of the *Aeneid* allegorists) which cast Ulysses as moral hero, rational leader, the only man who did not, after all, succumb to Circe's wicked brew.[102] But just as allegorical readers might stress either Aeneas's entrapment by lust in *Aeneid* 4 or his rational renunciation of same at the end of the book, so one might choose to regard Ulysses' initial rational control over Circe or his subsequent, lengthy passivity under her sway. Dante clearly fell into the latter group ("Quando mi diparti' da Circe, che *sottrasse* me più d'un anno . . .").[103]

In his magisterial essay, Padoan draws a compelling portrait of Ulysses as master rhetorician and cogent persuader from Virgil through the Middle Ages.[104] Despite Ulysses' eventual departure from Circe, a larger lust for worldly experience continues to dominate him.[105] We have seen that John of Salisbury nicely defines such philosophical libido in his discussion of the Epicureans and Adam and Eve (though for John, as we know, *scientia* has been at least partially redeemed through Christ). Many have noted that Ulysses' lust for knowledge resonates with original sin, for surely the first *fandi fictor* was the serpent of Genesis,[106] who led humanity into exile from its blissful *in-fantia*.

Mazzotta has provided the most insightful articulation of the rhetorical nature of Ulysses' sin. In Mazzotta's view, Ulysses peddles a "rhetoric . . . without foundation" in ethical quest, which is to say without direction within the sanctioned narrative of salvation history. For Ulysses, in the utopian space beyond the pillars of Hercules, "language seems to originate in the void."[107] The image of the vast, unlined open sea best expresses this vacant rhetoric, particularly when we recall that the *pelago* was for the Neoplatonists the fluid, libidinal body of the microcosmic infant defined by the wet nurse and her powerful flow. It is as though Ulysses has missed Grammar's most basic lesson—which is to drink and then turn away—and skipped ahead to an eternal, rhetorical whirlpool and thus death upon a great, milky sea.

Thus Ulysses is detained for more than a year under Circe, seductress and nurse of a sort, "là presso a Gaeta prima che sì Enëa la nomasse." Now we know that Dante appreciated the literary and allegorical tradition's intimations of Circe as nurse of foul milk. Guido del Duca makes this clear in *Purgatorio* 14 when he traces the degenerate flow of the Arno through its wretched valley and out to sea. The inhabitants of the Arno Valley have lost all reason and flee virtue as though it were a snake:[108] "hanno sì mutata lor natura/li abitator de la misera valle,/che par che Circe li avesse in pastura" (wherefore the dwellers in the wretched valley have so changed their nature that it seems as though Circe had them at pasture).[109] The various valley dwellers are then compared to Circe's animals with their beastly dietary habits.[110] The nutritional metaphor that Guido introduces rings with particular poignancy if we recall Dante's nostalgic reminiscence in the *De vulgari* of the Arno flow as an emblem of the nurse's milk in a pre-exilic, Edenic Florence ("quanquam Sarnum biberimus ante dentes . . .").

We know that there existed for Dante an ancient and familiar topos, inscribed upon the body of the wet nurse and her symbolic sister Lady Grammar, that connected nutrition to speech. We recall that the adult orator's speech still smacks of the nurse's milk for Macrobius and John of Salisbury (as for Quintilian and Cicero before them). Thus with Ulysses. Mazzotta has remarked that Ulysses hypnotizes his audience, that his hollow rhetoric carries a "melic aura."[111] Having rejected the grammar of the heterosexual family unit ("né dolcezza di figlio, né la pieta/del vecchio padre, né 'l debito amore/lo qual dovea Penelopè far lieta . . ."), on the verge of transgression with his pirate crew, Ulysses impersonates the enchantress. There where Aeneas buries Gaeta, Ulysses has absorbed Circe, or rather, Circe has absorbed him.[112]

Noms de lieu

Aeneas at once buries Gaeta and names a place. We have seen that Virgil and many of his readers recognized the symbolic importance of naming as a colonizing gesture and a means to a kind of immortality. Of course, we need not limit ourselves to Virgil commentary to recognize naming as a primordial defining human gesture, as in Adam's naming of the animals in Genesis[113] and Aristotle's *prima impositio,* a notion widely available in the Middle Ages from Boethius's commentary on the *De interpretatione.*[114]

Mazzotta observes that Aeneas's naming here traces his historical project and thus confirms that his speech is grounded in a preordained narrative. At the same time, Aeneas's naming "denounces Ulysses' own failure to name."[115] I would like to suggest that Dante's brief allusion in these verses to the act of naming or failing to name reflects the very cultural paradigm that we have uncovered at the breast of Lady Grammar. Lady Grammar was herself sometimes construed as the primordial namer.[116] Aeneas's burial of his wet nurse and naming of Gaeta are structurally coterminous. Likewise, I have argued that Ulysses' failure to name implies an exact parallel failure to bury the nurse. Indeed, there is a strong metaphorical logic by which we may say that the fluid wet nurse—as the sea closes over the ship in that final tercet and verse of *Inferno* 26—buries him.

Neoplatonic allegory has shown us that, in Aeneas's burial and naming of Gaeta, the macrocosmic text of universal history and the microcosmic text of individual moral development merge. At the crucial juncture between books 6 and 7, humanity turns from wandering to Rome, Republic and Empire, just as the human individual turns away from the things of childhood and toward manhood, away from maternal affection and toward paternal prohibition, away from the nurse's nutrition and toward whole speech, here archetypically present in the authoritative act of naming. The dilemma that thwarts Ulysses and defines Aeneas in *Inferno* 26 lies there on the enigmatic crease between nutrition and nomination.

This ancient paradigm for human development has cast fascinating reflections among twentieth-century theorists of language and selfhood. I have already suggested that medieval allegorizations of Grammar furnish an intriguing thematization of human subjectivity as defined by Julia Kristeva, forever shuttling between semiotic and symbolic. Dante's allusion in *Inferno* 26 adds the specific act of naming to the equation. For Jacques Lacan, naming becomes the foundational gesture of human selfhood as the signifier of paternal prohibition. This Name-of-the-Father/No-of-the-Father (at once *Nom-du-Père* and *Non-du-Père*)

> transforms the real, undifferentiated, mother-child unity. It bars the child's easy access to pleasurable contact with its mother, requiring it to pursue pleasure through avenues more acceptable to the father figure and/or mOther [that is, the Mother now as differentiated Other and thus Symbolic name, no longer Real body].[117]

Interestingly in the context of *Inferno* 26, for Lacan the mother's desire (both desire of and for the mother) can be a dangerous force that threatens to "engulf" and "swallow up" the would-be subject.[118] The developing (male) infant assimilates the paternal function as name and prohibition and a way out of the all-engulfing maternal body. This is for Lacan a crucial first step toward donning the "armour of subjectivity."[119] Need in the mother's body becomes symbolized desire as the subject-to-be takes his place in the signifying chain. Thus language and subjectivity are born upon the grave of the mother's desire.[120]

Lacan is, in a sense, very classical in his insistence on the barring and exclusion of maternal desire as constituent of the ego. We have seen that Kristeva's revision aims to attenuate the line between maternal semiotic and patriarchal symbolic. As Kelly Oliver has suggested, Kristeva wants to bring the body and its drives back into language.[121] For Kristeva, the semiotic body, whose first emblem is the mother-child symbiosis in the ill-defined space she calls *chora,* persists as a powerful, potentially subversive force throughout human mental life, forever exerting pressure on grammatical speech.

Like Lacan, Kristeva cites the place name as the primal signifier of the developing subject's conceptualization of discrete space, the subject/object dichotomy, symbolic logic and thus language. In an essay entitled "Place Names," Kristeva employs research in language acquisition and child psychology to trace this process in relation to her theory of the semiotic.[122] There Kristeva stresses the liminal, in-between status of the place name in the archaeology of the speaking subject. Moving toward full-blown syntax, subject and predicate, the place name remains very much involved in maternal dependency *(anaclisis),* structurally assimilable to the earliest vocalizations of desire, and infant laughter:

> Voice, hearing, and sight are the archaic dispositions where the earliest forms of discreteness emerge. The breast, given and withdrawn; lamplight capturing the gaze; intermittent sounds of voice or music—all these meet with anaclisis (according to a temporal sequence probably programmed, too, by the particular aptitude of each child), hold it, and thus inhibit and absorb it in such a way that it is discharged and abated through them . . . At that point, breast, light, and sound become a *there:* a place, a spot, a marker. The effect, which is dramatic, is no longer quiet but laughter. The imprint of an archaic moment, the threshold of space, the "chora" as primitive stability absorbing anaclitic facilitation, produces laughter. There is not yet an outside, and the things that made the newborn laugh at about two and one-half months . . . are simply markers of something in the process of becoming stability. But neither external nor internal, neither outside nor inside, such markers are noticeable only because they slow down anaclisis: they do not stop it.[123]

Kristeva argues that within this early pseudospace of infant laughter all of the conditions necessary to subjectivity and language proper are already present, long before the Lacanian mirror stage, intricately imbricated with maternal desire.[124]

These early riant vocalizations eventually distinguish themselves as topic comments, or place names.

We note that beginning with the "first point of psychic organization," light-giving marker or mother's face, which produced laughter along with the first vocalizations, the future speaker is led to separate such points into *objects* (transitional at first, then simply objects) and add to them *no longer laughter but phonation*—archetype of the morpheme, condensation of the sentence. As if *the laughter that makes up space had become, with the help of maturation and repression, a "place name."*[125]

Kristeva considers place names in their most basic form "*topic* demonstrative utterances" ("this is" or "that is," followed by a name or noun phrase) and notes their frequency among early speakers. "Given the frequency of *topic* demonstrative utterances beginning with the first grammatically constructed sentences, we might submit that the *entry into syntax constitutes a first victory over the mother,* a still uncertain distancing of the mother, by the simple fact of naming."[126]

Thus Kristeva concludes that the place name simultaneously substitutes and recalls desire in the mother's body. In the psychological development of the speaking subject, the place name marks the very fold between nutrition and nomination that I have located in the Ulysses canto. "We suggest that naming, always originating in a place (the *chora,* space, 'topic,' subject-predicate), is a *replacement* [at once a substitution and setting in place again] for what the speaker perceives as an archaic mother—a more or less victorious confrontation, never finished with her."[127] To be sure, Dante's allusion in *Inferno* 26 to Aeneas's burial of Gaeta signals a classical (or, if you will, Lacanian) victory of symbolic order over bodily desire, nomination over nutrition, picking up where the *De vulgari* left off. But the metaphorical deployment of the nurse's body in the remainder of the *Divine Comedy* will show that we would do well to heed Kristeva at this point, that this confrontation with the mother is "more or less victorious, never finished." The Christian resurrection of the nurse's body best articulated by John of Salisbury will play out in *Purgatorio* and *Paradiso.* Kristeva herself notes that the demonstrative "this" of the Christian Eucharist ("This is my body") provides a significant historical articulation of the subject's shifting status between need and naming. The developing speaker leads inevitably to the mystery of transubstantiation.[128]

Of course, Kristeva did not invent the notion of language in/as desire, familiar as it was to Dante from Augustine. Mazzotta has alluded to the importance of language and subjectivity in the Ulysses canto:

Like thievery which is a transgression of property, language forever eludes the possibility of universal, *proper* meaning. To say this is to talk of language as desire, originating in a condition of lack, in the Augustinian sense, and failing to achieve a stable, self-identity. The desire that subtends language (the "ardore" exposed by the tongues of fire) accounts for the inseparable link that exists between the promises of education and the seduction which actually takes place in Ulysses' speech.[129]

Dante's text in *Inferno* 26 perhaps unwittingly summons Lady Grammar as alluded to in *Aeneid* allegory. For to contemplate language's fragile positioning between education and seduction is to evoke the nurse and, and in a medieval educational context, *Grammatica lactans*. In the classical terms of *Inferno* 26, to bury and name the wet nurse is to escape language as seduction.

Virgil again represents this classical attitude toward the nurse with greater dramatic force in *Inferno* 20, where he holds forth on his own birthplace, the foundation and naming of Mantua on the bones of Manto. His account in verses 52–99, filled with the topology of rivers and marshes, echoes a central metaphor of the *De vulgari* by alluding to the parallel between the flow of water and the flow of language (see in particular vv. 76–77: "Tosto che l'acqua a correr mette co,/non più Benaco, ma Mencio si chiama" [As soon as the water starts to run, it is no longer named Benaco, but Mincio]),[130] and thus anticipates the poetics of *Purgatorio* 5 that we will investigate in the following chapter.[131] At present, we are struck by his portrait of the prophetess Manto as nurse-seductress: "E quella che ricuopre le mammelle,/che tu non vedi, con le trecce sciolte,/e ha di là ogne pilosa pelle . . ." (And she that covers her bosom, which you cannot see, with her loose tresses, and has on that side all her hairy parts . . .).[132] Manto's is one in a series of grotesque images that illustrate the distorted human form, head twisted backward on shoulders, that is the *contrapasso* of the soothsayers in the fourth *bolgia*. But the poet casts Manto alone in an erotic dialectic of concealment and revelation; he no sooner calls our attention to her breasts than he hides them behind seductive tresses.[133] And in that image of flowing hair, female allure, overlaying the breast, the primal scene of suckling shifts perilously from nurturing education to fatal seduction.

Manto, an enchantress like Circe, will meet at the hands of men the same end as Gaeta: bones and a name.

Li uomini poi che 'ntorno erano sparti
s'accolsero a quel loco, ch'era forte
per lo pantan ch'avea da tutte parti.
'Fer la città sovra quell'ossa morte;
e per colei che 'l loco prima elesse,
Mantïia l'appellar sanz'altra sorte.
(*Inf.* 20.88–93)

    Afterwards the people [men] who were scattered
round about gathered to that place, which was strong because of the
marsh it had on all sides. They built the city over those dead bones,
and for her who first chose the place they called it Mantua, without
other augury.

Virgil gained existence upon the dead bones of Manto. Aeneas's burial and naming of Gaeta, a virtuous act in the classical context that compares him to Ulysses, is replayed here by Virgil's male forebears and Manto, where the would-be nurse's twisted body bespeaks Christian morality and justice. Detached from the sanctioned narrative of salvation history, the story of Manto, her burial and naming, seems only a bizarre instance of pagan wizardry. Participation in that sanctioned narrative is all that separates Gaeta from Manto. But this is a narrative of which Dante's Virgil and Gaeta are, at best, vaguely aware through their faith in a historical truth that transcends the individual. In this sense, the classical burying and naming of the nurse represented by the *Aeneid* and its author, like so much else in Dante's poem, at once lauds Virgil's solid ancient *pietas* while mischievously alluding to his limitations within a Christian scheme largely beyond his ken, which is to say a Christian revalorization of the body in resurrection. We will explore in subsequent chapters the deconstruction of the classical subject and the reconstruction of a new Christian subject-*cum*-body in the poetics of *Purgatorio* and *Paradiso*. But first let us return to the endpoint of the journey in *Paradiso* 27 to complete the story of Aeneas's nurse.

Poppa and *prora* at the End of *Paradiso*

We recall that in *Paradiso* 27, Peter comes forth to decry the degeneration of the papacy and to describe the Church as the bride of Christ who was, as it were, nursed on the blood of the early popes.[134] The pilgrim's glance at earth (vv. 79–84) directly recalls Ulysses' *varco folle* and *Inferno* 26.[135] In the *Primum Mobile*, Beatrice's denunciation of the corruption of human will directly articulates the Christian rejection of classical/grammatical desire to bury the nurse mother. As we saw at the beginning of the chapter, Beatrice's words unite speech and nutrition in the mother's body. She resurrects the mother's body as an emblem of nutritional and linguistic propriety.[136]

As the canto comes to an end, Dante's text summons the bodies of Circe and Gaeta in a final note of Christian correction. Beatrice condemns Circe in no uncertain terms as sexual seductress and corruptor of human will: "Così si fa la pelle bianca nera/nel primo aspetto de la bella figlia/di quel ch'apporta mane e lascia sera" (Thus the white skin turns black at the first sight of the fair daughter of him that brings morning and leaves evening).[137] Given the strong textual ties between this canto and the other cantos 26–27 of the poem, Dante's reference to the resurrected mother should already have set our minds on Gaeta's burial in *Inferno* 26. At the very end of *Paradiso* 27, a subtle textual allusion again trains our vision on Gaeta's tomb. Employing a navigational metaphor by now familiar to us, Beatrice prophesies that human degeneration will eventually be set straight:

> *Ma prima che gennaio tutto si sverni*
> *per la centesma ch'è là giù negletta,*
> *raggeran sì questi cerchi superni,*
> *che la fortuna che tanto s'aspetta,*
> le poppe volgerà u' son le prore,
> sì che la classe correrà diretta,
> *e vero frutto verrà dopo 'l fiore.*
>
> (*Par.* 27.142–48; my emphases)

> But before January be all unwintered, because of the hundredth part that is neglected below, these lofty circles will so shine forth that the storm which has been so long awaited will turn round the sterns to where the prows are, so that the fleet will run straight; and good fruit will follow on the flower.

The final verse completes the branch-and-leaf metaphor that was central to the previous canto. Moreover, we note here that as in John of Salisbury a storm-tossed sea *(fortuna)*—far from a Neoplatonic image of peril—will provide moral correction.[138] Most strikingly, the conspicuous figure of *poppa* and *prora* makes its final appearance.[139] We will see that Beatrice controls both stern and bow upon her advent in *Purgatorio* 30. Coming as it does here at the end of a textual division, the *poppa* and *prora* figure visually recalls two other moments. The first, as we have seen, is when Ulysses loses control of stern and bow in the final verses of *Inferno* 26.[140] The second is from Virgil and comes at the structurally signifi-cant end of *Aeneid* 6: "Then [Aeneas] sailed directly to Caieta's port. Bow anchors out, the sterns rest on the beach."[141] Aeneas arrives in the future Gaeta at the very end of the first half of the poem. We have seen that this moment bears great moral significance for the *Aeneid* allegorists. Aeneas parks his ships stern to the shore, bow to the sea, so that they look already toward departure and the future founding of Rome. As we know, Caieta's body will be speedily buried and passed beyond at the beginning of the next book. But the attitude of Aeneas's ships here at the end of book 6 has already announced this outcome. Like the *infans* of *Convivio* 4.24, they have already turned away from the nursing mother. In the dramatic close of *Paradiso* 27, then, Beatrice redirects them toward this buried body ("le poppe volgerà u' son le prore") and the memory of Aeneas's nurse. Her fertile presence is confirmed by the fruitful flowering of the final verse. *Paradiso* 27 has at last sorted out the dangerous confusion between the seductive body and the educational body which threatened classical thought, as Circe is soundly condemned and Caieta resurrected in glory. Dante thus turns his metaphorical ships around to face the nursing body.[142]

The Nurse in *Inferno*

The metaphorical triumph of the wet nurse effected by Christianity can have no affirmative place in *Inferno*. Buried like Gaeta, the Christian nurse nonethe-less makes a ghostly appearance here and there via the negative image of irony.[143] Surely in Plutus's "nonsense" phrase at the opening of canto 7, "Pape Satàn, pape Satàn, aleppe!," we have an infernal parody of babytalk,[144] punc-tuated by the primal bilabial phoneme /p/, since ancient grammar a sign of corporeal infant desire second only to /m/.[145] In an interesting gender rever-sal, we might say that Plutus forgoes the Christian mother and links the desire of his infant phonetic production to an infernal father. Like his fellow stam-merer Nembròt (*Inf.* 31.67–81), Plutus produces a semiotic stream of per-manently precocious, unstable meaning and thus parodically recalls the semi-otic bond between infant and nurse.[146]

Head of the guardian troop of Centaurs on the banks of the blood river Flegetonte, Chirón seems a laughable, infernal anti-nurse: "E quel di mezzo, ch'al petto si mira, / è il gran Chirón, il qual nodrì Achille" (And the one in the middle, who gazes on his own breast, is the great Chiron, he who brought up [nourished, breast-fed] Achilles).[147] Dante's choice of *nodrì* here cannot be casual. What is more, the poet repeatedly draws attention to the breast of this nurse-tutor of seductive Achilles (vv. 70, 83, 97).[148] An ironic reference to the human-animal admixture in these beasts ("Già li er' al petto, /dove le due nature son consorte" [Who was now at his breast, where the two natures are consorted]),[149] in Chirón's case this harping on the breast makes more specific fun of his onetime status as nurse, particularly when the poet drops the neutral *petto* of verses 70 and 83 in favor of the base, fleshy *poppa* of verse 97: "Chirón si volse in su la destra poppa" (Chirón bent round on his right breast).[150]

The ex-nurse Chirón's positioning on a river gently evokes in infernal terms the macrocosmic analogy between the nurse's milky flow and the elemental flow of Mother Earth that we have seen in the *De vulgari* and that will gain special prominence in *Purgatorio 5*. Likewise among the panderers in the first bolgia, Venedico Caccianemico, who knows the pilgrim by his mother tongue (*chiara favella;* v. 53), spitefully identifies his fellow Bolognese sinners by evoking the poetic nexus between river flow and language acquisition while recalling the metaphorical breast:

> 'E non pur io qui piango bolognese;
> anzi n'è questo loco tanto pieno,
> che tante lingue non son ora apprese
> a dicer "sipa" tra Sàvena e 'Reno;
> e se di ciò vuoi fede o testimonio,
> rècati a mente il nostro avaro seno.
>> (*Inf.* 18.58–63)

> And I am not the only Bolognese who laments
> here; nay, this place is so full of them, that so many tongues are not
> now taught between Savena and Reno, to say *sipa;* and if of this you
> wish assurance or testimony, recall to mind our avaricious nature
> [breast].[151]

River flows help define Romagna in *Inferno* 27, Ulysses' companion canto and a canto well known for its cryptic references to the various mother tongues.[152] Malatesta's and Malatestino's political savagery is here figured as a "dental boring of holes": "'L mastin vecchio e 'l nuovo da Verrucchio, /che fecer di Montagna il mal govero, /là dove soglion fan d'i denti succhio" (And the old mastiff and the new of Verrucchio, who made the ill disposal of Montagna, ply their teeth where they are wont).[153] *Succhio* can of course be understood as *succhiello,* a "gimlet" or "auger" used to drill holes.[154] But it surely occurred to the poet that the juxtaposition of *denti* and *succhio* would elicit the sounds of the teething, weaning infant, *in dentium plantativa,* as he prepares to turn his back on maternal nurturing.[155] The pilgrim's odd locution casts this infamous father-son team as infernal anti-sucklings, engaged in a futile struggle to draw nourishment from hard teeth and bone. Guido's later crude definition of his mother ("Mentre ch'io forma fui d'ossa e di polpe / che la madre mi diè . . ." [While I was the form of the flesh and bones my mother gave me . . .])[156] reflects a similar mindset and a shortsighted, overly literal reading of the nurse mother.[157]

The classical terms of the nursing metaphor have thus already begun to shift by the time we reach the lowest circle of Hell. The poet expresses the rhetorical challenge of depicting the nadir of the universe in a pointed reference to babytalk: "Ché non è impresa da pigliare a gabbo / discriver fondo a tutto l'universo, / né da lingua che chiami mamma o babbo" (For to describe the bottom of the whole universe is not an enterprise to be taken up in sport, nor for a tongue that cries mamma and daddy).[158] Singleton has located the irony of the passage in understatement, litotes;[159] but the rhetorical dynamics here are somewhat more complex. For Dante is not simply jesting that babytalk is vastly insufficient to describe the center of all evil. Engaging the Christian logic of *sermo humilis* that will flower in the rest of the poem, he is more precisely suggesting that babytalk, the nurse's speech, is too good for such a task and thus utterly inappropriate in this setting.[160] We have here a parodic, Christian devaluation of classical high style that moves to recover the wet nurse and her nourishing flow.[161] The poet's intervention at the bottom of Hell thus looks forward to the nurse's resurrection in the realms of salvation.

FOUR

DECONSTRUCTING SUBJECTIVITY IN ANTEPURGATORY

But body is by nature fluid and the universe is made up of the body.

Plotinus, *Enneads* 2.1.3[1]

In turn, an earthly body cannot maintain its substance for long; rather it flows away like a raging stream and is overcome by its own flow.

Chalcidius[2]

Selfhood and the Body in *Purgatorio*

Thus far we have explored the significance of the nursing body to medieval conceptions of human selfhood in the narrow context of individual linguistic development (grammar) and the larger context of epic history (Virgilian allegory). Here we further expand our investigation of the nursing metaphor to encompass what is surely one of its major sources in intellectual history: the Platonic and Neoplatonic imaging of chaotic primal space—*chora, hyle,* and in Chalcidius's Latin *silva*—as "the wet nurse of creation." Here we will argue for the importance of *silva* in Dante's most compelling exposition of the mechanics of human personhood, canto 5 of the *Purgatorio*. More forcefully than any other canto of the *Comedy, Purgatorio* 5 probes the relationship between body and soul in the composite that is selfhood. To be sure, this canto underscores the distinction between temporal body and eternal soul in the human being, particularly as Bonconte da Montefeltro recalls the less felicitous fate of his father, Guido, in *Inferno* 27.

More interesting to our study, however, is what this canto can tell us about the role of body in the individual's sense of self in time and in history. What we discover is that the souls of antepurgatory had come to depend upon the apparent solidity of their temporal bodies as emblematic of a stable individual identity. They had not paid sufficient attention to the inherent fluidity of bodies so evident—as canto 5 dramatically attests—in the text of the created universe. *Purgatorio 5* shows us that temporal identity mistakenly depends upon bodily integrity, for just as the elemental body (of a person, of the earth, of the universe) is fragile and fluid, so is earthly personhood in time.

And yet, Christianity promises the restoration of the body at the end of time. Caroline Walker Bynum has recently traced Christian debates over the resurrection of the body from late antiquity through the fourteenth century.[3] Despite the variety and complexity of the views she analyzes, one idea emerges as constant in Bynum's study: with few exceptions, medieval thinkers defined personhood or selfhood as a composite of body and soul; body was integral to self. For most Christians, a strictly Platonic notion of selfhood as rational mind or soul was insufficient. In order for the blessed to enjoy complete happiness in Paradise, body must be restored. Soul alone is not ego. Aquinas is particularly clear on this point: "Moreover the soul, although it is a part of the body, is not the entire man, and soul alone is not self; so that even though the soul wins salvation in the next life, we cannot properly say that the self or the man has won salvation."[4] At the same time, it is clear that Scholastic theologians into the fourteenth century focused on rational soul as guarantor of personhood because that soul contained a virtual body.[5] As Bynum puts it, body was packed into soul. In an Aristotelian conceit with which all readers of *Purgatorio 25* will be familiar, soul was the eternal *forma* that gave shape to the *materia* of body. Thus even when deprived of elemental, earthly body, soul retained DNA-like the map of body and, indeed, could again inform with this shape whatever matter was at hand. Whence Dante's ingenious theory of aerial bodies as expounded by Statius in *Purgatorio 25*.

While earlier theologians went to great lengths to guarantee material identity between the earthly and resurrected bodies, after the schoolmen there was less insistence on material continuity. The Scholastics agreed that the resurrected body must be fully realized in flesh and in some sense identical to the earthly body—integral to personhood—in order for the notion of personal salvation to have real significance. But Aristotelian concepts of form and matter, act and potency, allowed them to move away in some degree from strict insistence on physical identity of earthly and resurrected body.[6] Somatomorphic soul assured continuity between the two. Still, for most thinkers—even those who insisted on material continuity—resurrected, glorified body was different from earthly body in one important, miraculous way: the glorified body, albeit fully in the flesh, was impassible, not subject to corruption and decay, forever safe from the change wrought by biological processes, nutrition and putrefaction. Thus Christian theologians redeem the body, since Plato a site of fluid instability and cultural horror. And here the nurturing, female body is paradigmatic, as Bynum confirms:

> Both medical literature and misogynist tracts characterized the female body as more changeable than the male. Closer to decay because colder and wetter than men's bodies, the female body was also closer to being food for worms because it was in all ways closer to food. Women were seen not only as more voracious and greedy than men but also as being themselves nutrition—for fetuses in the womb and infants at the breast. Although all body was feared as teeming, labile, and friable, female body was especially so.[7]

The principle theme of Bynum's study is that resurrection represented a triumph over corporeal fragmentation and dissolution. At the end of time, the body, and thus the person, is restored to perfect, eternal wholeness.

Now Dante accepts and, in *Purgatorio* 25, elaborates upon the Scholastic notion of somatomorphic soul, of bodily form packed into soul. At the same time, he agrees that both damnation and beatitude are imperfect without the fully fleshed body that all souls will regain only at the Last Judgment.[8] But this by no means signals the unalloyed continuity, much less strict identity, of personhood from earth to heaven. The point is never quite clear in Dante as it was never clear in the theologians who precede him. The concept of personhood or subjectivity was one to which they seldom addressed themselves directly.

Still, it is clear in Dante's poem that both components of person, body and soul, undergo significant change between death and the end of time. In every case, body decays and returns to the elements whence it came; Dante does not insist on its identical material reconstitution (as earlier thinkers had) at the end of time. Soul, at least for the saved in purgatory, gradually learns to forget and undo its sinful past in temporal body and recover only the good: this is the narrative of *Purgatorio* with its final sweet draughts of Lethe and Eunoe.[9] Thus despite the ideal, eternal corporealized self promised by the resurrection body, there is in Dante a sense of self in time and earthly body—what I will refer to as temporal body-ego—that must die away as the body dies away. One of the great lessons of purgatory and in particular antepurgatory, as we will see, is that individual, historical identity is illusory: a construct necessarily subject to dissolution because dependent upon elemental matter, a secondary and thus corruptible creation.

Poetically, *Inferno* is the realm of material, hard-edged bodies eternally undone and reconstituted according to the logic of *contrapasso*. *Purgatorio* is meant to draw us away from this historically and corporeally bound notion of self toward the ecstatic dissolution of *Paradiso*. Bynum has argued that the souls of Dante's blessed in some ways anticipate the wholeness of the resurrection body. She is correct to note that the individuality of earthly life—age, gender, status—seems to endure in *Paradiso* as some sense of individual personhood is guaranteed by somatomorphic soul. More significantly, however, this guarantee frees the poet to showcase without fear a poetics of dissolution and interpenetration that is at once spiritual and corporeal.[10] Thus I feel that Bynum's insistence on corporeal integrity does not reflect the poetics of *Paradiso*. Operating under the miraculous guarantee of individual survival in body, Dante's *Paradiso* indeed celebrates renewed corporeality, but its poetics everywhere emphasize not individual corporeal integrity but rather the dynamism and openness of the single body to the greater reality of divine love. If we are to take the images of *Paradiso* as emblematic, the function of the glorified body will be nutritive: continual nourishing interaction with other bodies which compromises corporeal borders without threatening individual survival.

Thus the image of the nursing body is central to this new intercorporeal eschatology. The very site of process and decay that, in a classical context, must be sacrificed for stable selfhood (and that continued to horrify medieval Christians) becomes the primary emblem for Dante's resurrection poetry. We have seen that Gaeta's only hope for eternity was corporeal sacrifice in exchange for symbolic nomination. Her burial and naming represented faith in human language and human history, a faith that—while locally virtuous—was imperfect from the larger perspective of Christian eternity. For all things human and temporal must fade, and here again language's naming function is paradigmatic for Dante.[11] *Paradiso* will represent the paradoxical promise of Christian salvation: individual corporeal selfhood and mystical dissolution in divine unity through eternity.

But it is the middle space of *Purgatorio* that proves most instructive in sounding Dante's notions of the body and selfhood. It is in *Purgatorio* that

Dante effects in verse the transition from corrupt historical body-ego to what will become eternal impassible self at the end of time.[12] In general, the terraces of purgatory dramatize the mortification of the flesh and thus the formal undoing of temporal body-ego in preparation for re-entry into terrestrial paradise. As in previous chapters, textual borders most interest us here as points of transition and definition. Framing the process of purgation on the seven terraces lie antepurgatory and terrestrial paradise. These textual borderlands represent, respectively, the deconstruction of historical body-ego and the reconstruction of a redeemed corporeal selfhood that is then repeatedly celebrated through the final vision of *Paradiso*. This chapter considers the deconstructive poetics of antepurgatory through a close *lectura* of *Purgatorio* 5, the canto where such poetics find sharpest focus. The final chapter will unravel the new Christian self assembled atop Mount Purgatory and affirmed in Paradise.

Silva from Plato to Dante

What I aim to demonstrate in particular in my close reading of *Purgatorio* 5 is the central metaphorical role of the wet nurse in the deconstruction of temporal body-ego and historical identity. We saw in the personification allegories of chapter 1 the significance of the nursing body—at once sustaining and threatening—to medieval conceptions of individual linguistic and moral development. Chapter 2 made use of these schemes to locate a kind of divided consciousness in Dante's linguistic theory as expressed in the texts of *Convivio* and *De vulgari*. There we translated the image of Lady Grammar as simultaneous nurturing mother and punishing master into a dialectical tension in Dante's writing about human language and development: a strictly rationalist imperative to turn away from and reject nurturing corporeality in uneasy coexistence with a longing for the nursing body which I labeled poetic. In the previous chapter, we investigated a classical source of male reason's fear of female nurturing in the intricate interplay between Circe and Caieta in Virgil and Ovid. We saw how these epic moments become significant as stages in individual educational and moral development through the long tradition of Virgilian allegory. Thus, conceptually, Lady Grammar and the epic Circe/Caieta merge as figures of female nursing. Most strikingly, we witnessed the gradual Christianization of allegorical readings of the nurse, which is to say a gradual reversal of the classical opposition to the nursing body in the new poetics of Christian charity. This gradual reaffirmation of the nurse as a site of Christian truth finds precise reflection in Dante's own metaphorical deployment of the nurse from *Inferno* to *Paradiso*.

In this chapter, we again discover that a metaphorical nursing body announces the fragility of any historical or time-bound notion of corporealized self. The souls of the late-repentant and violent dead in antepurgatory are still reeling from the recent separation of body from soul; the poet takes advantage of this liminal space to develop a poetics of personal deconstruction. The pilgrim's most substantial individual encounters—Manfredi in canto 3, Jacopo, Bonconte, and Pia de' Tolomei in canto 5—explore the problematics of temporal selfhood-in-body as it comes to an end. The meeting with Manfredi introduces themes that will find more perfect expression in canto 5: the materiality of the pilgrim's body in sunlight;[13] the soul's nostalgic yearning for recognition as an individual with a distinct historical/corporeal identity;[14] shock and lament over the reassimilation of body into the elements.[15]

But the important point is that the dissolution of body into elements dramatized in these cantos is intended to convey something larger. The dissolution of body is at the same time dissolution of what I have called temporal body-ego. Regardless of what may happen at the end of time, souls in preparation for beatitude must accept the radical undoing of the mental notion of self caught up in the trappings of historical identity to which they have become accustomed on earth. The apparent integrity and stability of body has sustained this notion; thus it is precisely the dissolution of body that signals its demise.

Purgatorio 5 conveys these ideas with particular force. For Dante individual temporal identity is intimately caught up with bodily integrity and both are illusory in their apparent stability. That is to say, both body and self are shown to be mere temporal, and thus temporary, constructs subject to dissolution by a greater reality. *Purgatorio* 5 conveys this reality by the metaphor of flow: the flow of the elements in the primordial universe and upon the body of Mother Earth *(alma mater),* and the alimentary flow of humors in the fluid human body, paradigmatically the nursing body. In *Purgatorio* 5, Dante exploits the Neoplatonic commonplace that matched macrocosmic universe to microcosmic human. More specifically, key to our understanding of the representations of elemental flow in this canto is the Platonic version of primal space and formlessness: *silva,* "the wet nurse of creation," ineluctable third term for Plato in the *Timaeus* and source of lengthy confabulation for Chalcidius in his fourth-century translation and commentary.

In the text of *Purgatorio* 5 are traces of *silva,* by definition invisible and beyond rational grasp. We will see, finally, that fragility of physical body and

temporal self is coterminous with the fragility of language as a stable symbolic entity. Here Dante invites us, then, to psychologize *silva*. The subtle
poetics of canto 5 superimpose the flow of language and temporal consciousness upon the material flow of elements. Just as the material flow of
elements threatens the integrity of an individual body, so a larger semiotic
flow ultimately undoes the word's effort to signify and delimit cleanly, and
just so a larger mental realm envelopes the ego's temporary identification
with its unified bodily image. In this canto, violence to the body is at once
violence to language and identity. Dante thus anticipates twentieth-century
theories of the human subject as a mirror illusion or trick of language (Lacan),
as ultimately "subject" to a greater maternal truth (Kristeva).

Silva constitutes the third term between Platonic Being and Becoming,
between what in Chalcidius will become *exemplar* and *simulacrum*.[16] She is
primal chaos without inherent quality or shape, but possessed in possibility
of all qualities and shapes. She is the receptacle space within which the primary elements of fire, air, water, and earth combine to create material substances. Neither wholly corporeal nor incorporeal, she subtends and thus sustains the perpetual transformations of the material universe. In metaphor,
she is consistently and repeatedly womb, mother, and wet nurse: "I imagine
her as the receptacle of all created things, as a kind of wet nurse."[17]

Plato's parallel accounts of the creation of the universe and of the human
being set the stage for the common Neoplatonic practice of drawing analogies between the macrocosmic universe and the microcosmic human, a practice that will receive its most dramatic elaboration many centuries later in
Bernardus Sylvestris's *Cosmographia*.[18] The minor gods construct the human
from a piece of the same immortal material that composed the world soul;
they set it in a body fashioned, like the material universe, from the four basic
elements. Plato underscores that these bodily materials are borrowed—as if
on loan ("faenus elementarium mutuati")—from the larger universe and will
have to be paid back someday ("quod redderetur cum opus foret"). Unlike
the world body, however, the human body is held together by tiny rivets *(gom-
phos)*, so minute as to be invisible. As we know, these rivets will eventually
fail, and this moment of failure is dramatized in *Purgatorio* 5.[19]

Thus the macrocosmic universe and microcosmic human are made from
the same materials, immortal soul-stuff and the four basic elements. For this
reason, Chalcidius explains, the ancients called man a miniuniverse ("unde
opinor hominem mundum brevem a veteribus appellatum"). Anticipating
the central metaphorical conceit of *Purgatorio* 5,[20] Chalcidius notes that the

blood-based humors flow out from the human body ("sanguis et cetera quae manant ex corpore") and thus eventually reconnect microcosm and macrocosm.[21]

Silva and Alma Mater

Chalcidius is careful not to equate *silva* to any concrete body; yet he explains that *silva,* while she cannot be known through pure reason nor touched with concrete sense, can nonetheless be apprehended by means of the bodies that inhabit her.[22] Metaphorically, earth, like *silva,* is a mother and a nurse already in Plato's text ("Terram vero matrem et altricem omnium terrenorum animantium").[23] Chalcidius moves easily in metaphor from the womb of *silva* to the womb of Mother Earth.[24] In her representation as an immense body shot through with life-sustaining flow, *silva* resembles Mother Earth, who is also a receptacle space of sorts that carries liquid sustenance through her vast system of rivers.[25]

In this she reflects the ancient Mother Earth goddess, *alma mater,* sometimes identified with Ceres, as Isidore explains: "She [Ceres and Earth] is sometimes called 'Mother,' because she gives birth to so many things; she is called 'Great,' because she generates so much food; she is called 'Nourishing' [*alma,* from *alere,* to nourish], because she nourishes [*alit*] all the creatures of the world with her bounty. Earth, then, is a great nurse who provides sustenance for all."[26] Thus the macrocosm/microcosm parallel takes on a somewhat more complex dynamic in some of the cosmogonists, as the structure of the individual human microcosm reflects sometimes the structure of the larger macrocosmic universe, sometimes the macrocosmic body of Mother Earth.

This metaphorical dynamic becomes particularly prominent in Bernardus Sylvestris in the twelfth century, where Mother Earth functions as a tangible, visible figure for the more enigmatic, imperceptible *silva.*[27] In Bernard, the analogy between the body of Earth and the human body is most apparent in his depiction of liquid flow: rivers flow through the body of Mother Earth to provide nourishment to her creatures just as milk flows through the body of the human mother to feed her offspring.[28] As we saw in chapter 3, perhaps Bernard himself has provided the most elaborate articulation of this notion in a well-known commentary on the first six books of the *Aeneid.* This commentator equates the turbulent sea of *Aeneid* 1 (whose narrative veils the joining of spirit and flesh) to the humor-filled body.[29] This liquid flow—ever reminiscent of *silva*—is at once bearer of nourishment and vice.[30]

He had earlier elaborated on these channels of nourishment—veins in the body, rivers on earth—in terms that foreshadow the drama of *Purgatorio* 5. For both veins and rivers are vulnerable, as it were, to rupture, in which case the life-sustaining liquid they contain flows out and away: "Just as in the human body there are channels for the humors, that is to say veins, through which blood flows and from which—when wounded—it spurts out, so on earth there are 'veins' which they call cataracts, through which water is drawn and from which—if pierced—it gushes forth."[31] For all their metaphorical similarity, however, there remains an important distinction between the microcosmic human body and the macrocosmic bodies of Mothers Earth and *silva:* whereas *silva* is self-sustaining and thus perpetual, the human body requires sustenance from without and even then can only maintain itself for a limited period. In the *Timaeus,* Plato asserts the perfect self-reliance of the corporeal universe, whose smooth spherical form figures cyclical perpetuity. The body of the world is complete and self-contained; nothing can or need be added, nothing can flow away. Outside, nothing exists. Unlike the individual body, the universal body feeds off the decomposition of its own elements and thus sustains itself in perpetuity.[32]

Bernard, in a poignant moment at the very end of the *Cosmographia,* converts this truth to tragedy by underscoring the fragile vulnerability of the individual human being in the powerful wake of universal flow:

> The nature of the universe outlives itself, for it flows back into itself, and so survives and is nourished by its very flowing away. For whatever is lost only merges again with the sum of things, and that it may die perpetually, never dies wholly. But man, ever liable to affliction by forces far less harmonious, passes wholly out of existence with the failure of his body. Unable to sustain himself, and wanting nourishment from without, he exhausts his life, and a day reduces him to nothing.[33]

This concluding passage from the *Microcosmos*—imbued, as we have seen, with the magnificent history of *silva,* the elements, and Mother Earth—constitutes an important intertext for the liquid poetics of *Purgatorio* 5. At death, the body—a temporary, microcosmic encapsulation of a much greater elemental flow—simply returns via Mother Earth to the womb of *silva,* the source of its existence. Individual blood flows back into terrestrial streams, rivers, and oceans to be vaporized and condensed. In *Purgatorio* 5, Dante trains his lens on the moment of individual death and attempts to gain laser-sharp focus. But what comes into view is hardly clear. What he sees, rather, is the blurred, ineluctable flow of river water as consciousness passes into silvan eternity. The confluence of individual testimonies that make up *Purgatorio* 5 dramatizes precisely this ever mysterious phenomenon of reassimilation by the nurturing mother's body. It is to a close reading of this canto that we now turn.[34]

Silva in *Purgatorio* 5

The dramatic opening of the canto plots beaming sunlight against the body of the pilgrim (vv. 1–9) and then, immediately, stable will and directed purpose against a flow of whispered language and consciousness. Virgil reproaches the pilgrim for allowing the chatter of the curious souls to halt his physical and mental progress toward salvation:

> *"Perché l'animo tuo tanto s'impiglia,"*
> *disse 'l maestro, "che l'andare allenti?*
> *che ti fa ciò che quivi si pispiglia?*
> *Vien dietro a me, a lascia dir le genti:*
> *sta come torre ferma, che non crolla*
> *già mai la cima per soffiar di venti,*
> *ché sempre l'omo in cui pensier rampolla*
> *sovra pensier, da sé dilunga il segno,*
> *perché la foga l'un de l'altro insolla."*
> (*Purg.* 5.10–18)

> "Why is your mind so entangled," said the master,
> "that you slacken your pace? What matters to you what is whispered
> here? Follow me and let the people talk. Stand as a firm tower which
> never shakes its summit for blast of winds; for always the man in
> whom thought wells up on thought sets back his mark, for the one
> thought weakens the force of the other."

These opening images of fluvial language and thought anticipate the fluvial geography that will figure so prominently in the rest of the canto. Here at the opening, mind is opposed to body in an obvious Platonic dualism.

But the poet grows instantly more subtle by suggesting that the pilgrim's focused purpose might get "caught up" or "entangled" in an aimless flow of thought and language. He thus already foreshadows the corporeal bases of human consciousness and language in the menacing stream of *silva*. Surely, Dante intends the careful reader to imagine this opening picture of ramiform human thought—catching up the pilgrim's straightforward bodily and mental motion ("Perché l'animo tuo tanto *s'impiglia* . . . che l'andare allenti?")—as homologous to a later picture of material entanglement, Jacopo del Cassero in the reeds and mire of the lagoon near Oriago ("Corsi al palude, e le cannucce e 'l braco *m'impigliar* sì ch'i' caddi"). The conspicuous presence of the verb *impigliare*,[35] as well as the evident similarity in situations (forward motion of a body is impeded by some entangling obstruction), joins these moments poetically. This clear textual correspondence intimates that directed thought quickly gets bogged down, as it were, in a kind of mental and linguistic swamp. We will have opportunity later to consider the elemental significance of swampland in a Chalcidean context.

In the linguistic realm, the pilgrim's progress is caught up by the whispered chatter ("s'impiglia . . . si pispiglia") of the recently deceased inhabitants of this antepurgatorial zone, who marvel at his corporeality. Whispering represented a kind of ghost language without solid ontological foundation, a mere *flatus vocis* or blowing wind ("soffiar di venti") dangerously close to the fragile bodily mechanics of speech.[36] Interestingly, Chalcidius himself blames the idle whispering of nurses ("nutricum . . . insussuratio") for diverting young minds toward false human glory away from the true good.[37] On whatever level, these complex images at the beginning of the canto set singleness of body and mind against a distracting torrent of fragmentation, at once corporeal, linguistic, and mental. As the canto develops, the controlling metaphor of ramification and flow will be closely aligned with Earth, the perpetual transformation of the elements, and thus the nurse *silva*.[38]

We know from the Neoplatonists that the human body has its own system of flowing branches of liquid in the circulation of the blood and the other humors. The pilgrim's shame in reaction to Virgil's reproach results in a blush and slyly calls to mind the corporeal river system that will overflow in the narratives that follow: "Che potea io ridir, se non 'Io vegno'?/Dissilo, alquanto del color consperso/che fa l'uom di perdon talvolta degno" (What could I answer if not, "I come"? I said it, overspread somewhat with that color which sometimes makes a man worthy of pardon).[39] This tercet in particular underscores the pilgrim's separateness and singularity as both a body and a mental being which has been evident since the start of the canto. As blood makes its inconspicuous entrance here, the poet gestures toward the tension between individual construct and larger dispersive system. The repetition of the first-person subject pronoun in verse 19 ("io ridir . . . 'Io vegno'") proclaims the pilgrim's shameful self-consciousness. This verse calls attention to the integral form of the first-person subject and pronoun. As I will argue below, the poet thus introduces here a deliberate program throughout the canto of alternating phonetic constitution and fragmentation of the grammatical subject pronoun *io*.

For it is nothing less than the notion of individual historical identity, one with the body and the subject pronoun,[40] that canto 5 deconstructs as it pays tacit homage to the power of *silva*. The segment that follows (vv. 22–63), leading up to the first encounter with Jacopo, plays on the theme of individual identity amidst collective anonymity. Dante goes to great lengths to describe the fluid, disordered motions of the troop of undifferentiated souls, who move as one and, in fact, form a musical chorus that sings for mercy ("Venivan genti innanzi a noi un poco, / cantando 'Miserere' a verso a verso" [Came people a little in front of us, singing the *Miserere* verse by verse]).[41] They marvel at the pilgrim's fleshy body and thus question his identity. At this point, two anonymous souls break off from the troop as the poet prepares structurally for the featured interviews with Jacopo, Bonconte, and Pia de' Tolomei ("E due di loro, in forma di messaggi, / corsero incontr'a noi e dimandarne: / 'Di vostra condizion fatene saggi'" [And two of them, as messengers, ran to meet us, and asked of us, "Let us know of your condition"]).[42]

Virgil assures them that the pilgrim's body is real flesh ("'l corpo di costui è vera carne") and, what is more, that the pilgrim may be able to help them ("Fàccianli onore, ed esser può lor caro" [Let them do him honor, and it may be dear to them]).[43] This sends the two envoys back to the pack with lightning speed: "Vapori accesi non vid'io sì tosto / di prima notte mai fender sereno, / né, sol calando, nuvole d'agosto, / che color non tornasser suso in meno" (Never did I see kindled vapors cleave the bright sky at early night, or August clouds at sunset, so swiftly as these returned above).[44] The simile has seemed to some commentators out of place and oddly exaggerated.[45] But here the poet conjures up a brooding late summer night sky, heavy clouds and distant streaks of lightning. A storm is approaching: that very metaphorical storm will set in motion the circulatory system of Mother Earth which will, later in the canto, drag Bonconte's body to its silvan fate. In the prominent *vapori accesi* at the beginning of verse 37, air mingles with fire in the upper atmosphere in anticipation of water's fall to Earth.[46] As we will see in somewhat closer detail below, for Plato and Chalcidius the cyclical conversion of the four elements is the most dramatic proof we possess of some underlying material unity. It is precisely the problem of elemental instability that leads Plato to *silva*.[47] Thus Dante anticipates canto 5's elemental theme from the start. Just as the pilgrim's blush in verses 20–21 evoked the microcosmic flow of blood within the body and its imminent flowing away at death, so the storm clouds here in verses 37–40 call forth the parallel macrocosmic flow of elements on Earth and their perpetual flowing away in *silva*.

The elemental instability pictured by Dante's simile perfectly matches the unstable collective motion of these antepurgatorial shadow-bodies.[48] The two messengers run to ogle the pilgrim ("corsero incontr' a noi") and rush back to the troop like lightning ("non tornasser suso in meno"), at which point the entire herd flocks back to the pilgrim out of control ("E, giunti là, con li altri a noi dier volta, / come schiera che scorre sanza freno" [And, arrived there, they with the others wheeled round toward us, like a troop that runs without curb]).[49] We recall here Chalcidius's repeated descriptions of *silva* as a powerful stream that cannot be checked, "more torrentis inrefrenabili, inrefrenabile motu."[50]

Amidst this chaotic motility, the restless souls plead with the pilgrim to identify one of them, to single them out, as it were, as body and ego. They envy the pilgrim's corporeal integrity and beg him to stop his forward motion:

> "O anima che vai per esser lieta
> con quelle membra con le quai nascesti,"
> venian gridando, "un poco il passo queta.
> Guarda s'alcun di noi unqua vedesti,
> sì che di lui di là novella porti:
> deh, perché vai? deh, perché non t'arresti?"
> (Purg. 5.46–51)

> "O soul that go to your bliss with those members
> with which you were born," they came crying, "stay your steps for a
> little; look if you have ever seen any of us, so that you may carry news
> of him yonder. Ah, why do you go? Ah, why do you not stay?"

They long nostalgically for news of their historical selves and hope to reaffirm their individual identities, but for all his visual effort ("perché ne' vostri visi guati") the pilgrim cannot distinguish a single individual ("non riconosco alcun"): their respective visages—markers of individuality in life—blur together.[51]

These are the violent dead and last-minute repentant, after all: these souls were snatched abruptly from human being and behave as if still stunned by that relatively recent aggression.[52] The pilgrim cannot restore them to their bodies or earthly identities, but he indulges their desire to speak, and thus the poet fulfills the canto's narrative and thematic promise. Paradoxically, the three autobiographical narratives that follow, while apparently promoting the notion of historical individuality, ultimately undo any human claims for stable identity. At every turn in these fateful histories, Dante the poet asserts the inexorable force of material and elemental flow, of the nurse *silva*. He thus shows Jacopo, Bonconte, and (to a lesser extent) Pia de' Tolomei to be "caught up" by a misplaced longing for an identity that was never "one" to begin with.

An anonymous *uno,* who will turn out to be Jacopo del Cassero, begins his account in verse 64. He asks the pilgrim to remember him to Fano and then moves quickly to the circumstances of his bloody demise. Here Dante begins to perform an intricate phonetic surgery on the first-person singular subject pronoun, *io,* linguistic guarantor, as Lacan teaches, of the unity of the subject.[53] In the discourses of both Jacopo and Bonconte, the first-person pronoun shifts repeatedly back and forth between its integral and truncated forms *(io . . . i')* before disappearing altogether with Pia de' Tolomei. Not surprisingly, with both Jacopo and Bonconte, the phonetic dissolution of the ego surfaces textually at the very moment of corporeal death. Thus both narratively and phonetically, these accounts rehearse the drama of the subject forever deflected between illusory unity—for Lacan a mirror reflection—and fragmentation in the real body. Somewhat less anachronistically for Dante, they rehearse the drama of individual human mental being, deluded in its sense of self-containment and self-sufficiency, as it flows back to its material bases at death.

Such phonetic play appears as soon as Jacopo alludes to his birth (in Fano) and death (near Padua, in the "womb of the Antenori"):

> *Quindi fu'io; ma li profondi fóri*
> *ond'uscì 'l sangue in sul quale io sedea,*
> *fatti mì fuoro in grembo a li Antenori,*
> *là dov' io più sicuro esser credea.*
>
> (*Purg.* 5.73–76)

> Thence I sprang; but the deep wounds whence
> flowed the blood in which I had my life were dealt me in the bosom
> of the Antenori, there where I thought to be most secure.

The statuesque past remote *io* is literally broken up from verse to verse, which is to say phonetically pulled apart and reintegrated into a larger, underlying semiotic stream, a linguistic *silva* of sorts. Jacopo's recollection of his birthplace, Fano, results in the integral form, *io,* followed closely by the wounds and bloody flow of his undoing. The temporary containment of elemental flow as blood in a body enables and sustains the possibility of ego.[54] Once the body is wounded, the blood is free to flow back into a greater system and the temporal ego flows away with it. Ironically, Jacopo's undoing comes to pass in a metaphorical womb ("in grembo a li Antenori"), but it is a treacherous womb. The allusion to Antenor evokes warring Greeks bent on the destruction of Troy as they wait silently for a metaphorical birth, as it were, from the womb of a fateful gift horse.[55]

There is much to note about gender in *Purgatorio* 5. I have already suggested that the passage from illusory unified selfhood to the loss of ego within the sequence of narratives reflects a movement from masculine to feminine. Locally, Jacopo returns to the womb to die, the Neoplatonists' *gremium telluris,* the womb of Mother Earth and ultimately *silva*. Paradoxically, Jacopo relates that the "I" thought itself safe there. But as far as the individual body and unified ego are concerned, the womb can be a very violent place, near as it is to the primal forces of elemental flow. Here Jacopo's "I" returns thinking to find protection, only to be slain at the hands of Azzo VIII and thus dissolve into its constituent humors.[56]

Jacopo laments his mistaken decision at Oriago to turn toward the marshy waters of the Po delta instead of seeking high ground in the relative elemental stability of the town La Mira. His turn toward the marsh is a race to death:

> *Ma s'io fosse fuggito inver' la Mira,*
> *quando fu' sovragiunto ad Oriaco,*
> *ancor sarei di là dove si spira.*
> *Corsi al palude, e le cannucce e 'l braco*
> *m'impigliar sì ch'i' caddi; e lì vid'io*
> *de le mie vene farsi in terra laco.*
>
> (*Purg.* 5.79–84)

> But if I had fled toward La Mira when I was surprised at Oriaco I should yet be yonder where men breathe. I ran to the marsh, and the reeds and the mire so entangled me that I fell, and there I saw form on the ground a pool from my veins.

These verses are curious in that there is virtually no mention of Jacopo's pursuers or their murderous aggressions: the poet erases their presence. The drama is entirely personal, between Jacopo and the elements. Human violence has disappeared. It is as though Jacopo has naturally dissolved back into the body of Earth. The earthly solidity ("terrena soliditas") of his body here merges with the aqueous solidity of marsh vegetation as blood flow returns to river flow.

Furthermore, these verses initiate the voyage across Italy that will inform the remainder of the canto while simultaneously moving from the microcosmic human body to the macrocosmic bodies of Mothers Earth and *silva*. We have come down from the fiery air of the upper atmosphere in verse 37 ("vapori accesi") to where air, earth, and water intermingle. Jacopo's body no longer traps air for sustenance through inhalation and exhalation, a privilege enjoyed only by animate beings.[57] His panicked race toward marshy waters signals, from a Chalcidian perspective, a plunge into the realm of elemental instability: unwittingly, Jacopo hurls himself headlong into the arms of *silva*. Significantly, all three of the canto's protagonists die where earth joins, and intermingles, with water. Jacopo and Pia de' Tolomei meet their ends in swampland ("disfecemi Maremma"), one on each of Italy's seaboards. In a famous passage from the *Ars poetica* which Dante repeatedly echoes, Horace sees the elemental instability of river flow and marshland *(palus)* as figures for the instability of all things human *(mortalia)* and in particular language ("multa renascentur quae iam cecidere").[58]

We recall that Bernardus Silvestris traced the geographical progression from shallow stream to river to marsh to lake in Earth's womb ("Per gremium telluris aque diffunditur humor, / Qui vada, qui fluvios, qui stagna lacusque facit").[59] Jacopo, *in grembo a li Antenori,* moves from marsh *(palude)* to a metaphorical and then all too literal lake *(laco)*. Clearly, he would have done better to keep to the manmade control and strict land / water division of the Brenta canal, upon which sits the small town of La Mira.

Just as earlier the pilgrim's mental processes had become entangled in the whispers of idle curiosity ("l'animo tuo tanto s'impiglia"), so Jacopo's body is caught up in the reeds and muck of the marsh ("le cannucce e il braco m'impigliar"). At that very moment, he looks on in amazement—almost as a kind of third person already outside of his self—as bodily blood flows back to join marsh, lake, and sea. We know from the *Aeneid* commentator that both the human body and the body of Earth have "veins" through which liquid flows and then flows away when these "veins" are wounded or pierced.[60] In verses 83–84, the integrated "I" (together and one for the very last time) witnesses, as though in a mirror, its own dissolution, once again represented by the poet in the phonetic disintegration of the first-person subject pronoun: "E le cannucce e 'l braco / m'impigliar sì ch'*i*' cadd*i;* e lì vid'*io* / de le mie vene fars*i* in terra laco."

Bonconte picks up ("Poi disse un altro") at once where Jacopo leaves off. He is at first, like Jacopo ("uno incominciò"), an anonymous voice in a largely undifferentiated chorus. When he then identifies himself, again very much like Jacopo ("Quindi fu'io"), he exhibits pride and nostalgia for his earthly subject, which he links first to a family lineage and then to an individual Christian name: "Io fui di Montefeltro, io son Bonconte" (I was of Montefeltro, I am Bonconte).[61] He underscores the loss of earthly status as a subject of any sort by noting that neither his widow nor any of his kin or acquaintances remember him, a source of shame and some confusion even now.[62]

The pilgrim wonders what became of Bonconte in his final hours after Campaldino.[63] He wants to know the final resting place of Bonconte's body, as though a grave marker could somehow endow a dead body with stable identity and a kind of eternal subjectivity. Appropriately, Bonconte is denied even this illusory comfort. What sort of power or fate could precipitate such an abrupt and complete erasure of individual presence?

Silva appears on the horizon as Bonconte recounts his end:

> *"Oh!" rispuos'elli, "a piè del Casentino*
> *traversa un'acqua c'ha nome l'Archiano,*
> *che sovra l'Ermo nasce in Apennino.*
> *Là 've 'l vocabol suo diventa vano,*
> *arriva'io forato ne la gola,*
> *fuggendo a piede e sanguinando il piano.*
> *Quivi perdei la vista e la parola;*
> *nel nome di Maria fini', e quivi*
> *caddi, e rimase la mia carne sola."*
> (*Purg.* 5.94–102)

> "Oh!" he answered, "at the foot of the Casentino a
> stream crosses, named the Archiano, which rises in the Apennines
> above the Hermitage. To the place where its name is lost I came,
> wounded in the throat, flying on foot and bloodying the plain. There I
> lost my sight and speech. I ended on the name of Mary, and there I
> fell, and my flesh remained alone."

Ingeniously, the poet superimposes the flow of blood, the flow of river water, and the flow of language as he challenges the reader to isolate the precise moment where and when one flow becomes another: where Archiano becomes Arno; when Bonconte's blood becomes river, lake, sea, and vapor; when individual human life—unable to sustain itself from without ("sic sibi deficiens, peregrinis indiget escis")—becomes one with the larger, more enduring flow of *silva*.

This time we find not only a wounded "I" ("io forato"), but an "I" wounded in the throat ("ne la gola"), the physical seat of language.[64] Language flows away with body and self. Dante has already intimated as much earlier in the canto by dramatizing the phonetic fragility of the first-person subject pronoun, as if to suggest that in the end the "I" is little more than a trick of language, a temporary and (like all language) arbitrary alignment of *signifié* and *signifiant,* forever on the move.[65] The poet chooses to highlight and contrast those river names, Archiano and Arno (implicitly here in verse 96 and again, more strikingly, in verses 125–26), one plainly representing a phonetic abbreviation and realignment of the other. *Arno* appears as a partial dissolution of *Archiano* because the remnants of *io* now vaguely embedded in the tributary are on their way to certain extinction, or perhaps better, evaporation, in the verses that follow.

Both Plato and Chalcidius dwell at some length on the difficulty inherent in naming the elements because they possess no substantial identity. They are mere accidental qualities that inhere temporarily in the spatial substance of *silva.* Plato's discourse on the transformation of the elements arises precisely at that moment in his text where he considers the imperviousness of *silva* to human reason:

> How should we describe her power and nature? I imagine her as the receptacle of all created things, as a kind of wetnurse. Now this statement about her is surely true, but it needs to be explained somewhat more clearly; but this is an extremely difficult matter that will necessarily muddle our mental vision and cause us to hesitate before fire and the other elements: when, for instance, should water be judged and labelled water rather than earth, since there is no one stable property in these bodies that points to their natural brotherhood.[66]

Thus Plato logically posits an invisible common mother, *silva.* He then details the great cycle of transformations that subtends *Purgatorio* 5 in order to emphasize that there is no clear dividing line between one element and the next:

> Let us begin with water, which we just mentioned: when it is condensed into ice, it certainly takes on the appearance of rock or a body of earthly solidity that will not easily dissolve; but this same water, when warmed and flowing in its various paths dissolves into liquid, air, and aerial vapors; then air burns dry and creates fire, which in turn is extinguished and

> grows more corpulent to make air, and then air grows more dense and
> gathers into clouds large and small, which when burst and wrung bring
> the rains and great flow of ponds and springs; and at last from water the
> mounds of earth are gathered.[67]

Of course, in *Purgatorio* 5 Dante has already alluded to the transformation of
air into fire, and we are about to hear Bonconte's account of condensation,
rain water, rivers, and pools.

More significantly, Bonconte's story gives prominence to the analogy
between elemental material and linguistic material. Just as, microcosmically,
the dissolution of body and self is one with the dissolution of language ("forato
ne la gola . . . perdei la vista e la parola"), so, macrocosmically, the dissolution of earthly solidity into river water, ocean, vapor, and fire is one with
semiotic flow. Where Archiano flows into Arno, the tributary loses its proper
name ("là 've 'l vocabol suo diventa vano").[68] As Plato makes clear in a passage that immediately follows the above-cited account of elemental conversion,[69] perpetual material flow gives the lie to language, or rather to that
cleanly delimited slice of language that is the substantive, noun, or pronoun.
The material phenomenon that appears temporarily as fire does not deserve
the stable permanence implied by the noun *fire;* rather, we should refer to
that appearance as "a fiery thing" ("igneum quiddam"). Likewise, air, earth,
and water. The only true reality that merits designation by pronoun ("'hoc'
vel 'illud'") is that perpetual space in which all these transformations take
place: *silva.* Plato condemns the linguistic habit of referring to the four elements as "fire," "air," "earth," and "water," as though these were fundamental,
stable substances and thus substantives. In an earlier, more minute linguistic
paradigm, he suggests that the basic universal building blocks might be analogous to letters of the alphabet *(initia),* whereas clearly the four elements do
not attain even to the status of syllables.[70]

In canto 5, Dante extends Plato's insight on elemental and linguistic instability to the human body and self: it is deceptive, if you will, to use the pronoun *ego/io* in order to designate what is at best a temporary "ego effect"
("egoisticum quiddam?"). Corporeal elements will not stop for a name, but
are forever on the move "in the manner," says Chalcidius "of a violently raging torrent" ("more torrentis inrefrenabili quodam impetu proruentis").[71]
This torrent will always leave its name behind ("fugiunt enim nec expectant
eam appellationem").[72] Plato thinks of a goldsmith who is continually mold-
ing his lump of molten gold into various forms: if you were to point to one

of these forms and ask, "What is that?" the only safe response would be "gold" and not "triangle" or "cylinder" or any of those fleeting, apparent realities.[73] Chalcidius embellishes Plato's illustration by noting that if you were to respond "pyramid," the gold might quickly transform *even as the words were being pronounced* ("mox et inter ipsa verba") and you would be a liar.[74]

Dante finds a way to respond linguistically to Plato's concern over the illusory stability of names. Like Plato and Chalcidius, he pictures elemental continuity as the flow of one powerful stream into another. He challenges the reader to contemplate the elusive boundary line, to point to a seamless flow of water and assert "that is Archiano" or "that is Arno."[75] But in choosing that particular geographic confluence, Dante undermines the deceptive stability of proper names that so troubled Plato, for Archiano and Arno lie so close to one another on some underlying phonetic continuum.[76] By juxtaposing Archiano and Arno, Dante breaches the phonetic wall of defense that protects substantive from substantive and suggests that one easily invades another, just as the fortress of the subject *io* must surrender to forces beyond the self.[77]

Like Jacopo ("in grembo a li Antenori"), Bonconte returns to a metaphorical space of maternity, this one specifically linguistic and Christian ("nel nome di Maria"). Bonconte uses his last moment of corporeal and subjective wholeness—of body and speech and sight—to launch his soul toward the Christian mother and salvation, just as the material body must return, as we know, to its own sort of material eternity in mother *silva*.

> *Io dirò vero, e tu 'l ridì tra ' vivi:*
> *l'angel di Dio mi prese, e quel d'inferno*
> *gridava: "O tu del ciel, perché mi privi?*
> *Tu te ne porti di costui l'etterno*
> *per una lagrimetta che 'l mi toglie;*
> *ma io farò de l'altro altro governo."*
> (*Purg.* 5.103–8)

> I will tell the truth, and do you repeat it among the living. The Angel of God took me, and he from Hell cried, "O you from Heaven, why do you rob me? You carry off with you the eternal part of him for one little tear which takes him from me; but of the rest I will make other disposal!"

This minidrama of salvation parodically recalls the less felicitous fate of Bonconte's father in *Inferno* 27,[78] but also Chalcidius's moralistic Christianization of the Demiurge and *silva* as the forces of good and evil.[79] Again in verse 103, it is as though the lesson that Bonconte urges the pilgrim to carry back to living humans regards the fragile instability of the corporeal "I" (*"Io dirò vero, e tu 'l ridì tra ' vivi"*). Appropriately, the corporeal sign of Bonconte's enlightenment and repentance *in extremis* is liquid. He forces one small tear out of that temporary liquid container that is the body, as though in recognition of the silvan destiny that awaits all humans.[80]

The following verses relate that destiny as they simultaneously detail the cycle of elemental conversion that is for Plato and Chalcidius, as we have seen, the mark of *silva*:

> *Ben sai come ne l'aere si raccoglie*
> *quell'umido vapor che in acqua riede,*
> *tosto che sale dove 'l freddo il coglie.*
> *Giunse quel mal voler che pur mal chiede*
> *con lo 'ntelletto, e mosse il fummo e 'l vento*
> *per la virtù che sua natura diede.*
> *Indi la valle, come 'l dì fu spento,*
> *da Pratomagno al gran giogo coperse*
> *di nebbia; e 'l ciel di sopra fece intento,*
> *sì che 'l pregno aere in acqua si converse;*
> *la pioggia cadde, e a' fossati venne*
> *di lei ciò che la terra non sofferse;*
> *e come ai rivi grandi si convenne,*
> *ver' lo fiume real tanto veloce*
> *si ruinò, che nulla la ritenne.*
>
>   (*Purg.* 5.109–23)

> You know well how in the air is condensed that
> moist vapor which turns to water soon as it rises where the cold
> seizes it. Evil will that seeks only evil he joined with intellect, and, by
> the power his nature gave, stirred the mists and the wind; then when
> day was spent, he covered with clouds the valley from Pratomagno to
> the great mountain chain and so charged the sky overhead that the
> pregnant air was turned to water. The rain fell, and that which the
> ground refused came to the gulleys and, gathering in great torrents,
> so swiftly rushed toward the royal river that nothing stayed its course.

As Singleton recalls, a similarly dramatic description of a summer storm was available to Dante in Virgil's first *Georgic*.[81] Sapegno sends us to Aristotle's account of elemental conversion in the *Meteorologia*.[82] I have argued that the entire canto—with its constant subtext of a nurturing, material flow through microcosm and macrocosm—owes a significant debt to Neoplatonism.

We should recall those bulbous summer storm clouds gathering at sunset ("di prima notte") earlier in the canto: here they burst ("come il dì fu spento"). Just as earlier, *vapori accesi* evoked the enigmatic border between fire and air, so here *umido vapor* lies somewhere on that continuum between air and water. Here the air collects or gathers itself ("l'aere si raccoglie") into clouds and mist ("nebbia") on the way to rainwater ("la pioggia"), which when too great to be contained by Earth's womb, spills over into puddles, lakes, and streams ("fossati"). So also for Plato air gathered into clouds and mist ("aer item crassior factus in nubes nebulasque concrescit"), which burst into rain, ponds, and streams ("pluviae stagnorumque et fontium largitas").

More particularly, to Plato's version Chalcidius joins an essentially Aristotelian explanation of elemental conversion based on the four qualities—hot, cold, dry, moist—that link the elements together.[83] Fire is hot and dry, air is hot and moist, water is cold and moist, earth is cold and dry. When, for instance, earth converts to water, dryness becomes moisture but cold remains.[84] These shared qualities unite the elements while extenuating the borders between them. Certainly, Chalcidius and Dante may have acquired such science in Aristotle's treatises *On Generation and Corruption, On Meteorology,* or *Physics.* But as Waszink notes, Aristotle aims plainly to provide a scientific explanation of elemental conversion via the theory of contrary qualities. Conversely, Chalcidius rehearses Aristotle's explanation in a Platonic context in order to prove the existence of invisible *silva*.[85] In the above example, since cold exists on its own outside of the various elements, it must exist within something; that something is *silva*.[86] For Chalcidius, the Aristotelian qualities are a kind of logical stepping-stone from the elements to *silva*. We cannot deny that Dante had his meteorology from Aristotle. But canto 5 moves beyond pure science to evoke a nurturing flow through microcosm and macrocosm within the bosom of a great, invisible nurse. Thus Chalcidius's Neoplatonic Aristotelianism offers a more suggestive and, perhaps, apposite text with which to understand Dante here.[87] Isidore announces plainly that it is the poets who transform Plato's *hyle* and Aristotle's prime matter into *silva*.[88]

Both Dante ("vapori accesi") and Chalcidius describe the ignition of air into fire ("ignito ergo aere et aliquatenus converso in naturam ignis") as moisture becomes dryness ("humor quidem ad siccitatem facit transitum"). Chalcidius details the conversion of elements and underlying transition of qualities from the ground up, from, that is, earth to water to air to fire; in the Bonconte episode, Dante moves in the opposite direction. But the borders they cross are the same. In Dante, moist air ("umido vapor"), which is hot by nature, rises to cold and becomes water ("che in acqua riede, tosto che sale dove 'l freddo il coglie").[89] In Chalcidius, water dissolves into air vapors ("resoluta in vapores aqua aeri") as cold becomes hot: the constant in both transformations is moistness ("humor porro communis manet").[90] In the end, all of these conversions point to the most ancient, primary receptacle.[91]

Bonconte then recalls the specific fate of his body:

> *Lo corpo mio gelato in su la foce*
> *trovò l'Archian rubesto; e quel sospinse*
> *ne l'Arno, e sciolse al mio petto la croce*
> *ch'i' fe di me quando 'l dolor mi vinse;*
> *voltòmmi per le ripe e per lo fondo,*
> *poi di sua preda mi coperse e cinse.*
>
>   *(Purg. 5.124–29)*

> The raging Archiano found my frozen body at its
> mouth and swept it into the Arno and loosed the cross on my breast
> which I had made of me when pain overcame me. It rolled me along
> its banks and along its bottom, then covered and wrapped me with its
> spoils.

Mention of the "Archian rubesto," a blood-red torrent, reminds readers that Bonconte's is not a singular destiny. Campaldino has occasioned a kind of mass return of individual corporeal humors to the collective maternal flows of Earth and *silva*.[92]

Here Dante's use of the adjective *gelato*, for Bonconte's frozen corpse, and then the verb *sciogliere*, to describe the dissolution of the salvific cross he had made of his arms before death, suggests that the conversion of Bonconte's body (or at least of its earthly component, *terrena soliditas*) to water involves a process of melting. This is notable because it is precisely that link in the chain of conversions—earth into water—that Plato's description in the *Timaeus* omits. As we have seen, Plato begins with water and notes that it can solidify into earth and stone or evaporate into air, which becomes fire when ignited, air again once extinguished, clouds and rainwater once condensed, and finally mounds of earth from water.[93] Chalcidius explains that earth must also convert to water for Plato's cycle to function, lest all be earth in the end. Plato does not mention it, Chalcidius posits, because there seems to be no visible proof of this conversion on earth.[94] Nonetheless it is clear that Chalcidius understands the conversion of water into solid rock and earth as a process of freezing and crystallization;[95] conversely, for Chalcidius earthly solidity melts into water, as he made clear in his Aristotelian discourse on contrary qualities ("Cum igitur terra late fusa convertetur aliquatenus in aquam").[96]

Why is Bonconte's cadaver suddenly frozen *(gelato)* in verse 124? Because it must melt *(sciogliere)* into water and flow away. His body becomes one with that powerful flow that eventually envelopes all ("di sua preda mi coperse and cinse"). Bonconte retrogresses back through the structures of subjective logic formed by the nourishing body at the breast through a kind of reverse pregnancy.[97]

Indeed, the entire metaphorical program of canto 5 might be said to perch on the enigmatic border between land and water, solid and liquid, cities and streams, as a figure for the fragility of body and the temporal body-ego. Bonconte's central account on relatively high land is shored up by two representations of death in swampland, Jacopo's *palude* and Pia de' Tolomei's Maremma, as though the poet were deliberately challenging Chalcidius's contention that the conversion of land to water is not apparent on earth. For surely, swampland depicts in an obvious way the precariousness of elemental boundaries that led Plato and Chalcidius to *silva* in the first place.[98]

The narratives of canto 5 trace an itinerary from one seaboard to the other, from swamp to swamp, and from solid bodies and selves to loss of same. In terms of gender, this is a movement from masculine to feminine and, more precisely, from (albeit wounded) male egocentrism to a kind of feminine resignation and wisdom. I have suggested that both Jacopo and Bonconte return to a metaphorical womb in death and have attempted to identify that womb as the Neoplatonist's *silva*. Just as each of these narratives returns individually to a maternal space, so the canto as a whole reverts to the feminine in the final lapidary words of Pia de' Tolomei:

> "*Deh, quando tu sarai tornato al mondo*
> *e riposato de la lunga via,*"
> *seguitò 'l terzo spirito al secondo,*
> "*ricordati di me, che son la Pia;*
> *Siena mi fé, disfecemi Maremma:*
> *salsi colui che 'nnanellata pria*
> *disposando m'avea con la sua gemma.*"
> (*Purg. 5.130–36*)

> "Pray, when you have returned to the world and have
> rested from your long journey," the third spirit followed on the second,
> "remember me, who am la Pia. Siena made me, Maremma unmade me,
> as he knows who with his ring had plighted me to him in wedlock."

Bonconte's quasi-spasmodic male pride of place and conquest, dramatically attested by a string of masculine toponymics (Montefeltro, Campaldino, Archiano, Ermo, Apennino; but at the very last, Maria), gives way to Pia de' Tolomei's knowing calm (Siena, Maremma). Canto 5 comes to rest in what Kristeva might define as a space of maternal semiosis. Pia de' Tolomei's supremely balanced self-presentation in verse 134 at once evokes and moves beyond the two that have come before. I have demonstrated that this canto invites us to contemplate the literal, phonetic constitution and dissolution of linguistic utterances as a reflection of the construction and deconstruction of selfhood. Juxtaposing *Siena* and *Maremma,* Pia de' Tolomei pronounces a more radical geo-semiotic reshuffling than, say, Bonconte's *Archiano/Arno.* She effortlessly moves the reader from a city to a swamp. The poet's choice of *Maremma* here for swamp, despite its geographical accuracy, is meant to seal canto 5 with a lasting emblem of the engulfing maternal sea that closes over all egos in the end.[99] Phonetically, *Maremma* envelopes an entire semantic program by weaving together the several strands of metaphorical motherhood that nourish this canto. Maremma is a swamp, to be sure. But also easily perceptible in that particular string of phonemes is the sea *(mare),* the seas *(maria),* mother and Virgin mother *(Maria, madre, mamma . . . Maremma).*[100] Pia de' Tolomei moves with admirable narrative simplicity from her treacherous husband back to the body of Mother Earth.

Conspicuously unlike her predecessors, she shows no misplaced nostalgic dwelling upon the "I." The first-person subject pronoun has vanished. Perhaps it has been transformed or, if you will, semioticized in the feminine end rhymes of verses 133 and 135: **Pia, pria.** Pia de' Tolomei recognizes her earthly being as all object from the first and, what is more, an object literally constructed and then deconstructed in time ("Siena mi fé, disfecemi Maremma").[101] In her self-presentation here in *Purgatorio,* she employs the feminine article before her proper name and thus articulates herself as a kind of third person. The strange sensation of seeing one's self as a kind of third-person construct—a sensation that overtook Jacopo and Bonconte only in their final moments, as they witnessed the dissolution of their bodies—had in some sense been with Pia de' Tolomei throughout earthly existence, built into her very Christian name.[102]

In addition, Pia de' Tolomei is the object of that final gerund, *disposando,* the last of a striking and programmatic use of gerunds in this canto.[103] Gerunds frame canto 5 from the poet's description of curious souls in the opening tercet ("quando di retro a me, drizzando 'l dito, una gridò") to Pia de' Tolomei's mournful recollection of convenient marriage in the final verse. We might expect this of a canto so taken up with the flow of individual consciousness and time beyond the grasp of language, inasmuch as the gerund is that part of speech that somehow hopes to capture this progressive flow. But as we know, the timeless mutability of *silva* will always exceed language and the temporal constructs of subjectivity. In this the gerund is as illusory, in the end, as the first-person subject pronoun. Notably, everyone and everything in *Purgatorio* 5—except Pia de' Tolomei—play the role of gerund subject: the anonymous soul of verses 3–4 ("drizzando 'l dito, una gridò"); the undifferentiated troop of verses 23–24 ("venivan genti innanzi a noi un poco, cantando Miserere"); the sun in a Latinate ablative absolute construction in verse 39 ("sol calando"); the pilgrim via Virgil in verse 45 ("però pur va, e in andando ascolta"); the undifferentiated souls again in verse 48 ("venian gridando"), and yet again in a crescendo of choral speech as they pronounce the dramatic double gerund of verses 55–56 ("sì che, pentendo e perdonando, fora di vita uscimmo a Dio pacificati"); this crescendo reaches its climax in verse 99 with Bonconte's story of death as dissolution and flowing away ("fuggendo a piede e sanguinando il piano").

The gerund then disappears only to resurface in the final verse, as quasi-parodic comment, on the lips of Pia de' Tolomei, whose husband is grammatical subject. Unlike Jacopo and Bonconte, she seems never to have acceded to subjectivity proper. She was rather always the object of male constructs, ringed in by her sometime husband's stone, done and undone by a structuring beyond her power. Placed here at the canto's very end as if in poignant contrast, she easily accepts—and thus expertly represents—the lesson of fragmented subjectivity, a lesson that Jacopo and Bonconte had so valiantly resisted in battle and about which they still perform a delicate dance of semi-understanding. Pia de' Tolomei seems never to have strayed very far from the central truth of canto 5: the inevitable flowing away of all corporeal, linguistic, and mental beings through brooks, streams, rivers, marshes, and oceans back to the great womb of Earth and Mother *silva.*

FIVE

RECONSTRUCTING SUBJECTIVITY IN *PURGATORIO* AND *PARADISO*

Sermo humilis and the Nursing Body of Christ

The preceding chapters have demonstrated a profound continuity in cultural attitudes toward the nursing body from antiquity through the Christian Middle Ages. Simultaneously site of sustenance and collapse, the very image of nursing challenged the temporal illusion of individual corporeal integrity and thus— as I argued in the previous chapter—of stable self-identity on earth in time. We have further seen that human language is a central element in cultural constructions of the nurse. The very physical source of language, the nurse nonetheless defies purely rational attempts to crystalize language as a finite symbolic system. In chapters 1 and 2, we saw how these complex cultural attitudes played out in depictions of Lady Grammar and in Dante's own theoretical texts. In chapter 3, we examined the nurse's body in an epic context and saw that the classical response to her enigmatic threat was sacrifice and burial in hope for a kind of eternal symbolic life in language. But this epic faith in the stability of names is shortsighted, as Dante conveys throughout *Purgatorio* and as Plato had made plain in the *Timaeus*. In *Purgatorio* 5, Dante shows us that language is itself a body, subject to fluid process, nutrition, and decay.

My labeling of the symbolic gesture against, or away from, the nurse as "classical" is convenient and in some ways reductive, but not without significant historical basis, particularly if we consider that Christianity—in a decidedly anticlassical and antigrammatical move—provides the counterdiscourse that embraces the nursing body and its correspondent linguistic dynamism. These binaries (classical/Christian, grammar/vernacular, patriarchal law/maternal nursing) are clear in Augustine, as we saw in chapter 1. Dante himself offers a dramatic reversal of attitude toward the nurse, from burial in the thoroughly classical *Inferno* 26 to resurrection in the thoroughly Christian *Paradiso* 27, as we saw in chapter 3. In *Purgatorio* 5, we are just over the border into salvation. Here classical and Christian come together in interesting ways. The antepurgatorial souls, recent arrivals in the spirit realm, are beginning to recognize the illusory nature of their temporal identities in body. But one of the lessons of that canto is that this understanding was substantially available to them on earth in the text of the created universe as explained by classical science. In its depiction of ceaseless material conversion, *alma mater* and through her invisible *silva, Purgatorio* 5 represents the all-engulfing maternal so feared by the classical subject.

For Ulysses, to be engulfed by the great sea bespoke despair and finitude. By contrast, in antepurgatory we are at the beginning of a new journey, a journey of salvation. Far from renouncing or attempting to bury the body in order to safeguard a rigid notion of selfhood, the poetics of *Purgatorio* and *Paradiso* will reaffirm the body—not as a static, cleanly bound unit, but as site of joyous process. Specifically, on top of Mount Purgatory, approaching and within the terrestrial paradise, Dante strategically deploys the nursing metaphor in order to map out a new Chrisitian paradigm for human selfhood: a paradigm that embraces the nurse's body and all that she represents about the motility of corporeal and linguistic borders.

Of course, the gradual reaffirmation of nursing corporeality we witness in the trajectory from *De vulgari* to *Inferno* to *Paradiso* reflects a much larger Christian discourse of maternalization, much of which we have explored in previous chapters. Many have written on the myriad facets of this phenomenon. In a theoretical vein, Julia Kristeva has discerned already in the semiotics of the New Testament a "nutritive opening up to the other, the full acceptance of archaic and gratifying relationship to the mother."[1] Caroline Bynum has also investigated at length the maternalization of Christ in late medieval spirituality, particularly among female mystics.[2] But it is the specifically linguistic import of the nursing body that most concerns our study of Dante the poet. I have argued that Dante's gradual opening to nursing corporeality is one with his ever more emphatic celebration of the mother tongue. Dante's metaphorical embrace of the nurse matches a linguistic ideology that accepts, indeed rejoices in, language—that central node of personhood—as fluid process. Here we must recall the specifically Christian rhetoric, or rather antirhetoric, that Erich Auerbach identified in a famous essay as *sermo humilis*.[3] After all, the rhetoric of the Christian

God is that of babes and sucklings.[4] Christian theologians posited linguistic simplicity and fluidity over and against hard-lined classical grammar and rhetoric. Appropriate to Christian charity was an open, gentle linguistic pedagogy that took its cue from Scripture, a nurse-tutor who provides gradual instruction.[5]

Thus we see the values of *sermo humilis* in Dante's new, properly inspired Christian poetics as communicated by the pilgrim's series of encounters with poets beginning in *Purgatorio* 21 through to the end of the canticle. I argued that the classical subject of history was undone in canto 5. Nevertheless, we must keep the classical, grammatical model of subject-building close at hand here at the end of *Purgatorio*. For we witness here no less than the rebirth and re-education of the pilgrim as subject-*puer* in a different, poetic grammar, which is to say a grammar continually open to nursing corporeality: an education that no longer hinges on turning away from the mother's body. Quite the contrary.

The broad outlines of this education are as follows: after a lengthy period of *infantia* and suckling among male poets, a period commensurate in Dante's scheme with absorption of right-minded poetic inspiration, the pilgrim turns away from the classical father toward the Christian mother and assumes a subject position/proper name for the very first time in the poem (canto 30).[6] The dramatic reversal of the gendered poles of the classical paradigm (from the *tetta de la madre* to the *correzione del padre*) are apparent. We will see, however, that, while Dante's text certainly suggests such a reversal on the relatively superficial level of a reading that simply matches characters with their historical gender, a deeper textual dynamic is at work to discard altogether binary thinking about gender at the very moment that the new subject emerges. Still, far from burying the nurse's body and her milk, the new subject will drink long and deep of the nurse's bosom in the earthly paradise.

Of course, the journey toward paradise regained is a journey toward reversal of a violated dietary prohibition. Time and again the pilgrim's impulse is figured as a "natural thirst" for what we may call Christian knowledge. One of the *Purgatorio*'s most amazing feats is the total fusion of poetic and Christian values that takes place in and around the sixth terrace of gluttony (cantos 21 and following), which allows the poet to feature the nutritional metaphor in all its complexity. Accordingly, the pilgrim's itinerary into paradise is punctuated by a series of ersatz trees of good and evil that underscore the universal moment of this individual path.[7]

Dante's Nurse-Poets

The pilgrim's extraordinary series of encounters with his poetic past begins in earnest with the Christ-like appearance of Statius in canto 21. Although we are here technically still on the fifth terrace of avarice and prodigality, we have in an important sense already left it behind, for the earthquake of Statius's liberation has already taken place (see 20.124–51 and 21.40–72). The opening verses of canto 21 at once envelope maternal nursing and Christian resurrection and thus inaugurate the text's probing of the new subject's semiotic origins:

> La sete natural che mai non sazia
> se non con l'acqua onde la femminetta
> samaritana domandò la grazia,
> mi travagliava, e pungeami la fretta
> per la 'mpacciata via dietro al mio duca,
> e condoleami a la giusta vendetta.
> 'Ed ecco, sì come ne scrive Luca
> che Cristo apparve a' due ch'erano in via,
> già surto fuor de la sepulcral buca,
> ci apparve un'ombra . . .
>
> (*Purg.* 21.1–10)

> The natural thirst which is never quenched, save with the water whereof the poor Samaritan woman asked the grace, was tormenting me, and our haste was urging me along the encumbered way behind my leader, and I was grieving at the just vengeance; and lo, as Luke writes for us that Christ, new-risen from the sepulchral cave, appeared to the two who were on the way, a shade appeared to us . . .

Dante links this dramatic image of Christian resurrection from Luke to the famous episode of the Samaritan woman as metaphorical nurse, abject female body ("femminetta samaritana"), purveyor of liquid nourishment. More importantly, the episode recalled for the medieval reader Christ's own function as nurse of the water of eternal life.[8] Thus already in the opening verses of canto 21 we discover, not very deeply embedded, the unburying ("surto fuor de la sepulcral buca") of the classical nurse in Christian resurrection, a paradigmatic image that anticipates Beatrice's more explicit statement in *Paradiso* 27.

This same canto will introduce the image of poetry as mother and wet nurse with Statius's famous description of the *Aeneid*, "La qual mamma/fummi, e fummi nutrice, poetando" (Which in poetry was both mother and nurse to me).[9] On the terrace of gluttony in the following canto, the Muses become lactating nurses on Parnassus, whose grottoes flow freely with the rich milk of poetic inspiration. Statius says to Virgil: "Tu prima m'invïasti/verso Parnaso a ber ne le sue grotte,/e prima appresso Dio m'alluminasti" (You it was who first sent me toward Parnassus to drink in its caves, and you who first did light me on to God).[10] And Virgil on Homer and the other ancient poets in Limbo:

> *"Costoro e Persio e io e altri assai,"*
> *rispuose il duca mio, "siam con quel Greco*
> *che le Muse lattar più ch'altri mai,*
> *nel primo cinghio del carcere cieco;*
> *spesse fiate ragioniam del monte*
> *che sempre ha le nutrice nostre seco."*
>
> > (*Purg.* 22.100–105)

> > "These, and Persius and I and many others," replied
> > my leader, "are with that Greek whom the Muses suckled more than
> > any other, in the first circle of the dark prison; oftentimes we talk of
> > that mountain which has our nurses ever with it."[11]

Like canto 21, canto 22 also opens with a reference to Christian thirst in the fourth beatitude recited by the guardian angel of the fifth terrace:

> *Già era l'angel dietro a noi rimaso,*
> *l'angel che n'avea vòlti al sesto giro,*
> *avendomi dal viso un colpo raso;*
> *e quei c'hanno a giustizia lor disiro*
> *detto n'avea beati, e le sue voci*
> *con* "sitiunt," *sanz'altro, ciò forniro.*
>
> > (*Purg.* 22.1–6)

> > Now the angel who had directed us to the sixth cir-
> > cle was left behind us, having erased a stroke from my face, and he
> > had declared to us that they whose desire is for righteousness are
> > blessed, his words completing this with *"sitiunt,"* without the rest.

Dante's fragmentary allusion to an emended text ("*'sitiunt,'*" "sanz'altro") fixes appropriately on the thirst metaphor in this canto and series of cantos where the wet nurse stands as purveyor of both virtuous classical and Christian nourishment.[12] At the end of the canto, the pilgrim and poets will encounter the first tree upside down, a crystal clear nectar flowing over its fronds. The gentle voice that emanates from within outlines *exempla* (from the mythological Golden Age, Old Testament and New) of what we might call nutritional humility: the Christian ideal of a *cibus humilis,* whose archetype the text has already projected as the nurse's milk.[13]

When the pilgrim then sees the emaciated gluttons in canto 23, he thinks of the ultimate anti-nurse and evokes the classical example of one starving Mary who, during the siege of Jerusalem by Titus, strangled and consumed the flesh of the infant son at her breast.[14] By contrast, Forese Donati, Dante's one-time poetic sparring partner, now espouses a humble Christian thirst and nutrition thanks to the tears of his wife, Nella: "Sì tosto m'ha condotto/a ber lo dolce assenzo d'i martìri/la Nella mia con suo pianger dirotto" (Thus soon has led me to drink the sweet wormwood of the torments my Nella with her flood of tears).[15] His subsequent diatribe targets the brazen Florentine women ("le sfacciate donne fiorentine"), to whom it will one day be forbidden to go about with fully bared breasts ("l'andar mostrando con le poppe il petto").[16] Such language participates in a larger textual dialectic of concealment and revelation of the breast, which, as we saw in chapter 4, shifts dangerously in the poet's heterosexual desire between mere erotic object and path to salvation, between seduction and education, as the text aims to merge the two.

These many embedded and apparent allusions to nursing in and around the terrace of gluttony are meant to suggest a new period of *infantia,* at once poetic and Christian. Appropriately, Forese's harangue against bare-breasted women also implicates the infant's physical and linguistic growth with a reference to babytalk: "Se l'antiveder qui non m'inganna,/prima fien triste che le guance impeli/colui che mo si consola con nanna" (If our foresight here beguiles me not, they will be sorrowing before he will cover his cheeks with hair who is now consoled with lullabies).[17] In fact, throughout these cantos we note a repeated focus on the line that separates silence from speech, set up by the pilgrim's desire to speak in order to reveal Virgil's identity to Statius at 21.103ff.[18]

Amidst the several allusions to nursing that continue in canto 24, Forese rehearses the primal speech act of demonstrative naming as the infant accedes to the position of new Christian subject:

"Qui non si vieta
di nominar *ciascun, da ch'è sì munta*
nostra sembianza via per la dïeta.
Questi," e mostrò col dito, "è Bonagiunta."
. . . .
Molti altri mi nomò *ad uno ad uno;*
e del nomar *parean tutti contenti.*

> (*Purg.* 24.16–19, 25–26; my emphases)

> "Here it is not forbidden *to name* each other, since
> our features are so wrung by the fast. This," and he pointed with his
> finger, "is Bonagiunta . . ." Many others he *named* to me, one by one,
> and at their *naming* all appeared content.

The gluttons' features are described as *munta* ("milked dry"; see Singleton
[Dante, *The Divine Comedy*] *ad loc.*) in verse 17, from *mungere,* "to milk,"
which perfectly captures Christian paradox, communicating simultaneously,
as it does, milky nutrition and physical emaciation. In this context, Ubaldino
dalla Pila and the bishop Bonifazio become teething infants: "Vidi per fame a
vòto usar li denti/Ubaldin da la Pila e Bonifazio/che pasturò col rocco molte
genti" (I saw, plying their teeth on the void for very hunger, Ubaldin da la Pila
and Bonifazio who shepherded many people with his staff).[19] Bonagiunta
stammers enigmatically: "El mormorava; e non so che 'Gentucca'/sentiv'io
là, ov' el sentia la piaga/de la giustizia che sì li pilucca" (He was murmuring,
and I know not what, save that I heard "Gentucca" there where he felt the
pang of the justice which so strips them).[20] As the pilgrim's address makes
clear, Bonagiunta is the very picture of desire on the threshold of language:
"'O anima,' diss'io, 'che par sì vaga/di parlar meco, fa sì ch'io t'intenda,/e
te e me col tuo parlare appaga'" ("O soul," said I, "that seem so eager to talk
with me, speak so that I may hear you, and satisfy both yourself and me by
your speech").[21] This allusional definition of a new infancy and a new speech
is, of course, immediately followed by Dante's manifesto of a new, mother-
tongue poetry, *dolce stil nuovo.*[22]

The righted, second tree *(pomo)*[23] on the terrace of gluttony is laden with
fruit and features beneath its branches starving gluttons who vainly reach out
in desire and give voice to that desire like *bramosi fantolini,* desirous incipi-
ent speakers.[24] The voice that comes from this tree recalls examples of nutritional excess—the drunken Centaurs and the Hebrews of Gideon's army
whose drinking brought about weakness of spirit—as the poet subtly evokes

the anti-nurse Chirón and *Inferno* 12 in a reference to the Centaurs' "double breasts."[25] In canto 25, Statius's discourse on generation will strive to articulate in Aristotelian terms the paradox of shadow bodies, which the pilgrim casts as a quandary involving principles of nutrition: "Come si può far magro/la dove l'uopo di nodrir non tocca?" (How can one grow lean there where the need of nourishment is not felt?).[26]

Even when we leave the terrace of gluttony behind and move on to lust in canto 26, Dante's text refuses to stray from the primal logic of infant appetite and maternal nutrition. Still among vernacular poets, the pilgrim's conversation with Guido Guinizzelli is sustained by references to appetite and feeding.[27] The poet names himself ("Son Guido Guinizzelli" [I am Guido Guinizzelli])[28] and Dante calls attention, again, to this founding act of speech ("Quand'io odo *nomar* sé stesso il padre" [When I hear *name* himself the father]).[29]

In between he frames a portrait of the power of maternal affection and nursing: "Quali ne la tristizia di Ligurgo/si fer due figli a riveder la madre,/tal mi fec'io ma non a tanto insurgo" (As in the sorrow of Lycurgus two sons became on beholding their mother again, so I became, but I do not rise to such heights).[30] The story is from Statius's *Thebaid* 5.499–730. Lycurgus, king of Nemea, had left his infant son in the charge of the nurse Hypsipyle, who leaves the boy alone momentarily in a wood in order to lead thirsty warriors to a nearby fountain (thus reinforcing her nursing role). When the infant is bitten and killed by a snake, the enraged Lycurgus is initially determined to put Hypsipyle to death, until he is won over by the outpouring of maternal affection by her two adult sons. In Statius, the sons weep for love and take turns clutching Hypsipyle to their bosoms ("alternaque pectora mutant").[31] While Dante's affection for Guido remains more mental than physical ("non a tanto insurgo"), it is nonetheless an affection of son for mother as the milk motif is passed down from Statius and Virgil.[32] This canto—as mentioned, one in the series of semiotic[33] cantos that reach across the entire poem—will conclude with the most dramatic affirmation of the mother tongue *(parlar materno)* in the *Comedy* as Arnaut Daniel recites three tercets in Provençal.[34] The semiotic eruption of the nurse-mother's tongue onto the page lies, then, at the very gates of earthly paradise, into which the poets will make their way in the following canto.

What finally draws the pilgrim through the wall of fire and into earthly paradise in canto 27 is the thought that Beatrice lies beyond.[35] Virgil uses his words to evoke Beatrice and, as it were, seduce the pilgrim. The thought of Beatrice captures the pilgrim's will as an apple wins over a young child, and Virgil is pleased with his rhetorical victory: "Ond'ei crollò la fronte e disse:

'Come!/volenci star di qua?'; indi sorrise/come al fanciul si fa ch'è vinto al pome" (At which he shook his head and said, "What? Do we desire to stay on this side?"; then smiled as one does to a child that is won with an apple).[36]

Not yet *ammiraglio* (*Purgatorio* 30.58), Beatrice is metaphorized here for the pilgrim-*puer* as *pomo*.[37] The reference recalls the earlier fruit-bearing trees we have seen on the terrace of the gluttons and the thematics of original sin.[38] More specifically, the *pomus* is the quasi-primal object, preceded only by the breast, in the Augustinian chain of human desire that must ultimately lead beyond all temporal objects to God: as the *infans* thirsts for the *uber,* so the *puer* or *parvulus* for the *pomum.*[39] Dante outlines this logic in *Convivio*:

> *Onde vedemo li parvuli desiderare massimamente un*
> *pomo; e poi, più procedendo, desiderare uno augellino; e poi, più oltre,*
> *desiderare bel vestimento; e poi lo cavallo; e poi una donna; e poi ricchezza*
> *non grande, e poi grande, e poi più. (Conv. 4.12.16)*

> Thus we see little children setting their desire first of
> all on an apple, and then growing older desiring to possess a little bird,
> and then still later desiring to possess fine clothes, then a horse, and
> then a woman, and then modest wealth, then greater riches, and then
> still more.

We have seen a playful iconographic tradition, current in Dante's Florence, that assimilates the breast and the generic piece of fruit or apple.[40] In the semiotics of Augustinian desire, the *pomus* conflates gluttony and lust, and thus barely conceals the image of the breast, object of an appetite where hunger and sexual desire commingle. Thus as the pilgrim prepares to re-enter paradise and don a new Christian selfhood, the classical hinge of human linguistic development away from the nursing body is evoked and implicitly questioned here in *Purgatorio* 26–27: midway between the burial of the classical nurse and the language of suckling in *Inferno* 26–27, and the resurrection of language as eternal flow and of the mother's body in *Paradiso* 26–27.[41]

In the new semiotics of Christianity, Dante reconnects temporal objects to their eternal end as the pilgrim accedes to a new subjectivity in the earthly paradise. Just as the breastlike object draws him into the garden, celebratory images of milk as spiritual nutrition characterize his sojourn with Matelda and Beatrice in the final cantos of *Purgatorio*. Canto 28 again stresses the pilgrim's thirst as he arrives at the two prelapsarian rivers, Lethe and Eunoe, which flow with a nectar whose sweetness surpasses all others.[42] Here Dante sheds his status as exile. These rivers will satisfy the poet's thirst for Arno as pre-exilic Florence and maternal breast ("quanquam Sarnum biberimus ante dentes") that we sensed in the *De vulgari*. These rivers flow with the Golden Age nectar dreamed of by ancient poets; in this flow, the human race, the root of human being, is innocent.[43]

The final verses of canto 28 frame the pilgrim looking backward at Virgil and Statius ("Io mi rivolsi 'n dietro allora tutto/a' miei poeti" [I turned then right round to my poets])[44] and then forward to Beatrice ("Poi a la bella donna torna' il viso" [Then to the fair lady I turned my face])[45] in a posture that we should now recognize as an allusion to individual moral development. We recall the classical paradigm of *Convivio* 4.24, where again the reflexive *(ri)volgersi* is operative as the infant turns away from the mother's breast toward the father's discipline ("si dee volgere a la correzione del padre"). Virgil and Statius make their final joint appearance here. As if out of supreme filial affection, Dante the poet allows Virgil a glimpse of the heavenly pageant at *Purgatorio* 29.55–57, as the pilgrim turns back—again, "Io mi rivolsi"—to find him "con vista carca di stupor."[46]

This sequential insistence on the pilgrim's retrospection in the verb *rivolgersi*[47] sets the reader up for Virgil's dramatic disappearance in *Purgatorio* 30:

> *Tosto che ne la vista mi percosse*
> *l'alta virtù che già m'avea trafitto*
> *prima ch'io fuor di püerizia fosse,*
> volsimi a la sinistra col respitto
> col quale il fantolin corre a la mamma
> *quando ha paura o quando elli è afflitto,*
> *per dicere a Virgilio: "Men che dramma*
> *di sangue m'è rimaso che non tremi:*
> conosco i segni de l'antica fiamma."*
>
> (*Purg.* 30.40–48; my emphases)

> As soon as on my sight the lofty virtue smote that had already pierced me before I was out of my boyhood, *I turned to the left with the confidence of a little child that runs to his mother* when he is frightened or in distress, to say to Virgil, "Not a drop of blood is left in me that does not tremble: I know the tokens of the ancient flame."

We are intended to recall Dante's temporal progression through the life stages ("prima ch'io fuor di püerizia fosse") here as he replays that progression in a new, spiritual key. The pilgrim's turning back over his left shoulder toward

Virgil as maternal breast *(mamma),* only to be confronted with absence and forced to face forward to the stern father-figure of Beatrice and adult self-hood, momentarily revives the classical paradigm while simultaneously undermining that paradigm's strict gender configurations.[48]

The pilgrim's sinister retrospection is a turning back toward ancient values ("conosco i segni de l'antica fiamma"), including Virgil's classical relation to the nurse as a seductive threat that must be buried.[49] Dante's text frustrates any attempt to discern fixed gender binaries in this Christian rebirth of the subject.[50] The pilgrim turns away from Virgil as metaphorical *mamma* toward Beatrice as paternal disciplinarian while simultaneously turning away from a classical father toward a Christian mother. The canto had announced this collapse of gender with the appearance of Beatrice on the triumphal chariot to the cry "Benedictus qui venis!" (v. 19), which recalls Christ's entry into Jerusalem on Palm Sunday,[51] and the Virgilian "Manibus date lilia plenis" (v. 21), with its evocation of paternal affection in *Aeneid* 6.[52]

If Virgil is a nurturing mother in the pilgrim's retrospective longing, he immediately becomes a sweet father upon disappearing:

> *Ma Virgilio n'avea lasciati scemi*
> *di sé, Virgilio dolcissimo patre,*
> *Virgilio a cui per mia salute die'mi;*
> *né quantunque perdeo l'antica matre,*
> *valse a le guance nette di rugiada*
> *che, lagrimando, non tornasser atre.*
>
> (*Purg.* 30.49–54)

> But Virgil had left us bereft of himself, Virgil sweet-
> est father, Virgil to whom I gave myself for my salvation; nor did all
> that our ancient mother lost keep my dew-washed cheeks from turn-
> ing dark again with tears.[53]

Mention of the ancient mother Eve places *matre* in end rhyme to Virgil's *patre* and adds to the general sense of gender conflation that characterizes the entire canto.

The Pilgrim as *infans/puer*

For all of the undoing of fixed notions of gender, however, Dante's text clearly means to recall, at least for the moment, the classical paradigm of subject building. At this climactic moment of the poem, the pilgrim is again a speechless, bawling *infans* caught between nutrition and nomination. The journey up through the seven terraces of Purgatory has effected the deconstruction of the classical subject. Here at the top of the mountain, the reborn pilgrim-infant comes to a new Christian subjectivity, a subjectivity that will embrace the wet nurse and acknowledge its status as "sub-ject" to a greater maternal flow. For the moment, we are meant to recall the movement toward selfhood as a separation from the breast. Thus the pilgrim, confronted with emptiness as he turns for "Virgilio-mamma," "la tetta de la madre," faces forward to confront "la correzione del padre" in the figure of Beatrice.

He faces forward to his destiny as subject, if you will, and at precisely this moment—for the first and only time in the entire poem—he is named:[54] "Dante, perché Virgilio se ne vada,/non pianger anco, non piangere ancora;/ché pianger ti conven per altra spada" (Dante, because Virgil leaves you, do not weep yet, do not weep yet, for you must weep for another sword).[55] From the breast to a name, from nutrition to nomination—we have seen this primal border delineated in the pilgrim's earlier meetings with the poets. Dante here calls extraordinary attention, however, to this most important act of naming: it is the sound of this name that turned him away from the breast and toward the angelic lady, now a reproachful admiral:

> *Quasi ammiraglio che in poppa e in prora*
> *viene a veder la gente che ministra*
> *per li altri legni, e a ben far l'incora;*
> *in su la sponda del carro sinistra,*
> *quando mi volsi al suon del nome mio,*
> *che di necessità qui si registra,*
> *vidi la donna che pria m'appario*
> *velata sotto l'angelica festa,*
> *drizzar li occhi ver' me di qua dal rio.*
>
> (*Purg.* 30.58–66)

> Like an admiral who goes to stern and bow to see
> the men that are serving on the other ships, and encourages them to
> do well, so on the left side of the chariot—when I turned at the
> sound of my name, which of necessity is registered here—I saw the
> lady, who first appeared to me veiled under the angelic festival, direct
> her eyes to me beyond the stream.

The verb *volgersi* ("mi volsi al suon del nome mio") again places the moment within the sequence of moral turnings we have seen. This time, however, the infantilized pilgrim turns toward the phonemes that will signify his very selfhood.

In Lacanian theory, the subject is nothing but this signifier, which assigns him a place in the symbolic order. This name offers the real mass of bodily drives a place in the symbolic order at the high price of exile. The signifier "takes the place" of the real as the *infans* becomes subject. In the symbolic order of language, the subject exists only as this name. He is an empty set, "a set which has no elements, a symbol which transforms nothingness into something by *marking* or *representing* it."[56] Thus for Lacan, the named speaking subject is necessarily alienated or exiled from his real body. I have already suggested that this twentieth-century psychoanalytic notion of the subject alienated from the body in language finds a precedent in the classical burial of the nurse as the foundation of culture. As we know from Augustine, the historical Christian subject was also profoundly alienated in language and desire; but unlike his classical counterpart, the Christian subject was exiled from a space to which he or she might someday return to be whole once again. The pilgrim finds himself well within this space in canto 30. By rehearsing the classical scene of naming—always a sign of alienation for the historical subject—within the ideal Christian space of earthly paradise, Dante poses a radical challenge to the classical paradigm. He forges a new subject: a named, speaking individual who is no longer in exile from the body or a transcendent self.[57]

The strictly gendered poles of the classical paradigm collapse. To be sure, Beatrice is a reproachful father-figure, an admiral who controls both *poppa* and *prora*. The figure of *poppa* and *prora* occurs only three times in the *Comedy*.[58] As we saw in chapter 4, it is an important figure of moral direction in allegorical readings of Virgil: Ulysses lost control of these anchored poles at the end of *Inferno* 26.[59] Beatrice will announce their historical correction at the end of *Paradiso* 27.

Despite her severity here, however, Beatrice's speech betrays her symbolic role as nurse-tutor. Much like the classical wet nurse and certain Christian conceptions of Lady Grammar, she gradually imparts the phonemes of speech to the pilgrim/incipient speaker. She dramatizes the maternal and corporeal bases of language in the musical motility of the body. She demonstrates the way in which the discrete units of symbolic language (of which the proper name is prototypical) arise from a larger semiotic stream. She constructs language phoneme by phoneme, syllable by syllable: "Non pianger anco, non piangere ancora;/ché pianger ti conven per altra spada." This is particularly evident as she names herself, where her alliterative fragmenting of the linguistic stream calls attention to language's underlying material sonority: "Guardaci ben! Ben son, ben son Beatrice."[60] We saw in the previous chapter that the poetics of *Purgatorio* 5 feature this same semiotic stream. There language and selfhood are pulled apart; here they are reconstructed.

Caught in Beatrice's all-powerful gaze ("drizzar li occhi ver' me di qua dal rio"), the nascent subject is traumatized by the sight of his self as object, by the form of his bodily unity in the mirror: "Li occhi mi cadder giù nel chiaro fonte;/ma veggendomi in esso, i trassi a l'erba,/tanta vergogna mi gravò la fronte" (My eyes fell down to the clear fount, but, seeing myself in it, I drew them back to the grass, so great shame weighed on my brow).[61] Shadow-body though Beatrice may be, her eyes here take on a curious physicality reminiscent of their power over the poet in temporal life, a power that will be explicitly recalled later in the canto.[62] But we soon learn that her apparent paternal austerity is only momentary (vv. 103ff.) and masks an underlying maternal charity. Dante's text thus again evokes the classical dynamics of selfhood as a construct permanently fixed outside of maternal affection only to undermine them. The pilgrim's sense of embarrassment as he contemplates his body in the Lacanian mirror is instantly reversed by the angelic choir's performance of the thirtieth psalm.[63] The poet makes plain Beatrice's ultimate status as mother, stern in her affection: "Così la madre al figlio par superba,/com'ella parve a me; perché d'amaro/sente il sapor de la pietade acerba" (So does the mother seem harsh to her child as she seemed to me, for bitter tastes the savor of stern pity).[64] Appropriately, the pilgrim's accession to this new model of subjectivity, founded on Christian mercy and open to maternal nurturing, is pictured in verses 85–99 as the melting of frozen, ice-hard snow into flowing, liquid streams.[65] From the frozen terror of the alienated mirror image, the new subject discovers maternal love in the corporeal music of flowing tears and sighs.[66]

The drama of speech comes to the fore in canto 31. From the other side of Lethe, Beatrice, nurse-tutor and mother still harsh in her rebuke, enjoins the *infans*-pilgrim, whose only vocalizations thus far have been tearful sighs, to speak:

> *"O tu che se' di là dal fiume sacro,"*
> *volgendo suo parlare a me per punta,*
> . . . .
> *ricominciò, seguendo sanza cunta,*
> *"dì, dì se questo è vero . . ."*
>
> (*Purg.* 31.1–2; 4–5)

> "O you who are on that side of the sacred river,"
> she began again, turning against me the point of her speech. . . "Say,
> say, if this is true . . ."

Dante then frames the pilgrim emerging from, and falling back into, Kristeva's *chora:* on the border between the body language of sobs and sighs and the discrete word, between semiotic and symbolic. The poet calls direct attention to the corporeal mechanics of speech as the pilgrim at last produces the affirmative adverb in response to Beatrice's demand. This simple monosyllable barely attains the status of a word, for it is legible more as visual body language than as a distinct vocal symbol, part of an uninterrupted continuum with the pilgrim's crying:

> 'Era la mia virtù tanto confusa,
> che la voce si mosse, e pria si spense
> che da li organi suoi fosse dischiusa.
> . . . .
> Confusione e paura insieme miste
> mi pinsero un tal "sì" fuor de la bocca,
> al quale intender fuor mestier le viste.
> (Purg. 31.7–9, 13–15)

> My power was so confounded that my voice moved
> and became extinct before it was set free from its organs . . .
> Confusion and fear, together mingled, drove forth from my mouth a
> *Yes* such that the eyes were needed to hear it.

The pilgrim's voice falls quickly back into tears and sighs:

> Sì scoppia' io sottesso grave carco,
> fuori sgorgando lagrime e sospiri,
> e la voce allentò per lo suo varco.
> (Purg. 31.19–21)

> So did I burst under that heavy load, pouring forth
> tears and sighs, and my voice failed along its passage.

Several tercets later, he arrives with great difficulty at a whole speech that is nonetheless one with lachrymose exhalations:

Dopo la tratta d'un sospiro amaro,
a pena ebbi la voce che rispuose,
e le labbra a fatica la formaro.
Piangendo dissi: "Le presenti cose
col falso lor piacer volser miei passi,
tosto che 'l vostro viso si nascose."

(*Purg.* 31.31–36)

After drawing a bitter sigh, I barely had the voice to
make answer, and my lips shaped it with difficulty. Weeping I said,
"The present things, with their false pleasure, turned my steps aside,
as soon as your countenance was hidden."[67]

As we witness the pilgrim in this liminal, maternal linguistic state, Beatrice
revives the role of nurse-tutor and upbraids him for his classical response to
her dead and buried body:

Pon giù il seme del pianger e ascolta:
sì udirai come in contraria parte
mover dovieti mia carne sepolta.

(*Purg.* 31.46–48)

Lay aside the seed of tears and listen: so shall you
hear how in opposite direction my buried flesh ought to have moved
you.

Such language foreshadows the metaphorically resurrected body at the end
of *Paradiso* 27. At this point the pilgrim stands at the edge of *pueritia;* but
shamed by self-recognition, he moves to cut off the gaze that announces his
selfhood as he retrogresses to the silence of *infantia:*

Quali fanciulli, vergognando, muti
con li occhi a terra stannosi, ascoltando
e sé riconoscendo e ripentuti,
tal mi stav'io.

(*Purg.* 31.64–67)

As children stand ashamed and dumb, with eyes on
the ground, listening conscience-stricken and repentant, so stood I.

Beatrice calls him back to the mirror of selfhood, as it were, and scolds him into *adulescentia* with a cutting and ironic reference to his adult beard:

> . . . *Quando*
> *per udir se' dolente, alza la barba,*
> *e prenderai più doglia riguardando.*
> (*Purg.* 31.67–69)

> Since you are grieved through hearing, lift up your
> beard and you will receive more grief through seeing.

Lest this traditional picture of male growth and phallic power be allowed to stand, the poet instantly deflates the image in the metaphor that follows. A mighty oak is uprooted ("si dibarba") by the wind as the poet recalls Hiarbas's utter lack of potency with mighty Dido:

> *Con men di resistenza si dibarba*
> *robusto cerro, o vero al nostral vento*
> *o vero a quel de la terra di Iarba,*
> *ch'io non levai al suo comando il mento;*
> *e quando per la barba il viso chiese,*
> *ben conobbi il velen de l'argomento.*
> (*Purg.* 31.70–75)

> With less resistance is the sturdy oak uprooted,
> whether by wind of ours or by that which blows from Iarbas' land,
> than at her command I raised my chin; and when by the beard she
> asked for my face, well I knew the venom of the argument.[68]

We might say that the old "I" and the new struggle against one another in this canto that returns the reader to the primal scene of suckling. At last, the old "I," the classical subject, falls, thoroughly undone by Beatrice's words:

> *'Tanta riconoscenza il cor mi morse,*
> *ch'io caddi vinto; e quale allora femmi,*
> *salsi colei che la cagion mi porse.*
> (*Purg.* 31.88–90; my emphases)

> Such contrition stung my heart that *I fell* over-
> come; and what I then became she knows who was the cause of it.

The phrase *io caddi* evokes the deconstruction of the "I" that we saw in *Purgatorio* 5.[69] This triumph of the Christian over the classical "I" is immediately marked by a scene of maternal nursing, as Matelda clutches the reborn pilgrim to her breast and offers him the purgative waters of Lethe:

> *Poi, quando il cor virtù di fuor rendemmi,*
> *la donna ch'io avea trovata sola*
> *sopra me vidi, e dicea: "Tiemmi, tiemmi!"*
> *Tratto m'avea nel fiume infin la gola,*
> *e tirandosi me dietro sen giva*
> *sovresso l'acqua lieve come scola.*
> . . . .
> *La bella donna ne le braccia aprissi;*
> *abbracciommi la testa e mi sommerse*
> *ove convenne ch'io l'acqua inghiottissi.*
>
> (*Purg.* 31.91–96, 100–102)

> Then when my heart had restored my outward
> sense I saw above me the lady I had found alone and she was saying,
> "Cling, cling to me!" She had brought me into the river up to the
> throat and, drawing me behind her, was moving over the water as
> light as a shuttle . . . The fair lady opened her arms, clasped my head
> and dipped me under, where it behooved me to swallow of the water.

After the allegory of the cart and tree in canto 32, the pilgrim remains a hesitant and uncertain speaker to the end of the canticle, as at *Purgatorio* 33.25–30:

> *Come a color che troppo reverenti*
> *dinanzi a suo maggior parlando sono,*
> *che non traggon la voce viva ai denti,*
> *avvenne a me, che sanza intero suono*
> *incominciai: "Madonna, mia bisogna*
> *voi conoscete, e ciò ch'ad essa è buono."*

> As with those who with excessive reverence are
> speaking in the presence of their superiors so that they do not bring
> the voice whole to their lips [teeth], so it was with me, and without
> full utterance I began, "My lady, my need you know and that which is
> good for it."

The reference to teeth in the context of attempted speech recalls medieval developmental schemes that marked a subdivision of *infantia* around age two, the time of weaning, teething, and first words.[70] Initially well over the pilgrim's head, Beatrice's speech eventually condescends to his intellect as she momentarily plays *magistra* to his *puer,* a configuration that looks forward to *Paradiso:*

> *Veramente oramai saranno nude*
> *le mie parole, quanto converrassi*
> *quelle scovrire a la tua vista rude.*
>
> (*Purg.* 33.100—102)

> But henceforth my words shall be as simple as may
> be needful to make them plain to your rude sight.

The Latin *rudis* was commonplace to describe the unformed young speaker at the beginning of his grammatical studies.[71]

In the final scene of the canticle, Beatrice orders Matelda to nurse the pilgrim once again, this time in the restorative waters of Eunoe. Dante takes the occasion here to define the linguistic sign as an instrument for the transmission of human will.[72] As *Purgatorio* comes to a close, the poet trains his retrospective lens on that moment of sweet suckling:

> *S'io avessi, lettor, più lungo spazio*
> *da scrivere, i' pur cantere' in parte*
> *lo dolce ber che mai non m'avria sazio;*
> *ma perché piene son tutte le carte*
> *ordite a questa cantica seconda,*
> *non mi lascia più ir lo fren de l'arte.*
> *Io ritornai da la santissima onda*
> *rifatto sì come piante novelle*
> *rinovellate di novella fronda,*
> *puro e disposto a salire a le stelle.*
>
> (*Purg.* 33.136—45)

> If, reader, I had greater space for writing, I would
> yet partly sing the sweet draught which never would have sated me;
> but since all the pages ordained for this second canticle are filled, the
> curb of art lets me go no further. I came forth from the most holy
> waves, renovated even as new trees renewed with new foliage, pure
> and ready to rise to the stars.

Thus the Christian subject is born: turning away from rigid classical notions of the self standing firm upon the nurse's grave and toward the milk of charity and salvation.

The Triumph of the Resurrected Breast

If the infant comes into a new Christian subjectivity atop the mountain of *Purgatorio,* as I have suggested, then we might expect to find in the metaphorical program of *Paradiso* a new schema of development. What is remarkable about the images of *Paradiso,* however, is the absence of any movement away from the mother's body. For all that the early cantos, and in particular *Paradiso* 5, involve classical science and thus, appropriately, allusions to weaning, Dante's text instantly reasserts the prevalence of the nurturing mother's body. Metaphorically, the new subject will remain one with mother's milk, and mother's speech, to the utmost height of paradise.

The image of the nursing body dominates *Paradiso.* From a Platonic and even Christian Neoplatonic perspective, it is of course extraordinary that a corporeal metaphor should reign in a text that purports to communicate a vision of ultimate truth. As mentioned, we must agree with Bynum that the metaphorical bodies of *Paradiso* aim on some level to anticipate the resurrection bodies that will come at the end of time.[73] For all the physicality of his imagery, however, the body Dante gives us in *Paradiso* is not that of the single, self-contained individual; rather we have images of continual corporeal interaction and, more than anything else, nurturing. As such, the body of *Paradiso* is a body of desire. Lino Pertile has explored the central function of desire in *Paradiso* in several important articles and shown that the mystical tension between desire and fulfillment allows *Paradiso* to exist, "for where there is no desire left to fulfill, there is no language and no poetry."[74] To the extent that the images of nursing corporeality in the *Paradiso* mean to prefigure the resurrection body, however, we must seriously consider the theological importance of desire even at the end of time. As Pertile has shown, there is a mystical tradition for which beatitude is not so much the end of desire as desire perfectly fulfilled through eternity.[75] The poetics of the nursing body nicely represent such a tradition.

The discussion that follows will necessarily be somewhat schematic, documenting the extraordinary presence of the nurturing body throughout this final leg of the pilgrim's journey. As demonstrated in chapter 4, however, *Paradiso* 27 gathers and gives focus to the imposing build of maternal imagery through *Purgatorio* and *Paradiso* by summoning, near the poem's end, the ghost of Gaeta.

Interestingly, Dante's invocation barely alludes to the nursing Muses of *Purgatorio* 22;[76] rather, the poet obscures them by focusing on the paternal peak of Parnassus, where Apollo (*padre* in v. 28) dwells:

> O buono *A*ppollo, a l'ultimo lavoro
> fammi del tuo valor sì fatto vaso,
> come dimandi a dar l'amato alloro.
> Infino a qui l'un giogo di *P*arnaso
> assai mi fu; ma or con amendue
> m'è uopo intrar ne l'aringo rimaso.
>
> (*Par.* 1.13–18)

> O good Apollo, for this last labor make me such a
> vessel of your worth as you require for granting your beloved laurel.
> Thus far the one peak of Parnassus has sufficed me, but now I have
> need of both, as I enter the arena that remains.[77]

We are here still with the poet at his writing desk and not yet in paradise. Although Dante's phrasing ("o divina virtù"; v. 22) hints at a fusion of Apollo with God the Father, the paternal language of this divine invocation is tainted by a decidedly human desire for earthly glory and an image of the poet laureate as Caesar.[78] At the same time, Dante remembers the painful consequences of desire for poetic glory in the satyr Marsyas.[79] The poet's slighting of the nurse-Muses here at the opening of *Paradiso* is deliberately planted in order to be dramatically reversed when we return to the poet's bench at the end of the canticle.

The early cantos of *Paradiso* renew the nutritional metaphor of hunger and thirst for spiritual knowledge familiar to us from *Purgatorio.*[80] As Beatrice elucidates the thorny doctrine of vows in the heaven of the Moon in *Paradiso* 5, she is again the purveyor of whole and precise speech.[81] She thus calls upon the pilgrim to sit at table and accustom his digestion to the hard food ("cibo rigido") of advanced doctrine.[82] This call to nutritional and digestive autonomy, evoking as it does a quasi-classical model of reason and knowledge as weaning, seems to cast its shadow, like the Earth,[83] through the heaven of the sun and the first ten, heavily doctrinal, cantos. Indeed, as the pilgrim ascends into full sunlight in canto 10, the poet announces that he must abandon the role of classical tutor, dispenser of solid food:

> *Or ti riman, lettor, sovra 'l tuo banco,*
> *dietro pensando a ciò che si preliba,*
> *s'esser vuoi lieto assai prima che stanco.*
> *Messo t'ho innanzi; omai per te ti ciba.*
>
> > (*Par.* 10.22–25)

> Now remain, reader, upon your bench, reflecting
> on this of which you have a foretaste, if you would be glad far sooner
> than weary. I have set before you; now feed yourself.

But already back in canto 5, Beatrice had admonished humans against hasty involvement in matters of doctrinal complexity, such as vows, and advised them to stick close to the basic language of Scripture for salvation.[84] Do not, she warns, be like the young lamb who foolishly abandons its mother's milk to struggle on its own:

> *Non fate com'agnel che lascia il latte*
> *de la sua madre, e semplice e lascivo*
> *seco medesmo a suo piacer combatte!*
>
> > (*Par.* 5.82-84)

> Be not like the lamb that leaves its mother's milk
> and, silly and wanton, fights with itself at its own pleasure.

Upon leaving the Earth's shadow, Dante's text turns to the story of Saint Francis of Assisi and what is perhaps the most sustained affirmation of the language of Christian paradox: Saint Francis's amorous embrace of the body of Lady Poverty offers a famous example of Christianity's embrace of the abject, maternal body in all its concrete physicality. Dante frames Francis's story as the elucidation of an enigmatic scriptural metaphor that juxtaposes nutrition, indeed "fatness," in its literal and spiritual senses.[85] Thus Saint Thomas holds forth on Saint Francis's rejection of physical, worldly sustenance in the metaphorical context of Christian grace as a spiritual "fattening."[86]

Saint Thomas's words characterize Franciscan spirituality as a direct reversal of the classical paradigm of growth and wisdom: the young Saint Francis turns, somewhat violently, against his father to take Lady Poverty as mistress lover:

Non era ancor molto lontan da l'orto,
ch'el cominciò a far sentir la terra
de la sua gran virtute alcun conforto;
ché per tal donna, giovinetto, in guerra
del padre corse, a cui, come a la morte,
la porta del piacer nessun diserra;
e dinanzi a la sua spiritual corte
et coram patre le si fece unito;
poscia di dì in dì l'amò più forte.

(*Par.* 11.55–63)

He was not yet very far from his rising when he
began to make the earth feel, from his great virtue, a certain
strengthening; for, while still a youth, he rushed into strife against his
father for such a lady, to whom, as to death, none willingly unlocks
the door; and before his spiritual court *et coram patre* he was joined to
her, and thereafter, from day to day, he loved her ever more ardently.

Et coram patre le si fece unito

Dante repeatedly characterizes the relationship between Francis and Poverty as
that of romantic lovers and thus intimates physical embrace. At the same time,
he firmly aligns Lady Poverty with the suffering body of Christ and abject corporeal death ("a cui, come a la morte,/la porta del piacer nessun diserra"). As
Poverty's second groom, Saint Francis, like all saints, rehearses the life of Christ
and particularly, in Dante's version, the crucified Christ as *corpus*. As Saint Francis
embraces Lady Poverty, so Lady Poverty melds with the crucified body and
reflects maternal grief from the *mater dolorosa* who weeps at the foot of the cross:

Questa [Povertà], privata del primo marito,
millecent'anni e più dispetta e scura
fino a costui si stette sanza invito;
né valse udir che la trovò sicura
con Amiclate, al suon de la sua voce,
colui ch'a tutto 'l mondo fé paura;
né valse esser costante né feroce,
sì che, dove Maria rimase giuso,
ella con Cristo pianse in su la croce.

(*Par.* 11.64–72)

> She [Poverty], bereft of her first husband, for eleven
> hundred years and more, despised and obscure, remained unwooed till
> he came; nor had it availed to hear that he who caused fear to all the
> world found her undisturbed with Amyclas at the sound of his voice;
> nor had it availed to have been constant and undaunted so that, where
> Mary remained below, she wept with Christ upon the Cross.[87]

Against the imposing patriarchy of Pietro Bernardone (v. 89), Poverty and Francis, a new *padre* and new *maestro* (v. 85), champion the *gente poverella* (v. 94) with an ever-growing retinue, whose very vestitional humility signals a radical openness to the body.[88]

As Saint Francis returns from Egypt to receive the stigmata on Italian soil, the poet gently evokes the Neoplatonic image of Mother Earth as fluvial, fertile womb:

> *E per trovare a conversione acerba*
> *troppo la gente e per non stare indarno,*
> *[S. Francesco] redissi al frutto de l'italica erba,*
> *nel crudo sasso intra Tevero e Arno*
> *da Cristo prese l'ultimo sigillo,*
> *che le sue membra due anni portarno.*
>   (*Par.* 11.103–8)

> And, finding the people too unripe for conversion
> and in order not to stay in vain, [Saint Francis] had returned to the
> harvest of the Italian fields, then on the harsh rock between Tiber and
> Arno he received from Christ the last seal, which his limbs bore for
> two years.

We saw in the previous chapter just how intimately geographic flow (water and the elements) and bodily nutritional flow (blood and milk) are linked in the poet's metaphorical logic. Here Saint Francis's characterization as abject Christian *corpus* is sealed as he assumes—as if in defiance of the apparent local hardness of material earth—the bloody wounds on a rock ("crudo sasso") between flowing rivers ("Tevero e Arno"). Thus flowing earth and flowing body, always gendered female, mark the saint's final triumph. In death, as Saint Francis's soul ascends heavenward, Dante calls attention to the saint's body, which merely transfers from one metaphorical womb (Poverty) to another (Earth):

'E del suo grembo l'anima praeclara
mover si volle, tornando al suo regno,
e al suo corpo non volle altra bara.

(*Par.* 11.115–17)

And from her bosom [womb] the glorious soul
chose to set forth, returning to its own realm, and for its body would
have no other bier.[89]

St. Thomas finishes the canto with a denunciation of Dominican corruption
as dietary degeneration. Here again (compare *Paradiso* 5.82–84), sheep stray
from maternal security and sustenance ("ovile") to sample strange new foods
("nova vivanda"), only to return desperate for milk ("di latte vòte").[90]

In *Paradiso* 12 in the words of Saint Bonaventure, the life of Saint Dominic
becomes an ideal picture of prophetic infancy, of speechlessness as a site of
Christian truth. Saint Bonaventure's version stresses Saint Dominic's conception and growth amidst female figures: his mother (v. 60), his wife Lady
Faith (v. 62), and his godmother (v. 64). Most strikingly in the context of our
study, his wet nurse, guardian of infancy and babytalk, often found the young
boy saint seated upon the earth (like the corpse of Saint Francis), fully conscious and yet speechless: or rather, speaking very clearly, through his silence,
the language of Christian revelation:

Spesse fiate fu tacito e desto
trovato in terra da la sua nutrice,
come dicesse: "Io son venuto a questo."

(*Par.* 12.76–78)

Oftentimes his nurse found him silent and awake
upon the ground, as though he would say, "I am come for this."[91]

The metaphorical glorification of the body—maternal, nurturing, suffering, site of life and death—that we witness in these cantos finds specific
doctrinal confirmation in *Paradiso* 14, where Solomon enunciates the principle of the resurrected body.[92] These wise souls seem to yearn for union
with their glorified bodies ("disio d'i corpi morti"), a union that will mean
perfection of pleasure and illumination. This union will reconfirm their affec-
tive ties on earth, for family and friends and, first of all, for *mamma*.[93] As the
pilgrim ascends midcanto to the heaven of Mars, the Cross that radiates forth

Cristo in triple rhyme is compared to the mysterious Milky Way, as in John of Salisbury.[94]

Jeffrey Schnapp has located in the central cantos 15 and 16 of *Paradiso* a transfiguration of the idea of history in the classical, which is to say rigidly patriarchal, sense.[95] Here where the pilgrim encounters his illustrious forefather, the crusader Cacciaguida, we might expect a glorification of history as male succession. Instead Dante undercuts patriarchy at every turn. In its place, he celebrates a different history, one that consists largely of motherhood: female labor, female speech, indeed female eloquence. Cacciaguida's conservative discourse on Florence in the good old days centers on the ideal women of old, whose defining feature is a humility in dress and appearance,[96] in labor,[97] and especially in speech. Linguistically, the women of Cacciaguida's generation consoled infants cribside with babytalk:

> *L'una vegghiava a studio de la culla,*
> *e, consolando, usava l'idïoma*
> *che prima i padri e le madri trastulla.*
> (*Par.* 15.121–23)

> The one kept watch in minding the cradle, and,
> soothing, spoke that speech which first delights fathers and mothers.

At the same time, they wove tales as they wove cloth: popular, which is to say vernacular, tales of the founding of Florence:

> *L'altra, traendo a la rocca la chioma,*
> *favoleggiava con la sua famiglia*
> *d'i Troiani, di Fiesole e di Roma.*
> (*Par.* 15.124–26)

> Another, as she drew the threads from the distaff,
> would tell her household about the Trojans, and Fiesole, and Rome.

This translation of foundational myths into a female, vernacular idiom—intimately associated here as elsewhere with babytalk and the semiotics of the maternal body—represents a bold deflation of patriarchal privilege and reason as Latin, antimaternal, and acorporeal. Lest we be tempted to dismiss this female speech as lowly and limited, Dante immediately equates it to the pinnacle of political power in humble Cincinnatus, and the very height of rhetorical skill in Cornelia, mother of the Gracchi and ancient proverbial example of female reason and eloquence.[98]

In *Paradiso* 16, Florence of old is again *ovile*,[99] a place of gentler and more innocent speech.[100] Cacciaguida then traces the pilgrim's ancestry from the Virgin to his own mother as a succession of female birth labors.[101] His subsequent account of the degeneration of Florence denounces racial contamination[102] and political corruption as false motherhood. The Florentines' relationship to their political leader (Cesare, the Holy Roman Emperor) has been that of an evil stepmother *(noverca)* to an adopted son rather than one of natural, maternal affection:

> *Se la gente ch'al mondo più traligna*
> *non fosse stata a Cesare noverca,*
> *ma come madre a suo figlio benigna . . .*
>   *(Par.* 16.58—60)

> If the folk who are the most degenerate in the
> world had not been a stepmother to Caesar, but like a mother, benignant to her son . . .

The metaphorical result of this antagonistic mother-son relationship has been, appropriately, a kind of political indigestion.[103]

The discourse of nutritional hardness thus makes a brief reappearance in the following canto as the pilgrim learns of his poetic mission in exile. He will turn his back on Florence, evil stepmother (again, *noverca*), as Hippolytus turned his back on Athens and Phaedra.[104] He will know the bitterness of a foreign diet in his exile from the maternal body.[105] Much like Lady Grammar's rod, his own words will be bitter at first taste but will ultimately provide life-giving nutrition ("vital nodrimento")[106] to the world.[106] Thus exile and nutritional difficulty ultimately give way to life-giving nourishment as the very words and text of the *Commedia* are implicitly assimilated to the nurse's milk.

In canto 18, we return to a charitable vision of language as joy in maternal nutrition, as the souls of earthly rulers spell out their luminous creed ("DILIGITE IUSTITIAM QUI IUDICATIS TERRAM")[107] like flocks of birds content for the meal they have drawn from a flowing river.[108] The pilgrim experiences this language corporeally, as food, as music, as visual sensation; the phonetic flow that will eventually bear the symbolic meaning of whole speech is pulled apart into its constituent vowels and consonants.[109] This violation of language as fixed symbolic unity continues as the *M* of *TERRAM* becomes first a heraldic lily and then the imperial eagle.[110] Individual subjectivity is lost in the mystic chorality of the eagle's speech, which is akin to a babbling brook, lute and fife music.[111] Having spoken, the eagle circles above the pilgrim like a mother stork who has just fed her young.[112] As the pilgrim ascends to Saturn and a radiant Jacob's ladder in canto 21, Beatrice becomes a metaphorical wet nurse, source of visual nutrition and supervisor of the pilgrim's desire and speech.[113] Later in the canto, Saint Peter Damian espouses nutritional and vestitional humility.[114]

The image of the nurse dominates the remainder of *Paradiso* through to the final vision of canto 33. As we move from Saturn to the heaven of the Fixed Stars, cantos 22, 23, and 24 all open with elaborate nutritional figures. At the opening of *Paradiso* 22, Beatrice is a loving mother who comforts the pilgrim/child with her speech.[115] At the opening of *Paradiso* 23, Beatrice is a mother bird in predawn darkness who hovers above her nesting brood in eager anticipation of the rising sun so that she may find food for them. Dante's text underscores the sweet virtue of this female labor ("gravi labor") as it aligns the advent of Christ in the image of the rising sun with maternal nurturing.[116] This same canto recalls the Muses as wet nurses whose sweet milk makes the poet's tongue fat, *pingue,* a word we remember from Saint Thomas in *Paradiso* 10 and 11;[117] thus, in a word, the milk of poetic inspiration and the milk of Christian grace converge.[118] The canto closes with the triumph of the ascendent Virgin, *regina coeli,* and the flaming souls who reach upward after her "just like the young infant speaker *(fantolin)* who reaches in love for its mother after having tasted her milk."[119] At the opening of *Paradiso* 24, Beatrice's words reaffirm Christ as nurse: the blessed souls sup from the Lamb of God, who is at once a fountain that flows with everlasting satisfaction.[120]

When Saint John appears toward the end of *Paradiso* 25 to examine the pilgrim on charity, Dante pictures him at the breast of Christ-Pelican and recalls John's special relationship to Christ through maternal affection:

> *Questi è colui che giacque sopra 'l petto*
> *del nostro pellicano, e questi fue*
> *di su la croce al grande officio eletto.*
> (*Par.* 25.112–14)

> This is he who lay upon the breast of our Pelican,
> and this is he who was chosen from upon the Cross for the great
> office.[121]

Christ's special affection for John qualifies John as an authority on charity. The specifically linguistic content of his Scripture qualifies him as an authority on language.[122] Thus it is, appropriately, John in *Paradiso* 26 who expounds, with Adam's help, what we might call the new Christian grammar: a grammar whose central tenet is charity and whose primary emblem is the mother's nursing body. As Dante's text has repeatedly asserted, love and language come together in the mother's body. John and Adam divide canto 26 along these lines, as John holds forth on charity and Adam on language.[123] But the theme of language in charity, and vice versa, pervades the entire canto.[124]

The pilgrim's final words to John best conjoin the canto's two themes:

Le fronde onde s'infronda tutto l'orto
de l'ortolano etterno, am' io cotanto
quanto da lui a lor di bene è porto.
(*Par.* 26.64–66)

> The leaves wherewith all the garden of the Eternal
> Gardener is enleaved I love in measure of the good borne unto them
> from Him.

The figure of God as vine-keeper and the Word as vine is John's.[125] The figure is, of course, nutritional; indeed, in his reading of this image, Pertile recalls that the Song of Songs directly compares bunches of grapes on the vine to the lover's breasts.[126] Dante drops the Eucharistic specificity of the vine in favor of the more vegetally generic *fronde*. The things of man are as a tree and leafy branches, forever changing form, dividing and diverging in growth. Each fleeting form is worthy of human love to the extent that it bears invisible divine love, and thus fruit. God's Word, Christ, can be borne along in the flow of human words. We recall that Dante used this same ramiform structure to denote linguistic history as dispersion in the *De vulgari*. Intimately related to the ramiform flow of liquid streams on the Neoplatonic body of Mother Earth,[127] the leafy linguistic forest of the Italian peninsula is the grammarian's hunting ground for the illustrious vernacular.[128] In the treatise, the illustrious grammarian plays the role of vine-keeper, *in loco Dei*; the pilgrim's central citation of John in *Paradiso* 26 thus provides a Christian correction to that earlier grammatical arrogance. Adam himself uses the branch-and-leaf figure from Horace to define human linguistic dispersion at the end of the canto: "Ché l'uso d'i mortali è come fronda/in ramo, che sen va e altra vene"

(For the usage of mortals is as a leaf on a branch, which goes away and another comes).[129] Whereas the *De vulgari* grammarian had sought to stem geocorporeal linguistic flow through an aggressive process of cutting away, the *Paradiso* 26 poet merges classical and scriptural texts to celebrate this same flow as an outpouring of divine love.[130]

I have suggested that, in the classicizing canto 26 of *Inferno*, Ulysses drowns in the Neoplatonic sea of the mother's body as seduction without end. In this classical context, the only antidote to the nurturing threat is Aeneas's burial of Gaeta. *Paradiso* 26 offers a new Christian sea of right love ("amor . . . diritto") and thus a new Christian body. In a pointed allusion to Ulysses' sea, the pilgrim details the elements of this new love:

> *Tutti quei morsi*
> *che posson far lo cor volgere a Dio,*
> *a la mia caritate son concorsi:*
> *ché l'essere del mondo e l'esser mio,*
> *la morte ch'el sostenne perch'io viva,*
> *e quel che spera ogne fedel com'io,*
> *con la predetta conoscenza viva,*
> tratto m'hanno del mar de l'amor torto,
> e del diritto m'han posto a la riva.
>
> > (*Par.* 26.55–63; my emphases)

> > All those things whose bite can make the heart turn
> > to God have wrought together in my love; for the being of the world
> > and my own being, the death that He sustained that I might live, and
> > that which every believer hopes, as do I, with the living assurance of
> > which I spoke, *have drawn me from the sea of perverse love and placed*
> > *me on the shore of right love.*

Thus we discover that there is a good sea of right love and the pilgrim now stands upon its shore in burning thirst.[131]

Before Adam, the pilgrim is again a picture of desire in language.[132] His playful circumlocution for Adam at 26.91–92, "O pomo che maturo/solo prodotto fosti" (O fruit that were alone produced mature), resonates on many levels, similar to Dante's previous use of *pomo* to describe Beatrice as object of desire in *Purgatorio* 27. We noted in our discussion of that canto that, among its several allusive possibilities, *pomo* evoked for Dante and his contemporaries the breast as rounded object of human appetite.[133] The pilgrim's address of Adam as *pomo* in itself suggests a conception of human history that is open to female corporeality in a way very much opposed to the antimaternal *De vulgari* grammarian and his idealized *vir sine lacte*. The pilgrim's second circumlocution for Adam as the ancient father of an imposing matriarchy confirms this altered view.[134]

Adam reveals that his sin, like Ulysses', was not gluttony per se, but rather the transgression of a boundary at once semiotic and nutritional.[135] His final words underscore his presence, however brief, atop the mountain of Purgatory in poignant contrast to Ulysses' final words in *Inferno* 26, which announce his tragic failure to reach this same space.[136] But most of Adam's speech here concerns the new history of language.[137] Through Adam, Dante at last allows that postlapsarian human language has always been a dispersive flow, even before Babel.[138] Linguistic diversity is a constant of human experience, as Arnaut Daniel so dramatically demonstrated at the end of *Purgatorio* 26. I have suggested that this view of language as continual semiotic stream—an affirmation of the mother tongue in all its variety—is one that Dante associated closely with the nurturing maternal body and Christian charity. The poet saw the inevitability of linguistic variation even in the names of God, who was once called *I* and then, further down in time, *El*.[139] He might also have seen it in the names of the wet nurse, who, as we know, was once *Caieta* and is now *Gaeta*. As we know from chapter 4, her shade will appear in *Paradiso* 27, where Dante will make explicit this embrace of the mother's fluid body obliquely alluded to here in the images of canto 26. Now that John and Adam have explicated the new Christian grammar as fluid and nurturing in canto 26, Beatrice can call for the resurrection of the classical nurse's body in canto 27.

The remainder of the poem climactically affirms Christian subjectivity as a regression to the primal scene of suckling. The image of the nurse proliferates in these final cantos. The exiled *De vulgari* grammarian who longed for the pre-exilic breast of mother Arno is at last satisfied by the waters of a greater river. In the Empyrean, the pilgrim visually drinks in the rounded, overflowing river of light like an infant who, awakening late from a nap, moves eagerly for his mother's milk.[140] At the end of canto 30, Beatrice exclaims that blind greed has made of humanity "a starving infant who chases away his nurse."[141] In the following canto, Saint Bernard appears as a father, but a thoroughly Christianized father filled with maternal affection.[142]

The final canto of *Paradiso* opens with Bernard's prayer to the Virgin and dramatically affirms Christian love as a female value.[143] But even at this great height, Dante again asserts his metaphorical conception of Christian charity not merely as female, but as corporeal and nurturing. At a loss to convey the power of the final vision, a simple point of light, he can only return to the primal scene of suckling at the nursing mother's body:

> *Omai sarà più corta mia favella,*
> *pur a quel ch'io ricordo, che d'un fante*
> *che bagni ancor la lingua a la mammella.*
>
> (*Par.* 33.106–8)

> Now will my speech fall more short, even in
> respect to that which I remember, than that of an infant who still
> bathes his tongue at the breast.

The interpenetrating rings of light that he then attempts briefly to describe[144] rather pale in comparison to this fleshy juxtaposition of speech and milk in the greatest heaven. The poet who had somewhat neglected the nursing Muses at the beginning of the canticle here gives way to the semiotic power of the nurse.[145] Poet and pilgrim finally merge to leave the reader, in this culminating moment of deepest truth, with that simple image of the infant at the mother's breast.

NOTES

Introduction

1. "He [Dante] railed at great length against his fellow citizens, for they had deliberately taken from him the teat of his nurse." From the *Centiloquio* in Sapegno, *Poeti minori del trecento,* 418.

2. The true story of this early virgin martyr, who was sometimes identified with Marina or Margherita Pelagia, is in any case obscure; see the *Bibliotheca sanctorum,* vol. 11, cols. 124–28. For the full account of her life and martyrdom, see the *Acta sanctorum* for 8 October, vol. 4, 24–41, which cites various *Passiones,* including Rabanus Maurus: "VIII Idus Octobris Natale Reparatae, virginis et martyris, quae passa est in Caesarea, urbe Palaestinae, sub Decio praeside. Haec cum nollet idolis sacrificare, primo adhibita est illi olla plumbo fervente impleta, postea abscissae sunt illi mamillae, et lampades ardentes adhibitae" (The 8th of October is the birthdate of Reparata, virgin and martyr, who suffered death in Caesarea, a city of Palestine, under the rule of Decius. When she refused to make sacrifices to the pagan idols, first her body was seared with a vial of molten hot lead, then her breasts were cut off, and she was further tormented with burning torches).

3. Despite the fact that it was a church, the Duomo represented an important piece, perhaps the most important piece, of the vast civic building program undertaken by the growing *comune* in the thirteenth and early fourteenth century. The cathedral's very dedication to Santa Maria del Fiore was meant to allude to the symbol of Florentine state power, the heraldic lily or *giglio.*

4. For Julia Kristeva's initial formulation of the semiotic, see *Desire in Language* and *Revolution in Poetic Language.* For Kristeva's formulation of the "nurturing horror" in Western culture, see in particular *Powers of Horror.* For a clear introduction to the Lacanian notion of subjectivity that informs Kristeva's semiotic, see Kaja Silverman, *The Subject of Semiotics,* particularly pp. 149–93.

5. See Plato, *Timaeus* 48ff. (ed. and trans. Cornford), where *chora* is primal chaos, a receptacle space between Being and Becoming, "the wet nurse of creation." Plato's *chora* will translate into Chalcidius's *silva;* see chapter 4.

6. Kristeva, *Revolution in Poetic Language,* 28—29: "Drive facilitation, temporarily arrested, marks *discontinuities* in what may be called the various material supports susceptible to semiotization: voice, gesture, colors. Phonic (later phonemic), kinetic, or chromatic units and differences are the marks of these stases in the drives. Connections or *functions* are thereby established between these discrete marks which are based on drives and articulated according to their resemblance or opposition, either by slippage or by condensation. Here we find the principles of metonymy and metaphor indissociable from the drive economy underlying them." See also Kristeva, *Powers of Horror,* 72: "Through frustrations and prohibitions, this [maternal] authority shapes the body into a territory having areas, orifices, points and lines, surfaces and hollows, where the archaic power of mastery and neglect, of the differentiation of proper-clean and improper-dirty, possible and impossible, is impressed and exerted. It is . . . a primal mapping of the body that I call semiotic to say that, while being the precondition of language, it is dependent upon meaning, but in a way that is not that of linguistic signs nor of the symbolic order they found."

7. Kristeva, *Revolution in Poetic Language,* 28: "The semiotic *chora* is no more than the place where the subject is both generated and negated, the place where his unity succumbs before the process of charges and stases that produce him." More generally, the maternal body represents the collapse of the very binary life/death and thus, for Kristeva, must inform any definition of horror. See also Rosi Braidotti, "Mothers, Monsters, and Machines," in *Nomadic Subjects,* 75—94, especially p. 81: "Julia Kristeva . . . connects this mixture [of simultaneous attraction to and repulsion from the monster] to the maternal body as the site of the origin of life and consequently also of the insertion into mortality and death. We are all of woman born, and the mother's body as the threshold of existence is both sacred and spoiled, holy and hellish; it is attractive and repulsive, all-powerful and therefore impossible to live with." See also Luisa Muraro, *L'ordine simbolico della madre.*

8. For a reading of Lady Grammar in light of recent definitions of cultural monstrousness, see my essay, *"A la tetta de la madre s'apprende."*

9. And yet Kristeva is by no means a simple ally of feminist theory, which has often criticized her for what it has construed as a dangerous biological essentialism that condemns women to eternal mute exile from symbolic power. For this debate, see Kelly Oliver, ed., *Ethics, Politics, and Difference in Julia Kristeva's Writing.* For one of Kristeva's most influential and incisive critics, see Judith Butler, *Gender Trouble,* especially pp. 79—93. For a reassessment and, in many ways, defense of Kristeva that has influenced my reading, see Kelly Oliver, *Reading Kristeva.*

10. Mary Douglas, *Purity and Danger.*

11. See Douglas, *Purity and Danger,* 121, as cited by Kristeva, *Powers of Horror,* 69: "Matter issuing from [the orificies of the body] is marginal stuff of the most obvious kind. Spittle, blood, milk, urine, faeces or tears by simpling issuing forth have traversed the boundary of the body." The threat of corporeal humors to subjective and corporeal integrity is the central poetic idea of *Purgatorio* 5; see chapter 4.

12. Douglas, *Purity and Danger,* 69: "The mistake is to treat bodily margins in isolation from all other margins . . . Pollution is a type of danger which is not likely to occur except where the lines of structure, cosmic or social, are clearly defined"; Kristeva, *Powers of Horror,* 121.

1. Lady Grammar between Nurturing and Discipline

1. *De vulgari* 1.9.11 (ed. and trans. S. Botterill).

2. For more on this, see below.

3. The bibliography on medieval *grammatica* is vast. Some of the best discussions of medieval grammar are in books on rhetoric. Before Irvine, the most informative modern treatments of the subject were James J. Murphy, *Rhetoric in the Middle Ages,* and Charles Sears Baldwin, *Medieval Rhetoric and Poetic to 1400,* especially pp. 87–99 and 130–32. For a general, introductory history, such classics as John Edwin Sandys, *A History of Classical Scholarship,* and Ernst Robert Curtius, *European Literature and the Latin Middle Ages,* have much to offer. Fundamental are: Charles Thurot, *Notices et extraits de divers manuscrits latins;* Paul Abelson, *The Seven Liberal Arts;* and, more recently, Louis Holtz, *Donat et la tradition de l'enseignement grammatical.* Though outdated, Robert Henry Robins, *Ancient and Medieval Grammatical Theory in Europe* provides a useful historical outline and brief theoretical summaries from the point of view of a "modern" linguist. See also Richard William Hunt, *The History of Grammar in the Middle Ages;* Geoffrey L. Bursill-Hall, "The Middle Ages," whose interests are primarily speculative; Jeffrey F. Hunstman, "Grammar," 66–71. For a survey that treats both grammar and rhetoric, and the potential confusion between the two, see Louis John Paetow, *The Arts Course at Medieval Universities.* For a bibliographic survey through 1970, see Aldo D. Scaglione, *Ars Grammatica.*

4. Martin Irvine, *The Making of Textual Culture.* In the preface, Irvine announces his intention to treat the twelfth to fourteenth centuries in a second volume. Irvine provides an encyclopedic survey of writers, schools, and texts while arguing that grammar was constitutive of textual culture from antiquity forward. Another important recent study on grammar's social significance is Robert A. Kaster, *Guardians of Language.* On reading and commentary generally in medieval grammar, see: Alastair J. Minnis, *Medieval Theory of Authorship;* Alastair J. Minnis and A. B. Scott, eds., *Medieval Literary Theory and Criticism c. 1100—c. 1375;* and most recently Susan Reynolds, *Medieval*

Reading. The battle between grammar and rhetoric for the interpretation of the poets is a central theme of Rita Copeland, *Rhetoric Hermeneutics and Translation in the Middle Ages,* in part. pp. 11–21; on this, see also Reynolds, 73ff. On translation, and the interaction between Latin and vernacular with regard to grammar and particular focus on emerging French in the thirteenth and fourteenth centuries, see also Serge Lusignan, *Parler vulgairement.*

5. On the etymology of *grammatica,* see Isidore, *Etymologiarum* 1.5, cited and discussed by Irvine, *The Making of Textual Culture,* 217; see also pp. 2, 23, 36.

6. Thus the Alexandrian grammarian Dionysius Thrax (born c. 166 B.C.) included as the sixth and noblest component of grammar the critical reading of poetry. Aristotle's inclusion of limited observations on gender and syntax in chapters 20–23 of the *Poetics* bears witness to this early commingling of linguistics and literature. For a useful survey of early meanings, see Sandys, *A History of Classical Scholarship,* 6–10; Hunstman, "Grammar," 66–71. See Irvine, *The Making of Textual Culture,* for grammar in Plato (pp. 25–30), Aristotle (pp. 30–34), and the Stoics (pp. 34–39).

7. For the classical Latin arts of grammar, see Heinrich Keil, ed., *Grammatici latini.* On Roman and early medieval grammar, see Irvine, *The Making of Textual Culture,* 49–87.

8. For Varro's definition, see Sandys, *A History of Classical Scholarship,* 179: "Ars grammatica, quae a nobis litterae dicitur, scientia est eorum, quae a poetis, historicis, oratoribusque dicuntur ex parte maiore" (The art of grammar, which we call letters, is for the most part the science of those things said by poets, historians, and orators). For a broader survey of definitions in classical Latin, see the *Thesaurus linguae latinae,* vol. 6, fasc. 11, *s.v. grammatica* and *grammaticus,* which cites Seneca, *Epistles* 88.3: "Grammaticus circa curam sermonis versatur et, si latius evagari vult, circa historias, iam ut longissime fines suos proferat, circa carmina" (The grammarian busies himself with the management of speech and, if he wishes to stray a bit farther, with histories, and, when he really stretches his sights as far as possible, with poems). See also the *Oxford Latin Dictionary, grammatica* and *grammaticus.* For medieval Latin, see the entries in Charles DuCange and G. A. L. Heschel, *Glossarium mediae et infimae latinitatis.* Grammar's power to organize and mold natural speech led in some instances to an association with magic and the occult, as in the Old French *gramaire:* see F. Godefroy, *Dictionnaire de l'ancienne langue française,* vol. 4; see also Walther von Wartburg, *Französisches etymologisches Wörterbuch,* which gives as one definition for *gramaire,* "livre de sorcellerie" (book of sorcery). Whence the modern English *glamour;* see the *Oxford English Dictionary,* vol. 4. All English translations are my own unless otherwise indicated.

9. Quintilian, *Institutionis oratoriae libri duodecim;* see the opening of book 2; and a definition of *grammatica,* 1.4.1: "Haec igitur professio, cum brevissime in duas partis dividatur, recte loquendi scientiam et poetarum enarrationem" (This profession may

be most briefly considered under two heads, the art of speaking correctly and the inter-pretation of the poets). English trans. of Quintilian are from Butler, with some changes.

10. Martianus thus rejects two (architecture and medicine) of the nine basic disciplines established by Varro, *Disciplinarum libri novem;* see Murphy, *Rhetoric in the Middle Ages,* 43–45.

11. See Lady Grammar's words in Martianus Capella, *De nuptiis* 3.230: "Officium vero meum tunc fuerat docte scribere legereque; nunc etiam illud accessit, ut meum sit erudite intellegere probareque, quae duo mihi [vel] cum philosophis criticisque videntur esse communia" (My duty then had been to write and read in a learned man-ner; now they have added to that, so that erudite understanding and demonstration would be mine, which two things I share with the philosophers and the critics).

12. Cassiodorus, *Institutiones* 2.1.3: "Grammatica vero est peritia pulchre loquendi ex poetis illustribus auctoribusque collecta" (Grammar is skill in beauti-ful speech acquired from famous poets and writers); quoted by Murphy, *Rhetoric in the Middle Ages,* 67, n. 81; translation by Margot H. King, *"Grammatica Mystica,"* 147. The entire work has been translated into English by Leslie W. Jones under the title *Introduction to Divine and Human Readings.* See also Irvine, *The Making of Textual Culture,* 195–209.

13. Isidore, *Etymologiarum* 1.5.1: "Grammatica est scientia recte loquendi, et origo et fundamentum liberalium litterarum." Isidore had earlier drawn a distinc-tion between "common" and "liberal" letters at 1.4.1: "Litterae autem aut sunt com-munes aut liberales. Communes dictae, quia multi eas in commune utuntur, ut scribere et legere. Liberales, quia eas tantum illi noverunt qui libros conscribunt recteque loquendi dictandique rationem noverunt" (Letters are either common or liberal. There are those called common, because many people make use of them in common, as in writing or reading. Those called liberal, because only those who com-pose books and who have learned the rule of proper speech and composition have come to know them); see Murphy, *Rhetoric in the Middle Ages,* 73–76. Isidore devotes the entire first book of the *Etymologiarum* to *grammatica.* For a summary and schema-tization of Isidore's treatment in English, followed by translated extracts, see Ernest Brehaut, *An Encyclopedist of the Dark Ages,* 89–95. On Isidore and grammar, see Irvine, *The Making of Textual Culture,* 209–44.

14. *Rabani Mauri de clericorum institutione* 3.18, in *Patrologia latina* 107, cols. 294–420, and on grammar cols. 395–96: "Grammatica est scientia interpretandi poetas atque historicos, et recte scribendi loquendique ratio" (Grammar is the sci-ence of interpreting poets and historians, and the rule of writing and speaking cor-rectly); see Murphy, *Rhetoric in the Middle Ages,* 83–84.

15. See Murphy, *Rhetoric in the Middle Ages,* 144–45: "What seems to have hap-pened is that the monolithic *ars grammatica* of Donatus and Priscian, even when but-tressed by centuries of approving commentary, simply broke up into its constitutent

parts around the year 1200. The philosophical tensions inherent within it finally proved unbearable to a great many intelligent students of language. It proved impossible to carve out a single *ars* which could accommodate sensible principles concerning every one of the questions that had been brewing since Quintilian's time." See also Hunstman, "Grammar," 62.

16. John of Garland's treatise *De arte prosayca, metrica et rithmica* represents this branch. Murphy, *Rhetoric in the Middle Ages,* 142–62, points out that the *rithmus* constituted a method of rhythmical prose used in hymn and letter writing, distinct from the better-known *cursus.* See Giovanni Mari, ed., *I trattati medievali di ritmica latina.*

17. Alberich of Montecassino (fl. late eleventh century) is generally regarded as the medieval father of this discipline, which has remoter origins in late antiquity; see Murphy, *Rhetoric in the Middle Ages,* 194–268; Baldwin, *Medieval Rhetoric and Poetic to 1400,* 206–23.

18. See Murphy, *Rhetoric in the Middle Ages,* 269–355; Baldwin, *Medieval Rhetoric and Poetic to 1400,* 228–54; and Thomas Marie Charland, *Artes praedicandi.*

19. See Murphy, *Rhetoric in the Middle Ages,* 162–93, and in part. p. 136, where he lists and dates the six major works of this branch: "Matthew of Vendôme's *Ars versificatoria* (ca. 1175); Geoffrey of Vinsauf's *Poetria nova* (1208–13) and *Documentum de modo et arte dictandi et versificandi* (after 1213); Gervase of Melkely's *Ars versificaria* (c. 1215); John of Garland's *De arte prosayca, metrica, et rithmica* (after 1229); and Eberhard the German's *Laborintus* (after 1213, before 1280)." The texts of Matthew, Geoffrey, and Eberhard, as well as summaries of Gervase and John, are in Edmond Faral, ed., *Les arts poétiques du XIIe et du XIIIe siècle.* See also *The Parisiana poetria of John of Garland.* Matthew and Geoffrey are also available in several English editions.

20. The enduring standards of Donatus (c. 310–c. 380) and Priscian (fl. c. 500) begin to give way in some degree after 1200 to the new versified teaching grammars of Alexander of Villedieu (c. 1170–1240) and Eberhard of Béthune (d. c. 1212); see Murphy, *Rhetoric in the Middle Ages,* 146–52.

21. The best introductions to speculative grammar are Jan Pinborg, *Die Entwicklung der Sprachtheorie im Mittelalter;* and Geoffrey L. Bursill-Hall, *Speculative Grammars of the Middle Ages.*

22. Thus, to cite one of several nearly identical speculative definitions, Siger de Courtrai (fl. c. 1310–20): "Gramatica est sermocinalis scientia" (Grammar is the science of discourse); cited by Bursill-Hall, "The Middle Ages," 197.

23. "Gramatica una et eadem est secundum substantiam in omnibus linguis, licet accidentaliter varietur"; cited by Murphy, *Rhetoric in the Middle Ages,* 154, n. 43, from the *Grammatica Graeca.* Fredborg ("Universal Grammar") has detected the notion of a universal, logical grammar at least as early as the twelfth century.

24. Chartrian humanism confined rhetoric to persuasive discourse and embraced grammar as the passionate pursuit of the *auctores* and their language. Such devotion to Lady Grammar took on ever greater zeal as her followers waged a losing battle against the inexorable onslaught of Dame Logic from Paris. The struggle between grammatical humanism and the new Aristotelian logic received a dramatic rendering in the thirteenth century in Henri d'Andeli's Old French allegorical poem, *The Battle of the Seven Arts.*

25. Much has been written on many facets of this problem. For an extensive treatment of initial reactions in the early Church, see Gerard L. Ellsperman, *The Attitude of the Early Christian Latin Writers;* Eduard Norden, *Die antike Kunstprosa,* 670–87. For a thorough and lucid review of Christian attitudes from Clement of Alexandria to Bernard of Clairvaux, see Franco Simone, "La 'Reductio Artium ad Sacram Scripturam.'" In "Grammaire et théologie aux XIIe et XIIIe siècles," Marie Dominique Chenu examines twelfth- and thirteenth-century theologians' appropriation of grammar. Many of the general histories cited above deal briefly with this problem as well; see in particular, Paetow, *The Arts Course at Medieval Universities,* 20–23; Sandys, *A History of Classical Scholarship,* 617–78; Curtius, *European Literature and the Latin Middle Ages,* 446–67; Vivien Law, *The Insular Latin Grammarians,* 30–41; Jan Ziolkowski, *Alan of Lille's Grammar of Sex,* 109–39. There exists also a wealth of studies that deal with individual figures. The following were particularly helpful: Henri de Lubac, "Saint Grégoire et la grammaire"; Jacques LeClercq, "Smaragde et la grammaire chrétienne"; many of the essays in *Arts libéraux et philosophie au moyen âge* are of interest in this light, and, in particular, Marcia Colish, "Eleventh-Century Grammar in the Thought of St. Anselm," 785–95; and Robert Darwin Crouse, "Honorius Augustodunensis," 531–39. For further bibliography, see Ziolkowski, *Alan of Lille's Grammar of Sex.*

26. Irvine, *The Making of Textual Culture,* 162–69.

27. Irvine, *The Making of Textual Culture,* 169–89. While wanting to reject pagan learning after his conversion, Augustine could not help but pause before his once beloved Cicero; see in part. *Confessions* 3.4. For a definition of *grammatica* in Augustine, see *Soliloquia* 2.2.19 (*Patrologia latina* 32, col. 894): "Est autem grammatica vocis articulatae custos et moderatrix disciplina" (Grammar is the guardian of the spoken word and she is the moderator through discipline). See also G. Bellissima, "Sant'Agostino grammatico." For more on Augustine and the *disciplina* of grammar, see below.

28. Ziolkowski, *Alan of Lille's Grammar of Sex,* 111. Saint Jerome's difficult love for classical learning reached dramatic climax in his oft-cited dream of reproach. The narrative can be found in Ellsperman, *The Attitude of the Early Christian Latin Writers,* 160–61, from *Epistles* 30.1–6. In a state of feverish rapture, Jerome is interrogated and reproached by a voice in the glaring light: "Interrogatus condicionem

Christianum me esse respondi. Et ille, qui residebat: 'mentiris,' ait, 'Ciceronianus es, non Christianus'" (I was asked to state my condition and replied that I was a Christian. But He who presided said: "Thou liest; thou art a Ciceronian, not a Christian"; trans. Ellsperman). Even Gregory the Great, who has often been characterized as a spokesperson for anticlassicism, admitted to the utility of grammar for Christianity; see de Lubac, "Saint Grégoire et la grammaire," and Irvine, *The Making of Textual Culture,* 189–95.

29. An anonymous tenth-century manuscript nicely captures this view: "Grammatica . . . tunc vera est, quando in suis litteris et syllabis et pedibus et partibus orationis . . . sine ullo vitio constat. Tunc mendax est, quando de fabulis gentium exempla ponit" (Grammar . . . is true when, without any mistake, it agrees in its letters and syllables and feet and parts of speech. It is false when it sets forth examples from the pagan tales). Thus Christian accommodations of Donatus and Priscian arose at least as early as the seventh century. Characteristic of these new Christian grammars was the at least partial replacement of classical citations by texts from the Vulgate or early Christian poetry. The ninth-century Smaragdus deserves special mention as the most zealot advocate of this cause, if only for the sheer quantity of original scriptural citations contained in his revision of Donatus. See Holtz, *Donat et la tradition de l'enseignement grammatical,* 245–71, and Smaragdus, *Liber in partibus Donati,* xlvi–xlix, l–lviii; Law, *The Insular Latin Grammarians,* 30–41; LeClercq, "Smaragde et la grammaire chrétienne." What is more, Christian grammarians were consistent in their willingness to overlook or reverse classical rules when faced with an exception from the Vulgate. Gregory the Great has provided the *locus classicus* for this attitude in the *Epistula missoria ad Leandrum Hispalensem, Patrologia latina 75,* col. 516B: "Non barbarismi confusionem devito, situs motusque et praepositionum casus servare contemno, quia indignum vehementer existimo ut verba caelestis oraculi restringam sub regulis Donati" (I do not avoid the addition of a barbarism, I despise keeping the proper constructions and prepositional cases, because I vehemently deem it shameful that the words of the celestial oracle be bound under the rules of Donatus); see Thurot, *Notices et extraits de divers manuscrits latins,* 523; de Lubac, "Saint Grégoire et la grammaire," 185; Charles Homer Haskins, "The Early *Artes Dictandi* in Italy," 96; Holtz, *Donat et la tradition de l'enseignement grammatical,* 254–56, and Smaragdus, *Liber in partibus Donati,* lii–liii; Sandys, *A History of Classical Scholarship,* 618; Ziolkowski, *Alan of Lille's Grammar of Sex,* 115, n. 19.

30. Dante, *De vulgari eloquentia* (ed. and trans. Pier Vincenzo Mengaldo).

31. Maria Corti, *Dante a un nuovo crocevia;* Gian Carlo Alessio, "La grammatica speculativa e Dante"; Marianne Shapiro, *"De Vulgari Eloquentia."* Many of the modistic texts articulated a distinction between the initial founders or *inventores* of grammar, who first discerned and set down the universal forms of language, and later

practitioners or *positores,* who carried out the far more pedestrian task of treatise-writing and teaching. Corti, 37–46, argues that Dante recognized this distinction at *De vulgari* 1.9.11; on this, see also the earlier edition of the treatise ed. and trans. by Aristide Marigo, lxi, n. 2.

32. See Zygmunt G. Barański, *"Sole nuovo, luce nuova,"* which collects and translates into Italian essays written in English and published elsewhere. When possible, I will cite the original English versions in what follows. For a recent summary of Barański's work on Dante and medieval poetics, see Zygmunt G. Barański, "Dante and Medieval Poetics," in Amilcare A. Iannucci, ed., *Dante: Contemporary Perspectives.*

33. *Paradiso* 12.137–38: "E quel Donato/ch'a la prim'arte degnò porre mano" (And that Donatus who deigned to set his hand to the first art). Thirteenth-century encyclopedias promulgate this basic notion of *grammatica* as the first science and gateway to knowledge as defined by Isidore. See Vincent of Beauvais (c. 1190–c. 1264), *Speculum doctrinale,* books 1 and 2 and for a definition, 2.1. Closer to home for Dante is Brunetto Latini, *Li livres dou tresor,* who, while primarily interested in rhetoric, describes the entire *trivium* beginning with grammar at 1.4.7: "La premiere est science gramatique, ki est fondement et porte et entrée des autres sciences; ki nos ensegne a parler et escrire et lire a droit sans vice de barbarisme et de solercisme" (The first is the grammatical science, which is the foundation and door and entryway of the other sciences; which teaches us to speak and write and read correctly without the vice of a barbarism or solecism).

34. The word *disciplina* developed two distinct meanings: field of study and punishment or flagellation. DuCange and Niermeyer suggest that the latter meaning originated in monastic culture, where *disciplina* referred both to punishment and to the instruments of punishment *(virgae ipsae).* The etymological association between fields of study and disciplinary control is evident as well in the word *ars, artis,* which was (falsely) derived from the adjective *artus* (narrow; constricted); typical among ancient grammarians is Servius, *Commentarius in arte Donati* (Keil, *Grammatici latini,* vol. 4, p. 405): "Vel certe ideo ars dicitur, quod artis praeceptis cuncta concludat. Id est angustis et brevibus" (Or surely another explanation is that it is called "art" because it delimits all things within narrow rules, that is to say rules which are strictly defined and succinct); cp. Augustine, *De civitate Dei* 4.21; Isidore, *Etymologiarum* 1.12; John of Salisbury, *Metalogicon* 1.12; Boncompagno da Signa, *Rhetorica novissima* 3.1, p. 257: "'Ars' dicitur ab 'arto artas,' quoniam artista quilibet motu rationabili debet artare suos auditores ad credendum ea que de arte proponit" (Art is thus called from the verb "to constrict," since every artist must make use of rational means to constrict his listeners into believing those things which he proposes about the art); for further references see Daniel McGarry's note at 1.12 in his translation of the *Metalogicon.* Also, Roger Dragonetti, "La conception du langage poétique," 55–56, n. 1; Alessio, "La grammatica speculativa e Dante," 82–83.

According to DuCange and Niermeyer, s.v., *grammatica* also bears the etymological suggestion of rectilinearity (from the Greek, *gramma,* line) and therefore was metaphorically equated to the "moral straight path" in society; see Eugene Vance, *Mervelous Signals,* 238; Howard R. Bloch, *Etymologies and Genealogies,* 52–53.

35. As such, grammar functioned as a kind of initiation rite. This idea has been developed at some length by Walter J. Ong, "Latin Language Study as a Renaissance Puberty Rite." Although Ong suggests that this phenomenon culminated with the Renaissance humanists, he acknowledges that it developed throughout the Middle Ages. "The fact that school pupils were all boys of course encouraged rule by the rod. In the Middle Ages not only does this environment and rule persist, but there is evidence that the specifically initiatory cast of the punishment grew more intense and evident . . . [In order to enter grammar school,] the boy must acknowledge the equation of learning and flogging, and thereby face courageously into learning as into an initiation, something of itself taxing and fearsome" (p. 124). But see also Irvine, *The Making of Textual Culture,* 21: "Thus when a student entered the ranks of the *litterati* through the grammatical curriculum, he or she was learning far more than the obvious subject matter of the discipline: a student was being inducted into a whole social system, internalizing the structures of authority that were reproduced and guaranteed by *grammatica.*" See also Lusignan, *Parler vulgairement,* 86, who notes that throughout the Middle Ages Latin was the language of reason and discipline, the vernacular of the nurse and maternal affection: "Il n'est pas surprennant de voir se dégager de certains textes l'impression que si la raison parle latin, le coeur penche du coté du vernaculaire." For a rosier portrait of Latin language learning in the twelfth century, see James J. Murphy, "The Teaching of Latin as a Second Language in the 12th Century."

36. Irvine, *The Making of Textual Culture,* 2: "In its foundational role, *grammatica* also created a special kind of literate subjectivity, an identity and social position for *litterati* which was consistently gendered as masculine and socially empowered." Irvine (p. 8) believes *grammatica* constituted a fundamental cultural paradigm of the sort discussed by Thomas Kuhn; see also Kaster, *Guardians of Language.*

37. Paul F. Gehl, *A Moral Art,* part. 1–42.

38. Giorgio Petrocchi, *Vita di Dante,* 13: "i primi studi si svolsero esclusivamente in ambiente laico, presso uno dei tanti *doctores puerorum* che esercitavano la professione nella città di Firenze, fors'anche alla scuola d'un Romano 'doctor puerorum populi sancti Martini 'di cui un documento dello stesso 1277 (la scuola che si conosca, più vicina alle case degli Alighieri). L'educazione che Dante poté ricevere da fanciullo presso un 'doctor puerorum' fu certo un'istruzione elementare di grammatica, come da *Conv.,* II, xii, 2–4, non soltanto sugli ardui testi di Cicerone e sugli esametri di Virgilio (ben conosciuti solo più tardi e forse solo durante il soggiorno a Bologna), ma sul latino molto più agevole dei *Disticha Catonis,* del *Liber Esopi,* dell'*Elegia* di Arrigo da Settimello." On Dante's schooling more generally, see

Petrocchi, 31. For grammar education in Dante's Florence generally, see Gehl, *A Moral Art,* and Charles T. Davis, "Education in Dante's Florence." To state that females were always and everywhere excluded from medieval grammatical education is an overgeneralization; nonetheless, it is beyond argument that, as an institution, grammar was overwhelmingly male. Based on Villani's *Cronica* (11.94), Davis (p. 415) notes that, in the early fourteenth century, Florentine schools taught reading to both boys and girls, but only boys then entered grammar school proper.

39. On the distance between Latin grammar and mother tongue in late antiquity, see Henri-Irénée Marrou, *Saint Augustin e la fin de la culture antique,* 13–14; on the relationship between Greek and Latin learning, pp. 27–46, and especially p. 28: "L'enseignement du latin était moins celui d'une langue vivante que d'une langue littéraire fixée dans les classiques"; on the increasing distance between Latin and mother tongue, see Murphy, "The Teaching of Latin as a Second Language in the 12th Century," and Hans Wilhelm Klein, *Latein und Volgare in Italien.*

40. See, for instance, Cicero (106–43 B.C.), *Tusculanae Disputationes* 3.1.2: "Ut paene cum lacte nutricis errorem suxisse videamus" (trans. King: So that it seems as if we drank in deception with our nurse's milk). This anxiety over the nurse's character eventually expresses itself as a wholesale condemnation of the natural mother who entrusts her infant to a wet nurse; see Aulus Gellius (c. 123–65), *Noctes Atticae* 1.12, and especially 1.12.6: "Quod est enim hoc contra naturam imperfectum atque dimidiatum matris genus, peperisse ac statim a sese abiecisse? Aluisse in utero sanguine suo nescio quid quod non videret, non alere nunc suo lacte quod videat, iam viventem, iam hominem, iam matris officia inplorantem?" (trans. Rolfe: For what kind of unnatural, imperfect, and half-motherhood is it to bear a child and at once send it away from her? To have nourished in her womb with her own blood something which she could not see, and not to feed with her own milk what she sees, now alive, now human, now calling for a mother's care?). Cp., some two and a half centuries later, Macrobius, *Saturnalia* 5.11; and see Marilyn Yalom, *A History of the Breast,* 24–26.

41. *Institutiones oratoriae* 1.1.4–5: "Ante omnia ne sit vitiosus sermo nutricibus; quas, si fieri posset, sapientes Chrysippus optavit, certe quantum res pateretur optimas eligi voluit. Et morum quidem in his haud dubie prior ratio est, recte tamen etiam loquantur. Has primum audiet puer, harum verba effingere imitando conabitur, et natura tenacissimi sumus eorum quae rudibus animis percepimus: ut sapor quo nova inbuas durat, nec lanarum colores quibus simplex ille candor mutatus est elui possunt. Et haec ipsa magis pertinaciter haerent quae deteriora sunt. Nam bona facile mutantur in peius: quando in bonum verteris vitia? Non adsuescat ergo, ne dum infans quidem est, sermoni qui dediscendus sit" (Above all see that the child's nurse speaks correctly. The ideal, according to Chrysippus, would be that she should be a philosopher: failing that he desired that the best should be chosen, as far as possible. No

doubt the most important point is that they should be of good character: but they should speak correctly as well. It is the nurse that the child first hears, and her words that he will first attempt to imitate. And we are by nature most tenacious of childish impressions, just as the flavor first absorbed by vessels when new persists, and the color imparted by dyes to the primitive whiteness of wool is indelible. Further it is the worst impressions that are most durable. For, while what is good readily deteriorates, you will never turn vice into virtue. Do not therefore allow the boy to become accustomed even in his infancy to a style of speech which he will subsequently have to unlearn).

42. Despite his enlightened, "maternal" view of language education throughout, we should note that Quintilian still metaphorizes this stage of the development of the *puer* as a "leaving the womb" ("exire de gremio") at 2.1.1, and the beginning of formal study with peers has all the qualities of a religious rite at 1.2.20: "Neque enim est sanctius sacris iisdem quam studiis initiari" (For initiation in the same studies has all the sanctity of initiation in the same mysteries of religion).

43. *Institutiones oratoriae* 1.1.15–17 is particularly clear on this point. While Chrysippus has stated that the wet nurse should be given dominion over the first three years of the child's formation, Quintilian insists that these are years in which the mind is open to the basics of linguistic ability and disagrees with those who would delay reading lessons until age seven (i.e., *pueritia* proper); cp. 1.1.21: "Sed est sua etiam studiis infantia" (But studies, like men, have their infancy).

44. "Aesopi fabellas, quae fabulis nutricularum proxime succedunt." *Institutiones oratoriae* 1.9.2, cited by Copeland, *Rhetoric Hermeneutics and Translation in the Middle Ages,* 23.

45. *Institutiones oratoriae* 1.1.21: "Sed est sua etiam studiis infantia, et ut corporum mox fortissimorum educatio a lacte cunisque initium ducit, ita futurus eloquentissimus edidit aliquando vagitum et loqui primum incerta voce temptavit et haesit circa formas litterarum" (But studies, like men, have their infancy, and as the training of the body which is destined to grow to the fullness of strength begins while the child is in his cradle and sucking milk from his mother's breast, so even the man who is destined to rise to the heights of eloquence was once a squalling babe, tried to speak in stammering accents and was puzzled by the shapes of letters).

46. *Institutiones oratoriae* 1.1.6: "In parentibus vero quam plurimus esse eruditionis optaverim. Nec de patribus tantum loquor: nam Gracchorum eloquentiae multum contulisse accepimus Corneliam matrem, cuius doctissimis sermo in posteros quoque est epistulis traditus, et Laelia C. filia reddidisse in loquendo paternam elegantiam dicitur, et Hortensiae Q. filiae oratio apud triumviros habita legitur non tantum in sexus honorem" (As regards parents, I should like to see them as highly educated as possible, and I do not restrict this remark to fathers alone. We are told that the eloquence of the Gracchi owed much to their mother Cornelia,

whose letters even today testify to the cultivation of her style. Laelia, the daughter of Gaius Laelius, is said to have reproduced the elegance of her father's language in her own speech, while the oration delivered before the triumvirs by Hortensia, the daughter of Quintus Hortensius, is still read and not merely as a compliment to her sex). On Cornelia as example of female eloquence, see Dante, *Paradiso* 15.129. The very concept of an eloquent female was for many an oxymoronic freak of nature, indeed a monster; see Pliny, *Natural History* 7.69, and, in the twelfth century, Johannes de Hauvilla, *Architrenius,* 1.10.248–50: "Mascula Graccorum tribuit gestamina matri;/Malleolosque ferens duplici cum folle viriles,/Conlectura fuit gemini Cornelia sexus" (trans. Wetherbee: Nature assigned the actions of a man to Cornelia, the mother of the Gracchi, and it was held that she was bisexual, possessing the little walnuts of a man in their double pouch); cp. pp. 255–56, n. 15.

47. See *proemium* to Book 1 at 26: "Illud tamen in primis testandum est, nihil praecepta atque artes valere nisi adiuvante natura" (There is however one point which I must emphasize before I begin, which is this. Without natural gifts technical rules are useless); cp. 2.19.

48. See in part. 2.19. The notion of natural grammar will find expression throughout the medieval period and a particularly energetic champion in John of Salisbury in the twelfth century; on natural grammar in the twelfth century, see Ziolkowski, *Alan of Lille's Grammar of Sex,* 104–7.

49. "Deinde quod, si cui tam est mens inliberalis ut obiurgatione non corrigatur, is etiam ad plagas ut pessima quaeque mancipia durabitur . . . Iam si minor in eligendis custodum et praeceptorum moribus fuit cura, pudet dicere in quae probra nefandi homines isto caedendi iure abutantur, quam det aliis quoque nonnunquam occasionem hic miserorum metus" (Secondly if a boy is so insensible to instruction that reproof is useless, he will, like the worst type of slave, merely become hardened to blows. Further if inadequate care is taken in the choices of respectable governors and instructors, I blush to mention the shameful abuse which scoundrels sometimes make of their right to administer corporal punishment or the opportunity not infrequently offered to others by the fear thus caused in the victims).

50. Saint Jerome, *Lettres,* vol. 5, epistle 107.

51. "Nutrix ipsa non sit temulenta, non lasciva, non garrula."

52. "Hortensiae oratio in paterno sinu coaluit."

53. In addition to the fundamental works of Marrou, *Saint Augustin et la fin de la culture antique;* Pierre Courcelle, *Recherches sur les Confessions de saint Augustin;* and Peter Brown, *Augustine of Hippo;* the following have helped form my understanding of Augustine's linguistic psychology (the linguistic origin of the subject, the association of language and exile, the problem of grammar), particularly with regard to the *Confessions:* Kenneth Burke, "Verbal Action in St. Augustine's

Confessions"; Eugene Vance, "Augustine's *Confessions* and the Grammar of Selfhood"; "Augustine's *Confessions* and the Poetics of the Law"; *Mervelous Signals*, 1–50; Margaret W. Ferguson, "Saint Augustine's Region of Unlikeliness"; and more recently, Brian Stock, *Augustine the Reader*. On Augustine's early linguistic education in general, see Marrou, 1–26; Brown, 28–39; and on his relationship to grammar, Stock, 24–33. On Augustine's concept of subjectivity, particularly as it relates to the Cartesian *cogito,* see Goulven Madec, *"In te supra me"*; Gareth B. Matthews, *Thought's Ego in Augustine and Descartes,* in part. pp. 151–68 on language and learning; and Stock, 259–73. For an extensive, up-to-date bibliography, see Stock.

54. See Margaret Miles, "Infancy, Parenting, and Nourishment."

55. *Confessions* 1.6.7: "Exceperunt ergo me consolationes lactis humani, nec mater mea vel nutrices meae sibi ubera implebant, sed tu mihi per eas dabas alimentum infantiae secundum institutionem tuam et divitias usque ad fundum rerum dispositas" (trans. Warner: I was welcomed then with the comfort of woman's milk; but neither my mother nor my nurses filled their own breasts with milk; it was you who, through them, gave me the food of my infancy, according to your own ordinance and according to the way in which your riches are spread throughout the length and depth of things).

56. *Confessions* 1.6.7: "Tu etiam mihi dabas nolle amplius, quam dabas, et nutrientibus me dare mihi velle quod eis dabas: dare enim mihi per ordinatum affectum volebant quo abundabant ex te" (You also granted me not to desire more than you supplied; and on those who suckled me you bestowed a desire to give to me what you gave to them).

57. *Confessions* 1.6.7: "Nam tunc sugere noram et adquiescere delectationibus, flere autem offensiones carnis meae, nihil amplius" (Then all I knew was how to suck, to be content with bodily pleasure, and to be discontented with bodily pain; that was all). Cp. 1.7.11: "Ita imbecillitas membrorum infantilium innocens est, non animus infantium" (It is clear, indeed, that infants are harmless because of physical weakness, not because of any innocence of mind).

58. *Confessions* 1.7.11: "Vidi ego et expertus sum zelantem parvulum: nondum loquebatur et intuebatur pallidus amaro aspectu conlactaneum suum" (I myself have seen and known a baby who was envious; it could not yet speak, but it turned pale and looked bitterly at another baby sharing its milk); cp. Lacan, *Écrits,* 20.

59. *Confessions* 1.6.8: "Itaque iactabam et membra et voces, signa similia voluntatibus meis, pauca quae poteram, qualia poteram." Cp. 1.6.10: "Eram enim et vivebam etiam tunc et signa, quibus sensa mea nota aliis facerem, iam in fine infantiae quaerebam" (So even then I had life and being, and by the end of my infancy I was already trying to find signs by which I could make my feelings intelligible to others).

60. *Infantia* was etymologically defined by all medieval encyclopedists as the life stage characterized primarily by lack of speech. See Isidore, *Etymologiarum*

11.2.9: "Infans dicitur homo primae aetatis; dictus autem infans quia adhuc fari nescit, id est loqui non potest" (Man is called "in-fant" in the first stage of life; he is called thus because he does not yet know how to speak [*fari,* to speak]).

61. *Confessions* 1.8.13 contains Augustine's famous account of beginning to discern words and word meanings in the speech of those around him. But his emphasis is everywhere on the incremental nature of this process still very much caught up in the universally significant bodily semiosis of the *infans:* "Non enim eram infans, qui non farer, sed iam puer loquens eram . . . cum gemitibus et vocibus variis et variis membrorum motibus edere vellem sensa cordis mei . . . hoc autem eos velle, ex motu corporis aperiebatur, tamquam verbis naturalibus omnium gentium, quae fiunt vultu et nutu oculorum ceterorumque membrorum actu et sonitu vocis indicante affectionem animi in petendis, habendis, reiciendis fugiendisve rebus" (For I was no longer an infant, incapable of speech; I was now a speaking boy . . . By making all sorts of cries and noises, all sorts of movements of my limbs, I desired to express my inner feelings . . . That they meant this object and no other one was clear from the movements of their bodies, a kind of universal language, expressed by the face, the direction of the eye, gestures of the limbs and tones of the voice, all indicating the state of feeling in the mind as it seeks, enjoys, rejects, or avoids various objects).

62. *Confessions* 1.9.9–10: "Deus, deus meus, quas ibi miserias expertus sum et ludificationes. . . ."

63. *Confessions* 1.9.14: "Multiplicato labore et dolore filiis Adam"; cp. *De civitate dei* 21.14; 22.22; see Stock, *Augustine the Reader,* 15–16.

64. *Confessions* 1.9.14: "Nam puer coepi rogare te, auxilium et refugium meum, et in tuam invocationem rumpebam nodos linguae meae et rogabam te parvus non parvo affectu, ne in schola vapularem" (For when still a boy I began to call upon you, my Help and my Refuge, and in praying to you I broke through the knots of language; I was small, but it was with no small earnestness that I prayed to you that I should not be beaten at school).

65. *Confessions* 1.9.15: "Sed delectabat ludere et vindicabatur in nos ab eis qui talia utique agebant. Sed maiorum nugae negotia vocantur, puerorum autem talia cum sint, puniuntur a maioribus, et nemo miseratur pueros vel illos vel utrosque. Nisi vero approbat quisquam bonus rerum arbiter vapulasse me, quia ludebam pila puer et eo ludo impediebar, quominus celeriter discerem litteras, quibus maior deformius luderem" (But what we liked to do was to play, and for this we were punished by those who were themselves behaving in just the same way. But the amusements of older people are called "business," and when children indulge in their own amusements, these older people punish them for it. And no one is sorry for the children; no one is sorry for the older people; no one is sorry for both of them. I doubt whether any good judge of things would say that it was a good thing for me, as a boy, to be beaten for playing some ball game simply on the grounds that by playing

this game I was impeded in my studies, the point of which was that I should be able to perform, when I grew older, in some game more unbecoming still).

66. *Confessions* 1.13.20: "Adamaveram enim latinas, non quas primi magistri, sed quas docent qui grammatici vocantur. Nam illas primas, ubi legere et scribere et numerare discitur, non minus onerosas poenalesque habebam quam omnes graecas" (For I was very fond of Latin, not the elementary grammar but the literature. As to the rudiments—reading, writing, and arithmetic—I found these just as boring and troublesome as all my Greek studies); cp. Burke, "Verbal Action in St. Augustine's *Confessions,*" 68–69. Quintilian had also made a distinction between the teacher of the most basic elements *(praeceptor)* and the teacher of language and literature *(grammaticus),* a distinction that will endure in some form through to Dante's Florence; see Gehl, *A Moral Art,* 20–42, and in part. p. 30. But for abstract thinkers like Quintilian and Augustine, as we have seen, any early language education might be considered a part of *grammatica,* broadly construed. See in particular Marrou, *Saint Augustin et la fin de la culture antique,* p. 10, n. 1, who cites *De ordine* 2.12, where Augustine labels this early instruction "an infancy of grammar" ("velut quaedam grammaticae infantia"); on Augustine's knowledge of Greek and the relationship between Greek and Latin learning in late antiquity, see Marrou, 27–46.

67. Cp. Quintilian, *Institutiones oratoriae* 1.1.12: "A sermone Graeco puerum incipere malo, quia Latinum, qui pluribus in usu est, vel nobis nolentibus perbibet" (I prefer that a boy should begin with Greek, because Latin, being in general use, will be picked up by him whether we will or no). Quintilian's choice of *perbibet* here subtly recalls the suckling imagery elaborated elsewhere. In this regard, see also Isidore, *Etymologiarum* 9.1 *(De linguis gentium).* 10: "Omnem autem linguam unusquisque hominum sive Graecam, sive Latinam, sive ceterarum gentium aut audiendo potest tenere, aut legendo ex praeceptore accipere. Cum autem omnium linguarum scientia difficilis sit cuiquam, nemo tamen tam desidiosus est ut in sua gente positus suae gentis linguam nesciat. Nam quid aliud putandus est nisi animalium brutorum deterior? Illa enim propriae vocis clamorem exprimunt, iste deterior qui propriae linguae caret notitiam" (Each and every man, however, is able to grasp one language entirely, be this Latin or Greek or one of the other languages, upon hearing it spoken or hearing his teacher read. For although a knowledge of all the languages is difficult for any man, no one can be so indolent as not to know the language of his own people once having lived among them. How could such a creature be judged as anything but worse off than brutes? For even animals express themselves with the clamor of their own voices; he who lacks an acquaintance of his own language is thus inferior). It would appear, then, that Isidore in the early seventh century, like Quintilian several centuries before him, still considered grammatical Latin in some sense his mother tongue.

68. With less personal intensity, Augustine will elaborate a similar view in book 4 of the *De doctrina christiana.* To paraphrase from 4.3: "Rules are not going to help

those who lack a naturally eloquent disposition and those who are naturally eloquent have little need for rules; imitation is the preferred method of learning, as it parallels the infant's acquisition of the mother tongue"; cp. Quintilian, *Institutiones oratoriae* 2.19.

69. Cp. *De civitate dei* 19.7: "Linguarum diversitas hominem alienat ab homine" (The diversity of languages separates man from man); cited by Benvenuto Terracini, "Natura ed origine del linguaggio umano," 240.

70. *Confessions* 1.14.23: "Cur ergo graecam etiam grammaticam oderam talia cantantem? Nam et Homerus peritus texere tales fabellas et dulcissime vanus est. Mihi tamen amarus erat puero. Credo etiam graecis pueris Vergilius ita sit, cum eum sic discere coguntur ut ego illum" (But why, then, did I hate Greek literature, which is full of such things? For Homer too is skillful at putting together this sort of story and there is great sweetness in his vanity; yet when I was a boy he was not to my taste. I think that Greek children must feel just the same about Vergil, when they are forced to study him as I was forced to study Homer).

71. *Confessions* 1.14.23: "Videlicet difficultas, difficultas omnino ediscendae linguae peregrinae, quasi felle aspergebat omnes suavitates graecas fabulosarum narrationum. Nulla enim verba illa noveram et saevis terroribus ac poenis, ut nossem, instabatur mihi vehementer" (No doubt it was a question of difficulty; and this difficulty of mastering a foreign language was like a bitter gall spread over all the sweetness of Greek stories and fables. For I simply did not know the words, and strict measures were taken, punishments and cruel threats, to make me learn them).

72. *Confessions* 1.14.23: "Nam et latina aliquando infans utique nulla noveram et tamen advertendo didici sine ullo metu atque cruciatu inter etiam blandimenta nutricum et ioca adridentium et laetitias adludentium. Didici vero illa sine poenali onere urgentium, cum me urgeret cor meum ad parienda concepta sua, et qua non esset, nisi aliqua verba didicissem non a docentibus, sed a loquentibus, in quorum et ego auribus parturiebam quidquid sentiebam. Hinc satis elucet maiorem habere vim ad discenda ista liberam curiositatem quam meticulosam necessitatem" (There had been a time too, of course, in my infancy, when I did not know any Latin words either; yet simply by paying attention I learned Latin without any fears or torments; I learned it in the caressing language of my nurses and in the laughter and play and kindness of those about me. In this learning I was under no pressure of punishment, and people did not have to urge me on; my own heart urged me on to give birth to the thoughts which it had conceived, and I could not do this unless I learned some words; these I learned not from instructors but from people who talked to me and in whose hearing I too was able to give birth to what I was feeling. It is clear enough from this that free curiosity is a more powerful aid to the learning of languages than a forced discipline). For all the simple innocence of this scene of language acquisition among nurses, however, Augustine's choice of *blandimenta* (*blandior,* to flatter,

charm, entice, allure) suggests a physical seduction; cp. Seneca in a letter to Lucilius, where the corrupting elements of the sensible world, the very things that tempted and tossed Ulysses upon the sea, include "insidiosa blandimenta aurium" (insidious invitations [that] caress our ears); cited by Dante Della Terza, "Tradition and Exegesis," 4. On Ulysses, the Sirens and Circe, see chapter 3.

73. For a recent survey of the popularity of wet nursing from Homeric times through the Renaissance within the larger cultural history of the breast, see Yalom, *A History of the Breast,* and especially pp. 15, 19, 25, 36–37, 69–73, 84–85. On wet nurses in medieval and Renaissance Italy, see Clarissa W. Atkinson, *The Oldest Vocation,* pp. 57–63; Louis Hass, *The Renaissance Man and His Children,* pp. 89–132; Christiane Klapisch-Zuber, *Women, Family, and Ritual in Renaissance Italy,* 132–64; Iris Origo, *The Merchant of Prato,* pp. 214–16; Shulamith Shahar, *Childhood in the Middle Ages,* 53–76;

74. On the first meaning (breast, dug) and development of *mamma,* see the *Oxford Latin Dictionary* and DuCange, s.v. On "mother tongue," see Leo Spitzer, "Muttersprache und Muttererziehung." Spitzer investigates the origins of the phrase *lingua materna* in Latin and the vernaculars (earliest example from 1119 in an account of the *magister scholarum Argentinensis Hesso*); of particular interest is an exhaustive catalogue of scriptural and patristic references to mother's milk on pp. 29–43. Spitzer summarizes on p. 29: "Es wird sich zeigen dass Erziehung und Unterweisung eines Kindes im Religiösen und überhaupt in allem wahren Wissen im Mittelalter oft durch die Metapher des mütterlichen Nährens und Stillens ausgedrückt wird"; see also Otto Behagel, "Lingua materna." On Latin and grammar in Dante with particular attention to the expression "mother tongue," see Richard Baum, "Dante—fabbro del parlar materno."

75. Cp. Jacques Derrida, *Of Grammatology,* 152–53. Derrida discusses the wet nurse in Rousseau (who in *Emile,* much like Aulus Gellius before him, condemns giving a child out to nurse as a kind of original sin): "Nature draws away at the same time as the Mother, or rather 'Mamma,' who already signified the disappearance of the true mother and has substituted herself in the well-known ambiguous manner . . . It is at the moment when the mother disappears that substitution becomes possible and necessary."

76. Cp. Vance, *Mervelous Signals,* 13–16; and Ong, "Latin Language Study as a Renaissance Puberty Rite."

77. *Confessions* 2.3.6: "Quin immo ubi me ille pater in balneis vidit pubescentem et inquieta indutum adulescentia, quasi iam ex hoc in nepotes gestiret, gaudens matri indicavit, gaudens vinulentia, in qua te iste mundus oblitus est creatorem suum et creaturam tuam pro te amavit, de vino invisibili perversae et inclinatae in ima voluntatis suae. Sed matris in pectore iam inchoaveras templum tuum et exordium sanctae habitationis tuae."

78. See Burke, "Verbal Action in St. Augustine's *Confessions*," 66 and 97.

79. *Confessions* 3.4.8: "Hoc nomen salvatoris mei, filii tui, in ipso adhuc lacte matris tenerum cor meum pie biberat et alte retinebat."

80. *Confessions* 4.1.1: "Aut quid sum, cum mihi bene est, nisi sugens lac tuum aut fruens te cibo, qui non corrumpitur?"

81. Miles, "Infancy, Parenting, and Nourishment," 355.

82. See Ong, "Latin Language Study as a Renaissance Puberty Rite."

83. In addition to Gozzoli, see the school scene in the Forum at Pompeii, where a boy receives a thrashing in *catomus* ("over the shoulders") position; reproduced in Stanley F. Bonner, *Education in Ancient Rome,* 118. Many centuries later, see the seventeenth-century Flemish engraving in the Uffizi (reproduced in the iconography catalogue of the Kunsthistorisches Institut in Florence, cat. no. 311 506). In the left foreground, a large Lady Grammar (with two small students) stands and copies onto a large tablet from another tablet on the floor; in the right background, a student "mounts the horse" as a seated and bearded old *grammaticus* raises his switch to strike the boy's bare behind. Needless to say, this recurrent image of the old man with a rod striking the young naked boy from behind recalls the centuries-old association between grammatical pedagogy and sodomy. This is not the place to explore that fascinating tradition, so central to Dante's portrayal of Brunetto Latini, his beloved *magister,* in *Inferno* 15. On pedagogical sodomy in the ancient world, Henri-Irénée Marrou, *A History of Education in Antiquity,* remains fundamental. Compare also the passage from Quintilian's *Institutiones oratoriae* 1.3 cited above. On the continued presence of sodomy in the classroom through to Dante's day, see Gehl, *A Moral Art,* 196. In the Gozzoli fresco, there seems to be a calculated sodomitical pun in the thrice-repeated figure of one boy hanging on the shoulders of another: we see it in the two older boys in the center of the frame, in the young boy mounting the horse, and again in two small boys to the right of the central arcade in the grammar school. On Gozzoli, see Ahl, *Benozzo Gozzoli,* particularly pp. 121–42 and plate 154.

84. At 1.7.2 in reference to Babel and the confusion of tongues, the third of humankind's great infractions and punishments (after Eden and the Flood): "Sed, sicut proverbialiter dici solet, 'Non ante tertium equitabis,' misera miserum venire maluisti ad equum" (But, just as the saying goes, "You will not mount a horse until the third time," so you preferred in your wretchedness to come to a wretched horse). For more on this passage, see the following chapter. In Gozzoli's painting, the bearded master who delivers the whipping resembles his counterpart on the other side of the frame. Beside him stands a studious young boy with open book; thus Gozzoli's design echoes the good boy/bad boy motif we will see at Chartres. As the arcaded columns communicate a strong vertical rhythm in the background, so the upright figures of the masters and young boys organize the foreground. The two masters are notable for their heavy beards and reddish robes. The three small boy figures—Augustine being

introduced by his parents, the boy being whipped, and the studious boy—may all mean to convey subsequent moments of Augustine's grammar experience. The three resemble one another in size and physiognomy, all have blond hair and the same greenish robe. As we know from the *Confessions,* the young Augustine was at various times both an excellent student and a victim of beatings. Two fifteenth-century Boethius manuscripts (MS 222 of the Pierpont Morgan Library, fol. 39r, and MS *français* 1098 of the Bibliothèque Nationale in Paris, fol. 40v) convey the notion of Lady Grammar as the student's guide into adult society. In these pictures, Philosophia introduces Boethius to the Liberal Arts, but Lady Grammar stands apart from her other sisters and is the immediate focus of the introduction; for reproductions, see Pierre Courcelle, *La Consolation de la Philosophie dans la tradition littéraire,* fig. 54, 1–2. The most interesting illustration of this type, however, is Botticelli's fresco of, it seems, Lady Grammar introducing Lorenzo il Magnifico to Philosophy and the other Arts. Executed before 1486 for the Villa Lemmi in Florence, it is now in the Louvre. According to Phillipe Verdier, ("L'iconographie des arts libéraux," 343 and n. 101), the fresco later became identified with the marriage of Lorenzo Tornabuoni and Giovanna degli Albizzi; cp. Paola Casciano (in Lorenzo Valla, *L'arte della grammatica*), who identifies the figures as Matteo degli Albizzi, his wife, and the Arts.

85. For a thorough introduction to Martianus, his text, and his influence on medieval thought, see *Martianus Capella and the Seven Liberal Arts,* vol. 1: *The Quadrivium of Martianus Capella.* The second volume of this translation contains the first five books of Martianus's poem and is somewhat misleadingly titled *The Marriage of Philology and Mercury.* Books 1 and 2 depict the betrothal and marriage of Mercury and Philology; 3 through 9 treat the Seven Arts in traditional order; appendix A contains an extensive bibliographical survey. All subsequent English translations are from this edition. For a catalogue of the many manuscripts of the *De nuptiis,* see Claudio Leonardi, "I codici di Marziano Capella." E. L. Burge, R. Johnson, and W. H. Stahl note that, although parts of the *De nuptiis* were very popular throughout the Middle Ages (in particular the treatment of Geometry), as a technical manual of grammar Martianus's Book 3 went virtually unused thanks to the enormous popularity of Donatus. They note, for instance, that of the well over one hundred manuscripts listed by Leonardi, aside from those that contain the entire text, only two (nos. 77 and 189) contain all of Book 3 (*Martianus Capella and the Seven Liberal Arts,* 103). Nevertheless, as an allegorization and basis for iconographical depictions, Martianus's portrait remained unparalleled. The two major ninth-century commentators on the *De nuptiis,* Remigius of Auxerre and John Scotus Eriugena, may be taken as emblematic of Martianus's fate. Both are extremely brief on book 3, ignoring the technical sections almost entirely; their interest falls instead on the initial allegorical section, which is treated in some detail. Both of these commentaries have been edited by Cora Lutz.

86. For a discussion of critical reactions to the *De nuptiis* and an attempt at a defense of Martianus's poem, see Cora E. Lutz, "Remigius' Ideas on the Origins of the Seven Liberal Arts."

87. Book 3.220 in Burge, Johnson, and Stahl, "Bibliographical Survey of the Seven Liberal Arts." For Eriugena (?815–?877), see *Iohannis Scotti Annotationes in Marcianum,* 75 (line 84.14): "Ars de genituris hominum quae magica dicitur." Cp. the gloss of Remigius of Auxerre (841–c. 908), *Remigii Autissiodorensis Commentum in Martianum Capellam* 2, 6 (line 84.13): "Genethlia enim Grece genitura dicitur, inde genethliaci dicuntur mathematici qui de genituris hominum disputant" (Genethlia is the word for "procreation" in Greek, wherefore the mathematicians who discuss the generation of mankind are called genethliacs). We should recall in this magical context the evolution of *grammatica* into the Old French *gramaire* as wizard, magician, or book of sorcery, and into modern English *glamour;* see Godefroy, *Dictionnaire de l'ancien langue française,* vol. 4; and Wartburg, *Französisches etymologisches Wörterbuch, s.v. gramaire;* as well as the *Oxford English Dictionary,* vol. 4, *s.v. grammar.* For a definition of Lady Grammar from the perspective of late twentieth-century theories of cultural monstrosity, see my *"A la tetta de la madre s'apprende."*

88. The two possibilities for *teres* as (1) "smooth and rounded" or simply (2) "polished" led to some confusion in the iconographical tradition (i.e., the roundness of the *ferculum* is not always recognized). The *ferculum* will sometimes be a carrying tray, sometimes simply a box.

89. *De nuptiis Philologiae et Mercurii* 3.223–24: "Gestabat haec autem teres quoddam ex compactis annexionibus ferculum, quod levi exterius elephanto praenitebat, unde velut medendi sollers magistra curandorum vulnerum insignia proferebat. Nam ex eodem scalprum primo vibranti demonstrabat acumine, quo dicebat circumcidi infantibus vitia posse linguarum dehincque nigello quodam pulvere, qui ex favilla confectus vel sepia putaretur, illato per cannulas eadem resanari."

90. *De nuptiis Philologiae et Mercurii* 3.224: "Tunc etiam quoddam medicamen acerrimum, quod ex ferulae flore caprigenique tergoris resectione confecerat, rubri admodum coloris exprompsit, quod monebat faucibus adhibendum, cum indocta rusticitate vexatae fetidos ructus vitiosi oris exhalant."

91. Unlike, it seems, our modern English translators, the two major ninth-century commentators on Martianus (and again John of Salisbury in the twelfth century, as we will see) have no trouble recognizing Martianus's double meaning about grammar. John Scotus Eriugena (ed. Lutz, p. 76, line 83.5) wastes no words: "MEDICAMEN ACERRIMUM flagellum dicit" (A VERY SHARP MEDICINE means a whip). Remigius of Auxerre (ed. Lutz, p. 4, line 83.4) treats the passage in some detail: "QUODDAM ACERRIMUM id est durum et saevum, MEDICAMEN. Significat autem flagellum quo pueri caeduntur. QUOD subaudis medicamen, CONFECERAT id est composuerat, EX FLORE FERULAE ET EX RESECTIONE id est recisione, CAPRIGENI

TERGORIS id est caprini corii. Manifeste flagellum significat quod haberet manubrium ex ferula. ADMODUM id est valde, RUBRI COLORIS QUOD subaudis medicamen, MONE-BAT id est imperabat vel docebat, subaudis ipsa Grammatica, ADHIBENDUM FAUCIBUS id est oribus, puerorum. Cum enim dorsa eorum caeduntur, oris vitia corriguntur" (A VERY SHARP that is hard and cruel, MEDICINE. This means the whip with which the boys are beaten. WHICH the understood medicine, SHE HAD MADE that is composed, FROM CANE AND THE CLIPPINGS, that is cuttings, FROM A GOAT'S BACK that is from the hide of a goat. Clearly this describes a whip that has a handle made of cane. FULLY that is intensely, RED IN COLOR WHICH, the understood medicine, SHE ADVISED that is she ordered or taught, Grammar herself being understood, WAS TO BE APPLIED TO THE THROATS that is to the mouths, of the schoolboys. For since their backsides are beaten, the vices in their mouths are corrected). This last comment adds a dose of irony to Martianus's already playful description.

92. See Lutz, "Remigius' Ideas on the Origins of the Seven Liberal Arts."

93. At *De nuptiis* 7.739, Martianus writes that the infant's first teeth come in at seven months and the adult teeth at seven years (the beginning of *pueritia*).

94. Cassiodorus, *Epistolae variae* 9.21 (*Patrologia latina* 69, col. 787): "Mater gloriosa facundiae . . . magistra verborum"; cited by Dragonetti, "La conception du langage poétique," 42, n. 3.

95. "Non barbarismi confusionem devito, situs motusque et praepositionum casus servare contemno, quia indignum vehementer existimo ut verba caelestis oraculi restringam sub regulis Donati. Neque enim haec ab ullis interpretibus in scripturae sacrae auctoritate servata sunt. Ex qua nimirum quia nostra expositio oritur, dignum profecto est, ut quasi edita soboles speciem suae matris imitetur" (I do not avoid the addition of a barbarism, I despise keeping the proper constructions and prepositional cases, because I vehemently deem it shameful that the words of the celestial oracle be bound under the rules of Donatus. Indeed these rules are not observed by any interpreters under the authority of Sacred Scripture. And because my commentary is born from such authority, it is actually quite fitting that the new-born babe take on the looks of her mother). We recall that the passage is from the end of the *Epistola missoria ad Leandrum Hispalensem* (5.53a), *Patrologia latina* 75, col. 516. Cp. de Lubac, "Saint Grégoire et la grammaire," 194.

96. *Liber in partibus Donati:* "Ut teneat gremio natos desiderat omnes,/more patris nutrit, matris amore fovet."

97. *Liber in partibus Donati:* Preface, 36–37: "Dulcia depromit, promittit et aurea regna,/lactea cum solido pocula pane dabit."

98. *Liber in partibus Donati:* "Ut dulciter . . . artis cum caelestis mellis dulcedine facilius possit gluttire." We might recall here that Barański, *Sole nuovo* (passim), identifies Dante's plurilinguistic poetics with a fundamentally scriptural linguistics; here a key

Christian grammarian identifies the language of Scripture with grammatical education in the nursing body. Cp. *De vulgari* 1.1.1 (my emphases): "Non solum aquam nostri ingenii ad tantum *poculum* aurientes, sed, accipiendo vel compilando ab aliis, potiora miscentes, ut exinde potionare possimus *dulcissimum hydromellum*" (I will not bring to so large a cup only the water of my own thinking, but will add to it more potent ingredients, taken or extracted from elsewhere, so that from these I may concoct the sweetest possible mead). Cp. also Bartholomeus Angelicus, *De rerum proprietatibus* (c. 1209), on the *nutrix* at 6.9 (my emphases): "Cibum primo masticat, & masticando puero edentulo præparat, *ut facilius transglutiat cibum*" (She first chews the food, and by chewing prepares it for the toothless lad, so that he may more easily swallow it).

99. Marie-Thérèse d'Alverny, "La sagesse et ses sept filles." D'Alverny concludes only that the image derives from the union of two older images, Philosophy as mother and Philosophy as source or stream of knowledge. She does not discuss the image of Philosophy's first daughter, Lady Grammar, as nursing mother. But Lady Philosophy was already a *nutrix* for Boethius, *De consolatione philosophiae* 2.prose 4.1 ("virtutum omnium nutrix"); see chapter 2, "Lady Philosophy as *Nutrix* and *Magistra*," in Jaroslav Pelikan, *Eternal Feminines,* especially p. 37.

100. "Legimus, Salomone dicente, per quem ipsa [sapientia] se cecinit: Sapientia aedificavit sibi domum, excidit columnas septem (Prov. 9:1) quae sententia, licet ad divinam pertineat sapientiam . . . tamen sapientia liberalium litterarum septem columnis confirmetur, nec aliter ad perfectam quemlibet deducit scientiam, nisi his septem columnis, vel etiam gradibus exaltetur" (We read in the sayings of Solomon, through whom Wisdom sang: "Wisdom has built herself a house, she has hewn out seven pillars." And although this saying refers to divine wisdom . . . nevertheless wisdom is reinforced by the seven columns of the liberal arts, and in no other way can it lead anyone to perfect knowledge, unless he is raised up by these seven columns or steps). Cited by d'Alverny, "La sagesse et ses sept filles," 245.

101. Martianus's popularity will endure throughout the High Middle Ages. In addition to the two major commentaries of John Scotus Eriugena and Remigius already mentioned, Lutz has also edited a commentary attributed to the unknown "Dunchad," *Dunchad: Glossae in Martianum,* which may be the work of Martin of Laon; cp. Lutz, "Remigius' Ideas on the Origins of the Seven Liberal Arts," 38, n. 3. In any event, this latter commentary leaves out Book 3 in its entirety. In their introduction, Burge, Johnson, and Stahl *(Martianus Capella and the Seven Liberal Arts)* mention other anonymous Cambridge manuscripts containing commentaries on Martianus which I have been unable to consult. They further note Martianus's popularity among certain Italian intellectuals of the tenth century. Bernardus Silvestris (fl. c. 1150) may also have left a commentary fragment, *The Commentary on Martianus Cappella's "De nuptiis Philologiae et Mercurii" Attributed to Bernardus Silvestris.* For more on this latter commentary, see chapter 3.

102. *Super caelestem hierarchiam* 1 (*Patrologia latina* 122, 139–40): "Septem disciplinas, quas philosophi liberales appellant, intelligibilis contemplativae plenitudinis, qua Deus et creatura purissime cognoscitur, significationes esse astruit . . . Ut enim multae aquae ex diversis fontibus in unius fluminis alveum confluunt atque decurrunt, ita naturales et liberales disciplinae in una eademque internae contemplationis significatione adunantur, quem summus fons totius sapientiae, qui est Christus, undique per diversas theologiae speculationes insinuat" (The seven disciplines, which the philosophers have designated "liberal," are seen to be the symbols of intelligible contemplation in all its plenitude, wherein God and His creature are most purely recognized . . . Just as many waters from different sources converge and flow together in the bed of a single river, so the natural and liberal disciplines are gathered in one and the same figure, the figure of internal contemplation, the supreme source of all wisdom, which is Christ, whence it thus meanders through the various branches of theology); cited by d'Alverny, "La sagesse et ses sept filles," 250, n. 4.

103. See d'Alverny, "La sagesse et ses sept filles," 255.

104. "Discus erat tereti formatus imagine mundi,/arboris unius quem decorabat opus./Huius Grammatica ingens in radice sedebat,/gignere eam semet seu retinere monens./Omnis ab hac ideo procedere cernitur arbos,/ars quia proferri hac sine nulla valet./Huius laeva tenet flagrum, seu dextra machaeram,/pigros hoc ut agat, radat ut haec vitia./Et quia primatum sapientia gestat ubique,/compserat illius hinc diadema caput./Et quia te sensus bonus, aut opinatio gignit,/ambae hic adsistunt, celsa Sophia, tibi."

105. "Verba philosophiae ad suos sectatores: quisquis alumne velis varias cognoscere rerum/Causas, nutricem me cole corde piam"; cited by d'Alverny, "La sagesse et ses sept filles," 253.

106. "Unica regina, specialis Virgo, supina/Spes, septem natas non carne viri generatas/Lactat per partes quas septem credimus artes/Turbaque mammarum superatur lacte duarum/Nec plus quam flamme didicerunt fallere mamme/Has ergo formosas credo satis et speciosas/He vincunt dominas quidvis cantando marinas/Ipsam silvanam superant venando Dianam/Cinthia tam bellis cedit super sui astra puellis/His non astricta vult esse Proserpina victa/Non est mortalis quales sunt femina talis" (Extraordinary queen, special Virgin, overflowing/Hope, she nurses her seven newborns—not born of the flesh of man—/Through members which we believe to be the seven arts/The group is overcome by the milk of her two breasts/No more than flames did these breasts learn to deceive/I therefore judge them to be sufficiently shapely and beautiful/They overcome in singing whichever of the sea mistresses [Sirens]/in hunting they surpass even the sylvan Diana/Cynthia above the stars yields to such beautiful girls/Proserpina longs not to be set beside them in defeat/A woman of their sort is not mortal). Bibliothèque Nationale, MS

Lat. 3110; d'Alverny, "La sagesse et ses sept filles," 274–78, publishes only extracts and a description.

107. "Nam velut in solio quaedam residebat imago/Quae, bene si novi, philosophia fuit./Huic sua manebant fluido velut ubera lacte/Virgo tamen facie, fronte severa tamen . . . /Haec digitum dextrae tendebat more magistrae/Effigies septem discipulae suberant" (For as in a throne was seated a certain image/which, if I discerned correctly, was Philosophy./Her breasts were continually streaming forth a liquid, as though it were her milk/A Virgin in appearance, yet with a severe countenance . . . /She held out the forefinger of her right hand in the manner of a school teacher/The images of the seven disciplines were below her); d'Alverny, "La sagesse et ses sept filles," 260.

108. *Anselm der Peripatetiker, Rhetorimachia* 2.20–23: "'Quem enim lactavimus in sua infancia, quem in ipsa cibavimus adolescentia noster est iuvenis,' dixit rethorica. 'Vera quippe sunt hec,' iurat grammatica" ("This youth—whom we suckled in infancy and nourished in adolescence—belongs to us," said Rhetoric. "These things are certainly true," attested Grammar). Anselm's allusion to the three early life stages—*infantia* (and *pueritia), adulescentia, iuventus*—suggests a conceptual alignment with the three branches of the trivium present, each appropriate to a specific age: grammar for infancy and boyhood, rhetoric for adolescence, dialectic for young adulthood. We will see that conceptual associations between the life stages and the arts will figure prominently in the metaphorical structure of Dante's *De vulgari.*

109. Most of the major studies on liberal arts iconography are from the nineteenth or early twentieth centuries. In chronological order: M. von Böck, *Die sieben freien Künste im 11. Jahrhundert;* August Aymard, *Ancienne peinture murale représentant les arts libéraux;* E.-F. Corpet, "Portraits des arts libéraux d'après les écrivains du moyen âge"; E.-E. Viollet-Le-Duc, "Arts (libéraux)"; Gabriel Meier, *Die sieben freien Künste im Mittelalter;* Julius von Schlosser, "Beiträge zur Kunstgeschichte aus den Schriftquellen des frühen Mittelalters"; Emile Mâle, "Les arts libéraux dans la statuaire du moyen-âge"; Eduard Norden, "Die Stellung der Artes liberales im mittelalterlichen Bildungswesen" (in *Die antike Kunstprosa,* 670–87); A. Filangieri di Candida, "Martianus Capella e le rappresentazioni delle arti liberali"; Paolo D'Ancona, "Le rappresentazioni allegoriche delle arti liberali"; Emile Mâle, *The Gothic Image;* Karl Künstle, *Ikonographie der christlichen Kunst;* Raimond van Marle, *Iconographie de l'art profane;* Rudolf Wittkower, "'Grammatica' from Martianus Capella to Hogarth"; Donald Lemen Clark, "The Iconography of the Seven Liberal Arts"; Ludwig H. Heydenreich, "Eine illustrierte Martianus Capella–Handschrift"; Adolf Katzenellenbogen, "The Representation of the Seven Liberal Arts"; P. Verdier, "L'iconographie des arts libéraux "; M. W. Evans, *The Personification of the Arts from Martianus Cappella to the End of the Fourteenth Century;* see also Burge, Johnson, and Stahl, "Bibliographical Survey of the Seven Liberal Arts." I have also consulted the

Princeton Index of Christian Art and the iconography catalogue of the Kunsthistorisches Institut, Florence.

110. For instance, d'Alverny ("La sagesse et ses sept filles," 253) reports that wall decorations in the monastery of Saint Gall (founded 610) probably included depictions of the arts, which are reflected in the poetry of the period.

111. D'Ancona ("Le rappresentazioni allegoriche delle arti liberali," 215) refers to three allegorical tapestries of the *De nuptiis:* one from the tenth century given to the monks at Saint Gall by Edviga of Schwabia; and two from the twelfth century, one given to the church of Sant'Antonio in Piacenza, the other by Agnese, prioress of Quedlimburg monastery; fragments of this latter survive (see Verdier, "L'iconographie des arts libéraux," 341, n. 95, and 343, n. 101). MS S. Marco 190 in the Laurenziana, Florence, follows Martianus closely and, according to Heydenreich, was influential for two late fifteenth-century Italian manuscripts, Codex Urbinas lat. 329, in the Vatican (c. 1480), and Marciano lat., Signatur cl. XIV, n. 35, fol. 24v, in the Marciana, Venice (1490), with illuminations by Attavante; see also the manuscript from St. John's College mentioned by Reynolds, *Medieval Reading,* 18.

112. The vast majority are of this type. For some relatively accessible illustrations see: MS lat. 7900A, fol. 127v, in the Bibliothèque Nationale, Paris (early tenth century; Verdier, "L'iconographie des arts libéraux," pl. 7); Herrade of Landesburg's *Hortus deliciarum,* in the Strasbourg Library (late twelfth century; *Arts libéraux et philosophie au moyen âge,* pl. 1); archivolt in the right (Royal) portal of the cathedral at Chartres (1145–55; for best detail, see Viollet-le-Duc, "Arts [libéraux]," 2), which was imitated some two centuries later at the cathedral in Freiburg im Breisgau (Künstle, *Ikonographie der christlichen Kunst,* pl. 38). Almost all of the French Gothic cathedrals included representations of the arts; see Katzenellenbogen, "The Representation of the Seven Liberal Arts" and *The Sculptural Programs of Chartres Cathedral;* MS 1041–42, fol. 1v, of the Bibliothèque Geneviève, Paris (twelfth or thirteenth century; Verdier, "L'iconographie des arts libéraux," pl. 4); bas-relief by Andrea Pisano (or da Pontedera) on Giotto's Campanile (1336–43); Fra Filippino Lippi, "The Glory of St. Thomas," in the Caraffa Chapel, Santa Maria Sopra Minerva, Rome (1488–93; Lady Grammar on far right).

113. D'Alverny, "La sagesse et ses sept filles," 255; van Marle, *Iconographie de l'art profane,* 211ff.; D'Ancona, "Le rappresentazioni allegoriche delle arti liberali," 212–13; Künstle, *Ikonographie der christlichen Kunst,* 47. D'Alverny (p. 268) also refers in passing to sixteenth-century descriptions of eleventh-century pavement mosaics of the Arts in Saint-Remi, Reims, which are now destroyed.

114. A rather nondescript Grammar flanks Lady Philosophy on the left in the late eleventh-century manuscript studied by d'Alverny (MS lat. 3110, fol. 60, Bibliothèque Nationale, Paris); for a reproduction, see d'Alverny, "La sagesse et ses

sept filles," pl. 3. Many of the illustrations I discuss have recently been reproduced (some in color) by Casciano (Lorenzo Valla, *L'arte della grammatica*).

115. For a reproduction, see van Marle, *Iconographie de l'art profane,* 206, fig. 231. Cp. also Viollet-Le-Duc, "Arts (libéraux)," 1–2; D'Ancona, "Le rappresentazioni allegoriche delle arti liberali," 216; Katzenellenbogen, "The Representation of the Seven Liberal Arts," 49; Künstle, *Ikonographie der christlichen Kunst,* 147–48.

116. Reproduced by van Marle, *Iconographie de l'art profane,* 207, fig. 232; Katzenellenbogen, "The Representation of the Seven Liberal Arts," 48 (Katzenellenbogen's essay mistakenly exchanges the titles of his figures 8 and 9, thus erroneously labeling this miniature "Hortus Deliciarum").

117. There are good reasons to identify this figure as *Grammatica*, not the least of which is her positioning as the first of the Arts at Sapientia's right hand. But the cup this figure bears is rather too generic for a positive identification; and as far as I can tell the notion of Grammar as opener of the door to wisdom (i.e., key-bearer) enters the iconographical tradition only in the Italian Renaissance (see Andrea da Firenze and Luca Della Robbia). By contrast, the figure on Sapientia's lower left— winged and thus usually called Astronomia—carries an open book in one hand and a long rod in the other: for centuries the standard implements of Grammar.

118. On the idea of natural grammar in the twelfth century, see Ziolkowski, *Alan of Lille's Grammar of Sex,* 104–7. For general background on the nature/art dilemma, see Winthrop Wetherbee, *Platonism and Poetry;* cp. also Curtius's brief excursus, "Poetry and Scholasticism," in *European Literature and the Latin Middle Ages,* 480–84.

119. On the ever increasing distance between Latin and vernacular, see, for instance, Klein, *Latein und Volgare in Italien.*

120. *Metalogicon* 1.6; 833c–834a (references are to book and chapter numbers; the number and letter that follow the semicolon refer to Migne's column divisions, which Webb reproduces in his text): "Greca plebs et Hebrea sine preceptorum dif-ficultate lingue sue compendio utitur; et tam Galli quam Britones et alie itidem gentes commercium verbi ante a nutricum sinu quam a cathedra doctorum excipi-unt. Nutricis linguam plerumque redolet etas virilis; nec potest interdum ab eo quod tenerior etas ebiberat doctorum diligentia erudiri." All English translations of the *Metalogicon* are from McGarry, with slight modifications.

121. In fact, John plays the role of Cornificius with such comfort and at such length that, in his English translation, McGarry feels obliged to interpolate "[Cornificius argues]" to remind the reader that this is not really John talking.

122. An argument could be made for the influence of Book 1 of the *Metalogicon* on Book 1 of the *De vulgari,* particularly there where Dante relies on the distinc-tion between *naturalis* and *artificialis* to proclaim the vernacular's superiority.

123. *Metalogicon* 1.8; 836c: "Prodest utique natura, sed eatenus aut numquam aut raro, ut sine studio culmen optineat." For a general introduction to medieval concepts of nature and the allegorical Natura, see Curtius, *European Literature and the Latin Middle Ages;* and George D. Economou, *The Goddess Natura in Medieval Literature.*

124. On the linguistic nature of Edenic sinfulness, see Barański, "Dante's Biblical Linguistics."

125. For a survey of patristic and Scholastic readings of Babel, see Arno Borst, *Der Turmbau von Babel;* Paolo Rotta, *La filosofia del linguaggio;* Lusignan, *Parler vulgairement,* 49–59; Paul Zumthor, *Babel ou l'inachèvement.*

126. *Metalogicon* 1.8; 835bc: "Quare ergo, doctissimi Cornificiani, peritiam omnium non habetis linguarum? Quare non saltem Hebream nostis? Quam, ut aiunt, *natura parens* primigenis tradidit et generi conservavit humano, donec unitatem scidit impietas et confusione linguarum prostrata est elatio que in celum conscendere non virtute sed viribus moliebatur, turre constructa. Quare non hanc, que ceteris naturalior est, ut sic dicatur, natura docente loquuntur?" (Emphasis mine).

127. On the medieval notion of Hebrew as the natural, default language for humans, we recall the experiment carried out at the Sicilian court of Frederick II, recorded by Salimbene da Parma, wherein several infants were isolated from all linguistic exposure in hopes that they would speak Hebrew. The infants eventually died. For a recent account in English, see Umberto Eco, *The Search for the Perfect Language,* xii. But see also the quote from Salimbene in Lusignan, *Parler vulgairement,* 60, where Salimbene notes that the infants died because deprived of their nurses's caresses, a passage that strongly evokes Augustine and Kristeva's semiotic: "Non enim vivere possent sine aplausu et gestu et letitia faciei et blanditiis baiularum et nutricum suarum" (They could not survive without the clapping and gestures and happy smiles and caresses of their caretakers and wet nurses); we recall Augustine's recollection of Latin learning *inter blandimenta nutricum.*

128. *Metalogicon* 1.9; 837a: "Sed licet alique artium contingentium et docentium virtutem eloquii naturam attingant, illa tamen, que *ad placitum* fere est, naturaliter sciri non potest, quia nec naturalis est; *non est enim eadem apud omnes.*" Emphasis mine.

129. Cp. Karin Margareta Fredborg, "Universal Grammar." For a more categorical twelfth-century response (c. 1150) to the natural/artificial controversy, cp. in particular the Spaniard Dominicus Gundissalinus in the *De divisione philosophiae.* Under the rubric *De grammatica,* Gundissalinus divides the art in two: (1) early acquisition of words and their meanings, and (2) formal study of the rules of speech. The first is learned through imitation, is natural and arbitrary; the second is learned through study, is artificial and universal: "Unde ad evitanda hec vicia sciencia lingue,

que omnium scienciarum naturaliter prima est, primum in duo dividitur. Scilicet in scienciam considerandi et observandi quid unaque dictio significet apud gentem illam cuius lingua est, et in scienciam observandi regulas illarum dictionum. Illa est sciencia intelligendi ad quid significandum singule dictiones sint imposite. Ista est sciencia ordinandi singulas dictiones in oracione ad significandum concepciones anime. Illa naturaliter solo auditu addiscitur a parvulis, hec doctrina et studio addiscitur ab adultis. Illa solo usu audiendi, ista regulis magisterii apprehenditur. Illa variatur apud omnes secundum diversitatem linguarum, hec pene eadem est apud omnes secundum similitudinem regularum" (Whence in order to avoid these vices the science of language—which of all the sciences is naturally the first—is first off divided into two parts: that is, into the science of considering and observing what each and every word means in one's own native tongue, and the science of observing the rules of those words. The former is the science of understanding the meanings to which individual words are attached. The latter is the science of ordering individual words in speech to express the concepts of the soul. The former is picked up by children naturally just from listening, the latter is learned by adults through rules and study. The former is grasped just through the habit of listening, the latter by the rules of the grammar teachers. The former varies among all peoples according to the diversity of tongues, but the latter is virtually the same among all due to the unity of rules).

130. *Metalogicon* 1.11; 838a: "Est autem ars ratio que compendio sui naturaliter possibilium expedit facultatem. Neque enim impossibilium ratio prestat aut pollicetur effectum; sed eorum que fieri possunt, quasi quodam dispendioso nature circuitu compendiosum iter prebet, et *parit (ut ita dixerim)* difficilium facultatem. Unde et Greci eam methodon dicunt, quasi compendiariam rationem, que nature vitet dispendium, et amfractuosum eius circuitum dirigat, ut quod fieri expedit, rectius et facilius fiat." English translation from McGarry, emphasis mine. Cp. Vance's discussion of nature as female, passive principle perfected by the (male) social order in Bernardus Sylvestris and Alan of Lille (*Mervelous Signals,* 236–38).

131. *Metalogicon* 1.11; 838ab: "Natura enim, quamvis vivida, nisi erudiatur, ad artis facilitatem non pervenit, artium tamen omnium parens est, eisque, quo proficiant et perficiantur, dat *nutriculam rationem.*" English translation by McGarry, with modifications. Emphasis mine.

132. *Metalogicon* 1.11; 839b: "Quia artium natura mater est, merito in iniuriam parentis redundat contemptus earum."

133. *Metalogicon* 1.13; 840a: "Grammatica scientia recte loquendi scribendique et origo omnium liberalium disciplinarum. Eadem quoque est totius philosophie *cunabulum, et (ut ita dixeram) totius litteratorii studii altrix prima; que omnium nascentium de sinu nature teneritudinem excipit, nutrit infantiam,* cuiusque gradus incrementa in philosophia provehit, et *sedulitate materna* omnem philosophantis producit et custodit etatem"* (emphasis mine). John's addition to Isidore's standard definition

consists precisely of the suckling image. On grammar as cradle, cp. Geoffrey of Vinsauf, *Poetria nova* (c. 1200–1202), as cited by Léopold Delisle, "Les écoles d'Orléans au XII et au XIII siècles," 144; Johannes de Hauvilla, *Architrenius* 3.8.173; and Adelard of Bath and Alan of Lille, in the *De planctu naturae,* as discussed below.

134. "Although it is not natural, grammar imitates nature."

135. *Metalogicon* 1.14; 840cd: "Ceterum cum hec ad placitum sit, non a natura videtur esse profecta; siquidem naturalia eadem sunt apud omnes, hec autem apud omnes non eadem est. Artium vero matrem superius collectum est esse naturam."

136. Cp. discussion of 1.9 *supra*. While it is not at present my purpose to prove or disprove Dante's reliance on *Metalogicon* 1 in the opening of the *De vulgari,* I have suggested that a strong case for such a link could be made. Such a case would not overlook John's insistence on custom as the "supreme arbiter of speech" along with his citation in chapter 16 of Horace, *Ars poetica,* 70–72: "Multa renascentur quae iam cecidere, cadentque/quae nunc sunt in honore vocabula." These verses were intimately bound up with Dante's own thoughts about grammar. He cites them in Italian translation at the end of his famous comparison of Grammar to the moon in *Convivio* 2.13.10. Adam paraphrases them as part of his discourse on the natural variation of language in *Paradiso* 26.137–38. And they are everywhere lurking in the margins of the *De vulgari*; see in particular 1.9.7.

137. *Metalogicon* 1.21; 851d–852a: "Eo spectat quod Marcianus in Nuptiis Mercurii et Philologie Gramaticam inducit cum scalpro et ferula et unguentaria pixide medicorum. Scalpro siquidem oris vitia purgat et infantium linguas, qui ad artem philosophie, *ea prelactante cibante et ducente*, ituri sunt, radit, dum erudit; et ne barbarismo, aut soloecismo balbutiant, in sermone preformat; peccantes autem castigat ferula; *et unguento honestatis et utilitatis, que ex ea provenit, patientium mitigat penam.*" Emphasis mine.

138. *Metalogicon* 1.21; 852a.

139. *Metalogicon* 1.24; 854d: "Et quoniam memoria exercitio firmatur, ingeniumque acuitur ad imitandum ea que audiebant, alios admonitionibus, alios flagellis et penis urgebat" (In view of the fact that exercise both strengthens and sharpens our mind, Bernard would bend every effort to bring his students to imitate what they were hearing. In some cases he would rely on exhortation, in others he would resort to punishments, such as flogging).

140. *Metalogicon* 1.24; 855b: "Si quis autem ad splendorem sui operis alienum pannum assuerat, deprehensum redarguebat furtum; sed penam sepissime non infligebat" (And if, to embellish his work, someone had sewed on a patch of cloth filched from an external source, Bernard, on discovering this, would rebuke him for his plagiary, but would often refrain from beating him [McGarry's translation, modified]).

141. See in part. *Metalogicon* 1.25; 856c: "Sed quia isti hesterni pueri, magistri hodierni, heri vapulantes in ferula, hodie stolati docentes in cathedra . . ." (Those who only yesterday were mere boys, being flogged by the rod, yet who today are [grave] masters, ensconced in the [doctor's] chair and invested with the [official] stole . . .).

142. *Metalogicon* 1.24; 854cd: "Ergo pro capacitate discentis aut docentis industria et diligentia, constat fructus prelectionis auctorum. Sequebatur hunc morem Bernardus Carnotensis, exundantissimus modernis temporibus fons litterarum in Gallia, et in auctorum lectione quid simplex esset et ad imaginem regule positum ostendebat; figuras gramatice, colores rethoricos, cavillationes sophismatum, et qua parte sui proposite lectionis articulus respiciebat ad alias disciplinas, proponebat in medio; ita tamen ut non in singulis universa doceret, sed pro capacitate audientium dispensaret eis in tempore doctrine mensuram" (The fruit of the lecture on the authors is proportionate both to the capacity of the individual student and to the industrious diligence of the teacher. Bernard of Chartres, the greatest font of literary learning in Gaul in recent times, used to teach grammar in the following way. He would point out, in reading the authors, what was simple and according to rule. On the other hand, he would explain grammatical figures, rhetorical embellishment, and sophistical quibbling, as well as the relation of given passages to other studies. He would do so, however, without trying to teach everyone everything at once. On the contrary, he would dispense his instruction in measured quantity according to the capacity of his listeners).

143. John cites both Quintilian and Augustine in this very chapter. He notes Quintilian's use of the word *prelectio* in *Institutiones oratoriae* 2.5 in order to introduce his own distinction between *lectio* and *prelectio;* he further cites *Institutiones oratoriae* 1.8 regarding grammar classroom methods (853d).

144. *Metalogicon* 1.24; 855a: "Vespertinum exercitium, quod declinatio dicebatur, tanta copiositate gramatice refertum erat, ut siquis in eo per annum integrum versaretur, rationem loquendi et scribendi, si non esset hebetior, haberet ad manum, et significationem sermonum, qui in communi usu versantur, ignorare non posset." English translation by McGarry, with modifications.

145. "In hac autem septem artium liberalium synodo, ad cultum humanitatis conducta, prima omnium grammatica procedit in medium, matrona vultuque habituque severo. Pueros convocat, rationes recteque scribendi recteque loquendi prescribit; ydiomata linguarum decenter transmutit, expositionem omnium auctorum sibi debitam profitetur: quicquid dicitur auctoritati eius committitur." This famous passage is cited by A. Clerval, "L'enseignement des arts libéraux à Chartres et à Paris," 284; also in French translation in A. Clerval, *Les écoles de Chartres,* 224. See also P. Delhaye, "'Grammatica' et 'Ethica' au XIIe siècle," 70; Ziolkowski, *Alan of Lille's Grammar of Sex,* 92, whose English translation I follow closely. For a general description of the

Heptateuchon, see Paetow, *The Arts Course at Medieval Universities,* 12–13; Murphy, *Rhetoric in the Middle Ages,* 117.

146. On Chartrian humanism see Clerval, *Les écoles de Chartres;* regarding the pervasiveness of grammar at Chartres in the eleventh and twelfth centuries see in part. pp. 108–9, 223–24. See also Wetherbee, *Platonism and Poetry;* Paetow, *The Arts Course at Medieval Universities.* I note here for the sake of completeness the absence of grammatical imagery relevant to our survey in two well-known figures of Thierry's generation. Hugh of St. Victor (1097–1141) offers nothing in the way of personification or imaginative portraiture, neither in his cursory treatment of Grammar in the *Didascalicon* nor in the largely technical *De grammatica.* Honorius Augustodinensis's *De animae exsilio et patria (Patrologia latina* 175), wherein the Arts are represented as cities along the path of the Christian pilgrim, gives a rather prosaic picture of Grammar with none of the personal attributes that concern our investigation.

147. See above and Margaret Miles, "The Virgin's One Bare Breast"; Jerome Mazzaro, "Dante and the Image of the 'Madonna Allattante.'"

148. Godfrey de Breteuil, *Fons philosophiae,* stanza 33: "Primi ripe fluminis presidet Donatus/Puerorum series stipat ejus latus/Quorum potu lacteo reficit hiatus/Virga quoque faciles corrigit erratus" (Here's Donatus on the first river bank presiding;/Close-ranked boys against his side eagerly colliding,/For he fills their gaping mouths, milky drinks providing;/From his cane faults frequently earn them a good hiding). On disciplinary practices in medieval grammar schools, see Charma's note 6 (with references to the lives of Lanfranc and Saint Anselm).

149. *De eodem et diverso,* ed. Willner, 17–18: "Sunt igitur mihi septem virgines hae, quarum naturam moresque singillatim expediam, ut, quam omnium tibi malis, proprio arbitro eligas. Omnes enim simul amplecti maius, quam quod tuo ingenio competeret, esset. Hae itaque prima, quam vides dextera ferulam gestantem, laeva codicem lituris innumeris distinctum, una liberales artes ingredientes cunabulis suis nutrit primoque lacte imbuit. Sine cuius nutrimento frustra ad sapientiam tendas" (The seven virgins you behold belong to me, and I will explain their nature and customs one by one, so that, of your own free will, you can pick and choose from among them all the one you prefer. It would of course be best, within the realm of your capabilities, to embrace them all alike. This first one [Grammar], whom you see wielding a rod in her right hand, in her left a book marked with innumerable corrections, is she who gives suckle with the very first milk to those just entering into the study of the liberal arts. Without her nourishment you will strive in vain toward wisdom). For more twelfth-century allegorical portraits of Grammar, see the passages by Stephen of Tournai (1150?–1203) and Walter of Châtillon (c. 1135–after 1189) reproduced by Curtius, *European Literature and the Latin Middle Ages,* 45. Grammar is an authoritative matron in both. In particular, Walter portrays her rather

satirically as an imperious military leader: "Inter artes igitur, que dicuntur trivium,/Fundatrix grammatica vendicat principium./Sub hac chorus militat met-
rice scribentium" (Among the *artes* which are called the *trivium,* grammar takes
precedence as the first foundation. Under her serves the troop of those who write
in verse [trans. Trask]). For the complete poem, see Karl Strecker, ed., *Moralisch-
Satirische Gedichte,* poem 3, 41, 7. For another satirical treatment, see the anonymous erotic parody published by Paul Lehmann, *Die Parodie im Mittelalter,* 223.
Here the rod becomes an object of sexual parody; speaking, it seems, is the new,
parodic *grammaticus:* "Non posco manum ferule,/non exigo sub verbere/partes
orationis./Prociantur tabule,/queramus, quid sit ludere/cum virginale specie,/que
primule, non tercie/sit declinacionis" (I do not demand the hand for the rod, I
don't require the parts of speech on pain of beatings. Let the writing tablets be
thrown aside, let us inquire what it is to play with a virginal form of the first, not
the third, declension).

150. *De planctu naturae,* ch. 14, prose 7, vv. 12–14: "Alii, dum in artis gramatice vagientes cunabulis eiusdem lactantur uberibus, Aristotilice subtilitatis apicem
proficentur." There is a similar moment in the Prose Prologue of the *Anticlaudianus:*
"Hoc igitur opus fastidire non audeant qui adhuc nutricum vagientes in cunis, infe-
rioris discipline lactantur uberibus" (Let those not dare to show disdain for this work
who are still wailing in the cradles of the nurses and are being suckled at the breasts
of the lower arts [trans. Sheridan]).

151. *Anticlaudianus,* vv. 390–403: "Cum flos virgineus non deffloretur in illa/nec
proprium frangat Veneris fractura pudorem./Sunt tamen in multo lactis torrente
natantes./Mamme, subducti mentite damna pudoris./Dum suspirat adhuc lactan-
tis ad ubera matris,/infantem cibat iste cibus liquidoque fovetur,/quem solidum
non pascit adhuc, dum pocula lactis/lactea delibat etas potuque sub uno/et cibus
et potus in solo lacte resultat./Asperat illa manum scutica qua punit abusus/quos
de more suo puerilis combibit etas./Verberibus sic asperat ubera, verbera mol-
lit/uberibus. Facto pater est et mater eodem,/verbere compensat patrem, gerit
ubere matrem."

152. Smaragdus is the only other instance we have seen where Grammar is
explicitly both mother and father. Furthermore, Alan's passage seems to recall
Smaragdus's unique description of the mixing of milk and small amounts of bread.
Alan's rhetorical exuberance has transformed Smaragdus's simple *lactea pocula* into
pocula lactis lactea.

153. In the imitative fourteenth-century *De consolatione rationis,* Peter of
Compostella focuses on the curiosity of a lactating virgin while leaving discipline
out altogether. "Prima quidem, que ver florum venatur honorem./Et nec virgineum
veneris fractura pudorem/Auferat, ac lactis torrente carere putetur,/Infantes cibat
iste cibus nec pigra moretur" (The first maiden, spring of budding youth, hunts for

honor. Although the cleft of Venus does not mar her virginal integrity, nor can she be said to lack milky torrents, this food nourishes the infants so that she does not die from inactivity). On Peter, see Peter Dronke's introduction to Bernardus Silvestris, *Cosmographia,* 13: "Peter's derivative *De consolatione rationis* has long been erroneously placed in the early twelfth century, and has even been suggested as a source for Bernard and Alan." On the paradox of the lactating virgin, see Charles T. Wood, "The Doctor's Dilemma," especially p. 719.

154. See Künstle, *Ikonographie der christlichen Kunst,* 148.

155. Katzenellenbogen, *The Sculptural Programs of Chartres Cathedral,* 24.

156. Viollet-Le-Duc, "Arts (libéraux)," 2–3: "L'un étudie, l'autre tend la maïn pour recevoir une correction; sa figure est grimaçante" (One studies, the other holds out his hand to receive a correction; he has a grimacing expression).

157. Künstle, *Ikonographie der christlichen Kunst,* 150 (my translation). For a photograph, see 151, Bild 38.

158. MS S. Marco 190.

159. Heydenreich, "Eine illustrierte Martianus Capella–Handschrift," 61; "Bitter root, sweet fruit."

160. Henri d'Andeli, *The Battle of the Seven Arts,* vv. 240–41: "Icele pesme gent amare / Poinstrent sor Gramaire lor mere" (These bad spiteful people attacked Grammar, their mother).

161. Jean Le Teinturier D'Arras, *Le Mariage des Sept Arts,* vv. 23, 33–34, 41: "Blanches furent con flors de lis / . . . L'ainsnee s'assist primeraine, / Qui de biauté passoit Helaine . . . Lor mere fu, si com moi samble" (They were white as lilies . . . The eldest sat down first, She who surpassed even Helen in beauty . . . It seems to me she was their mother). In her opening speech (vv. 46–47), Grammar reminds the other Arts that she gave birth to them ("De moi vo nessence prendez, / De moi venez"). Jean merges the source / stream image that we saw in Godefroy of St. Victor with the breast motif. The anonymous quatrain version (also edited by Långfors) employs much the same imagery.

162. Cited by Paetow, *The Arts Course at Medieval Universities,* 42.

163. From the *Ars poetica* in Faral, ed., *Les arts poétiques du XIIe et du XIIIe siècle:* "Magister Johannes de Hauvilla, cuius ubera disciplinae rudem adhuc mihi lactaverunt infantiam, multas quidem elegantias adinvenit."

164. *Laborintus* in Faral, ed., *Les arts poétiques du XIIe et du XIIIe siècle,* vv. 73–80: "Nascitur hic plorans. Licet hoc generale sit omen, / ploratus tamen hic particulare tenet: / iste genas lacrimis oneratas saepe videbit, / nec fiet lacrima prosiliente pius. / Masculus 'a' profert omnis dum prodit ad auras: / ex radice trahit primi parentis Adae: / hic cum vagitu speciali ructuat 'alpha!,' / quod rudibus pueris

syllibicando legit." On the misery of scholarly life, cp. Johannes de Hauvilla, *Architrenius,* chapter 3. For a closer reading of nursing imagery in Eberhard, see my "Dante, Boncompagno da Signa, Eberhard the German and the Rhetoric of the Maternal Body."

165. Faral, *Les arts poétiques du XIIe et du XIIIe siècle,* 39.

166. *Laborintus,* vv. 135–36: "Inter vos gradus est soror in limine prima/primo, quae lactis ubera plena gerit."

167. *Laborintus,* vv. 171–74: "Vester sic praeco, qui fati lege vocatur,/ubera grammaticae sobrietate bibat./Si de lacte satur fuerit, contemnet alumnos/nec stomacho pascet esuriente rudes."

168. Isidore, *Etymologiarum* 10.3 (letter A): "Alumnus ab alendo vocatus, licet qui alit et qui alitur alumnus dici potest; id est qui nutrit et qui nutritur; sed melius tamen qui nutritur" (*Alumnus* comes from *alendo,* even though the one who is doing the nourishing as well as the one who is nourished can be called *alumnus;* that is to say, both the one who nurtures and the one who is nurtured; but it is best used to refer to the one who is nurtured); cp. the adjective *almus* in the discussion of *alma mater* in chapter 4.

169. Arrigo da Settimello, *Henrici Septimellensis Elegia sive De Miseria,* vv. 509–10: "Prima fovet pueros, alia silogizat, amenat/tertia colloquiis." Dante may well have studied this text as a young grammar student; see Petrocchi, *Vita di Dante,* 13.

170. "Nam hic parvulus suavius lactabitur, hic adultus uberius cibabitur." Cited by Paget Toynbee, "Dante's Latin Dictionary," 100.

171. Bonvesin da la Riva, *Vita scholastica,* vv. 5–12: "Reginam cernet nitido velamine comptam./Aspectu miram, virginitate meram./.../veri thesauri fertilitate gravem" (He there sees a queen adorned with shining white robes./She is wondrous in appearance, pure in her maidenhood /.../ pregnant with the fertility of a true treasure).

172. For a closer reading of nursing imagery in Boncompagno, see my "Dante, Boncompagno da Signa, Eberhard the German and the Rhetoric of the Maternal Body"; on Boncompagno, see also Ronald G. Witt, "Boncompagno and the Defense of Rhetoric."

173. *Rhetorica novissima* 9.3: "Prima quidem volvebatur laborioso impulsu, sed procedebat ex ea lac quod dabatur his qui erant in dentium plantativa." Cp. the *Rhetorica antiqua* (or *Buoncompagnus*), where Boncompagno provides rhetorical *formulae* to ridicule the "adult grammarian" as an oxymoronic perversion, "an old goat sucking at the udders of a young nanny" (Virgilio Pini, *Testi riguardanti la vita degli studenti a Bologna nel sec. XIII,* 12). For Boncompagno, the infant/student must nurse at the breast of grammar as briefly as possible and then turn away (Pini, 9–12).

Boncompagno further recalls his early grammar studies in Florence in terms parallel to those of Dante in the *De vulgari,* 1.6.3 ("quanquam Sarnum biberimus ante dentes"): "Tamen te certificio, quod inter floride civitatis Florentiae ubera primitive scientie lac suscepi" (Just the same I assure you that it was amidst the breasts of that most florid city of Florence that I took in the milk of the first art). We have already seen reference to teething/weaning as metaphor for acquisition of language skills in Martianus Capella, but the idea has a much older history; see Pliny the Elder, *Natural History* 7.15; cp. Boncompagno's reference to Saint Jerome's foreign language training in the *Boncompagnus* 1.23.3 (Pini, 48). For the phrase *in dentium plantativa* to characterize a subdivision of the life stage of *infantia,* see Bartholomeus Angelicus's encyclopedic *De rerum proprietatibus* (c. 1230; trans. 1309 into Mantuan vernacular) at 6.1; see also 6.9 on the *nutrix* (cited above). Thus straight teeth made for straight speech, and the wet nurse, Lady Grammar, governed both teething and language acquisition. Several medieval thinkers pointed to the appearance of teeth at age two as demarcating a subdivision of *infantia;* see Shahar, *Childhood in the Middle Ages,* 21–31.

174. *Rhetorica novissima,* 9.5: "Verumtamen quemlibet grammaticum assimilo illi qui est in dentium plantativa, qui lac sugit, recitat sicut puer, et cum dicit a, e, i, o, u, tamquam infantes vagire videtur. Iudicat enim de solis vocibus, quia bene sustinet et defendit regulariter esse dictum 'musca parit leonem' et 'angelus est cimera.'"

175. For a photograph, see d'Ancona, "Le rappresentazioni allegoriche delle arti liberali," 147; see also d'Ancona, 220. Nicola's other great pedestal monument, in the Baptistery at Pisa, does not include the Arts.

176. D'Ancona, "Le rappresentazioni allegoriche delle arti liberali," 221; for photograph, p. 152.

177. Cp. d'Ancona, "Le rappresentazioni allegoriche delle arti liberali," 221: "Affettuoso è l'atteggiamento della *Grammatica* piegata verso un allievo, il quale sembra intento a scrivere gl'insegnamenti della sollecita istitutrice." Rowley claims that the personifications of the Trivium found below Ambrogio Lorenzetti's "Allegory of Good Government" in the Sala Della Pace in the Palazzo Pubblico in Siena (early fourteenth century) are based on Giovanni's sculptures. In the case of Grammar, he must have in mind solely the Perugia fountain (not the Pisa pulpit), for Lorenzetti's figure leans gently over her pupil to consult an open book; see George Rowley, *Ambrogio Lorenzetti,* vol. 1, 106.

178. For photograph, see Michael Ayrton, *Giovanni Pisano, Sculptor,* fig. 324; Enzo Carli, *Giovanni Pisano,* fig. 109.

179. For photograph, see Ayrton, *Giovanni Pisano, Sculptor,* fig. 312; Carli, *Giovanni Pisano,* fig. 119.

180. For photograph, see van Marle, *Iconographie de l'art profane*, fig. 240. The reliefs are now on display (along with Luca Della Robbia's extraordinary reinterpretations from a century later) in the Museo dell'Opera del Duomo in Florence. See van Marle, *Iconographie de l'art profane*, 223ff.; Giulio Carlo Argan, *Storia dell' arte italiana*, vol. 2, 174; d'Ancona, "Le rappresentazioni allegoriche delle arti liberali," 228: "La *Grammatica*, una tozza figura muliebre, è rappresentata seduta, con la disciplina nella destra e la sinistra sollevata verso tre fanciulli, che la stanno ad ascoltare . . . Triste impressione fanno queste figure, paragonate con quelle che circa un secolo innanzi Nicola aveva effigiate nel pulpito di Siena." The tomb of King Robert in the Church of Santa Chiara, Naples (c. 1345), appears to have inherited at least in part the classical grace of Nicola and Giovanni. Grammar is the first figure on the left, behind the statue of Robert's body, and the only figure in profile. In addition to her flowing hair and garments and open book, however, there seems to be little significant detail. For photograph, see van Marle, *Iconographie de l'art profane*, 219, fig. 246. According to d'Ancona, the monument is by Pacio and Giovanni da Firenze. Regarding Grammar, see d'Ancona, "Le rappresentazioni allegoriche delle arti liberali," 270: "Tiene nelle mani un libro aperto e sembra meditarne profondamente i concetti: i capelli finissimi le incorniciano l'ovale del volto e il manto le cade al fianco rompendosi in armoniche pieghe."

181. Clark, "The Iconography of the Seven Liberal Arts," 6.

182. D'Ancona, "Le rappresentazioni allegoriche delle arti liberali," 283.

183. There were also tapestries of the arts in the Spanish Chapel; a fragment showing Arithmetic and Astronomy survives in the Memorial Art Gallery at the University of Rochester. In the *Centiloquio* (canto 55, which is dedicated to Dante), the Florentine poet Antonio Pucci (1310–88) portrays the seven Liberal Arts weeping over Dante's death; Lady Grammar calls Dante "caro signor mio e sposo" ("my dear lord and husband"); see Natalino Sapegno, *Poeti minori del trecento*, 349–420. Pucci may be imitating an earlier allegorical poem, "Morale delle sette arti," possibly by Pietro Alighieri; see Alessandro d'Ancona, ed., *In lode di Dante: Capitolo e sonetto di Antonio Pucci;* Giuseppe Corsi, *Rimatori del trecento*, 201–2.

184. Venturi, *Gallerie Nazionali Italiane* 4 and 5.

185. Bartolomeo di Bartoli da Bologna, *La canzone delle virtù e delle scienze,* ed. Leone Dorez, 76–77. See also J. von Schlosser, "Giustos Fresken in Padua und die Vorläufer der Stanza della Segnatura."

186. Bartolomeo di Bartoli da Bologna, *La canzone delle virtù e delle scienze,* 21 (my translation).

187. Bartolomeo di Bartoli da Bologna, *La canzone delle virtù e delle scienze,* 38. "Bella, gentile, legiadra è Gramaticha./E questa gioven che cum la mamilla/al fantulin distilla/el senno litterale, ond'el cognosse/più per quel lacte e posse/perfecto fare et

haver sapientia." There is here, I think, a pun on *seno* (breast); thus, "senno litterale" is both "knowledge of letters" and "the literal breast." For the link between suckling and mother tongue in a fourteenth-century French vernacular text, see the Boethius translator from Meun cited by Lusignan, *Parler vulgairement,* 71, who excuses himself for speaking the Meun dialect instead of Parisian: "Mais me raporte et me compère/Au parler que m'aprist ma mère/A Meun, quant je l'alaitoie" (But I compare myself to the speech my mother taught me in Meun when I was nursing at her breast).

188. Bartolomeo's verses with illuminations exist in a manuscript in the library of the Musée Condé in Chantilly, the one studied by Dorez and mentioned above (Image 5, p. 35); a second manuscript is in the Gabinetto Delle Stampe in Rome and has been studied by Adolfo Venturi, *Gallerie Nazionali* 4 and 5; a third manuscript in the Biblioteca Ambrosiana in Milan (MS B. 42) contains similar illuminations without Bartolomeo's poems (Image 6, above, p. 36). For a complete facsimile of the Chantilly manuscript, as well as select photographs from the other two, see Bartolomeo di Bartoli da Bologna, *La canzone delle virtù e delle scienze* (in particular p. 81, table 13). Dorez discusses the relationship among the various manuscripts. He also (p. 73) refers to two other related manuscripts that carry the same illustrations alongside Augustinian definitions of the Arts, but which replace Bartolomeo's poetry with various bits of moral and historical prose; cp. Clark, "The Iconography of the Seven Liberal Arts," 6. One is in the Biblioteca Nazionale in Florence (BANCO RARI 38; image 7, above, p. 37), the other is in the Nazional Bibliotech in Vienna (Ser. Nov. 2639, fol. 2v; formerly in the Ambras collection); both contain writings of Convenevole da Prato. In the MS Paris Lat. 8500 (Bibliothèque Nationale, Paris) of Northern Italian origin (second half of the fourteenth century), Grammar has abandoned the whip altogether in order to squeeze both breasts (Image 8, above, p. 38). This manuscript contains Cassiodorus's *Liber secularum litterarum* and, according to de Nolhac, was once owned by Petrarch.

189. Of further interest in these manuscripts are Bartolomeo's associations between the various cycles of seven (Arts and Virtues), which Dorez (Bartolomeo di Bartoli da Bologna, *La canzone delle virtù e delle scienze,* 90) links to a specifically Augustinian milieu; in the Augustinian Church of the Eremitani in Padua discussed above, the cycles of the Arts and Virtues were complemented by the seven Mechanical Arts, the seven Planets, and the seven Ages of Man. Dante will of course exploit the correspondences between the Arts and the Planets in *Convivio* 2 (Grammar = the moon); he will also discuss the Ages of Man in a somewhat modified version (he defines four or five) in *Convivio* 4; cp. Bartolomeo di Bartoli da Bologna, table 3. There is a second set of illustrations in a summary tree diagram at the end of the Arts section of the Chantilly manuscript (there is a corresponding "tree" at the end of the Virtues section). These illustrations recapitulate the earlier drawings in miniature and with somewhat less detail.

2. The Primal Scene of Suckling in *De vulgari eloquentia*

1. "It is the quiet shore of contemplation that I set aside for myself, as I lay bare, under the cunning, orderly surface of civilizations, the nurturing horror that they attend to pushing aside by purifying, systematizing, and thinking; the horror that they seize on in order to build themselves up and function?" Julia Kristeva, *Powers of Horror,* trans. L. S. Roudiez, 210.

2. Paul F. Gehl, *A Moral Art.*

3. Gehl, *A Moral Art,* 227. For more on classroom etiquette and discipline, see pp. 193–201.

4. Gehl, *A Moral Art,* 128–29.

5. Christiane Klapisch-Zuber, "Blood Parents and Milk Parents: Wet Nursing in Florence, 1300–1530," in *Women, Family, and Ritual in Renaissance Italy,* 132–64; in the same volume, see also "The 'Cruel Mother': Maternity, Widowhood, and Dowry in Florence in the Fourteenth and Fifteenth Centuries," 117–31. For an anthropological reading of female body fluids as a threat to the bodily integrity of the male (and the male social order), see Mary Douglas, *Purity and Danger,* 121 and 140–58; cf. Julia Kristeva, *Powers of Horror,* 56–89.

6. We will have occasion below to consider in greater detail Dante's definition of the life stages.

7. *Convivio* 4.24.14. *Convivio* English trans. by Lansing.

8. Cp. Guinizzelli, *Foco d'amor 'n gentil cor s'apprende,* cited in Battaglia, *s.v. voce;* Dante at *Inferno* 5.100–101, "Amor, ch'al cor gentil ratto s'apprende, prese costui della bella persona . . . ," where *s'apprende* is in end rhyme with *discende* and *m'offende.*

9. For an initial survey of acceptations, see Salvatore Battaglia, *Grande dizionario della lingua italiana, s.v. apprendere.*

10. See Charles DuCange and G. A. L. Heschel, *Glossarium mediae et infimae latinitatis, s.v. apprehendere.*

11. Cp. Jacopo da Lentini: "Non è da blasmare/omo che cade in mare—se s'apprende," cited in Battaglia; *Grande dizionario della lingua italiana, s.v. apprendersi,* acceptation 10 *(appigliarsi, aggrapparsi, afferrarsi),* where it is cited along with *Convivio* 4.24.4.

12. On the relative dating of the two works, see Pier Vincenzo Mengaldo's edition of the *De vulgari* (1968), vi–xxi.

13. On the dialectic of concealment and revelation with regard to the veiled female body in a completely different context, see Robert Pogue Harrison, *The Body of Beatrice.*

14. Cp. Stefano Rizzo, "Il *De vulgari eloquentia* e l'unità del pensiero linguistico di Dante," 72.

15. Ned Lukacher, *Primal Scenes,* 24. My post-Freudian conception of the primal scene is entirely indebted to Lukacher, who defines the structure as "an intertextual event that displaces the notion of the event from the ground of ontology. It calls the event's relation to the Real into question in an entirely new way. Rather than signifying the child's observation of sexual intercourse, the primal scene comes to signify an ontologically undecidable intertextual event that is situated in the differential space between historical memory and imaginative reconstruction, between archival verification and interpretive free play" (p. 24). For Lukacher's review of the primal scene in Freud, see in particular pp. 25–38 and 45–58. For the primal scene in Freud, see in particular *The Case of theWolf-Man;* see also Jean Laplanche and J.-B. Pontalis, *The Language of Psychoanalysis, s.v.*

16. See for instance Pio Rajna, *Il trattato "DeVulgari Eloquentia";* A. Ewert, "Dante's Theory of Language"; Roger Dragonetti, "La conception du langage poétique"; Cecil Grayson, "'Nobilior est vulgaris'"; PierVincenzo Mengaldo, "Gramatica"; Ileana Pagani, *La teoria linguistica di Dante;* Aldo D. Scaglione, "Dante and the Ars Grammatica"; Angelo Mazzocco, *Linguistic Theories in Dante and the Humanists.*

17. As we have seen in Quintilian, *Institutiones* 1.4.1; Cassiodorus, *Institutiones* 2.1.1-3; Isidore, *Etymologiae* 1.5.1.

18. Before Dante, this usage was common with the early Provençal grammarians, RaimondVidal (fl. late twelfth / early thirteenth century) and Uc Faidit (fl. first half of the thirteenth century), and remained current at least through the sixteenth century. See Raimond, *Las rasos de trobar* at 71.7; 71.16; 73.21; 73.37; 73.40; and Faidit, *Donats Proensals* at 1.4; 2.6; 4.6; 11.34; and 16.15 (both in J. H. Marshall's edition); it is also found in some early French translations of Latin texts; see Serge Lusignan, *Parler vulgairement,* 147; cp. Mengaldo's note 5 at *De vulgari* 1.1.3 (1979 ed.), and his "Gramatica."

19. This grouping can be found in writers as various as the pre-modist Petrus Helias (fl. c. 1150), Roger Bacon (1214?–94), and the author of the Tuscan verse paraphrase of Brunetto Latini's *Trésor.* See Petrus in Charles Thurot, *Notices et extraits de divers manuscrits latins,* 126–27; for an illuminating discussion of Petrus's relation to the later *modistae,* see Karin Margareta Fredborg, "Universal Grammar"; Roger Bacon, *Opus minus,* 33 (ed. Brewer; cited by Mengaldo, in the *De vulgari* edition of 1979, 31); for the paraphrase of Brunetto, see Mengaldo, "Gramatica"; cp. also Mengaldo's note at *De vulgari* 1.1.3 (1979); Henri de Crissey in Thurot, 131; Lusignan, *Parler vulgairement,* 59–61.

20. See in particular Maria Corti, *Dante a un nuovo crocevia;* Gian Carlo Alessio, "La grammatica speculativa e Dante"; Marianne Shapiro, *"DeVulgari Eloquentia,"*

133–74; Umberto Eco, "Languages in Paradise"; for a non-modistic interpretation, see Franco Lo Piparo, "Sign and Grammar in Dante."

21. The word *gramatica* (and related forms in Italian and Latin: *gramatice, gramatici*) appears seven times in the *De vulgari,* eight times in the *Convivio,* and once in the *De monarchia* (3.8.5). For a more thorough perusal of these usages, see my unpublished doctoral dissertation, "The Whip and the Wet Nurse," 58–100.

22. *Convivio* 2.11.9; 2.12.4; and, somewhat more problematically, 2.13.8. This last instance occurs by way of introduction to his fantastic metaphorical assimilation of Grammar to the Moon, which is anything but orthodox; cp. also *Paradiso* 12.138 ("la prim'arte").

23. *De vulgari* 1.11.1; 1.11.7; 2.7.6; *Convivio* 3.2.18; 4.6.3.

24. *De vulgari* 1.9.11: "Hinc moti sunt inventores gramatice facultatis: que quidem gramatica nichil aliud est quam quedam inalterabilis locutionis ydemptitas diversibus temporibus atque locis. Hec cum de comuni consensu multarum gentium fuerit regulata, nulli singulari arbitrio videtur obnoxia, et per consequens nec variabilis esse potest. Adinvenerunt ergo illam ne, propter variationem sermonis arbitrio singularium fluitantis, vel nullo modo vel saltim imperfecte antiquorum actingeremus autoritates et gesta, sive illorum quos a nobis locorum diversitas facit esse diversos" (This was the point from which the inventors of the art of grammar began: for their *gramatica* is nothing less than a certain immutable identity of language in different times and places. Its rules having been formulated with the common consent of many peoples, it can be subject to no individual will; and, as a result, it cannot change. So those who devised this language did so lest, through changes in language dependent on the arbitrary judgment of individuals, we should become either unable, or, at best, only partially able, to enter into contact with the deeds and authoritative writings of the ancients, or of those whose difference of location makes them different from us). All citations of the *De vulgari* are from Mengaldo (1979); English translations are from Botterill. Cp. *De vulgari* 1.1.3; 1.10.2; and *Convivio* 1.11.14. Traditionally, these uses in the *De vulgari* would fall under category three of my typology, but it is in these passages that critics such as Corti and Shapiro detect specific speculative influence, and thus a less historical, more abstract, sense. In point of fact, categories three and four of my typology are closely related: the former denotes those few select historical languages that derive their universality from an original association with divinity; the latter denotes a more secular (radical Aristotelian) principle that inheres in all languages. Perhaps nowhere are points of contact between the two more apparent than in the Henri de Crissey passage cited by Thurot, *Notices et extraits de divers manuscrits latins,* 131.

25. For other texts relevant to Dante's articulation of the acquisition of vernacular vs. Latin here, see Lusignan's discussion of, and citations from, Giles of Rome, *De regimine principum* (*Parler vulgairement,* 40–47) and Roger Bacon.

26. This apparent reversal has remained a central issue of *De vulgari* criticism for centuries; for a solid introduction, see Grayson, "'Nobilior est vulgaris'"; and more recently, Zygmunt G. Barański, *"Sole nuovo, luce nuova."*

27. Julia Kristeva, *Revolution in Poetic Language.*

28. Cp. Jacques Derrida, *Of Grammatology,* 152–56, on the wet nurse in Rousseau.

29. All citations of *Convivio* are from the Busnelli and Vandelli edition; English translations are from Richard Lansing.

30. Dante will of course refute the Averroistic moon-spot hypothesis in *Paradiso* 2.49–111.

31. See chapter 2, "Sacrifice and Grammar," in Giuseppe Mazzotta, *Dante's Vision and the Circle of Knowledge,* 34–55.

32. Horace, *Ars poetica,* 60–63; cp. *Paradiso* 26, 137–38. On natural linguistic variation, cp. *Convivio* 1.5.9–10, where Dante announces his intention to write the *De vulgari.* In his *Greek Grammar,* Roger Bacon discusses regional variations in spoken Latin; see Lusignan, *Parler vulgairement,* 72. On symbolic views of the moon generally, see Ernst Robert Curtius, *European Literature and the Latin Middle Ages.*

33. Aristide Marigo, in his edition of the *De vulgari;* Dragonetti, "La conception du langage poétique," part. p. 29; Corti, *Dante a un nuovo crocevia,* part. pp. 33–76; Robert Hollander, "Babytalk in Dante's *Commedia,*" 83.

34. His account is largely scriptural; see Barański, "Dante's Biblical Linguistics."

35. *De vulgari* 1.4.1: "Nunc quoque investigandum esse existimo cui hominum primum locutio data sit, et quid primitus locutus fuerit, et ad quem, et ubi, et quando, nec non et sub quo ydiomate primiloquium emanavit" (I think it now also incumbent upon me to find out to which human being that power was first granted, and what he first said, and to whom, and where, and when; and also in what language that primal utterance was made).

36. On the rhetorical construction of authority in the *De vulgari,* see Albert Russell Ascoli, *"Neminem ante nos."*

37. *De vulgari* 1.6.1 (my emphases).

38. Ascoli has also sensed the implications of Dante's gendered terminology; see *"Neminem ante nos,"* 200–201 and n. 28. Mengaldo glosses these phrases by recalling the commonplace tradition of Adamic circumlocutions, although Dante's motherless, milkless man appears to be without precedent. Most prominent was the "not of woman born" *mortuus et non natus* topos, which Dante himself will adopt at *Paradiso* 12.26: "quell'uom che non nacque." I would point out that even this more generic formula implies a radical detachment from the maternal body, which is equated to original sin, the stain of postlapsarian existence.

39. *De vulgari* 1.6.3. Cp. also *Convivio* 1.3.5: "Veramente io sono stato legno sanza vela e sanza governo, portato a diversi porti e foci e liti dal vento secco che vapora la dolorosa povertade" (Truly I have been a ship without sail or rudder, brought to different ports, inlets, and shores by the dry wind that painful poverty blows).

40. Regarding Dante's exile as a kind of individual Babel, cp. *Convivio* 1.3.4: "Poi che fu piacere de li cittadini [di . . .] Fiorenza, di gittarmi fuori del suo dolce seno,. . . *per le parti quasi tutte a le quali questa lingua si stende, peregrino, quasi mendicando, sono andato*" (Since it was the pleasure of the citizens of the most beautiful and famous daughter of Rome, Florence, to cast me out of her sweet bosom . . . *I have wandered like a pilgrim, almost like a beggar, through virtually all the regions to which this tongue of ours extends* [my emphases]). In this passage, the hopeful *questa lingua* would conjure "Italian," which—as we know from the *De vulgari*—is a purely conceptual and at times mythical unity that for Dante evokes the Babelic reality of the Italian peninsula. For a closer consideration of this passage, see below.

41. Barański, "Dante's Biblical Linguistics," 109, also notes the marginalization of the other two human catastrophes given the centrality of language to human history for Dante; on Dante and Babel, see also pp. 121–26. On the relation among grammar, vernacular, and Latin with reference to Babel, see Lusignan, *Parler vulgairement*, 15–47, and on the *De vulgari* specifically pp. 44–46.

42. *Paradiso* 26, 124–38. Adam essentially undoes the significance of Babel as a distinct historical event and is (in my view, purposefully) vague even on the nature of the alleged Edenic idiom. His definition is wholly negative ("whatever it was, it is no longer").

43. Cp. Eberhard the German's *Laborintus*, vv. 73–80, in Faral, which ironically links the suffering of the *grammaticus* to original sin. On the symbolic conflation of the three great human crimes, cp. *De genesi ad litteram* 9.12, in Dragonetti, where Augustine maintains that there was a universal language, not before Babel, but before the Flood (he thus contradicts his opinion in *De civitate dei* 16.3–5); see Dragonetti, "La conception du langage poétique," 18. On Babel as a second Fall, see Glauco Cambon, "Dante and the Drama of Language," 33 and 39.

44. On the content of these stylistic examples, cp. Mengaldo's note *ad loc.* and also *Linguistica e retorica di Dante,* 281–88.

45. Compare this to Barański, "Dante's Biblical Linguistics," 109, who argues more generally that for Dante of *De vulgari* 1 there is a "basic equation between history, language, and morality."

46. See Bonvesin de la Riva, *Vita scholastica,* and the anonymous *Rudium doctrina* for similar uses; for further references see Mengaldo's note *ad loc.*

47. See *Convivio* 1.1.4–15 and in part. 1.1.11: "Per che ora volendo loro apparecchiare, intendo fare un general Convivio di ciò ch'i' ho loro mostrato, e di quello pane

ch'è mestiere a così fatta vivanda, sanza lo quale da loro non potrebbe essere mangiata" (Wishing now to set their table, I intend to present to all men a banquet of what I have shown them and of the bread which must necessarily accompany such meat, without which it could not be consumed by them). Cp. *Convivio* 1.3.2: "Lo mio scritto, che quasi comento dir si può, è ordinato a levar lo difetto de le canzoni sopra dette, ed esso per sè fia forse in parte alcuna un poco duro" (My writing, which can almost be called a commentary, is intended to remove the defect of the canzoni mentioned above, and this may itself prove to be perhaps a little difficult [hard, like bread] in part).

48. Bartholomeus Angelicus, *De rerum proprietatibus,* 6.9, *s.v. nutrix:* "Cibum primo masticat, et masticando puero edentulo praeparat, ut facilius transglutiat cibum."

49. *Convivio* 1.1.12: "E però ad esso non s'assetti alcuno male de' suoi organi disposto, però che né denti né lingua ha né palato" (Therefore I would not have anyone be seated there whose organs are ill-disposed because he lacks teeth, tongue, or palate).

50. *Convivio* 1.1.16: "E se ne la presente opera, la quale è Convivio nominata e vo' che sia, più virilmente si trattasse che ne la Vita Nuova, non intendo però a quella in parte alcuna derogare, ma maggiormente giovare per questa quella; veggendo sì come ragionevolmente quella fervida e passionata, questa temperata e virile esser conviene" (If in the present work, which is called *The Banquet,* as I wish it to be, the subject is treated more maturely [in a more virile manner] than in *The New Life,* I do not intend by this in any way to disparage that book but rather more greatly to support it with this one, seeing that it understandably suits that one to be fervid and passionate, and this one tempered and mature [virile]).

51. *Convivio* 1.1.17: "Chè altro si conviene e dire e operare ad una etade che ad altra; perché certi costumi sono idonei e laudabili ad una etade che sono sconci e biasimevoli ad altra, sì come sotto, nel quarto trattato di questo libro, sarà propria ragione mostrata" (For it is proper to speak and act differently at different ages, because certain manners are fitting and praiseworthy at one age which at another are unbecoming and blameworthy, as will be shown below with appropriate reasoning in the fourth book).

52. *Convivio* 1.13.4.

53. *Convivio* 1.13.5.

54. Cp. *Convivio* 1.1.4: "L'altra è lo difetto del luogo dove la persona è nata e nutrita" (The other is the handicap that derives from the place where a person is born and bred [nourished]).

55. In his discussion of the *De vulgari,* the trecento poet Antonio Pucci describes Dante's exile from Florence as a loss of the breast; see the epigraph to the introduction and Sapegno, *Poeti minori del trecento,* 418–19.

56. "Childhood in Tuscany at the Beginning of the Fifteenth Century," in *Women, Family, and Ritual in Renaissance Italy,* 95—96; cp. Bartholomeus Angelicus 6.1; Shulamith Shahar, *Childhood in the Middle Ages,* 21—31.

57. In *Convivio* 1.4, Dante clearly demonstrates his penchant for using traditional categorical definitions as figures where he asserts that the great majority of humans live by the senses and not by reason, and thus in a kind of lifelong *puerizia* of the mind ("puerizia, non dico d'etate ma d'animo").

58. *De vulgari* 1.16.1 and 4, and 1.18.3: "Redolentem ubique et necubi apparentem . . . in qualibet redolet civitate nec cubat in ulla . . . velut acola peregrinatur."

59. Cp. Lacan's notion of the *Nom/n-du-Père;* see, in particular, Jacques Lacan, "On a question preliminary to any possible treatment of psychosis," in *Écrits,* 179—225; cp. Laplanche and Pontalis, *The Language of Psychoanalysis, s.v.*

60. Isidore remarks that the pre-dental infant period of *infantia* is characterized by fluidity *(fluida);* see *Sancti Isidori Liber Numerorum, Patrologia latina* 83, col. 188, as cited by Shahar, *Childhood in the Middle Ages,* 23.

61. Kristeva, *Powers of Horror,* 8.

62. Kristeva, *Powers of Horror,* 45.

63. On the link between nourishment in general and abjection, see Douglas, *Purity and Danger;* Kristeva, *Powers of Horror,* 75—79. On the scriptural foundations of food taboos, see the chapter in *Powers of Horror* entitled "Semiotics of Biblical Abomination," 90—112; particularly relevant to our present argument is the discussion of milk in Deuteronomy, p. 105.

64. *De vulgari* 1.8.1—2: "Ex precedenter memorata confusione linguarum non leviter opinamur per universa mundi climata climatumque plagas incolendas et angulos tunc primum homines fuisse dispersos. Et cum radix humane propaginis principalis in oris orientalibus sic plantata, nec non ab inde ad utrunque latus per diffusos multipliciter palmites nostra sit extensa propago, demumque ad fines occidentales protracta, forte primitus tunc vel totius Europe flumina, vel saltim quedam, rationalia guctura potaverunt" (The confusion of languages recorded above leads me, on no trivial grounds, to the opinion that it was then that human beings were first scattered throughout the whole world, into every temperate zone and habitable region, right to its furthest corners. And since the principal root from which the human race has grown was planted in the East, and from there our growth has spread, through many branches and in all directions, finally reaching the furthest limits of the West, perhaps it was then that the rivers of all Europe, or at least some of them, first refreshed the throats of rational beings).

65. *De vulgari* 1.10.4. For precedents in Lucan and Fazio degli Uberti, see Mengaldo's note *ad loc.*

66. Much traditional criticism on the *De vulgari* has tended to marginalize Dante's larger theoretical speculating on language and to see the treatise as a mere *rhetorica Dantis*. But Barański, "Dante's Biblical Linguistics," 110–12, is surely correct when he notes that the *De vulgari*'s philosophizing about the nature and origins of language lies closer to the heart of Dante's enterprise than the rhetorical niceties of book 2.

67. *De vulgari* 1.12.9; 1.13.5; 1.14.3; 1.14.7; 1.15.6. He breaks conspicuously with this formula only for Sordello; see Zygmunt G. Barański, "'Sordellus . . . qui . . . patrium vulgare deseruit.'"

68. *De vulgari* 1.18.1: "Nam sicut totum hostium cardinem sequitur ut, quo cardo vertitur, versetur et ipsum, seu introrsum seu extrorsum flectatur, sic et universus municipalium grex vulgarium vertitur et revertitur, movetur et pausat secundum quod istud, quod quidem vere paterfamilias esse videtur" (For, just as the whole structure of a door obeys its hinge, so that in whatever direction the hinge moves, the door moves with it, whether it opens towards the inside or the outside, so the whole flock of languages spoken in the cities of Italy turns this way or that, moves or stands still, at the behest of this vernacular, which thus shows itself to be the true head of their family [father of the family]).

69. Cp. Mengaldo's note *ad loc.*

70. See *De vulgari* 1.1.1: "Cum ad eam non tantum viri sed etiam mulieres et parvuli nitantur."

71. On the metaphorical link between the primal forest *(silva)* and Neoplatonic primal space as wet nurse *(silva* in Chalcidius), see chapter 4; on the primal forest in general, see Robert Pogue Harrison, *Forests*.

72. Not surprisingly, the nine words that the grammarian does then accept as exemplary of the new illustrious vernacular *(pexa)* embody the three great subject matters worthy of treatment in the new idiom, based upon the highest aspirations, respectively, of the three components of the Aristotelian soul (vegetative, animal, rational): *salus, venus, virtus*. Words commonplace in the lexicon of the vernacular poets, they are already firmly inscribed within a patriarchal system of linear, ordered thought: *amore, donna, disio, virtute, donare, letitia, salute, securtate, defesa*. In this light, the distance that separates the ideal *donna* of the *dolce stil nuovo* from the physical, vernacular *femina* is particularly significant; cp. Mengaldo's note *ad loc.*

73. On Dante's selective editing of Scripture, see Barański, "Dante's Biblical Linguistics," particularly under the subheading "Rewriting Genesis," 112–14.

74. Proverbs 1:8–15 (my emphases). English translations of the Vulgate are taken from *The Holy Bible. Translated from the Latin Vulgate*. "Audi, fili mi, disciplinam patris tui *et ne dimittas legem matris tuae*, ut addatur gratia capiti tuo et torques collo tuo. Fili mi, *si te lactaverint peccatores*, ne adquiescas eis; si dixerint: 'Veni nobiscum, insidiemur sanguini . . .' fili mi, ne ambules cum eis."

75. *Lacto* commonly conveyed the figurative meaning "to entice, seduce, deceive" at least as early as Terence (190?–159 B.C.); see *Thesaurus linguae latinae, s.v.*

76. *Convivio* 4.24.17–18: "E se non è in vita lo padre, riducere si dee a quelli che per lo padre è ne l'ultima volontade in padre lasciato; e se lo padre muore intestato, riducere si dee a colui che la Ragione commette lo suo governo. E poi deono essere obediti maestri e maggiori, c[ui] in alcuno modo pare dal padre, o da quelli che loco paterno tiene, essere commesso" (If the father is no longer living, it redounds to him to whom the Law entrusts his son's guidance. And next in order teachers and elders should be obeyed, to whom he seems in some way to have been entrusted by the father or by him who stands in the father's place).

77. *Convivio* 4.24.17 (my emphases).

78. Colossians 3:20 (my emphases): "Filii, obedite *parentibus* per omnia: hoc enim placitum est in Domino."

79. Barański, "Dante's Biblical Linguistics," 116–19, reminds us that such linguistic misogyny is perfectly in line with a tradition that begins with Paul and his commentators, who praise womanly silence as a virtue, and Gregory, who holds forth in the *Moralia in Job* on the insidiousness of female speech.

80. "Appellavitque Adam nominibus suis cuncta animantia et universa volatilia caeli et omnes bestias terrae."

81. For a critical review of the problem, see Mengaldo's note *ad loc.*

82. Warman Welliver mentions it but makes nothing of it. Marigo, André Pézard, and Mengaldo overlook it entirely.

83. "Dixitque Adam hoc nunc os ex ossibus meis et caro de carne mea haec vocabitur virago quoniam de viro sumpta est."

84. "Quamobrem relinquet homo patrem suum et matrem et adhaerebit uxori suae et erunt duo in carne una."

85. For the threat of gender confusion ("the heteroclite gender") to grammar and patriarchy in other late medieval texts, see R. Howard Bloch, *Etymologies and Genealogies;* cp. also Dante's scorn for Romagnolo in the *De vulgari* 1.4 as a transsexual idiom.

86. In "Dante's Biblical Linguistics" (in part. pp. 112–16), Barański notes in *De vulgari* 1 (in terms strongly parallel, I think, to my own) a rational, philosophical voice and a more personal voice; Barański identifies closely this latter with scriptural *sermo humilis* and in particular Genesis. At the opening of chapter 5 of this book, I will make explicit the conceptual link between what I defined here, with Kristeva's help, as the language of the semiotic nursing body and the *sermo humilis* of Scripture. While Barański's readings are not overtly psychoanalytic, he nonetheless detects in *De vulgari* 1 a "programmed subjectivity," the result of Dante's highly

personalized use of Genesis; he also refers to the presence of several "repressed" Biblical moments in the treatise, moments obfuscated by rational, philosophical discourse. Also, in "'Significar per verba'" ("*Sole nuovo, luce nuova*," chapter 2) Barański argues that Dante moves from a traditional grammar of linguistic separation and strict categorization in the *De vulgari* to a poetics of integration in the *Comedy;* that Dante came to an awareness of this new poetics while composing the treatise: "When this fact came to him, he emblematically foresook the *De vulgari* in mid-sentence," for the comic mode of the poem, which "abandons the traditional drive towards separation, and instead makes a virtue of integration" (p. 11). I am arguing that the nursing body, particularly as constructed within grammatical discourse, is the most compelling image of this new poetics of integration in tension with more traditional rules of separation.

3. The Body of Gaeta: Burying and Unburying the Wet Nurse in *Inferno*

1. Quotations of the *Comedy* are from *La Commedia secondo l'antica vulgata,* Giorgio Petrocchi, ed. (Milan: Mondadori, 1966–67), as reproduced by Charles Singleton ed. and trans., *The Divine Comedy.* English translations are from Singleton.

2. *Paradiso* 27.82–83.

3. Giuseppe Mazzotta, *Dante, Poet of the Desert,* 215; Jeremy Tambling, *Dante and Difference;* Kevin Brownlee, "*Inferno* XXVI." Peter S. Hawkins, "Virtuosity and Virtue," investigates ties among the cantos 24–26.

4. Franco Fido, "Writing Like God."

5. *Paradiso* 27.124–26.

6. See, above all, *Psalm* 8:3: "Ex ore infantium et lactentium perfecisti laudem propter inimicos tuos, ut destruas inimicum et ultorem" (Out of the mouth of infants and of sucklings thou hast perfected praise, because of thy enemies: that thou mayest destroy the enemy and the avenger). Dante cites this verse in part in his letter to the Italian Cardinals, *Epistola* 11.10: "Nam etiam in «ore lactentium et infantium» sonuit iam Deo placita veritas" (For even from the mouth of babes and sucklings has been heard the truth well pleasing to God); cp. Matthew 21:16.

7. *Paradiso* 27.127–29.

8. On babytalk in Dante's *Commedia,* see Robert Hollander, "Babytalk in Dante's *Commedia.*" As far as I can tell, André Pézard is the only critic to have read this passage in light of other nutritional metaphors in the poem and *Convivio* 4.24.14; see *Dante sous la Pluie de Feu,* 113–21, and in part. p. 119 (notes 1 and 2). In addition to *Psalm* 8, Pézard cites Frate Egidio (p. 117, n. 1), "Tutta la Scrittura che favella di Dio, sì ne parla quasi balbettando, sì come fa la madre che balbetta col figliuolo" (All

of Scripture speaks of God in the manner of a stammering baby, just as the mother stammers in babytalk to her young child).

9. *Aeneid* 6.899–901; 7.1–7: "Ille viam secat ad navis sociosque revisit;/tum se ad Caietae recto fert litore portum./Ancora de prora iacitur; stant litore puppes./Tu quoque litoribus nostris, Aeneia nutrix,/aeternam moriens famam, Caieta, dedisti;/et nunc servat honos sedem tuus, ossaque nomen/Hesperia in magna, si qua est ea gloria, signat./At pius exsequiis Aeneas rite solutis,/aggere composito tumuli, postquam alta quierunt/aequora, tendit iter velis portumque relinquit." Text of the *Aeneid* is from the Loeb Classical Library edition of Virgil; English translations are from Virgil, *The Aeneid,* trans. Robert Fitzgerald.

10. See Servius's commentary *ad loc.:* "TV QVOQVE sicut Misenus, Palinurus etiam." On Servius, see Martin Irvine, *The Making of Textual Culture,* 126–42.

11. On this point, see the article "Caieta" by Alessandro Barchiesi in the *Enciclopedia virgiliana.* I have also consulted the following: Alessandro Barchiesi, "Palinuro e Caieta"; Henriette Boas, *Aeneas's Arrival in Latium;* Eduard Fraenkel, "Some Aspects of the Structure of *Aeneid* VII"; Reinhold Merkelbach, "Aeneia Nutrix"; Ettore Paratore, "Caieta in Virgilio."

12. Servius 7.1: "Ut in principio diximus, in duas partes hoc opus divisum est: nam primi sex ad imaginem Odyssiae dicti sunt, quos personarum et adlocutionum varietate constat esse graviores, hi autem sex qui sequuntur ad imaginem Iliados dicti sunt, qui in negotiis validiores sunt: nam et ipse hoc dicit <45> maius opus moveo" (As I said in the beginning of my commentary, this work is divided into two parts: for the first six books are said to be in the image of *The Odyssey,* as they are weighed-down with a great variety of characters and speeches, and these six that follow, which are more straightforward in their material, are said to be in the image of *The Iliad:* for the poet himself says [verse 45], "A greater task awaits me").

13. See, for instance, Fraenkel, "Some Aspects of the Structure of *Aeneid* VII," 1: "If ever a poet was sensitive to the effects of symmetry and clearly marked arrangement, it was Virgil. And yet here, at one of the most conspicuous points of the Aeneid, he allows himself a glaring asymmetry"; and Barchiesi, "Palinuro e Caieta," 10: "Ci si può chiedere se questo congedo da una vecchia nutrice, mai ricordata altrove dal poeta, meriti il posto di rilievo che gli attribuisce l'economia dell'opera, giusto all'inizio della seconda esade—in modo tale che il *maius opus* iliadico si apre con un'apostrofe ad un personaggio non soltanto minore, ma umile e socialmente marginale." On textual criticism, see Fraenkel, 1, n. 2; cp. Paratore, "Caieta in Virgilio," who reads this moment to support his theory that the first six books were written later.

14. Barchiesi, "Palinuro e Caieta," 9–11.

15. On a modern map of Italy, one need only locate Gaeta and San Felice Circeo.

16. *Aeneid* 7.9–14: "Adspirant aurae in noctem, nec candida cursus/Luna negat, splendet tremulo sub lumine pontus./Proxima Circaeae raduntur litora terrae,/dives

inaccessos ubi Solis filia lucos/adsiduo resonat cantu, tectisque superbis/urit odoratam nocturna in lumina cedrum,/arguto tenuis percurrens pectine telas."

17. *Aeneid* 7.15–20: "Hinc exaudiri gemitus iraeque leonum/vincla recusantum et sera sub nocte rudentum,/saetigerique sues atque in praesepibus ursi/saevire, ac formae magnorum ululare luporum,/quos hominum ex facie dea saeva potentibus herbis/induerat Circe in voltus ac terga ferarum."

18. *Aeneid* 7.21–24: "Quae ne monstra pii paterentur talia Troes/delati in portus, neu litora dira subirent,/Neptunus ventis implevit vela secundis,/atque fugam dedit, et praeter vada fervida vexit."

19. Donatus, *ad loc.*, contrasts the good Trojans' fortune to the fate of some of Diomedes' men, who were changed to seabirds (see *Aeneid* 11.271–75): "Ne conversi in monstra bestiarum mutarentur informia pii Troiani. ecce dixit Troas perindeque causam qua ab his malis liberari meruerunt: pii fuerunt, inquit, nec debuerunt illis aequari qui pro nefariis actibus eiusmodi supplicia perferebant. hos tetigit quos supra mutatos dixit, de quibus Diomedes etiam locutus est in undecimo libro" (Nor are the good Trojans transformed into ugly, monstrous beasts. Here he also stated the cause for which the Trojans deserved to be freed from such evils: they were good, he says, and they should not be equated to those other men who had to endure such torments because of their evil actions. He referred to those men who, as he said above, had been transformed. Diomede also spoke of such men in the eleventh book).

20. We should recall the dual etymology of the Latin *monstrum* in *monstro* (to exhibit, to show) and *moneo* (to advise, to warn).

21. *Odyssey* 10.212–317: "Wolves and mountain lions lay there, mild in her soft spell, fed on her drug of evil . . . she prepared a meal of cheese and barley and amber honey mixed with Pramnian wine, adding her own vile pinch, to make them lose desire or thought of our dear father land . . . The lady Kirke mixed me a golden cup of honeyed wine adding in mischief her unholy drug."

22. Lino Pertile, "Dante e l'ingegno di Ulisse," underscores Dante's indebtedness to Ovid for his Ulysses in the *Comedy*.

23. Ovid, *Metamorphoses* 14.273–81: "Nec mora, misceri tosti iubet hordea grani/mellaque vimque meri cum lacte coagula passo,/quique sub hac lateant furtim dulcedine, sucos/adicit. accipimus sacra data pocula dextra./quae simul arenti sitientes hausimus ore,/et tetigit summos virga dea dira capillos,/(et pudet et referam) saetis horrescere coepi,/nec iam posse loqui, pro verbis edere raucum/murmur et in terram toto procumbere vultu" (At once she bade her maidens spread a feast of parched barley-bread, of honey, strong-wine, and curdled milk; and in this sweet drink, where they might lie unnoticed, she slyly squeezed some of her baleful juices. We took this cup which was offered by her divine hand. As soon as we had thirstily drained the cup with parched lips, the cruel goddess touched the

tops of our heads with her magic wand; and then [I am ashamed to tell, yet will I tell] I began to grow rough with bristle, and I could speak no longer, but in place of words came only hoarse, grunting sounds, and I began to bend forward with face turned entirely to the earth). All English trans. of Ovid are from Miller.

24. *Metamorphoses* 14.387, 403, 413: "Ter iuvenem baculo tetigit . . . illa nocens spargit virus sucosque veneni . . . ora venenata tetigit mirantia virga." For the specifically linguistic powers of Circe's potions in an early fourteenth-century reading of Ovid, see Pierre Bersuire, *Metamorphosis Ovidiana Moraliter . . . Explanata*, Liber XIIII, Fo. lxxxviii (Fa. ix, P–Q), in the 1509 manuscript facsimile published by Stephen Orgel in *The Philosophy of Images*. This text focuses on Picus's transformation into a magpie, a chatty bird with a very long tongue that catches many ants; i.e., the verbose man ("in picum cum lingua prolixa: id est hominem vagum et verbosum mutatur") captures many foolish listeners ("formicas id est fatuas mulieres . . . fatuos auditores") with his excessive rhetoric *(multiloquium)*. On the moral dangers of *multiloquium*, cp. below, John of Salisbury, *Policraticus* 8.24 (817b; 822d).

25. *Metamorphoses* 14.299–301: "Spargimur ignotae sucis melioribus herbae / percutimurque caput conversae verbere virgae, / verbaque dicuntur dictis contraria verbis."

26. Eberhard the German, *Laborintus* (in Faral) 231–32: "Corrige delicta verbis et verbere, verbis / Asperius, virgis conveniente modo."

27. "Annua nos illic tenuit mora."

28. "Litora adit nondum nutricis habentia nomen."

29. But compare 14.435: "Talia multa mihi *longum* narrata per *annum* [my emphases]" (Many such things I heard and saw during *a long year*).

30. Could Dante have known Donatus's commentary on the *Aeneid* at 6.901 ("ancora de prora iacitur; stant litore puppes")? "Portum Caietae ex persona poetae melius accipimus; *Aeneas enim nondum loco ipsi dederat nomen* [my emphases]" (We should best understand that the poet tells us that the port is Gaeta; *for Aeneas had not yet given the name to that place*).

31. *Metamorphoses* 14.156–61: "Troius Aeneas sacrisque ex more litatis / litora adit nondum nutricis habentia nomen. / Hic quoque substiterat post taedia longa laborum / Neritius Macareus, comes experientis Ulixei. / Desertum quondam mediis sub rupibus Aetnae / noscit Achaemeniden" (Making due sacrifices here, he next landed on a shore which did not yet bear his nurse's name. Here also Neritian Macareus, a comrade of all-suffering Ulysses, had stayed behind after the long weariness of his wanderings. He recognizes Achaemenides, whom they had left long since abandoned midst the rocks of Aetna).

32. See in part. 14.218–20: "Hanc procul adspexi longo post tempore navem / oravique fugam gestu ad litusque cucurri / et movi: Graiumque ratis Troiana recepit!" (And then, after a long time, far in the distance I saw this ship, and I begged

them by gestures to save me, I rushed down to the shore and I touched their hearts: a Trojan ship received a Greek!).

33. *Metamorphoses* 14.436–40: "Resides et desuetudine tardi/rursus inire fretum, rursus dare vela iubemur,/ancipitesque vias et iter Titania vastum/dixerat et saevi restare pericula ponti:/pertimui, fateor, nactusque hoc litus adhaesi" (At length, grown sluggish and slow through inactivity, we were ordered to go again upon the sea and again to spread our sails. The Titaness had told us of the dubious pathways of the sea, their vast extent, and all the desperate perils yet to come. I own I was afraid to face them and, having reached this shore, I stayed behind). Several critics have noted the suggestive similarity to *Inferno* 26.106: "Io e' compagni eravam vecchi e tardi." It seems that Fornaciari was the first to suggest that Ulysses' *orazion picciola* in *Inferno* 26 merely picks up where Ovid's Macareus leaves off; see Giorgio Padoan, "Ulisse *fandi fictor* e le vie della sapienza," 32; Antonino Pagliaro, "Il canto XXVI dell'*Inferno*," 28.

34. *Metamorphoses* 14.242–47: "Amissa sociorum parte dolentes/multaque conquesti terris adlabimur illis,/quas procul hinc cernis (procul est, mihi crede, videnda/insula visa mihi!) tuque o iustissime Troum,/nate dea, . . . /moneo, fuge litora Circes!" (Grieving for our lost companions and with many lamentations, we finally reached that land which you see at some distance yonder. [And, trust my word, I found 'twas best to see it at a distance.] And you, most righteous Trojan, son of Venus, . . . I warn you, keep away from Circe's shores!).

35. *Metamorphoses* 14.441–44: "Finierat Macareus, urnaque Aeneia nutrix/condita marmorea tumulo breve carmen habebat:/HIC _ ME _ CAIETAM _ NOTAE _ PIETATIS _ ALUMNUS/EREPTAM _ ARGOLICO _ QUO _ DEBUIT _ IGNE _ CREMAVIT."

36. *Metamorphoses* 14.445–46: "Solvitur herboso religatus ab aggere funis,/et procul insidias infamataeque relinquunt tecta."

37. Looking retrospectively at Caieta through medieval nurses and Lady Grammar, Ovid's choice of *alumnus*—foster son, surrogate son, student or pupil, charge of the wet nurse or substitute mother (from *alere; to nourish*)—is particularly suggestive; cp. *alma mater*, below.

38. Servius, Virgil's late fourth-century commentator, explains at 7.1: "AENEA NUTRIX hanc alii Aeneae, alii Creusae, alii Ascanii nutricem volunt. Lectum tamen est in philologis in hoc loco classem Troianorum casu concrematam, unde Caieta dicta est, 'apo tu chaiein'" (AENEAN NURSE some think this is Aeneas's nurse, some Creusa's, some Ascanius's. Nevertheless we read in the scholars that by chance the Trojan fleet was burned in this place, whence the name Caieta, *apo tu chaiein*). Compare to this Servius's contemporary, Aurelius Victor, in the *Origo gentis romanae*, 10.4–5: "Inde profectum pervenisse in eum locum, qui nunc portus Caietae appellatur, ex nomine nutricis eius, quam ibidem amissam sepeliit. At vero Caesar et

Sempronius aiunt Caietae cognomen fuisse, non nomen, ex eo scilicet inditum, quod eius consilio impulsuque matres Troianae taedio longi navigii classem ibidem incenderint, graeca scilicet appellatione 'apo tu chaiein,' quod est incendere" (Whence having made progress they came to that place which is now called the port of Caieta, from the name of his nurse, whom he buried there in the same manner. On the other hand, Caesar and Sempronius say that Caieta was a kind of nickname, not a proper name, given to her because it was through her urging and counsel that the Trojan women, worn out from the long journey, burnt the fleet. That is to say, her name is from the Greek, *apo tu chaiein,* which means "to burn"). On this etymology, see Barchiesi, "Caieta," and Paratore, "Caieta in Virgilio," 318.

39. See the above discussion of *Aeneid* 7.21 ("quae ne monstra pii paterentur talia Troes"). On the complex history of *pietas* from Virgil to Dante, see Robert Ball, "Theological Semantics," in particular p. 12: "Like its Greek equivalent *eusebia, pietas* fundamentally denotes the correct hierarchical relationship of a man to his superiors, and especially to father figures: the gods, the head of the family, and the fatherland." It should come as no surprise, then, that the cremation and burial of the nurse, the surrogate mother, connotes an act of *pietas.* On p. 20 and again on p. 251 (n. 7), Ball remarks that the allusion to Caieta in *Inferno* 26 is meant to link the two journeys and thus contrast Aeneas's *pietas* to Ulysses' lack thereof; but he describes the specific reference to Caieta as gratuitous (p. 20). I have argued that the specific choice of Caieta is charged with narrative and cultural significance.

40. The definitive study of Virgil commentary (and larger questions of Virgil's literary heritage) from late antiquity through the Renaissance remains Domenico Comparetti, *Virgilio nel Medioevo.* On Virgil's late antique commentators, see in particular chap. 5. Stanley Tate Collings, *The Interpretation of Virgil,* also provides a general survey of Virgil commentary through Dante. For a briefer introduction, see O. B. Hardison, Jr., ed., *Medieval Literary Criticism,* 64–69; see also Alastair J. Minnis, *Medieval Theory of Authorship;* Martin Irvine, *The Making of Textual Culture,* 118–21.

41. For Caieta, see pp. 3–5 in the Georges edition (hence Donatus). The famous grammarian Aelius Donatus also wrote an influential commentary on the *Aeneid,* now lost, but reflected in the commentary of Servius; see Irvine, *The Making of Textual Culture,* 121–26.

42. We should recall here the image of buried bones and teeth that will sprout again in life found in many early Christian discussions of resurrection; see my discussion of Caroline Bynum's work on the resurrection body in the next chapter and also Caroline Walker Bynum, *The Resurrection of the Body,* 31 and 54.

43. Donatus, 4–5: "'Litoribus,' inquit, 'nostris,' hoc est Italiae: quid tam pulchrum tamque egregium provenire potuisset quam illic condi reliquias eius ibique Aeneae nutricis nomen excellere ubi qui ipsius uberibus nutritus esset fuerat cum posteris regnaturus perindeque esset aeterna utriusque memoria, scilicet illius semper per se et

per posteros imperantis et illius perpetua sepulchri consecratione? celeberrima Aeneia nutrix qualem vel ubi memoriam consequi debuit cuiusque erat totum quicquid per Aenean Romanis rebus prospere videretur feliciterque conlatum?" (He says *litoribus nostris,* which means Italy: what more beautiful or honorable thing could have come to pass than to have buried her remains there where her name would also be esteemed through history, where he who by those very breasts had been suckled would reign with his successors just as both their names would endure in eternal memory: that is to say, the name of the ruler would live on in glory through his actions and those of his successors, and her name would live on through the perpetual consecration of her grave? For what other sort of memorial [where else?] should the illustrious nurse of Aeneas have received, she who—as would be seen—had successfully and happily conferred all things upon the Romans through Aeneas?).

44. Donatus, 6: "Post curam Caietae depositam oportunitas navigandi matura et commoda subinde successerat" (After the careful burial of Caieta immediately followed time ripe for sailing).

45. Leslie George Whitbread, ed. and trans., *Fulgentius the Mythographer,* 103–53. This volume offers a thorough introduction to Fulgentius and his works, and also contains translations of the *Mythologiae* and lesser works. See also the introduction and translation in Hardison, *Medieval Literary Criticism,* 64–80, from which all English translations here are taken. See Domenico Comparetti, *Virgil in the Middle Ages,* 104–18, on Christian allegorizations of Virgil and on Fulgentius in particular; pp. 110–11 provide a useful summary of Fulgentius's allegorical reading of the *Aeneid.* On Fulgentius, see Irvine, *The Making of Textual Culture,* 155–60.

46. On the problem of authorship and relevant bibliography on this famous Chartrian commentary, see Julian W. Jones and Elizabeth F. Jones, eds., *The Commentary,* ix–xiv; see also Winthrop Wetherbee, *Platonism and Poetry,* 105 and n. 76; Alastair J. Minnis and A. B. Scott, eds., *Medieval Literary Theory and Criticism c. 1100–c. 1375,* 112–26. For a discussion of this commentary and the commentary on Martianus also commonly attributed to Bernard, see Wetherbee, 104–25, and Brian Stock, *Myth and Science,* 33–40; Peter Dronke (introduction to Bernardus Silvestris, *Cosmographia,* 3) accepts both commentaries as the work of Bernard. For a more general discussion of medieval allegories of the *Aeneid,* see Comparetti, *Virgil in the Middle Ages,* 104–18; Padoan, "Ulisse *fandi fictor* e le vie della sapienza," 34–38. Comparetti, 211–23, is fairly convinced that Dante did not know Fulgentius, but he certainly knew one or both of Fulgentius's twelfth-century imitators, Bernardus Silvestris (whom Comparetti knows, erroneously, as Bernard of Chartres) and John of Salisbury; for Dante's knowledge of Bernardus's commentary, see also Ernst Robert Curtius, *European Literature and the Latin Middle Ages,* 354–55; and Theodore H. Silverstein, "Dante and Vergil the Mystic," especially pp. 78–82.

47. Thus the lyre player Iopas of *Aeneid* 1 becomes for Fulgentius a wet nurse, purveyor of song and speech to the silent infant; see Helm's edition of Fulgentius (hence Fulgentius), 93, lines 12–16; Hardison, *Medieval Literary Criticism,* 74 (my emphases): "Iopas e | nim Grece quasi | siopas dictus est, id est taciturnitas puerilis. *Infantia enim blandiloquiis semper nutricum <et> cantibus oblectatur; unde et crinitum eum posuimus vertici muliebri similimum*" (Iopas in Greek is *siopas [siope]*—that is, the silence of a child. *Infants are always soothed by the sweet words and songs of nurses; and to symbolize this I described Iopas with long hair like that of a woman*). At *Aeneid* 1.740, Iopas is described as *crinitus*.

48. Fulgentius, 103–4, lines 14–20, 1–4; Hardison, *Medieval Literary Criticism,* 79: "In septimo vero Caieta nutrice sepulta, id est magistriani timoris proiecta gravidine—unde et Caieta dicta est quasi coactrix aetatis; nam et aput antiquos caiatio dicebatur puerilis cedes . . . nam evidenter monstratur quia in modum disciplinae posita est, dum diximus: 'Aeternam moriens famam Caieta dedisti'; disciplina doctrinae quamvis studendo desciscat, aeternum tamen memoriae semen hereditat. Ergo pedagogantis suspectione sepulta ad desideratam olim pervenitur Ausoniam." We should note that as *coactrix aetatis,* Caieta is not so much "forcer of youth" as a forcer or compeller of a life stage *(aetas):* she sets in motion and presides over the generational transition from one life stage to the next.

49. Fulgentius, 104, lines 3–7; Hardison, *Medieval Literary Criticism,* 79: "Ergo pedagogantis suspectione sepul | ta ad desideratam olim pervenitur Ausoniam, id est ad boni crementa, quo omnis sapientum voluntas avida alacritate festinat,—Ausonia enim apo tu ausenin, id est cremento—sive etiam quod usque in hac aetate crementa sint corporum" (Therefore, having buried school matters, Aeneas arrives at his much-desired Ausonia—that is, "increase of good" toward which the desire of wise men eagerly hastens. *Ausonia* is from *apo tu ausenin [apo toi auxanein]*—that is, "of increase." Another explanation is that even at this age the body continues to grow). It seems to me that the clear implication of Fulgentius's locution *usque in hac aetate* is that growth takes place "all the way up to this age," in which growth is then perfected or completed. For Fulgentius on Circe and Ulysses, see *Mythologiae* 2.7–9. Macrobius writes that *grammatica* is the gateway to Roman *pietas;* see Irvine, *The Making of Textual Culture,* 13.

50. For a fuller account of this Neoplatonic image, see the following chapter.

51. *Expositio,* Jones and Jones, *The Commentary,* 4: "Dea vero partus dicitur quia calore et humore partus concipitur, formatur, alitur. Unde dicitur Iuno quasi novos iuvans" (She is called the goddess of childbirth because childbirth is conceived, formed, and nourished through warmth and moistness. Whence she is called Juno, which means "she who assists newborns"). Bernardus uses the Aristotelian theory of contrary qualities to assign Jupiter, Juno, Neptune, and Pluto places in the elemental universe (respectively, fire, air, water, and earth).

52. On this nondiscriminating picture language, see Jones and Jones, *The Commentary*, 12. At 1.516 (Jones and Jones, 13), Aeneas's men are compared to his body, which at this stage leads him along for he does not yet command it through reason/speech: "Socios videt nube tectus et non videtur ab eis nec alloquitur eos . . . non alloquitur eos qui nec revocat membra a turpibus nec propellit ad honesta" (Hidden away in this cloud, he sees his men and is not seen by them, nor does he speak to them . . . he does not speak to them as he fails to summon his members away from wicked temptation [i.e., Dido] and urge them toward virtue). Bernardus's description of Iopas at 1.740 alludes to the wet nurse and Lady Grammar (Jones and Jones, 13): "Suscipitur in epulis et carminibus Iope: alimentis educatur et garrulitate puerili permulcetur. Iopas enim puerilis taciturnitas dicitur; quamvis enim sonum emitat, vocem tamen perlevem non format" (He is carried into the banquet and the songs of Iopas: as the infant is brought up and educated with nourishment and he delights in the prattle of children. For Iopas means "the silence of children"; for even though he makes a sound, he nevertheless cannot form even the slightest whole word).

53. Jones and Jones, *The Commentary*, 14: "In hoc secundo volumine secunde etatis, id est pueritie, describitur natura. Infantia est illa pars prima vite que est a nativitate usque dum homo naturaliter loquatur. Pueritia est illa secunda pars vite humane que incipit ex quo homo incipit esse sub disciplina custodie et protenditur usque dum a custodia exeat. Unde infantia dicitur ab in et for, faris; pueritia vero a pure, id est custodia. In hoc maxima est differentia infantie et pueritie quod pueri loquuntur, infantes vero loqui non possunt naturaliter ideoque nichil aliud mistice in hoc volumine secundo significatur nisi initium et possibilitas loquendi" (In this second book the nature of the second life stage, that is *pueritia,* is described. *Infantia* is that first part of life which runs from birth through to when the individual begins to speak naturally. *Pueritia* is the second part of human life, which starts when the individual comes under the discipline of a guardian and extends all the way to when he leaves the guardian. For which *infantia* comes from *in* and *for, faris* [to speak]; *pueritia* instead from *pure,* which is to say "guardianship." The biggest difference between *infantia* and *pueritia* is that boys *[pueri]* can speak whereas infants cannot by nature. Thus there is no other mystical meaning represented in this second book except the beginning and possibility of speech).

54. Jones and Jones, *The Commentary,* 22: "Filia Solis dicitur quia omnis opulentia ex semine eius, id est solis calore agente in terra, procreatur. Hec propinat pocula ex herbis, id est voluptates ex temporalibus bonis, quibus socii Ulixis, id est socii sapientis, id est insipientes, in belvam mutantur. Belva fit ex homine dum homo qui naturaliter rationalis et immortalis erat secundum animam nimia delectatione temporalium fit irrationalis et mortalis" (She is called the daughter of the Sun because all luxuriance is born of such seed, that is to say of the Sun's heat acting upon the earth. She offers cups filled with a magic herbal brew, that is to say with the sensual

pleasures of worldly goods, by means of which Ulysses' men—that is the companions of the wise man, or the unwise—are changed to wild beasts. A wild beast is made from a man when the man, who was by nature rational and immortal in his soul, becomes irrational and mortal for having taken excessive pleasure in the things of this world). On Circe, compare the Martianus commentary, 4.244–74 (Bernardus Silvestris, *The Commentary,* ed. Haijo Jan Westra, 91–92); and, of course, Boethius, *De consolatione philosophiae,* 4, meter 3, especially vv. 5–7 (Solis edita semine/Miscet hospitibus novis/Tacta carmine pocula) and vv. 18–24.

55. See 3.707 (Jones and Jones, *The Commentary,* 23): "Sepelit patrem in Drepano. Drepanus quasi 'drimus pes,' id est acerbitas puerilis, interpretatur que est iracundia que pueros maximo fervore solet infestare. In iracundia pater sepelitur cum oblivioni deus datur. Iracundi enim pene apostatantur. Sepultura quedam oblivio est" (He buries his father in Drepanum. Drepanum can be understood as *drimus pes,* that is childish bitterness, which refers to the rage that tends to infest young boys with great fervor. His father is buried in rage as God is given up to oblivion. For the wrathful almost forget their faith. Burial is a kind of oblivion).

56. Jones and Jones, *The Commentary,* 25: "Increpat Mercurius Eneam oratione alicuius censoris. Discedit a Didone et desuescit a libidine" (Mercury scolds Aeneas with the speech of a severe moral judge. He gets him away from Dido and frees him from the habit of lust).

57. Jones and Jones, *The Commentary,* 26: "Quattuor certamina, dimissa Didone, ad honorem patris celebrat quia dimissa luxuria quattuor virtutum exercicia in virili etate deo immolat" (Having abandoned Dido, he celebrates four contests in honor of his father because once lust has been left behind in the manly age he offers up to God his practice of the four virtues). Jones and Jones, 27: "Monetur imagine patris ad inferos descendere visurus ibi patrem, id est cogitatione quadam imaginaria quam de creatore habet" (He is advised by the image of his father—that is, by a kind of imaginary vision of the Creator he has—to descend to the underworld where he will actually see his father).

58. See 5.840 (Jones and Jones, *The Commentary,* 28): "Tunc moritur Palinurus nauta. Palinurus dicitur quasi palans noron, id est errabundus visus. Hic hactenus naves Enee duxit, id est voluntates, sed dum ammonetur Eneas videre patrem, moritur Palinurus, id est demigrat errabundus visus" (Then the seaman Palinurus dies. Palinurus means *palans noron,* that is "errant vision." Up to this point, he steered Aeneas's ships, that is his will, but when Aeneas learns that he is to see his father, Palinurus dies, that is "errant vision" departs); cp. 6.337–38 (Jones and Jones, 83), where Dido and Palinurus reappear to Aeneas as memories of an earlier life stage and errors overcome.

59. Jones and Jones, *The Commentary,* 60: "Misenum in sepulcrum ponere est gloriam oblivioni mandare quod monet intelligentia" (Placing Misenus in his tomb

equals sending concern for human glory into oblivion, which rational intelligence advises); cp. 6.189 (Jones and Jones, 63).

60. Trivia is Diana as goddess of the underworld and crossways. *Aeneid* 6.13: "Iam subeunt Triviae lucos atque aurea tecta" (Here Trojan captains/Walked to Diana of the Crossroads' wood/And entered under roofs of gold); the Fairclough translation reads, simply, "Now they pass under the grove of Trivia and the roof of gold." For Diana as Trivia in Dante, see *Paradiso* 23.25–30.

61. See Jones and Jones, *The Commentary*, 30–31: "Relicto errabundo visu incipit rationalis spiritus voluntatem suam ratione que est gubernaculum regere a quibusdam eam cohibendo et ad quedam propellendo et tunc appellit classem nemori Trivie, id est applicat studiis eloquentie voluntatem" (Having abandoned errant vision, the rational spirit begins to rule his will through reason, which is a kind of rudder, holding it back from certain things and propelling it toward others; and then he directs his fleet to the wood of Trivia, which is to say he applies his will to the study of eloquence). Compare pp. 32–34 and in particular 6.5 (Jones and Jones, 33): "Nota ordinem: prius obvertuntur naves pelago, deinde applicantur litoribus quia prius contraponende sunt voluntates libidinibus carnis, deinde applicande incohationibus studii" (Take note of the order of events here: first the ships are turned to face the open sea, then they are anchored to the shore because first the will must be opposed to the desires of the flesh, then applied to the elementary stages of study).

62. Jones and Jones, *The Commentary*, 36, at 6.13: "Quia dixerat Eneam subire lucos TRIVIE, id est studia eloquentie, ostendit qualiter id fiat. Hoc autem fit per instructionem in actoribus. Sunt namque poete ad philosophiam introductorii, unde volumina eorum 'cunas nutricum' vocat Macrobius." Bernardus takes the phrase *cunas nutricum* from *In Somnium Scipionis* 1.2.8, but violates Macrobius's meaning there. For Macrobius, the fables recited in nurseries may delight the infant ear, but can have nothing to do with philosophy. On the movement from open sea to shore as allegorical representation of the movement away from lust toward the arts and reason, see also Jones and Jones, 38, and in part. "Hee namque artes mentis occulum corporeis sensibus turbatum rursus illuminant" (For these arts shed light on the eye of the mind, which has been altogether muddled by the bodily senses). For Macrobius on Virgil, see Irvine, *The Making of Textual Culture*, 142–48.

63. *Aeneid* 6.305–10; cp. *Inferno* 3.112–17.

64. Jones and Jones, *The Commentary*, 78–79: "In omnibus integumentis per patres et matres accipimus preceptores, per filios et filias eos qui doctrina eorum formantur, id est discipulos" (In all allegorical coverings we should understand fathers and mothers to mean teachers, sons and daughters those formed by their instruction, that is students).

65. Jones and Jones, *The Commentary*, 79: "Duas vitas et duas mortes et duas sepulturas in integumentis philosophia intelligit. Una vita secundum Stoicos est lib-

ertas anime in virtutibus et scientiis manens que ab eisdem Stoicos philosophia dicitur. Altera est secundum Epicureos corporearum voluptatum servitus quam solam isti vitam arbitrantur. Est ergo illa vita anime, haec carnis. Prima mors est prime vite finis, oppressio viciorum que est vera mors. Altera mors est viciorum mortificatio quam Plato ait philosophantibus appetendam. Hanc mortem persuadebat qui dicebat 'mortificate membra vestra.' Una sepultura est cognitorum intimatio in firma memoria in qua sepliende sunt virtutes et scientie. Altera sepultura est in qua Misenus et Palinurus sepeliendi sunt, scilicet involutio in oblivionem." The logic here is, to say the least, confusing for readers used to Dante's understanding of *seconda morte* in *Inferno* 1.117; cp. Apocalypse 20:14 and 21:8. On the Christian idea of two deaths as it relates to Aeneas and Ulysses in *Inferno* 26, see John Freccero, "Dante's Ulysses," in his *Dante: The Poetics of Conversion,* 148–49.

66. *Policraticus* 8.24 is entitled *Epicureos numquam assequi finem suum* (Epicureans Never Attain Their Goal). For the Latin text of the *Policraticus* I have used the edition of C. C. J. Webb; English translations are from Joseph B. Pike, *Frivolities of Courtiers.*

67. See 815b–c: "De loco voluptatis exclusus est homo, ex quo libido praevaluit, eo quod vita iocunda et tranquilla frui non potest cui coeperit libido dominari. Maluit facere quod libuit quam quod iussus est et proiectus in locum miseriae in terram laboris missus est, ut ei et semini suo terra spinas et tribulos germinet et in sudore vultus comedat panem suum qui in rectitudine voluntatis obediens sine difficultate et labore plenam poterat habere voluptatem . . . Si ergo sudatur in eo qui confirmat cor hominis et etiam in sumendo quod letificat, quid est quod sine labore sibi natura mortalis credat indultum?" (Man was excluded from the place of pleasure from the moment that lust prevailed for the reason that life can be neither pleasing nor tranquil for one who has begun to be swayed by it. Man preferred to do what he pleased rather than what he was commanded and was cast out into the place of misery, into the land of labor, in order that the earth put forth, for him and his seed, thorns and thistles, and that he, who obedient in rectitude of desire might have had full pleasure with no difficulties and labor, should eat his bread by the sweat of his brow . . . If therefore there is sweating for that which strengthens man's heart and that gives him joy even in partaking, what is there that mortal man should suppose conceded to him without labor?). Cp. 819b: "Ad arborem scientiae manum extendit, gulam implevit" (Man stretched out his hand to the tree of knowledge, satisfied his greed [gluttony]). One might recall in this context *Purgatorio* 3.37–45.

68. In 815c–d, John plays with the rhetoric of Genesis 3:16: "Parit ergo in dolore filios virtutum quae sine labore parit sobolem vitiorum. Natura namque peccatrix ad malum prona est et corrupta ab adolescentia sua, quae etas origini vicinatur, ut sine labore et erecta sine difficultate et gratia stare non possit. Parit itaque vitia, filias utique non filios, sine dolore sed procul dubio ad dolorem; sed in dolore filios, sed plane ad gaudium non dolorem" (She therefore who brings forth offspring of

sin without labor brings forth in sorrow children of the virtues; for sinful nature is prone to evil and is corrupt from its youth, an age that is near to its origin, so that without labor or difficulty it can fall, and cannot be lifted up to goodness without labor, and when lifted up it cannot stand without difficulty and without grace. She therefore brings forth sins, daughters, not sons, without sorrow but indubitably for sorrow; on the other hand sons in sorrow, but assuredly for joy, not sorrow).

69. *Policraticus* 816c-d: "Exinde inclinata est ad malum natura hominis, cuius quasi quaedam infantia praecessit innocens, dum a colloquiis pervertentibus et perversis abstinuit. Siluit homo et mansit innocens, immisso sopore obdormivit innocens, expergefactus et agnoscens auxilium simile quod ei fabricaverat Deus, innocenter locutus est magnalia Dei; sed ex quo factus verbosior per ostium curiositatis eductus exercuit cum temptatore verbi commercium." John's notion of speech as a kind of sinful adult commerce echoes such Augustinian locutions as, for instance, "venditores grammaticae vel emptores" (*Confessions* 1.13); and rhetoricians as "salesmen of words" *(De doctrina christiana)*.

70. Acts 2:11: "Cretes et arabes audivimus eos loquentes magnalia Dei" (Cretes and Arabians, we have heard them speak in our tongues the wonderful works of God).

71. See 816d: "Quasi ab infantia adolescens concepto calore intumuit et praevaricatus mandatum, cuius custodia ad gloriam fuerat profutura, corruptus est ut ex tunc mirabili et invicibili lege conditionis inflictae sibi unio reluctetur carnis et spiritus ut nulla ratione componi possint, nisi illius gratia intercedat qui fecit utraque unum et carnem in electorum fine faciet a spiritu absorberi" (As if he had attained maturity after childhood, he was swollen with the pride within him; and transgressing the command the keeping of which would have profited for his glory, he was corrupted, with the result that after the marvelous and inviolable law of the condition then imposed upon it, this union of flesh and spirit rebelled, so that in no way can the two be harmonized without the intervention of the grace of Him who hath made both one and will make flesh to be absorbed by spirit at the judgment of the elect).

72. *Policraticus* 816d–817a: "Si verbis gentilium uti licet Christiano, qui solis electis divinum et Deo placens per inhabitantem gratiam esse credit ingenium, etsi nec verba nec sensus credam gentilium fugiendos, dummodo vitentur errores, hoc ipsum divina prudentia in Eneide sua sub involucro fictitii commenti innuisse visus est Maro, dum sex etatum gradus sex librorum distinctionibus prudenter expressit" (If the words of the pagan may be employed by the Christian who believes that a nature divine and pleasing to God because of the grace inherent in it can belong to the elect alone [although I do not think that either the words or the thoughts of the pagans are to be shunned provided their errors are avoided], Virgil seems to have been by divine wisdom given a hint of this very fact. Under the cloak of poetic imagination in his

Eneid he subtly represents the six periods of life by the division of the work into six books).

73. Like Servius, John feels the first six books imitate the *Odyssey;* see 817a: "Quibus conditionis humanae, dum Odisseam imitatur, ortum exprimere visus est et processum, ipsumque, quem educit et provehit, producit et deducit ad Manes. Nam Eneas, qui ibi fingitur animus, sic dictus eo quod est corporis habitator; 'ennos' enim, ut Grecis placet, habitator est, 'demas' corpus et ab his componitur Eneas ut significet animam quasi carnis tugurio habitantem" (In these, in imitation of the *Odyssey,* he appears to have represented the origin and progress of man. The character he sets forth and develops he leads on and conducts down into the netherworld. For Eneas who therein represents the soul, is so named for the reason that it is a dweller in the body, for *ennos,* according to the Greeks, is "dwelling," and *demas* "body." The name Eneas is formed of these two elements to signify life dwelling, as it were, in a hut of flesh). Cp. Bernardus, Jones and Jones, *The Commentary,* 10; Macrobius, *Saturnalia* 10.182. For a brief comparative discussion of Fulgentius, Bernardus, and John, see David Thompson, *Dante's Epic Journeys,* 21–28.

74. *Policraticus* 817a–b: "Primus itaque liber Eneidos sub imagine naufragii manifestat infantiae, quae suis procellis agitatur, exponit tunsiones; et in fine suo habundantia cibi et potus adulta prosilit ad letitiam convivialem" (The first book of the *Aeneid* then, under the figure of a shipwreck, sets forth the manifest tribulations of childhood, which is shaken by its own tempests; and at the termination of the period the abundance of food and drink of manhood is in evidence at the gaiety of the banquet).

75. *Policraticus* 817b: "In confinio ergo adolescentiae prodeunt colloquiorum commercia, et eorum intemperies aut fabulas narrat aut veris falsa permiscet, eo quod multiloquio peccata deesse non possunt" (On the confines of boyhood conversation facilitates the interchange of ideas, and its freedom from restraint leads to the narration of stories and the mingling of the true and the false for the reason that a multitude of words cannot want sin). For *multiloquio,* cp. 822d, in the very last sentence of the *Policraticus* ("In multiloquio peccatum non deest"; in a multitude of words there does not want sin); and Proverbs 10:19: "In multiloquio non deerit peccatum, qui autem moderatur labia sua prudentissimus est" (In the multitude of words there will not want sin: but he that refraineth his lips is most wise). We recall such Dantean coinages in the *De vulgari* as *tristiloquium* (1.11.2) and *turpiloquium* (1.13.4), which were, according to Mengaldo, common in early Christian Latin; see Mengaldo (1979) *ad loc.* and compare, above, Fulgentius's (p. 93, line 14) *blandiloquiis nutricum.*

76. Much like Dante, as we have seen, in *Convivio* 4.24.

77. See *Policraticus* 817b–c and *Ars poetica* 161–68.

78. *Policraticus* 817b–c: "Prima ergo etas nutricem, secunda custodem habet,

tertia quo liberior, eo facilius errat, nondum tamen procedit ad crimina" (The first period, then, has its nurse; the second its guardian; the third, the freer it is the more easily it is led astray but not yet so far as to commit crime).

79. *Policraticus* 817b: "Quarta illicitos amores conciliat et ignem imprudenter conceptum in pectore ad amantis infelicem producit rogum. Neque enim inconcessis fatalem beatitudinem esse sub typo Mercurii ratio persuadet, docteque illum qui, dum fuerat parvulus, agebat ut parvulus, fuga irrefragabiliter apprehensa, evacuare quae erant parvuli" (The fourth period introduces illicit love and fans the flame unwisely lit within his heart, to kindle the pyre of the ill-fated queen; for reason, personified by Mercury, persuades that happiness is not ordained for forbidden love and teaches that he who, when he was a child, understood as a child, spoke as a child, and acted as a child, after he had irrevocably taken to flight puts away the things of a child). Compare 1 Corinthians 13:11.

80. *Policraticus* 817d: "Ergo et virilis etas puerilia et iuvenilia erubescit et, si a perversa voluptate et immundo amore navigii sui solvere non potest anchoram, praecidit et funem. Sic et patriarchae pudicus filius pallium reliquit adulterae, ne adulterii crimine involveretur" (Therefore mature manhood blushes at childish and youthful things, and if one has not power to weigh [pull up] anchor and flee from perverted pleasure and impure love, he will sever the cable). Compare *Aeneid* 4.575 ("tortosque incidere funis") and Genesis 39:12; for John on Circe, see *Policraticus* 1.4.

81. He thus covers all the categories Dante will use in *Convivio* 4.24.

82. *Policraticus* 817d: "Quinta maturitatem civilem promit, et etatem depingit vicinam senectuti, immo quae ipsam iam ingreditur senectutem. Nam et patrum honores recolit, maiorum memoriam veneratur, et, quasi ad tumulum Anchisae solemnes celebret ludos, in his ipsis exilii sui miseriam recognoscit" (The fifth period brings with it civic maturity and represents the period that is adjacent to old age, nay, that is already entering it. The protagonist reviews the honors held by his sires, venerates his ancestors, and, as if he were solemnizing games at the tomb of an Anchises, in them he recalls the misery of his exile).

83. *Policraticus* 817d–818a: "Dum vero hinc egreditur, transit ad sextum et amissis Palinuro et Miseno, duce scilicet navigii dormitante et temerarii praelii incentore, cum iam frigescat affectus viresque deficiant, non tam senectutem sentit quam senium et velut quendam descensum ad inferos, ubi quasi rebus inutiliter gestis totius anteactae vitae recognoscat errores" (As he emerges from this he enters the sixth period and suffers the loss of Palinurus and Misenus, the pilot who fell asleep and who incited to rash battle. Since by now his emotions are numbed and his powers waning, he experiences not so much old age itself as its decay and, as it were, a descent to the lower world, to review there the errors of his past life, as though all his achievements had come to naught).

84. *Policraticus* 818a: "Et discat alia via incedendum esse his qui volunt ad dulces Laviniae complexus et fatale regnum Italiae quasi ad quandam arcem beatitudinis pervenire" (He learns there that another way must be traveled by those who wish to attain the fond embraces of Lavinia and the destined kingdom of Italy as a sort of citadel of beatitude).

85. *Policraticus* 818a: "Licet autem de prima corruptione specialiter dictum sit, potest et de singulis manifesta ratione monstrari quia natura hominis ab adolescentia sua prona est ad malum" (Although this statement is specifically made in connection with the first sin, it can with clarity and reason be demonstrated with regard to every step, that man's nature from youth on is prone to evil).

86. *Policraticus* 818b: "Lata est ergo Epicureorum via et haud dubiam ducit ad mortem . . . Vana enim cultorem suum proturbant in tenebras exteriores, ad fletum oculorum, stridorem dentium, tinnitum aurium, et varias pressuras et penas inferorum, apud quos nullus ordo sed sempiternus horror inhabitat" (Broad therefore is the way of the Epicureans, and it leadeth indubitably to death . . . Vain blessings do indeed cast their votary into exterior darkness where there is weeping of eyes and gnashing of teeth, tingling of ears, the various tortures and afflictions of the damned, and where no order but everlasting horror dwelleth). Compare Matthew 7:13; Jeremiah 19:3.

87. *Policraticus* 818b–c: "Cap. 25. Quae via fidelissima sit ad sequendum quod Epicurei appetunt vel pollicentur" (The Safest Road to Follow to Reach What Epicureans Seek and Promise).

88. *Policraticus* 818d: "Via siquidem haec virtus est, duobus interiecta et artata limitibus, cognitione scilicet et exercitio boni. Nosse namque bonum et non facere meritum dampnationis est, non via beatitudinis" (Now this road is virtue, lying beween two boundaries, namely the knowledge and practice of goodness, and hemmed in by them. To be familiar with goodness and not to practice it is a cause for damnation, not the way to beatitude).

89. *Policraticus* 819c: "Ergo a ligno scientiae dum prohibitus illud ascenderet, nec revertetur ad vitam, nisi ad arborem scientiae redeat, et inde vertitatem in cognitione, virtutem in opere, vitam in iocunditate mutuetur. Rationis itaque acumen exerceat ut discernat inter bonum et malum" (Therefore man while climbing it, though forbidden, fell from the tree of knowledge and from truth, virtue, and life; he lost his way and will not return to life unless he return to the tree of knowledge and borrow from it truth by knowledge, virtue by deed, and life by joy. So let him exercise his wit in distinguishing between good and evil).

90. *Policraticus* 819d: "Ipse quoque labor dulcescat sibi et totam amaritudinem rerum praesentium (ut ait beatus Gregorius) spe temperet futurorum" (May his very labor be sweetened for him and may he temper [in the words of the blessed Gregory]

all the bitterness of things present with the hope of things to come). For the reference to Gregory the Great, Webb refers us to *Moralia in Iob* 8.8 §14.

91. *Policraticus* 819d: "In arbore ergo scientiae quasi quidam virtutis ramus nascitur, ex quo tota vita proficientis hominis consecratur. Neque enim ad genitorem vitae, Deum scilicet, alter redit, nisi qui virtutis ramum excisum de ligno scientiae praetendit" (Therefore there grows as it were on the tree of knowledge a sort of bough of virtue by which the entire life of the progressing man is consecrated. No other than he who stretches before him the bough of virtue cut from the tree of knowledge returns to the Creator of Life—that is God).

92. *Policraticus* 820a: "Hoc ipsum forte et Maro, qui, licet veritatis esset ignarus et in tenebris gentium ambularet, ad Eliseos campos felicium et cari genitoris conspectum Eneam admittendum esse non credidit, nisi docente Sibilla, quae quasi 'siosbole' consilium Iovis vel sapientia Dei interpretatur, ramum hunc Proserpinae, quae proserpentem et erigentem se a vitiis vitam innuit, consecraret" (Perhaps this is what Maro too perceived who, although ignorant of the truth and walking in the darkness of the heathen, did not believe that Aeneas should be admitted to the Elysian Fields of the blessed until, instructed by the Sibyl [the word Sibyl as if it were *siosbole*, is interpreted as meaning counsel of Jove or wisdom of God] he should offer up this bough of Proserpine whose name suggests life that creeps forward *[proserpens]* and raises itself from vice). John then cites *Aeneid* 6.136–44. On the Sybil, compare Servius at 3.445 and 6.12; Bernardus, Jones and Jones, *The Commentary*, 31.

93. See Jones and Jones, *The Commentary*, 30–31, 53.

94. *Policraticus* 819a: "'Est (inquam) via sublimis celo manifesta sereno; lactea nomen habet.' Serena tibi celum ne turbetur prae indignatione oculis animae tuae, et facile lacteam hanc agnosces viam."

95. *Policraticus* 820b–c: "Lactea haec est, innocentiae manifesta candore et alimentorum sedulitate nutricis explet officium et sola praeparat ad profectum; nam sine ea proficit nullus." Cp. *Convivio* 2.14.5–8; *Paradiso* 14.99; and, of course, John 14:6: "Ego sum via, veritas et vita." On the link between the celestial Milky Way and the wet nurse in a Neoplatonic context, see Macrobius, *Commentarium in Somnium Scipionis* 1.12.3, where the infant soul descends from the Milky Way.

96. *Policraticus* 820c: "Plus dicam; ipsam arborem scientiae et lignum vitae, in quo sunt omnes sapientiae et scientiae thesauri absconditi et in quo habitat plenitudo divinitatis corporaliter, extraxit (inscissa tamen substantia) et produxit in terram peregrinationis nostrae et plantavit in medio Ecclesiae, ut ab eo illustretur per scientiam, roboretur per virtutem, et exultet in misericordia uberi" (I will say more. Grace uprooted, without cutting into its trunk, brought out to the land of our wandering, and planted the very tree of knowledge and the wood of life [in it are all the

treasures of wisdom and knowledge and in it dwelleth all the fullness of the Godhead corporeally] in the midst of the Church, that she be illumined by knowledge, strengthened by virtue, and exult in rich pity [in the mercy of the breast]).

97. On the idea of *translatio studii* in a grammatical context, see Serge Lusignan, *Parler vulgairement*, 158–59; Rita Copeland, *Rhetoric Hermeneutics and Translation in the Middle Ages*, 103–7.

98. *Policraticus* 821c: "An perpetuitatem quaeris operibus? In memoria eterna erit iustus . . . Gratiamne linguae affectas? Labia iustorum distillant gratiam. Item: Memoria iusti cum laudibus, nomen impiorum putrescet . . . Et iusti in perpetuum vivent, et in pace sunt, licet mori insipientibus videantur." See Psalms 111:7 and 44:3; Proverbs 10:7; Wisdom 3:1–3.

99. See, again, *Convivio* 4.24.14. This important passage occurs within Dante's discussion of obedience as a necessary attribute of *adolescenza* and comes after his rejection of *Aeneid* allegory and other *auctores* at 4.24.9. It is as though here the philosopher wishes to strip the discussion of all extraneous matter and present the very core of the issue.

100. Dante's division and labeling of the life arc have been problematic for editors and readers alike, for they appear to correspond precisely to no one of his likely authorities in the matter. Albert and Thomas are themselves at odds here; see the preceding chapter and the editors' remarks at 4.24.2. When we add to this the linking of books of the *Aeneid* to the life stages, source attribution becomes a very complex endeavor indeed. Judging from their *apparati, Convivio* editors old and new feel Dante was following Fulgentius; Busnelli and Vandelli *(Convivio)* and Ageno ("Gerundio") cite from the *Continentia* to gloss 4.24.9 and 4.26.8ff., although Busnelli and Vandelli note the discrepancies between the two allegories. We saw above that Comparetti long ago rejected Fulgentius in favor of Bernardus or John; Collings *(The Interpretation of Virgil,* 25) concurs. Padoan ("Ulisse *fandi fictor* e le vie della sapienza," 36, n. 1) thinks that Bernardus is Dante's ultimate, if perhaps indirect, source for *Convivio* 4.26. D'Arco Silvio Avalle, "L'ultimo viaggio di Ulisse," 35, remarks that Servius was well known to Dante ("a lui ben noto"); cp. Erich von Richthofen, "Traces of Servius in Dante." In "Dante and Vergil the Mystic," Silverstein's conclusion must stand as the most sane pronouncement on the matter: "The fact seems to be that Dante followed no one allegory closely . . . Together these commentaries furnished a general tradition which affected Dante profoundly; but that tradition served essentially as a theme upon which he played his own variations" (p. 79, n. 5); for a useful summary of similarities and differences among Fulgentius, Bernardus, and John, see pp. 78–79 and p. 79, n. 4.

101. The most significant of these studies are: Padoan, "Ulisse *fandi fictor* e le vie della sapienza"; Thompson, *Dante's Epic Journeys* (on Ulysses and Aeneas, see in part. pp. 52–61); Freccero, "Dante's Ulysses"; Mazzotta, *Dante, Poet of the Desert*

(see in part. pp. 66–106). The bibliography on *Inferno* 26 is vast. In addition to the above, the following have been most helpful for my reading: Bruno Nardi, "La trage-dia d'Ulisse," in his *Dante e la cultura medievale;* Mario Fubini's *lectura* in *Letture dantesche;* and Fubini's article "Ulisse," in the *Enciclopedia dantesca;* Pagliaro, "Il canto XXVI dell'*Inferno*"; John A. Scott, "*Inferno* XXVI"; Avalle, "L'ultimo viaggio di Ulisse"; Mario Trovato, "The Semantic Value of *Ingegno*"; Pertile, "Dante e l'ingegno di Ulisse"; Teodolinda Barolini, "Dante's Ulysses."

102. On Neoplatonic readings of the *Odyssey,* Greek and Latin, see in part. Thompson, *Dante's Epic Journeys,* 13–18; Padoan ("Ulisse *fandi fictor* e le vie della sapienza," 36, n. 2) cites a passage from Giovanni del Virgilio that demonstrates clearly that the conception of Ulysses as positive hero was still very much alive among Dante's contemporaries. For a more general consideration of Dante's source for his version of Ulysses' end, see Nardi, "La tragedia d'Ulisse."

103. Bodo Guthmüller, "'Che par che Circe li avesse in pastura' (*Purg.* XIV, 42)," 250–56, notes that such a view of Ulysses was dominant in the Middle Ages.

104. Particularly suggestive in a grammatical context is Padoan's quotation ("Ulisse *fandi fictor* e le vie della sapienza," 29) from Statius, *Achilleid* 1.846–47, where the young Achilles is characterized as *rudis* and *simplex* before the persuasive powers of *varium Ulixem.*

105. Padoan, "Ulisse *fandi fictor* e le vie della sapienza," 51.

106. Padoan, "Ulisse *fandi fictor* e le vie della sapienza," 43. Ulysses, too, would eat of the tree of knowledge of good and evil; see *Inferno* 26.97–99: "L'ardore/ch'i' ebbi a divenir del mondo esperto/e de li vizi umani e del valore" (The longing that I had to gain experience of the world, and of human vice and worth).

107. See Mazzotta, *Dante, Poet of the Desert,* 81–87 and in part. pp. 81–82: "The *Convivio* ends with a neoplatonic interpretation of the *Aeneid;* the *Divine Comedy* begins with the resumption of a neoplatonic attempt at self-transcendence which fails and with the subsequent rediscovery of the *Aeneid* as the poem of history"; cp. Ulrich Leo, "The Unfinished *Convivio.*" In "Dante's Ulysses," Freccero thus suggests that Ulysses represents the futility of epic circularity, the pilgrim a more directed novelistic linearity that opens the possibility of individual transcendence; Aeneas lies somewhere in between these two extremes, as the *Aeneid* suggests the corpo-rate immortality of the Roman state at the expense of the individual. Gaeta is the perfect emblem of this intermediate sort of transcendence.

108. *Purgatorio* 14.37–38: "Virtù così per nimica si fuga/da tutti come biscia" (Virtue is fled from as an enemy by all, as if it were a snake).

109. *Purgatorio* 14.40–42. Cp. Mazzotta, *Dante, Poet of the Desert,* 106, n. 77. On Circe in general and these verses in particular, see also Guthmüller, "'Che par che Circe li avesse in pastura' (*Purg.* XIV, 42)."

110. *Purgatorio* 14.43–45: "Tra brutti porci, più degni di galle/che d'altro cibo fatto in uman uso,/dirizza poi il suo povero calle" (Among filthy hogs, fitter for acorns than for any food made for human use, it [the Arno] first directs its feeble course).

111. Mazzotta, *Dante, Poet of the Desert,* 87.

112. See Guthmüller, "'*Che par che Circe li avesse in pastura*' (*Purg.* XIV, 42)," 250–56, who cites Benoît de Sainte Maure, *Le roman de Troie,* to support his comment (p. 252) that Ulysses had to match Circe in witchery in order to overcome her at last: "Ulisse riesce a fuggire solo nel momento in cui arriva ad uguagliare nell'arte magica Circe, e diventare lui stesso un abile stregone."

113. Genesis 2:19–20; as we have seen, a passage with a curious presence, or rather absence, in the *De vulgari.*

114. See Susan Reynolds, *Medieval Reading,* 45–60.

115. Mazzotta, *Dante, Poet of the Desert,* 89–90.

116. In Adelard of Bath; see Reynolds, *Medieval Reading,* 46.

117. The quotation is from Bruce Fink, *The Lacanian Subject,* 56.

118. See Fink, *The Lacanian Subject,* 56, where he cites Lacan's Seminar 17, *L'envers de la psychanalyse.*

119. See Jacques Lacan, "The mirror stage as formative of the function of the I as revealed in psychoanalytic experience," in *Écrits,* 1–7 and in part. p. 4.

120. For this notion of buried maternal desire at the base of language and selfhood, see in part. the Lacanian diagrams reproduced by Fink, *The Lacanian Subject,* 57:

Name-of-the-Father	*Signifier*
Mother's Desire	Mother's Desire

We might particularize these diagrams to reflect our discussion:

Rome	*Aeneas*	*Gaeta as Name*
Gaeta	Gaeta	Gaeta as Body

121. See, for instance, *Reading Kristeva,* 3: "Kristeva has attempted to bring the semiotic body, replete with drives, back into structuralism. This attempt has also marked her point of departure from Lacanian theory. She argues that Lacan's bracketing of the drives 'castrates' Freud's discovery. Kristeva, protecting the father of psychoanalysis from this castration threat by his most prodigal son, reinscribes the drives in language. She attempts to protect Freud's body from Lacan's desire."

122. Julia Kristeva, *Desire in Language,* 271–94; Kristeva bases her descriptions on her own pschyoanalytic experience and the work of Melanie Klein, Winnicot, Halliday, R. Spitz, and others.

123. Kristeva, *Desire in Language,* 283.

124. Kristeva, *Desire in Language,* 283–85: "The inaugural sublimation, in most cases visual, brings us not only to the foundations of narcissism (specular gratification)

but to the riant wellsprings of the imaginary. The imaginary takes over from childhood laughter: it is a joy without words. Chronologically and logically long before the mirror stage (where the Same sees itself altered through the well-known opening that constitutes it as representation, sign, and death), the semiotic disposition makes its start as riant spaciousness. During the period of indistinction between 'same' and 'other,' infant and mother, as well as between 'subject' and 'object,' while no space has yet been delineated (this will happen with and after the mirror stage—birth of the sign), the semiotic *chora* that arrests and absorbs the motility of anaclitic facilitation relieves and produces laughter . . . At this stage we have the necessary conditions that, avoiding inhibition through laughter, constitute the semiotic disposition and insure its maintenance within the symbolic. The preconditions for language acquisition are given at this point; their modulations involve the entire neurotic gamut of inhibitions and anguish that characterizes the speaking being's destiny."

125. Kristeva, *Desire in Language,* 287; emphases in the original.

126. Kristeva, *Desire in Language,* 289.

127. Kristeva, *Desire in Language,* 291.

128. Kristeva, *Desire in Language,* 291: "[The demonstrative utterance] provides a presence, posited but indistinct, and an evocation of uncertain multiplicities, which would therefore explain why *this,* in its well-known evangelical usage, is at the same time Bread and Body of Christ: 'This is my body' . . . Could trans-substantiation (for this is what we are dealing with, and the child cannot help leading all of us, men and women, to it, for it is indeed such a key fantasy of our reproductive desire) be an indelible theming of this same fold between the 'space' of need (for food and survival) and a symbolic space of designation (of the body proper)? Could it be a fold that the archeology of shifters summarizes and is produced in all archaic designations of the mother, as well as in all experiences at the limits of corporeal identity— that is, the identity of meaning and presence?"; cp. Julia Kristeva, *Étranger à nous-mêmes,* 118–22.

129. Mazzotta, *Dante, Poet of the Desert,* 96. Mazzotta also suggests that language for Dante, as for Derrida, always "originates in the void," is always already cut off from its ground; p. 82: "Fraud is not simply the sin of Ulysses, but the very condition of discourse"; and p. 83: "[Ulysses' madness] lies in the belief that the distance [between words and history] can be bridged by an act of knowledge." But surely for Christians, as we have seen with particular force in John of Salisbury, there was at least one act of knowledge (for John, not entirely divorced from *scientia*) that could redeem language and restore *logos.*

130. *Inferno* 20.76–77. On this, cp. Isidore of Seville, *Etymologiarum* 13.19.7.

131. Virgil's description of the overflowing water of the Benaco in v. 74 as "ciò che 'n *grembo* a Benaco star non può" (all the water that in the bosom [womb] of

Benaco cannot stay) further foreshadows the macrocosmic poetics of Mother Earth that will inform *Purgatorio* 5.

132. *Inferno* 20.52–54. While Manto was not a nurse in the classical literature, Dante's focus on her *mammelle* here places her, metaphorically and structurally, *in loco nutricis*.

133. Singleton *ad loc.* cites Benvenuto on Manto's tresses: "In hoc tangit actum mulierum incantatricium, quae aliquando vadunt de nocte nudae cum crinibus sparsis" (Here he hints at the witches who sometimes go about at night, naked, with their hair loose).

134. *Paradiso* 27.40–45: "Non fu la sposa di Cristo allevata/del sangue mio, di Lin, di quel di Cleto,/per essere ad acquisto d'oro usata;/ma per acquisto d'esto viver lieto/e Sisto e Pïo e Calisto e Urbano/sparser lo sangue dopo molto fleto" (The spouse of Christ was not nurtured on my blood and that of Linus and of Cletus, to be employed for gain of gold; but for gain of this happy life Sixtus and Pius and Calixtus and Urban shed their blood after much weeping). The popes are thus *pastori* in *paschi* (vv. 55–56); compare *pasture* (v. 91).

135. *Paradiso* 27.82–84: "Sì ch'io vedea di là da Gade il varco/folle d'Ulisse, e di qua presso il lito/nel qual si fece Europa dolce carco" (So that, on the one hand, beyond Cadiz, I saw the mad track of Ulysses, and on the other nearly to the shore where Europa made herself a sweet burden). It is appropriate that the reference to Ulysses' mad breach—as I have argued, a kind of maternal seduction—be coupled with a reference to Europa, whose seduction brought monstrous pregnancy; Ovid, *Metamorphoses* 2.833–75.

136. *Paradiso* 27.130–35. "Tale, balbuzïendo ancor, digiuna,/che poi divora, con la lingua sciolta,/qualunque cibo per qualunque luna;/e tal, balbuzïendo, ama e ascolta / la madre sua, che, con loquela intera,/disïa poi di vederla sepolta" (One, so long as he lisps [stammers], keeps the fasts, who afterward, when his tongue is free, devours any food through any month; and one, while he lisps [stammers], loves his mother and listens to her, who afterward, when his speech is full, longs to see her buried). The proverbially variable moon, by contrast, evokes nutritional and linguistic promiscuity, as we again recall Ulysses on the verge of tragedy at *Inferno* 26.130–32: "Cinque volte racceso e tante casso/lo lume era di sotto da la luna,/poi che 'ntrati eravam ne l'alto passo" (Five times the light beneath the moon had been rekindled and as many quenched, since we had entered on the passage of the deep). On Dante's complex poetic relationship to the moon, particularly as a figure for natural linguistic variability and grammar, see chapter 2 on *Convivio* 2.8.9–10; and Giuseppe Mazzotta, *Dante's Vision and the Circle of Knowledge,* 34–35.

137. *Paradiso* 27.136–38. The strong poetic links between this canto and *Inferno* 26–27 and the common identification of Circe as *filia solis* in Virgil and Ovid and throughout the entire allegory tradition render problematic readings

that discern a reference to some other being or thing here (Aurora, sunlight, the moon). Michele Barbi, John Scott, and others have agreed that the reference is to Circe; see in part. John A. Scott, "Su alcune immagini tematiche di *Paradiso* XXVII," in *Dante magnanimo,* 195–237, and on this crux in part. p. 229; for a different reading, see Lino Pertile, *"Così si fa la pella bianca nera";* see also Natalino Sapegno, ed., *La divina commedia, ad loc.;* Antonio Martina, "Circe"; Guthmüller, "'*Che par che Circe li avesse in pastura*' (*Purg.* XIV, 42)," 248–49 (and for bibliography, n. 32).

138. This supports my above reading of *Paradiso* 26.62–63.

139. *Inferno* 26.139–42; *Purgatorio* 30.58; *Paradiso* 27.146–47. The word *poppa* held two common meanings for Dante: breast and ship's bow. For *poppa* as breast, see *Inferno* 7.27; *Inferno* 12.97; *Purgatorio* 23.102. For *poppa* as ship's bow, in addition to above, see *Inferno* 21.13; *Inferno* 26.140; *Purgatorio* 2.43. I am suggesting that both meanings are present in *Paradiso* 27. See also Salvatore Battaglia, *Grande dizionario della lingua italiana,* vol. 13, *s.v.*

140. *Inferno* 26.139–42: "Tre volte il fé girar con tutte l'acque;/a la quarta levar la poppa in suso/e la prora ire in giù, com'altrui piacque,/infin che 'l mar fu sovra noi richiuso" (Three times it whirled her round with all the waters, and the fourth time it lifted the stern aloft and plunged the prow below, as pleased Another, till the sea closed over us).

141. *Aeneid* 6.900–901: "Tum se ad Caietae recto fert litore portum./Ancora de prora iacitur; stant litore puppes."

142. On *poppa* and *prora* in *Paradiso* 27 in relation to Ulysses, see also Scott, *Dante magnanimo,* 232–33; Guthmüller, "'*Che par che Circe li avesse in pastura*' (*Purg.* XIV, 42)," 250–56.

143. On irony as the dominant rhetorical mode of *Inferno,* see Freccero, *Dante: The Poetics of Conversion,* 93–109.

144. Hollander, "Babytalk in Dante's *Commedia.*"

145. Dante's Latin commentators generally define *pape* as an expression of wonder or marvel, *interiectio admirantis;* see in particular Uguccione *s.v.* in the *Magnae Derivationes* as cited by Paget Toynbee, "Dante's Latin Dictionary," 112; see also Singleton, Sapegno, and Durling and Martinez *ad loc.* But there is an older tradition among the Latin grammarians that defines *papa* in terms of the infant's desire for nourishment or attention; see in particular the fourth-century Nonius Marcellus as cited *s.v.* in the *Thesaurus linguae latinae.* On *mamma* and *papa* in modern structural linguistics, see Roman Jakobson, "Why *Mama* and *Papa*?" Some of the early commentators hear in *aleppe* a reference to the first letter of the Hebrew alphabet; see Sapegno *ad loc.* We might recall in this context that Lady Grammar, the symbolic nurse, was responsible for teaching her charges their ABCs.

146. On Nimrod, see Zygmunt G. Barański, "Dante's Biblical Linguistics," 129–33.

147. *Inferno* 12.70–71.

148. See Statius, *Achilleid* 1.195–96; 2.395.

149. *Inferno* 12.83–84.

150. *Inferno* 12.97.

151. On the linguistic reality of Bologna, compare *De vulgari* 1.9.4. For the use of the affirmative adverb to identify a language, see *De vulgari* 1.10.1–2; compare *De vulgari* 1.14.2 on the Romagnoli of Forlì, who say *deuscì* in affirmation.

152. For river flows in *Inferno* 27, see vv. 30 and 52; on language games, see Freccero, "Dante's Ulysses," in *Dante: A Collection of Critical Essays,* 142–43.

153. *Inferno* 27.46–48. Durling and Martinez have "[they] drill with their teeth."

154. But *succhio* could also be "sap" or "juice," from *succhiare,* "to suck or drink in"; see Barbara Reynold, *Cambridge Italian Dictionary,* vol. 1, *s.v.*

155. We have seen references to the importance of teeth in the infant's development in chapter 2; Martianus Cappella's Lady Grammar wields a file. Sharpening one's teeth was a metaphor for acquisition and refinement of linguistic skills. See Isidore of Seville, *Etymologiarum* 11.2.9–10 on *infantia* as lack of speech: "Nondum bene ordinatis dentibus minus est sermonis expressio" (Since his teeth are not yet well ordered his speech is imperfect). See also above discussion of grammar in Boncompagno da Signa, *Rhetorica novissima;* compare Dante's own first eclogue to Giovanni del Virgilio, *Ecloge,* ed. and trans. Enzo Cecchini, p. 670, lines 65–66; Shulamith Shahar, *Childhood in the Middle Ages.*

156. *Inferno* 27.73–74.

157. We think here, of course, of Ugolino and Ruggieri (*Inferno* 32.124–39; 33.1–78), the most literal, and thus ghastly, reading of nourishment in Dante's poem; see Freccero, *Dante: The Poetics of Conversion,* 93–109 and 152–66.

158. *Inferno* 32.7–9.

159. See Singleton, *ad loc.;* cp. Hollander, "Babytalk in Dante's *Commedia.*"

160. For a more nuanced reading of the irony here, see Durling and Martinez *ad loc.*

161. We should remember the very opening of the canto where the poetic process is figured as juicing. *Inferno* 32.1–5: "S'ïo avessi le rime aspre e chiocce, / come si converrebbe al tristo buco / sovra 'l qual pontan tutte l'altre rocce, / io premerei di mio concetto il suco / più pienamente" (If I had harsh and grating rhymes, as would befit the dismal hole on which all the other rocks converge and weigh, I would press out more fully the juice of my conception).

4. Deconstructing Subjectivity in Antepurgatory

1. "Sed natura corporis fluida est et mundus constat ex corpore." Cited by Chalcidius at Chalcidius 75.

2. "Corpus porro terrenum hoc non diu constat, sed torrentis more praecipitis et ipsum effluit et ab effluentibus inundatur." Chalcidius 192.

3. Caroline Walker Bynum, *The Resurrection of the Body*. For a survey of the recent explosion in criticism on the medieval body, see the introduction by Peter Biller, 3–12, in Peter Biller and Alastair J. Minnis, eds., *Medieval Theology and the Natural Body*. Most of the essays in this volume deal with issues of gender and the body in various medieval discourses.

4. "Anima autem, cum sit pars corporis homini, non est totus homo, et *anima mea non est ego;* unde, licet anima consequatur salutem in alia vita, non tamen ego vel quilibet homo." Cited by Bynum, *The Resurrection of the Body*, 257, n. 114, from Aquinas's commentary on 1 Corinthians, chap. 15, lectio 2; in this same note, Bynum cites Thomas in the *Summa* (1a, q. 75, art. 4, reply obj. 2), where he argues that soul is only a piece of human being and cannot be considered self any more than a hand or a foot ("Unde manus vel pes non potest dici hypostasis vel persona, et similiter nec anima, cum sit pars speciei humanae"). Of particular interest here is the Scholastic use of the word *persona* to designate what we have been calling personhood, selfhood, or subjectivity; cp. Dante, *Paradiso* 14.43–45: "Come la carne gloriosa e santa/fia rivestita, la nostra persona/più grata fia per esser tutta quanta" (When the flesh, glorious and sanctified, shall be clothed on us again, our persons will be more acceptable for being all complete).

5. For Scholastic theories of body and selfhood in particular, see Bynum, *The Resurrection of the Body*, 135–37, 256–71.

6. See in part. Bynum, *The Resurrection of the Body*, 262.

7. Bynum, *The Resurrection of the Body*, 221.

8. Dante's references to the body of resurrection are numerous and occur in all three canticles of the *Comedy*. Solomon gives the most complete doctrinal exposition of the matter, however, in *Paradiso* 14.37–60. The pilgrim actually sees the resurrection of the bodies in *Paradiso* 30. For Bynum on Dante specifically, see *The Resurrection of the Body*, 298–305.

9. See in particular *Purgatorio* 31 and 33.

10. On this point, see Jacoff, "'Our Bodies, Our Selves,'" p. 131: "In *Paradiso* the shade bodies disappear as recognizable human forms. They are progressively dematerialized as Dante progresses up through the spheres."

11. A constant theme of *Purgatorio* in particular; see for instance Oderisi da Gubbio in *Purgatorio* 11 and in part. vv. 115–17.

12. Bynum discusses the significance of the rise of purgatory to the discourse of resurrection; see *The Resurrection of the Body,* 280–83, and in specific regard to Dante, pp. 306–7.

13. *Purgatorio* 3.16–18; 87–90.

14. *Purgatorio* 3.103–5; 112–27.

15. *Purgatorio* 3.124–32.

16. For the Latin text of the *Timaeus* with commentary, see Chalcidius, *Timaeus a Calcidio translatus.* Chalcidius's translation stops at 53C after Plato's treatment of *silva* and well before any detailed treatment of the microcosmic human body; the final eighty-seven chapters of his commentary (268–355) are on *silva.* For Chalcidius, see *Praefatio,* ix–cv, in Chalcidius, ed. J. H. Waszink; and J. C. M. van Winden, *Calcidius on Matter, His Doctrine and Sources.* For a recent, helpful reading of the *Timaeus,* see John Sallis *Chorology,* particularly pp. 91–145. For Platonism in the Middle Ages, see Raymond Klibansky, *The Continuity of the Platonic Tradition;* Ernst Robert Curtius, *European Literature and the Latin Middle Ages,* 106–27, 544–46; and especially Tullio Gregory, *Anima mundi.* The most imposing champion of Dante's Neoplatonism remains Bruno Nardi; see in part. *Saggi di filosofia dantesca,* 40–62, 63–72, 81–109, and *Studi di filosofia medievale.* On Dante and the *Timaeus,* see Freccero, *Poetics of Conversion,* in particular 181–85, 223–26, 237–40, 250–53; and "Dante e la tradizione del *Timeo.*" We should note that in both instances where Dante actually invokes the *Timaeus* by name (*Convivio* 3.5.6; *Paradiso* 4.49–60), he does so—at least apparently—to refute Plato in favor of Aristotle. For a recent treatment of the Neoplatonic macrocosm/microcosm analogy in Dante, particularly in the *rime petrose* and *Paradiso,* see Robert M. Durling and Ronald L. Martinez, *Time and the Crystal;* for Neoplatonism in the *De vulgari,* see pp. 22–32. Barański has emphasized the synchretic variety of Dante's intellectual background with particular emphasis on Neoplatonism; see in part. Zygmunt G. Barański, "Dante commentatore e commentato."

17. *Timaeus* 49A: "Opinor, omnium quae gignuntur receptaculum est, quasi quaedam nutricula." All citations of Plato and Chalcidius are from Chalcidius, *Timaeus a Calcidio translatus,* ed. J. H. Waszink; references are to the marginal page numbers and letters in Plato, *Timaeus,* in *Plato's Cosmology,* ed. and trans. F. M. Cornford, reproduced by Waszink. English translations of Chalcidius's Latin are my own, although I have regularly consulted Cornford's English rendering of the original Greek. Chalcidius repeatedly discusses the naming of *chora* or *hyle* in Latin, as well as her function as wet nurse; see Chalcidius 123, 248, 273, 278, 308, and 321.

18. For a history of the microcosm/macrocosm analogy, see Bernardus Silvestris, *The Cosmographia,* ed. Winthrop Wetherbee, introduction, 1–5 and, for bibliography, n. 10; also Macrobius, *Commentary on the Dream of Scipio,* 224, n. 7; and Lynn Thorndike, *A History of Magic.* For the centrality of this notion to Dante's poetics, see Durling and Martinez, *Time and the Crystal, passim* and in part. pp. 96–108.

19. See *Timaeus* 42E.

20. See also Macrobius, *Commentarium in Somnium Scipionis,* 2.12.10–11. For additional *loci* of the macrocosm/microcosm analogy in antiquity and the Middle Ages, see William Harris Stahl's note in Macrobius, *Commentarium in Somnium Scipionis,* 224, n. 7.

21. See Chalcidius 202. On the connection between blood and milk in medieval physiology, see Macrobius, *Saturnalia* 5.11; Isidore of Seville, *Etymologiarum* 11.1.77 (as cited by Charles T. Wood, "The Doctor's Dilemma," 719); Caroline Walker Bynum, *Fragmentation and Redemption,* 109–11. At *Timaeus* 44B, Plato notes that *silva* upsets the original harmony between orbits of the soul, Same and Different, but that once the individual begins to mature, and if he applies himself to rational study, he can almost regain the original harmony. Here we see clearly *silva* as precedent to the images of the wet nurse that would develop in antiquity and medieval grammar. Cp. Bernardus in the *Megacosmus* 2.7.6–10 (Bernardus Silvestris, *The Cosmographia,* 71), whose description of the materials of the infant universe striving toward rational order as *rudes* and *indisciplinatas* recalls a boisterous horde of grammar pupils at the beginning of their course of study.

22. See in particular Chalcidius 344–49.

23. *Timaeus* 40B–C.

24. Chalcidius 300.

25. Macrobius, *Saturnalia* 5.11, is perhaps the most explicit on the connection between the human and terrestrial wet nurses, the flow of milk and the flow of elements (for Dante, *alimenti);* cp. Aulus Gellius, *Noctes atticae* 12.1.12.

26. *Etymologiarum* 8.11.59–61: "Matrem vocatam, quod plurima pariat; magnam, quod cibum gignat; almam, quia universa animalia fructibus suis alit. Est enim alimentorum nutrix terra."

27. For an introduction to Bernard and his work, see Winthrop Wetherbee, *Platonism and Poetry,* 152–86; Bernardus Silvestris, *The Cosmographia,* 1–62; *Cosmographia,* 1–69. Also fundamental are Theodore H. Silverstein, "The Fabulous Cosmogony of Bernardus Silvestris"; and Brian Stock, *Myth and Science.*

28. See in particular *Megacosmos* 3.235–36, 241–44 (Bernardus Silvestris, *The Cosmographia,* 81).

29. Julian W. Jones and Elizabeth F. Jones, eds., *The Commentary,* 5 (lines 14–15): "His mare, id est humanum corpus quod est intrancium et exeuntium gurges humorum infestatur" ([The winds] assault the sea, that is to say the human body, which is a whirlpool of humors that continually flow in and out). On the human body as a whirlpool *(gurges)* with constant flow in and out, we should recall *Timaeus* 43A–B, where the gods attach soul to the liquid body ("inriguo fluidoque corpori . . . immenso

quippe inrigante et immoderate effluente gurgite . . ."). Likewise, the *Aeneid* commentator notes that Aeneas temporarily loses some of his men in the turbulent sea of book 1, just as the infant body recently joined to soul temporarily loses its rational powers, which can then be regained with age, disciplined instruction, and erudition ("etate et exercitio studii et doctrina"); see Jones and Jones, 11 (lines 10–11).

30. Jones and Jones, *The Commentary,* 10 (lines 15–18): "Mare corpus humanum intelligitur quia ebrietates et libidines que per aquas intelliguntur ab eo defluunt et in eo sunt commotiones vitiorum et per ipsum ciborum et potus meatus fit" (By "sea," the human body is understood, because drunkenness and lust, symbolized by the waters, flow out from it, and within the body reside the turbulent motions of vice, and through the body flows the channel of food and drink). Compare this passage to Chalcidius 92.

31. Jones and Jones, *The Commentary,* 8 (lines 1–4): "Quemadmodum in humano corpore sunt meatus humoris, id est vene, per quas sanguis desfluit et inde facto vulnere exilit, ita et in terra sunt vene quas cataractas vocant, per quas aqua deducitur et inde si fodiatur exilit." On "veins" in the earth, we should recall Dante, *Rime* C, 53ff. "Versan le vene le fummifere acque"; see also Brunetto Latini, *Tresor* 1.105.

32. See *Timaeus* 32–33, and in particular 33C–D; cp. Chalcidius 24 and 192; Macrobius, *Commentary on the Dream of Scipio* 2.12 (p. 225). On material death as mere transformation in Bernardus, see also *Microcosmos* 8.37–46 (Bernardus Silvestris, *The Cosmographia,* 110), and in part. vv. 45–46: "Forma fluit, manet esse rei, mortisque potestas/Nil perimit, sed res dissociat socias" (Form flows away, the essence of the thing remains; the power of death destroys nothing, but only disunites united parts).

33. *Microcosmos* 14.171–78 (Bernardus Silvestris, *Cosmographia,* 126–27): "Influit ipsa sibi mundi natura, superstes,/Permanet et fluxu pascitur usque suo:/Scilicet ad summam rerum iactura recurrit,/Nec semel—ut possit sepe perire—perit./Longe disparibus causis mutandus in horas,/Effluit occiduo corpore totus homo./Sic sibi deficiens, peregrinis indiget escis,/Sudat in hoc vitam denichilatque dies." On these final verses, see also Dronke (Bernardus Silvestris, *Cosmographia,* 48–49), who takes *dies* of v. 178 as the plural object of the verb *denichilat.*

34. I have consulted the following *lecturae:* Helmut A. Hatzfield, "*Purgatorio* V"; Giambattista Salinari, "Il Canto V del Purgatorio"; Peter Armour, "*Purgatorio* V"; for more bibliography and a survey of early commentary on this canto with particular attention to natural science, see Marcella Roddenwig, "*Purgatorio* V nella esegesi antica e moderna."

35. Dante uses the verb reflexively in v. 10 *(s'impiglia)* and then transitively in v. 83 *(m'impigliar sì).*

36. On *flatus vocis,* see Leo Spitzer, "Speech and Language."

37. Chalcidius 167: "Ex divulgatione autem succedit errori supra dicto ex matrum et nutricum votis de divitiis gloriaque et ceteris falso putatis bonis insussurratio" (On account of popular opinion another error follows the one mentioned above from the chatter of mothers and nurses, their vain whispering about wealth and glory and all sorts of other things falsely reputed good).

38. We should recall that one important source of Virgil's proverbial *torre ferma* image in vv. 14–15 is *Aeneid* 7.586–90, where a solid stone cliff sustains a beating by the elements, harsh winds, and the turbulent open sea: "Ille velut pelagi rupes immota resistit, / ut pelagi rupes magno veniente fragore, / quae sese, multis circum latrantibus undis, / mole tenet; scopuli nequiquam et spumea circum / saxa fremunt laterique inlisa refunditur alga" (Latinus, though, like a seacliff stood fast, like a sea-cliff that when the great sea comes to shatter on it, and the waves like hounds give tongue on every side, holds grandly on, though reefs and foaming rocks thunder offshore and seaweed flung against it streams away"); cp. *Aeneid* 10.693–96. But if for Virgil this is an image of eternal material stability, for Chalcidius we will see that even rocks eventually break down and dissolve back into the greater elemental cycle. Dante will suggest as much later in the canto with all the swamps. In this sense, Virgil's famous advice, while locally useful, ultimately speaks as much to his limitations as to his wisdom.

39. *Purgatorio* 5.19–21.

40. The equation between historical identity and body is evident in the testimonies that compose the bulk of the canto. In a psychoanalytic context, mental being equates itself with its self-contained bodily image in the mirror. For Lacan, this equation or "identity" (*idemptitas,* sameness) constitutes an illusory, "mistaken familiarity" and a "mis-recognition" *(méconnaisance);* see Jacques Lacan, "The Mirror Stage," in *Écrits,* 1–7; Jean Laplanche and J.-B. Pontalis, *The Language of Psychoanalysis, s.v.* "mirror stage."

41. *Purgatorio* 5.23–24.

42. *Purgatorio* 5.28–30.

43. *Purgatorio* 5.36. The poet ingeniously alludes to these souls' nostalgic desire for their recently lost bodies and identities in choosing this rather peculiar locution, as the end-tercet *caro* (v. 36) puns etymologically on the last word of the previous tercet, *carne* (v. 33), via the Latin feminine singular noun *caro, carnis.*

44. *Purgatorio* 5.37–40.

45. See, for instance, Charles S. Singleton (Dante, *The Divine Comedy,* vol. 2.2) on verse 40: "But, no matter how swiftly the two messengers may run back up the slope, and even though these are spirits, the hyperbole seems somewhat extreme, to say the least." Also, as Singleton comments, Grandgent explains that "vapori accesi" might refer to both lightning and meteors.

46. Cp. *Timaeus* 49C: "Aer porro exustus ignem creat rursumque extinctus ignis aera corpulentior factus instituit, aer item crassior factus in nubes nebulasque concrescit" (Then air burns dry and creates fire, which in turn is extinguished and grows more corpulent to make air, and then air grows more dense and gathers into clouds and mist); for a fuller discussion of this passage, see below; cp. Chalcidius 323–24.

47. See *Timaeus* 49 and Chalcidius 318–26 and below; cp. Chalcidius 303: "Si ergo has qualitates et quantitates, etiam formas figurasve volemus ratione animi separare, tum demum deliberare, quid sit illud, quod haec omnia inseparabiliter adhaerens complexumque contineat, inveniemus nihil aliud esse quam id quod quaerimus, silvam" (If therefore we wished to use the rational mind to separate out these quantities and qualities, and forms or figures, and then in the end ask what is that thing, which inseparable and unified contains all of these various forms, we would find it to be nothing other than what we are searching for, *silva*).

48. On the shadowy nature of bodies in the afterlife, see Statius's discourse on generation, *Purgatorio* 25.34–108. See also Jacoff's discussion of "body-biographies" in "'Our Bodies, Our Selves,'" p. 128.

49. *Purgatorio* 5.41–42.

50. See Chalcidius 325 and *passim* for other such locutions.

51. *Purgatorio* 5.58–59: "Although I gaze upon your faces, I do not recognize any."

52. *Purgatorio* 5.52–57: "Noi fummo tutti già per forza morti,/e peccatori infino a l'ultima ora;/quivi lume del ciel ne fece accorti,/sì che, pentendo e perdonando, fora/di vita uscimmo a Dio pacificati,/che del disio di sé veder n'accora" (We were all done to death by violence, and sinners up to the last hour. Then light from Heaven made us mindful, so that, repenting and pardoning, we came forth from life at peace with God, who fills our hearts with sad longing to see Him).

53. See Lacan, "The Mirror Stage."

54. Blood was considered the seat of the soul among the ancients; see Hatzfield, "*Purgatorio* V"; Armour, "*Purgatorio* V"; Singleton's note *ad loc.,* which quotes Benvenuto and Leviticus.

55. Antenor was the treacherous Trojan who was involved in betraying Troy to the Greeks and devising the strategy of the Trojan horse; according to legend, the Paduans were his descendents; see Singleton *ad loc.* and *Inferno* 32.88.

56. *Purgatorio* 5.77–78: "Quel da Esti il fé fare, che m'avea in ira/assai più che dritto non volea" (He of Este had it done, who held me in wrath far beyond what justice warranted).

57. On the four elements in the microcosmic human body, see Chalcidius 192 (cited above), 202 (cited above) and 303. Cp. the *Aeneid* commentator, Jones and

Jones, *The Commentary,* 8 (lines 4–6): "Item quemadmodum in humano corpore sunt arterie per quas hanelitus per corpus meat, ita in terra sunt caverne per quas aer immittitur" (Just as there are in the human body air passages by means of which breath flows through the body, so on earth there are cavities through which air is driven).

58. *Ars poetica,* vv. 60–72: "Ut silvae foliis pronos mutantur in annos,/prima cadunt; ita verborum vetus interit aetas,/et iuvenum ritu florent modo nata vigent-que./Debemur morti nos nostraque: sive receptus/terra Neptunus classes Aquilonibus arcet,/regis opus, sterilisve palus diu aptaque remis/vicinas urbes alit et grave sentit aratrum,/seu cursum mutavit iniquum frugibus amnis / doctus iter melius: mortalia facta peribunt,/nedum sermonum stet honos et gratia vivax./Multa renascentur quae iam cecidere, cadentque/quae nunc sunt in honore vocabula, si volet usus,/quae penes arbitrium est et ius et norma loquendi" (As forests change their leaves with each year's decline, and the earliest drop off: so with words, the old race dies, and, like the young of human kind, the new-born bloom and thrive. We are doomed to death—we and all things ours; whether Neptune, welcomed within the land, protects our fleets from northern gales—a truly royal work—or a marsh, long a waste where oars were plied, feeds neighboring towns and feels the weight of a plough; or a river has changed the course which brought ruin to corn-fields and has learnt a better path: all mortal things will perish, much less will the glory and glamour of speech endure and live. Many terms that have fallen out of use will be born again, and those will fall that are now in repute, if Usage so will it, in whose hands lies the judgment, the right and the rule of speech). Cp. *Convivio* 2.13.10; *Paradiso* 26.137–38.

59. *Megacosmos* 3.235–36 (in *Cosmographia*).

60. See above, note 31.

61. *Purgatorio* 5.85–88: "Poi disse un altro: 'Deh, se quel disio/si compia che ti tragge a l'alto monte,/con buona pïetate aiuta il mio!/Io fui di Montefeltro, io son Bonconte'" (Then said another, "Ah, so may that desire be fulfilled which draws you up the lofty mountain, do you with gracious pity help my own. I was of Montefeltro, I am Bonconte"). As a family name, Montefeltro is at least suggestive of geographical origin as well (and thus structurally assimilable to Jacopo's *Fano*). Singleton reads Bonconte's movement away from pride of family toward individual identity as sign of "a becoming humility"; and yet, within the larger Chalcidean context that we have sketched, even this attachment to personal identity betrays a limited, antepurgatorial vision.

62. *Purgatorio* 5.89–90: "Giovanna o altri non ha di me cura;/per ch'io vo tra costor con bassa fronte" (Giovanna, or any other, has no care for me, so that I go among these with downcast brow).

63. *Purgatorio* 5.91–93: "E io a lui: 'Qual forza o qual ventura/ti traviò sì fuor di Campaldino,/che non si seppe mai tua sepultura?'" (And I to him, "What force or what chance so carried you astray from Campaldino that your burial-place was never known?").

64. The unified "I" that here dissolves is one with sight (the subject's apparent bodily form in the mirror) and speech. While Jacopo made no direct reference to speech in the account of his death, his locution in verses 73–74 ("ma li profondi fóri/ond'uscì 'l sangue in sul quale io sedea") echoes well-known lines from *Inferno* 13, a disturbing meditation on speech and blood and radically wounded bodies ("Sì de la scheggia rotta usciva insieme/parole e sangue; ond'io lasciai la cima/cadere" [So from that broken twig came out words and blood together; whereon I let fall the tip]; *Inferno* 13. 43–45).

65. For this basic structuralist definition of the linguistic sign, see Ferdinand De Saussure, *Course in General Linguistics*. Cp. the pilgrim's words to Cacciaguida at *Paradiso* 16.18, which underscore the phonetic distinction between "io" and "i'": "voi mi levate sì, ch'i' son più ch'io" (you so uplift me that I am more than I).

66. *Timaeus* 49A–B: "Quam igitur eius vim quamve esse naturam putandum est? Opinor, omnium quae gignuntur receptaculum est, quasi quaedam nutricula. Atque hoc quod de ea dicitur verum est quidem, sed dicendum videtur paulo apertius; est tamen arduum eo | magis, quod praeconfundi mentis aciem necesse est et aestuare tam de igni quam de ceteris materiis, qui magis aquam iure aquam dici putarique oporteat quam terram, cum nulla sit certa et stabilis proprietas corporum quae cuiusque indicet naturalem germanitatem."

67. *Timaeus* 49B–C: "Principio ut de aqua, cuius modo fecimus mentionem, ordiamur: cum astringitur in glaciem, certe saxum terrenaeque soliditatis corpus et minime fusile apparet, eadem haec ignita et diffluens discretaque varie in humorem, spiritum et aereas auras dissolvitur, aer porro exustus ignem creat rursumque extinctus ignis aera corpulentior factus instituit, aer item crassior factus in nubes nebulasque concrescit, quibus elisis et expressis pluviae stagnorumque et fontium largitas demumque ex aqua terrenae moles aggerantur."

68. There are of course other such locutions in the poem, though none so linguistically incisive; cp., for instance, *Inferno* 20.76–78: "Tosto che l'acqua a correr mette co,/non più Benaco, ma Mencio si chiama/fino a Govèrnol, dove cade in Po" (Soon as the water starts to run, it is no longer named Benaco, but Mincio, as far as Govèrnolo, where it falls into the Po). We should also recall here that the four rivers of *Inferno* are in fact one flow under four different names; see *Inferno* 14.76–138.

69. *Timaeus* 49D–50A: "Quapropter de cunctis huius modi mutabilibus ita est habendum: hoc quod saepe alias aliter formatum nobis videtur et plerumque iuxta ignis effigiem non est, opinor, ignis sed igneum quiddam, nec aer sed aereum, nec

omnino quicquam velut habens ullam stabilitatem. Denique | ne pronominibus quidem ullis signanda sunt quibus in demonstratione uti solemus, cum dicimus 'hoc' vel 'illud'; fugiunt enim nec expectant eam appellationem quae de his tamquam existentibus habetur. Igitur ignem quoque eum esse vere putandum, qui semper idem est, et omne cuius proprietas manet. At vero id, in quo fieri singula haec videntur et demum dissolvi pereuntiaque ad alias inde transire formas, solum illud appellandum puto certo pronomine—recte quippe de eo dici posse 'hoc' vel 'illud'—, porro quod recipit qualitatem vel etiam verti potest in contrarias qualitates calidum dici vel candidum, proprioque et certo nomine appellari quod sit incertum et mutabile minime convenire" (For we should understand all of these mutable bodies in the following manner: that which often seems to us to take on this form or that and is generally in the shape of fire is not, in my opinion, "fire" but "a certain fiery substance," nor "air" but "an airy substance," nor anything else as though it had some stability. Nor should they be indicated by those pronouns we use to point things out, when we say "this" or "that"; for they slip away and do not wait for that name which is given to them as though they possessed real existence. Therefore, only that thing whose every property endures and is always the same should be considered "fire." Indeed, that thing in which all these individual elements seem to come into being and then dissolve away by changing form—only that thing can rightly be designated by a stable pronoun, since we can safely talk about it as "this" or "that." For that which takes on qualities and can be converted into other qualities might be called "warm" or "white," but it is wrong to use a genuine, stable noun to designate that which is unstable and mutable).

70. *Timaeus* 48B–C: "Nullus quippe ad hoc usque tempus genituram eorum indicavit, sed tamquam scientibus, quid sit ignis et cetera, sic loquimur et dicimus initia universitatis, constituentes ea quae ne syllabarum quidem locum vicemque pro veri examinis ratione obtinent" (For to this day no one has explained their generation, and yet we speak like people who knew what fire and the rest of them were, and we call them the basic building blocks of the universe, when rational examination shows that they do not even reach the level of syllables); on the linguistic analogy here, see Cornford (Plato, *Timaeus*), 161, n. 1. On this passage, cp. Chalcidius 272: "Quia sermonis elementa litterae sunt, post quas secundi ordinis syllabae, recte dixit quattuor haec mundana corpora ne in syllabarum quidem ordinem collocanda" (Since letters are the building blocks of language, after which come syllables on the second level, he correctly said that these four materials of the universe should not even be placed on the level of syllables). But the idea that the basic indivisible letters of the alphabet were analogous to the building blocks of the physical universe—both designated by the word *elementa*—was common to Roman grammar; see Martin Irvine, *The Making of Textual Culture,* 98–100, and in part. the passage he cites from Priscian, which makes clear that language was also a kind of physical body: "Litterae autem etiam elementorum vocabulo nuncupaverunt ad similitudinem mundi elementorum: sicut enim illa coeuntia omne perficiunt corpus, sic etiam haec

coniuncta literalem vocem quasi corpus aliquod componunt vel magis vere corpus" (But they call "letters" by the term "elements" from a similarity to the elements of the universe: just as elements of the universe come together to constitute every physical body, so letters conjoin to make a written word as if they were forming some sort of corporeal entity, which is to say a body [Irvine's translation modified]). Cp. William of Conches, *Philosophia mundi* 1.21, as cited by Dronke in Bernardus Silvestris, *Cosmographia,* 90–91. On human speech as a transitory flow in time, we must also recall Augustine, *The Confessions of St. Augustine* 11.6–8.

71. Chalcidius 325. Cp. *Microcosmos* 8.43–44 (Bernardus Silvestris, *Cosmographia,* 110): "Res eadem subiecta manet, sed forma vagatur / Atque rei nomen dat nova forma novum" (For the subject matter remains the same, though its form pass away, and a new form only gives this matter a new name). Thus Bernard explicitly draws the parallel between the name of a thing *(nomen rei)* and its temporary form, both of which are outlived by the perpetual flow of underlying material. As Wetherbee remarks *(Platonism and Poetry,* 179), Bernard's language here recalls "Horace's *Ars poetica* on the fortunes of language," a text and an idea (i.e., the continual decay and rebirth of linguistic forms), as we know, which were central to Dante's thinking about language; see in part. *Convivio* 2.13.9–10.

72. *Timaeus* 49E.

73. *Timaeus* 50A–B: "Si quis enim cunctas formas figurasque ex una eademque auri materia fictas iugiter et sine intermissione in alias atque alias reformet, tunc, si quis electa qualibet una figura quaerat quae sit, opinor posse firme et diligenter ac sine reprehensione responderi aurum illud esse nec addere trianguli cylindrive cuiusve alterius <formae> videbitur" (For if from the same piece of gold someone were to form continually and without pause all of the forms and figures into different forms and figures, and then if someone were to choose any one form and ask "what is it?," I think the only proper response you could give without reproach would be "gold," without adding "triangle" or "cyclinder" or any of those other forms that will appear).

74. Chalcidius 326: "Ne, si pyramidem esse responsum sit, illa in aliam figuram mox et inter ipsa verba responsionis migrante qui sic responderit mentiatur" (Lest, if one were to respond "pyramid," and the figure were to change quickly into another even as the words of the response flowed out, the respondent would be a liar).

75. I have visited this site amidst muddy fields in the Casentino and can assure the reader that the precise point of confluence of these two torrents is indeed elusive.

76. On this notion of an underlying phonetic stream that temporal language slices into, see the famous diagram in De Saussure, *Course in General Linguistics,* 112.

77. On the fortress or armor of subjectivity ("the armour of an alienating identity")—an extremely apt turn of phrase for this canto about military egos—see Lacan, "The Mirror Stage," in *Écrits,* 4.

78. See *Inferno* 27.112–29.

79. See Chalcidius 296–300.

80. For tears, liquid flow, or thaw as a sign of repentance and salvation (over and against icy or stony hardness) in a different context, see *Inferno* 33 and, more broadly, the entire Cocytus episode; on this theme, compare Durling and Martinez, *Time and the Crystal* on the *rime petrose*.

81. *Georgic* 1.322–27.

82. See Natalino Sapegno (Dante, *La Divina Commedia*), *ad loc.; Meteorologia* 1.9 and 2.4. In any case, descriptions of elemental conversion were widely available in encylcopedic texts; see Isidore, *Etymologiarum* 13.3.

83. Chalcidius 317–18. Cp. also the *Aeneid* commentator on evaporation and condensation, Jones and Jones, *The Commentary,* 6 (lines 3–12).

84. Chalcidius 317: "Cum igitur terra late fusa convertetur aliquatenus in aquam, tunc siccitas quidem eius mutata erit in humorem, frigus vero, quod commune est, perseverat in statu proprio" (When therefore earth, having dissolved, is commonly converted to water, surely dryness is changed into moistness, while cold, which is common to both, endures in its independent existence).

85. See Waszink (Chalcidius, *Timaeus a Calcidio translatus*) *ad loc.,* who refers the reader to the *De generatione et corruptione* B 3–4, 330 b 2-331 b 2 and *Physics* A 5–8.

86. Chalcidius 317: "Superest igitur, ut sit uspiam frigus, nec enim potest esse sine eo in quo est; hoc porro nihil esse aliud quam silvam ratio testatur" (Thus cold, since it is in both places [earth and water], endures, and it cannot exist without that thing in which it exists; furthermore, reason would demonstrate that this is nothing other than *silva*).

87. For a succint and lucid account of condensation and evaporation in Aristotle, see Patrick Boyde, *Dante Philomythes,* 74–95. Much of Dante's writing demonstrates his indebtedness to Aristotle for his basic understanding of meteorology, not the least of which is his own Scholastic investigation of water and earth, *Questio de aqua et terra.* While the concept of elemental conversion is only indirectly implicated in that treatise (see for instance 23.25–30), Dante alludes here to the common Scholastic notion of a *subiectum elementorum,* the primal elemental material prior to the definition of four distinct elements, akin to Plato's *silva;* cp. *Paradiso* 29.51, "il suggetto d'i vostri alimenti." For a broader discussion of the Aristotelean *prima materia* in Dante, see Boyde, *Dante Philomythes,* 60–63; Dante holds forth on the inscrutability of this concept in *Convivio* 3.15.6.

88. *Etymologiarum* 13.3.1: "Hanc hyle Latini materiam appellaverunt, ideo quia omne informe, unde aliquid faciendum est, semper materia, nuncupatur. Proinde

et eam poetae silvam nominaverunt, nec incongrue, quia materiae silvarum sunt"
(This *hyle* the Latins called *materia,* because everything that is without form, from
which something is to be made, is called *materia.* On account of which the poets
also gave her the name *silva* and not without reason, because these basic materials
come from the forests); cp. Brunetto Latini, *Tresor* 1.6–8. For a recent consideration of the forest as primal space, see Robert Pogue Harrison, *Forests.*

89. For other evaporation *loci,* see *Questio* 23.25–30; *Convivio* 4.18.4; the petrose, "Io son venuto" (vv. 14–21, 53–55; see also Durling and Martinez, *Time and
the Crystal,* 71–108) and "Amor tu vedi ben" (vv. 25–30; see also Durling and
Martinez, 138–64); *Purgatorio* 14.34–36 and 28.121–23.

90. Chalcidius 318: "Rursum dicimus aera duas qualitates habere, calorem et
humorem; constitit autem aquam quoque in duabus qualitatibus inveniri humoris
et frigoris. Erunt ergo et horum propria quae videntur contraria, aquae quidem frigus, aeris vero calor, sed communis his humor. Cum igitur resoluta in vapores aqua
aeri quod ex aqua conversum fluxit | quaeritur ac vindicatur, tunc, opinor, frigus
quidem ad calorem transitum facit, humor porro communis manet neque in aeris
nec in aquae gremio; esse tamen eum uspiam necesse est: erit igitur in silva" (In
turn, we say that air possesses two qualities, heat and moistness; but he established
that water too is found to have two qualities, moistness and cold. Thus there are
qualities proper to each element that seem contrary—cold for water, heat for air—
but moistness is common to both. Thus when water dissolves into air vapors, the
thing that flowed from water in conversion is sought and set free, for then, I believe,
cold makes a transition to heat, while moistness remains in common to both, for it
cannot be found contained in the womb of air or water; nevertheless it is necessary
that it be in both places: thus it will exist in *silva*).

91. Chalcidius 318: "Ex quo perspicuum est, quod in illa corporum mutua per-
mutatione invenitur silva antiquissima et principalis subiectio, perinde ut cera mol-
lis, in qua imprimuntur signacula, aut ut eorum quae generantur commune omnium
receptaculum" (From which it is very clear that in that mutual conversion is found
the most ancient and first foundation, *silva,* like soft wax in which seals are impressed,
or the common receptacle of all created things).

92. While Singleton and others (Longfellow) have taken *rubesto* as "robust,"
"mighty," or "raging" (as in *Inferno* 31.106), given the context it seems likely that the
poet here also aims to evoke the etymological association of that adjective to blood
red *(rubor, rubens, rubeo, rubesco),* particularly given the earlier reference to blushing
(vv. 20–21) and the literal presence of bloody rivers in both the Jacopo and Bonconte
histories. *Rubesto* emerged as a variant of *robusto* through etymological crossbreed-
ing with *rubicondo;* see Giacomo Devoto, *Avviamento alla etimologia italiana, s.v.*
Dante uses *rubicunde* at *Convivio* 4.25.8 to describe blushing virgins. On battlefield
rivers run red, cp. the pilgrim's words to Farinata on Montaperti in *Inferno* 10.85–86

("Lo strazio e 'l grande scempio/che fece l'Arbia colorata in rosso"); for rivers of blood generally in Dante, we of course recall Flegetonte.

93. *Timaeus* 49B–D.

94. Chalcidius 324: "Igitur secundum hanc orbitam rationemque circuitus terra quoque videtur in alia elementa mutari. Si enim sola non convertitur, ad postremum omnia terra fient, siquidem cetera in ipsam convertentur, ipsa autem in nihil eorum habebit conversionem. Sed quia probatio consistit in visu et numque visa est terra in aquam aliamve quam materiam converti, idcirco abstinuit ac refugit terrenae immutationis assertionem, ne pugnare adversum sensus videretur" (Thus following this cycle and cyclical reasoning, earth too appears to be converted into other elements. For if it alone were not to be converted, in the end all things would become earth, seeing as all of the elements would be converted into it while it would be converted into none of them. But because proof is established by sight and earth has never been seen to convert into water or any other element, he refrains from asserting that earth is converted so as not to appear to militate against sense). Boyde (*Dante Philomythes,* 58–60, 71–73) suggests that Dante would have had the example of a burning log as a transformation of earth (or at least, of a body of earthly solidity) into fire from Aristotle, *De generatione* 1.5.322a.15 and 10.327b.12.

95. In Chalcidius's translation, Plato writes that water "appears" to solidify into ice, stones, and earth ("saxum terraeque soliditatis corpus et minime fusile apparet"). In 323, Chalcidius explains that he is talking about freezing and crystallization, a notion Chalcidius may have picked up from any number of sources, as Waszink notes: "Acriter et nimium vigilanter 'apparet': quippe non in sua propria natura perseverans aqua solidatur et fit terra, siquidem est humida, sed quod [ea quae] subiacet, videlicet silva, contrariam naturam, hoc est siccitatem, suscipiens fit ex conversione terra, mutato repente habitu mutataque condicione apparens quod non erat. Sed aquam in saxum solidari dicit, quia in glacialibus et gelidis locis aqua diu constricta mutatur in saxum, quod crystallus vocatur ab Alpinis gentibus montium Raeticorum" (Very sharply and with excessive care he says "appears": since water that solidifies and becomes earth does not maintain its proper state, if it is indeed moist; but since that which lies beneath, *silva,* sustains the opposite quality, that is to say dryness, water becomes earth through conversion: it suddenly changes its habit and condition to appear that which it was not. But water is said to solidify into rock, because in glacial, icy places water that has been long frozen changes to rock, which is called crystal by the Alpine peoples of the Raetian mountains). Thus although Plato does not mention ice (see Cornford's translation at 49B–C: "This [water], when it is compacted, we see becoming earth and stones . . ."), Chalcidius adds the word for clarification ("cum astringitur in glaciem"). For this notion of crystallization in a variety

of classical sources, see Waszink (Chalcidius, *Timaeus a Calcidio translatus*) *ad loc.;* compare Isidore, *Etymologiarum* 16.13. For the history of this science through Dante's day and Dante's poetic deployment of crystallization, particularly in Cocytus and the *rime petrose* (and in part. "Io son venuto," vv. 59–61), see Durling and Martinez, *Time and the Crystal;* on the formation of stones via *congelatio,* see in part. pp. 37–38 (where Durling and Martinez cite Albertus Magnus, *Mineralium liber,* and Seneca, *Quaestiones naturales* 3.12).

96. Chalcidius 317. See also Isidore, *Etymologiarum* 13.3.2: "Terra diluatur in aquam" (Earth dissolves into water).

97. The entire description is of Earth as pregnant mother ("pregno aere," v. 118). On *cingere/incingere* in Dante, compare *Inferno* 8.45, and see M. Cortelazzo and P. Zolli, *Dizionario etimologico della lingua italiana, s.v. incinta,* who cite Isidore: "Incinta, id est sine cinctu; quia praecingi fortiter uterus non permittit" ("Pregnant," that is to say "not wearing a belt or girdle," because the womb cannot be constricted by a belt [during pregnancy]). We have already seen that Jacopo returns to a womb, and Bonconte to a space of maternity.

98. For Isidore on swamps as a place of death, see *Etymologiarum* 13.19; cp. Bernardus the *Aeneid* Commentator on 6.413, PALUDEM (Jones and Jones, *The Commentary,* 90, lines 2–3), where the Acheron ferryboat taking marsh water through its cracks figures the human flesh, whose imperfect solidity makes it vulnerable to the liquid passions: "Paludem Acherontis per rimas navis haurit, dum undas molestarum passionum per foramina sensuum et poros caro recipit" (The boat drinks in the marshy waters of Acheron through its cracks, as the flesh takes the waves of harmful passions through the holes of the senses and the pores).

99. Cp. Bonconte in v. 129: "Di sua preda mi coperse e cinse" ([The Archiano/Arno] covered and wrapped me with its spoils); but also Ulysses, *Inferno* 26.142: "Infin che 'l mar fu sovra noi richiuso" (Till the sea closed over us).

100. *Maremma* came into fourteenth-century Italian from the late Latin neuter plural *maritima* ("loca mari vicina"), built from the adjective *maritimus* (maritime, of the sea); see Carlo Battisti and Giovanni Alessio, *Dizionario etimologico italiano,* vol. 3, *s.v.*

101. Cp. Ciacco's words at *Inferno* 6.42: "Tu fosti, prima ch'io disfatto, fatto" (You were made before I was unmade).

102. See Singleton *ad loc.:* "The use of the article with a first name adds a touch of intimacy and familiarity, Pia repeating in this way the *la* which other people used in speaking *of* her, not *to* her" (emphases in original).

103. On Dante's use of the gerund in general, see the article "Gerundio," by Franca B. Ageno; Patrick Boyde, *Dante's Style in His Lyric Poetry,* 174–76.

5. Reconstructing Subjectivity in *Purgatorio* and *Paradiso*

1. Julia Kristeva, *Powers of Horror,* 115. It is, after all, a suffering, bleeding, and at the same time nutritive body that informs Christianity's central ritual, the Eucharist. Kristeva defines the Eucharist psychoanalytically as the introjection of a wounded ego-ideal and sees here the fundamental mechanism of a new, forever lapsing Christian subjectivity. This contrasts with an Old Testament semiotics of bodily pollution; see Kristeva, 90–132; cp. Kelly Oliver, *Reading Kristeva,* 125–31. On the link between Christian Eucharist and nursing body, see also Caroline Walker Bynum, *Fragmentation and Redemption,* 43–49. For a broader perspective on the relationship of women to food in this period, see Caroline Walker Bynum, *Holy Feast, Holy Fast;* see also Rudolph Bell, *Holy Anorexia.*

2. *Jesus as Mother* focuses on the twelfth-century maternalization of religious language and thought, particularly in Cistercian writing, which reflects a new devotion to Christ's humanity. Bernard of Clairvaux (1091–1153), Dante's guide in upper Paradise, is central here (see in part. pp. 110–20). Bernard speaks of breasts as "a symbol of the pouring out towards others of affectivity or of instruction" (p. 115); he contrasts the charitable *mater* to the worldly *magister* or *dominus.* "He also frequently attributes maternal characteristics, especially suckling with milk, to the abbot when he refers to him as father" (p. 116). In what will become an iconographic motif, Bernard redeems the suffering and blood of the Crucifixion as spiritual nourishment and milk ("suge non tam vulnera quam ubera Crucifixi"; p. 117); thus Christ bleeding from his side is assimilated to the lactating mother. See figures 3.10–14 (and, on Bernard, pp. 93, 157–60, 256–57) in Bynum, *Fragmentation and Redemption,* which collects essays that span Bynum's many interests, but contains a wealth of material and analysis on the maternalization of Christianity among late medieval woman mystics; see esp. pp. 79–118. For a recent study of Bernard's function as Dante's guide, see Steven Botterill, *Dante and the Mystical Tradition.* On the rise of the *madonna lactans* motif in Italian painting of the twelfth to fourteenth centuries, we again recall Margaret Miles, "Infancy, Parenting, and Nourishment."

3. Erich Auerbach, *"Sermo humilis."* On *sermo humilis* in connection with the Ulysses canto, see Giuseppe Mazzotta, *Dante, Poet of the Desert,* 88.

4. Psalm 8:3.

5. See *"Sermo humilis,"* 49, where Auerbach cites, for instance, Augustine, *De trinitate* 1.1: "Sancta Scriptura parvulis congruens, nullius generis rerum verba vitavit, ex quibus quasi gradatim ad divina atque sublimia noster intellectus *velut nutritus* assurgeret" (my emphases; Holy Writ, adapting itself to babes, has not been afraid to use expressions taken from any kind of thing, from which, as though drawing food from it, our understanding may rise gradually to things lofty and sublime); Auerbach, 51: "Scripture 'grows with children,' that is to say, children grow into an understanding of it . . . Thus the style of the Scriptures throughout is *humilis,* lowly

or humble. Even the hidden things *(secreta, recondita)* are set forth in a 'lowly' vein. But the subject matter, whether simple or obscure, is sublime. The lowly, or humble, style is the only medium in which such sublime mysteries can be brought within the reach of men. It constitutes a parallel to the Incarnation, which was also a *humilitas* in the same sense, for men could not have endured the splendor of Christ's divinity." On Scripture as nourishing milk in the *Confessions,* see in part. 3.5–6; for more on Augustine and the nurturing metaphor, cp. Miles, "Infancy, Parenting, and Nourishment," 360–61, and Brian Stock, *Augustine the Reader,* 70. Most recently, Zygmunt G. Barański has championed the idea that the poetics of the *Comedy* reflect a linguistic fluidity and openness akin to Scriptural *sermo humilis* while rejecting the strictly drawn categories of ancient and medieval grammar and rhetoric; see in part. chapter 1 of *"Sole nuovo, luce nuova,"* "L'(anti)-retorica di Dante: note sullo speri-mentalismo e sulla poetica della *Commedia*"; but also "Significar per verba" (part. pp. 14–15) and "Dante's Biblical Linguistics" (part. pp. 106, 135).

6. On the individual's return to *infantia* in order to be reborn and develop a new Christian selfhood, Augustine is again fundamental; see in part. Eugene Vance, "Augustine's *Confessions* and the Grammar of Selfhood," 17–19; Stock, *Augustine the Reader,* 23–25; Miles, "Infancy, Parenting, and Nourishment," 355.

7. The first appears upside down at 22.130–54, the second right side up at 24.103ff. Both prefigure the original tree in terrestrial paradise at 32.37ff. and 33.55ff. On these trees generally, see Lino Pertile, "L'albero che non esiste."

8. The resurrection reference is to Luke 24:13–16, which Charles S. Singleton (Dante, *The Divine Comedy*) cites. Singleton also cites the narrative of the Samaritan woman in its entirety from John 4:5–15. It is notable that the disciples have gone to town to find food ("Discipuli enim eius abierant in civitatem, ut cibos emerent") when Jesus finds himself at the well with the woman, who stresses her social infe-riority ("Quomodo tu, Iudaeus cum sis, bibere a me poscis") and thus marvels at Jesus' request for water ("Da mihi bibere"). Jesus contrasts the liquid nourishment he offers with the water of the well: "Omnis qui bibit ex aqua hac, sitiet iterum; qui autem biberit ex aqua quam ego dabo ei, non sitiet in aeternum, sed aqua quam ego dabo ei fiet in eo fons aquae salientis in vitam aeternam" (Everyone who drinks of this water will thirst again. He, however, who drinks of the water that I will give him will never thirst; but the water that I will give him will become in him a foun-tain of water, springing up unto life everlasting).

9. *Purgatorio* 21.96–97. We should also note that, phonetically, these verses evoke babytalk through their alliterative insistence on the bilabial /m/.

10. *Purgatorio* 22.64–66.

11. On the milk of poetic inspiration, cp. Dante's first Eclogue to Giovanni del Virgilio (*Ecloge,* ed. and trans. E. Cecchini) and in part. p. 662, line 2; p. 664, line 31; p. 668, lines 58–59.

12. Matthew 5:6: "Beati qui (esuriunt et) sitiunt iustitiam, quoniam ipsi satu-rabuntur" (Blessed are they who hunger and thirst for justice, for they will be satis-fied). Dante refers only to thirst at this point; he will complete his reference to this beatitude two cantos later, still on the terrace of gluttony, at *Purgatorio* 24.151–54. On the thrist and hunger metaphor, cp. also *Purgatorio* 23.34–36.

13. *Purgatorio* 22.139–54. The tree speaks of Mary's abstinence at the wedding feast of Cana; of virtuous Roman women who drank no wine; of Daniel's refusal of food; of the Golden Age appreciation for simple food and drink, acorns and river water; of John the Baptist's consumption of honey and locusts in the desert. For sources and citations, see Singleton *ad loc.*

14. *Purgatorio* 23.28–30: "Io dicea fra me stesso pensando: 'Ecco/la gente che perdé Ierusalemme,/quando Maria nel figlio diè di becco!'" (I said to myself in thought, "Behold the people who lost Jerusalem, when Mary struck her beak into her son!"). The account is in Flavius Josephus, *The Jewish War* 6.201–13. Singleton *ad loc.* cites Benvenuto da Imola, who takes his story from Vincent of Beauvais, *Speculum historiale* 10.5, and/or John of Salisbury, *Policraticus* 2.6. Benvenuto, drawing on John, dramatizes the horrific reversal of nutritional roles: "Nam assumpto infantulo quem lactabat . . . 'Veni ergo, mi fili, esto matri cibus'" (For having taken up the little infant she was nursing. . . [she said] "So come, my son, become nourishment for your mother"). Cp. John at 2.6 under the rubric "De Maria quae fame urgente comedit filiam: Erat namque ei sub uberibus parvulus fi-lius" (The Mary Who, Driven by Hunger, Ate Her Own Child [: For There Was a Small Child at Her Breasts]).

15. *Purgatorio* 23.85–87.

16. *Purgatorio* 23.101–2: "Nel qual sarà in pergamo interdetto/a le sfacciate donne fiorentine/l'andar mostrando con le poppe il petto" (When the brazen-faced women of Florence will be forbidden from the pulpit to go displaying their breasts with the paps). We should compare this revelatory gesture of the Florentine women to Dante's description of Eve at *Purgatorio* 29.26–27: "Femmina, sola e pur testé formata,/non sofferse di star sotto alcun velo" (A woman, alone and but then formed, did not bear to remain under any veil).

17. *Purgatorio* 23.109–11. On facial hair as signifier of the *adolescens,* cp. *Purgatorio* 31.68.

18. See *Purgatorio* 21.103–4: "Volser Virgilio a me queste parole/con viso che, tacendo, disse 'Taci';/ma non può tutto la virtù che vuole" (These words turned Virgil to me with a look that, silent, said, "Be silent." But the power that wills can-not do everything); 21.109–10: "Io pur sorrisi come l'uom ch'ammicca;/per che l'ombra si tacque, e riguardommi" (I only smiled, like one who makes a sign; at which the shade was silent, and looked into my eyes); and especially 21.115–17: "Or

son io d'una parte e d'altra preso:/l'una mi fa tacer, l'altra scongiura/ch'io dica; ond'io sospiro" (Now I am caught on the one side and the other: the one makes me keep silence, the other conjures me to speak, so that I sigh). At 22.115, Virgil and Statius fall silent: "Tacevansi ambedue già li poeti" (Now were both poets silent). At 23.21, the poet marks the silence and devotion of the gluttons: "D'anime turba tacita e devota" (A crowd of souls, silent and devout). Canto 24.1–3 then opens with the perfect complementarity of speech and moral progress: "Né 'l dir l'andar, né l'andar lui più lento/facea, ma ragionando andavam forte,/sì come nave pinta da buon vento" (Speech made not the going, nor did the going make that more slow; but, talking, we went on apace even as a ship driven by a fair wind). Silence nonetheless remains a virtue, as in Statius's covert reference to male genitalia at 25.43–44: "Ancor digesto, scende ov'è più bello/tacer che dire" (Digested yet again, it descends there whereof to be silent is more seemly than to speak).

19. *Purgatorio* 24.28–30. Cp. Ovid, *Metamorphoses* 8.824–27. *Purgatorio* 24.20–24 refers to Pope Martin IV's gluttonous appetite for Vernaccia wine and the eels of Bolsena, which, the chronicler Pipino relates, he used to soak in milk before stewing; see Singleton, *ad loc*. Thirst and drink are also thematized in Dante's reference to the winebibber Marchese, podestà of Faenza, at *Purgatorio* 24.31–33.

20. *Purgatorio* 24.37–38. For the historical identity of Ubaldino and Bonifazio and the possible meaning of the mysterious "Gentucca," see Singleton, *ad loc*.

21. *Purgatorio* 24.40–42.

22. See *Purgatorio* 24.49–63.

23. For the full resonance of *pomo,* see my discussion below of *Purgatorio* 27.45.

24. Note the continual references to desire and speech acts in this passage, *Purgatorio* 24.100–11: "E quando innanzi a noi intrato fue,/che li occhi miei si fero a lui seguaci,/come la mente a le parole sue,/parvermi i rami gravidi e vivaci/d'un altro pomo, e non molto lontani/per esser pur allora vòlto in laci./Vidi gente sott'esso alzar le mani/e gridar non so che verso le fronde,/quasi bramosi fantolini e vani/che pregano, e 'l pregato non risponde,/ma, per fare esser ben la voglia acuta,/tien alto lor disio e nol nasconde" (And when he had gone on so far ahead of us that my eyes became such followers of him, as my mind was of his words, the laden and verdant branches of another tree appeared to me, and not far distant, because only then had I come round there. Beneath it I saw people lifting up their hands and crying I know not what toward the leaves, like eager and fond little children, who beg, and he of whom they beg answers not, but to make their longing full keen, holds aloft what they desire and hides it not).

25. *Purgatorio* 24.121–26: "'Ricordivi,' dicea, 'd'i maladetti/nei nuvoli formati, che, satolli,/Tesëo combatter co' doppi petti;/e de li Ebrei ch'al ber si mostrar molli,/per che no i volle Gedeon compagni,/quando inver' Madïan discese i colli'"

("Remember," the voice was saying, "the accursèd ones that were formed in the clouds who, when gorged, fought Theseus with their double breasts; and the Hebrews who at the drinking showed themselves soft, wherefore Gideon would not have them for comrades when he came down the hills to Midian").

26. *Purgatorio* 25.20–21.

27. *Purgatorio* 26.84, 103.

28. *Purgatorio* 26.92.

29. *Purgatorio* 26.97.

30. *Purgatorio* 26.94–96.

31. My account is taken from Singleton, *ad loc.*

32. But Guido is also a father *(padre)* in v. 97 as Dante prepares to collapse these gendered binaries in the earthly paradise.

33. I use the word *semiotic* here both in the general sense of being concerned with the ways in which signs function and language functions as a system of signs, and in the narrower sense defined by Kristeva (see introduction) as a signifying system intimately related to the nurse-mother's body.

34. *Purgatorio* 26.140–47.

35. Virgil to the pilgrim at *Purgatorio* 27.35–36: "Or vedi, figlio:/tra Bëatrice e te è questo muro" (Now see, son, between Beatrice and you is this wall).

36. *Purgatorio* 27.43–45.

37. *Pome* was a common variant in early Italian prose and verse; see Singleton, *ad loc.* Again in this canto, cp. Virgil's words to the pilgrim at *Purgatorio* 27.115–17: "Quel dolce pome che per tanti rami/cercando va la cura de' mortali,/oggi porrà in pace le tue fami" (That sweet fruit which the care of mortals goes seeking on so many branches, this day will give your hungerings peace).

38. *Purgatorio* 22.131–32: "Un alber che trovammo in mezza strada,/con pomi a odorar soavi e buoni" (A tree which we found in the midst of the way, with fruit sweet and good to smell). *Purgatorio* 24.103–4: "Parvermi i rami gravidi e vivaci/d'un altro pomo" (The laden and verdant branches of another tree appeared to me), under whose branches the souls reach out as *bramosi fantolini* (v. 108).

39. On the objects of human desire, see in part. *De doctrina christiana* 1. In the *Confessions,* book 1 takes up *infantia* and *pueritia* and focuses on the breast as primal object of desire; book 2 moves on to *adulescentia* and sexual lust, but also features the famous pear tree (2.4), laden with fruit—"Arbor erat pirus in vicinia nostrae vinae, pomis onusta" (Near our vineyard there was a pear tree, loaded with fruit)—as the prototypical object of fetishistic desire and sin.

40. A tradition that grew from an association between Eve's breast and the apple of original sin; see chapter 1, and Marilyn Yalom, *A History of the Breast,* 4, 18, 40.

In the twelfth century, see Johannes de Hauvilla, *Architrenius,* 2.1.22-23: "Bina mamil-larum distinguit pomula planum/vallis arans sulcum" (A valley divides the twin fruits *[pomula]* of her breasts like a straight and level furrow). For this motif in fourteenth-century Florence, we recall Andrea da Firenze's portrait of Lady Grammar (c. 1365) in the Spanish Chapel of Santa Maria Novella.

41. Barański has defined *Purgatorio* 27 as a structural node of retrospection and anticipation which connects Purgatory to terrestrial paradise; see *"Sole nuovo, luce nuova,"* chapter 7, "Funzioni strutturali della retrospezione nella *Commedia*: l'esem-pio del canto XXVII del *Purgatorio."*

42. *Purgatorio* 28.133.

43. As Matelda explains at *Purgatorio* 28.139–44: "Quelli ch'anticamente poe-taro/l'età de l'oro suo stato felice,/forse in Parnaso esto loco sognaro./Qui fu inno-cente l'umana radice;/qui primavera sempre e ogne frutto;/nettare è questo di che ciascun dice" (They who in olden times sang of the Age of Gold and its happy state perhaps in Parnassus dreamed of this place. Here the root of mankind was innocent; here is always spring, and every fruit; this is the nectar of which each tells).

44. *Purgatorio* 28.145–46.

45. *Purgatorio* 28.148.

46. *Purgatorio* 29.55–57: "Io mi rivolsi d'ammirazion pieno/al buon Virgilio, ed esso mi rispuose/con vista carca di stupor non meno" (I turned round full of wonder to the good Virgil, and he answered me with a look no less charged with amazement). Statius will accompany the pilgrim through to the end of the canticle; see *Purgatorio* 32.28–30; 33.134–35.

47. On the central figure of turning *(aversio, perversio, reversio, conversio)* in Augustine, see Stock, *Augustine the Reader,* 37–39.

48. Jeffrey Schnapp, "Dante's Sexual Solecisms"; Rachel Jacoff, "Transgression and Transcendence."

49. We might recall in this context *Inferno* 12.97: "Chirón si volse in su la destra poppa" (Chiron bent round on his right breast).

50. For a recent consideration of gender in Dante and a survey of the relevant critical literature, see Carolynn Lund-Mead, "Dante and Androgyny."

51. See Matthew 21:4–9, and Singleton, *ad loc.:* "The welcoming cry in the masculine is remarkable in view of the fact that it is Beatrice who comes."

52. *Aeneid* 6.883.

53. Cp. Robert Hollander, "Babytalk in Dante's *Commedia,"* on this passage.

54. On the rhetorical proscription against self-nomination, cp. *Convivio* 1.2.3 and the references in Busnelli and Vandelli *ad loc.;* see also Ernst Robert Curtius, *European Literature and the Latin Middle Ages,* Excursus 17, 515–19. For a recent,

insightful reading of naming and silence in this canto, see Dino Cervigni, "Beatrice's Act of Naming." Cervigni (p. 90) cites Leo Spitzer, "Note on the Poetical and Empirical 'I' in Medieval Authors," *Traditio* 4 (1946), 414–22. Spitzer (p. 417) reads Beatrice's pronunciation of Dante's name as the moment when the pilgrim becomes a "true Christian personality."

55. *Purgatorio* 30.55–57.

56. Bruce Fink, *The Lacanian Subject,* 52. On the alienation inherent in Lacan's understanding of the subject, see Fink, 49–68. On the role of the proper name in this alienation, see p. 53: "The empty set as the subject's place-holder within the symbolic order is not unrelated to the subject's proper name. That name is often selected long before the child's birth, and it inscribes the child in the symbolic. A priori, this name has absolutely nothing to do with the subject; it is as foreign to him or her as any other signifier. But in time this signifier—more, perhaps than any other—will go to the root of his or her being and become inextricably tied to his or her subjectivity. It will become the signifier of his or her very absence as subject, standing in for him or her."

57. We recall that the pilgrim has his body in paradise, a scene that prefigures all souls' reunion with the resurrected body at the end of time. On the importance of the body in medieval Christian definitions of selfhood, particularly in regard to the resurrected body, see my discussion of Bynum at the beginning of the previous chapter.

58. *Inferno* 26.139–42; *Purgatorio* 30.58; *Paradiso* 27.146–47. Cp. *Inferno* 21.13, where *poppa* is paired with *proda; poppa* stands alone at *Purgatorio* 2.43; and *prora* alone at *Inferno* 8.29; *Paradiso* 23.68. On the etymological connection between this *poppa* (stern) and the *poppa* (breast) of *Inferno* 7.27; 12.97; and *Purgatorio* 23.102, see below.

59. *Inferno* 26.139–42: "Tre volte il fé girar con tutte l'acque;/a la quarta levar la poppa in suso/e la prora ire in giù, com'altrui piacque,/infin che 'l mar fu sovra noi richiuso" (Three times it whirled her round with all the waters, and the fourth time it lifted the stern aloft and plunged the prow below, as pleased Another, till the sea closed over us). Cp. *Inferno* 26.124: "E volta nostra poppa nel mattino" (And turning our stern to the morning).

60. It is as though Beatrice simultaneously defines herself as the good ("sono il bene") and good sound ("suono bene"). Such semiotic play on Beatrice's name will reappear at *Paradiso* 7.14, and on Dominic's name at *Paradiso* 12.67–81. The semiotic play inherent in medieval etymologizing and the doctrine of *nomina sunt consequentia rerum*—by which the reified, literal surface of language as a word-unit fixed in the symbolic system is breached to uncover a richer, more dynamic, potentially unlimited field of signifiers—reflects the values of *sermo humilis* inasmuch as these practices refuse to grant the privilege of stability and finality to any one lin-

guistic register. On *nomina sunt consequentia rerum,* see Bruno Nardi, "Nomina sunt consequentia rerum"; on medieval etymology, see Curtius, *European Literature and the Latin Middle Ages,* Excursus 14, 495–501; R. Howard Bloch, *Etymologies and Genealogies.*

61. *Purgatorio* 30.76–78. See Jacques Lacan, "The Mirror Stage," in *Écrits,* 1–7. In terms of gender, this moment reverses the traditional alignment of the power-bearing gaze with the male subject upon the female object as discussed by contemporary feminist film theory; see Kaja Silverman, *The Acoustic Mirror,* and Laura Mulvey, *Visual and Other Pleasures.*

62. *Purgatorio* 30.121–23: "Alcun tempo il sostenni col mio volto:/mostrando li occhi giovanetti a lui,/meco il menava in dritta parte vòlto" (For a time I sustained him with my countenance: showing him my youthful eyes I led him with me turned toward the right goal). We again note the oblique appearence of the key verb *volgere* in the past participle *volto,* here in rhyme with the substantive *volto.*

63. *Purgatorio* 30.82–99. See Psalm 30:2–9, and especially the opening verse: "In te, Domine, speravi, non confundar in aeternum" (In you, O Lord, I take refuge; let me never be put to shame).

64. *Purgatorio* 30.79–81.

65. *Purgatorio* 30.85–91: "Sì come neve tra le vive travi/per lo dosso d'Italia si congela,/soffiata e stretta da li venti schiavi,/poi, liquefatta, in sé stessa trapela,/pur che la terra che perde ombra spiri,/sì che par foco fonder la candela;/così fui sanza lagrime e sospiri" (Even as the snow, among the living rafters upon the back of Italy, is congealed, blown and packed by Slavonian winds, then melting, trickles through itself, if only the land that loses shadow breathes, so that it seems a fire that melts the candle; so was I without tears or sighs). Singleton, *ad loc.,* notes that the passage recalls Augustine's moment of conversion in *Confessions* 8.12. We should of course recall here that the bottom of Hell is an ice-hard place of frozen tears; on hardness as the figure of infernal despair, cp. John Freccero, *Dante: The Poetics of Conversion,* 93–109, 152–66.

66. *Purgatorio* 30.97–99: "Lo gel che m'era intorno al cor ristretto,/spirito e acqua fessi, e con angoscia/de la bocca e de li occhi uscì del petto" (The ice that was bound tight around my heart became breath and water, and with anguish poured from my breast through my mouth and eyes). The brief allusion made here to the analogy between the microcosmic corporeal flows and the macrocosmic geographical flows of elemental conversion was elaborately developed in *Purgatorio* 5; see chapter 4.

67. Again note the use of the verb *volgere (volser).*

68. See Singleton, *ad loc.:* "Iarbas, or Hiarbas, was king of the Gaetulians in North Africa at the time Dido founded Carthage; he was among those who sued in vain for her hand (Virgil, *Aen.* IV, 36, 196, 326; Ovid, *Fasti* III, 552–54)." Anna's

words to Dido at *Aeneid* 4.35–38 (Fitzgerald translation) are particularly relevant: "Esto; aegram nulli quondam flexere mariti,/non Libyae, non ante Tyro; despectus Iarbas/ductoresque alii, quos Africa terra triumphis/dives alit" (Granted no suitors up to now have moved you,/Neither in Libya nor before, in Tyre—/Iarbas you rejected, and the others,/Chieftains bred by the land of Africa/Their triumphs have enriched).

69. Cp. Jacopo del Cassero at *Purgatorio* 5.82–83; my emphases: "Le cannucce e 'l braco/m'impigliar sì ch'*i' caddi*" (The reeds and the mire so entangled me that I fell); and Bonconte da Montefeltro at *Purgatorio* 5.98–102; my emphases: "Arriva' io forato ne la gola,/. . . /. . . e quivi/*caddi*" (I came, wounded in the throat . . . and there I fell). We recall also that the verb is etymologically linked to the dead earthly body via *cadaver,* a link explicit since Tertullian; see Caroline Walker Bynum, *The Resurrection of the Body,* 35.

70. See Shulamith Shahar, *Childhood in the Middle Ages,* 23, 265, nn. 8, 9.

71. See my earlier discussion of *De vulgari* 2.6.4 in chapter 3.

72. *Purgatorio* 33.130–32: "Come anima gentil, che non fa scusa,/ma fa sua voglia de la voglia altrui/tosto che è per segno fuor dischiusa" (As a gentle spirit that makes no excuse, but makes its will of another's will, as soon as that is disclosed by outward sign).

73. See Bynum, *The Resurrection of the Body,* 298–307, and above, chapter 4.

74. Lino Pertile, "A Desire of Paradise," 163; but see also "Paradiso: A Drama of Desire" and "'La punta del disio.'" On the inherent impossibility of representing Paradise and Dante's poetic solution, see also Freccero, *Dante: The Poetics of Conversion.*

75. On this, see in part. "Paradiso: A Drama of Desire." For more on Dante and mysticism, see Giuliana Carugati, *Dalla menzogna al silenzio;* Botterill, *Dante and the Mystical Tradition.*

76. See *Purgatorio* 22.64–66; 100–105.

77. On the two peaks of Parnassus, see Natalino Sapegno, ed. (Dante, *La divina commedia*), *ad loc.,* who refers us to Lucan, *Pharsalia (The Civil Wars)* 5.72, and Ovid, *Metamorphoses* 1.316ff. Of the two peaks, Cirra was sacred to Apollo, Nisa to the Muses.

78. *Paradiso* 1.22–30: "O divina virtù, se mi ti presti/tanto che l'ombra del beato regno/segnata nel mio capo io manifesti,/vedra'mi al piè del tuo diletto legno/venire, e coronarmi de le foglie/che la materia e tu mi farai degno./Sì rade volte, padre, se ne coglie/per trïunfare o cesare o poeta,/colpa e vergogna de l'umane voglie" (O divine Power, if you do so lend yourself to me that I may show forth the image of the blessed realm which is imprinted in my mind, you shall see me come to your beloved tree and crown me with those leaves of which the matter and

you shall make me worthy. So rarely, father, are they gathered, for triumph of caesar or of poet—fault and shame of human wills).

79. *Paradiso* 1.19–21: "Entra nel petto mio, e spira tue/sì come quando Marsïa
traesti/de la vagina de le membra sue" (Enter into my breast and breathe there as
when you drew Marsyas from the sheath of his limbs). The Phrygian satyr Marsyas
challenged Apollo to a contest of song/poetry to be judged by the Muses, who
decided in favor of Apollo. As punishment, Marsyas was bound to a tree and flayed
alive. Ovid, *Fasti* 6.697–708; *Metamorphoses* 6.383–91.

80. *Paradiso* 2.19; 3.91–96; 4.1–6.

81. *Paradiso* 5.16–18: "Sì cominciò Beatrice questo canto;/e sì com'uom che
suo parlar non spezza,/continüò così 'l processo santo" (So Beatrice began this canto,
and as one who does not interrupt his speech [one who does not split or fragment
his speech], she thus continued her holy discourse); cp. *Paradiso* 5.48.

82. *Paradiso* 5.37–39: "Convienti ancor sedere un poco a mensa,/però che 'l
cibo rigido c'hai preso,/richiede ancora aiuto a tua dispensa" (It behooves you to sit
a while longer at table, for the tough food which you have taken requires still some
aid for your digestion). Cp. *Convivio* 1.1, where Dante is purveyor of fallen crumbs,
perhaps somewhere between the nurse's milk and solid adult food; see in part. 1.1.12.

83. See *Paradiso* 9.118–19. The Earth's shadow is cast over these first—at once
perfect and somehow less than perfect—regions of paradise.

84. *Paradiso* 5.73–81.

85. Proverbs 11:25: "Anima quae benedicit impinguabitur" (He who confers
benefits will be made fat).

86. The citation from Proverbs appears three times in Dante's text before and
after Saint Thomas's account of the life of Saint Francis: *Paradiso* 10.96; 11.25; 11.139.

87. On the paradoxical power of poverty to stand up even to the might of a
Caesar, Dante recalls the poor fisherman Amyclas; see Lucan, *Pharsalia* 5.515–31;
cp. *Convivio* 4.13.12, where avarice destroys the natural bond of affection between
father and son. On Christ's material poverty at the Crucifixion, cp. Mark 15:24: "Et
crucifigentes eum diviserunt vestimenta eius, mittentes sortem super eis, quis quid
tolleret" (Then they crucified him, and divided his garments, casting lots for them
to see what each should take).

88. *Paradiso* 11.85–87: "Indi sen va quel padre e quel maestro/con la sua donna
e con quella famiglia/che già legava l'umile capestro" (Then that father and master
goes his way, with his lady and with that family which was already girt with the lowly
cord). On this vestitional theme, cp. Dante's reference in vv. 79–81 to Bernardo da
Quintavalle, one of Saint Francis's early followers and himself a former wealthy merchant, who "si scalzò prima, e dietro a tanta pace corse" (first bared his feet, following such great peace, and running); cp. vv. 81–82. Medieval versions of the life

of Saint Francis featured his undressing in the public square before his father, a "divestment" in both its literal and economic acceptations; Singleton notes that Dante's version relies heavily on those of Saint Bonaventure and Thomas of Celano. We might also recall Giotto's famous portrait of this scene in the basilica at Assisi.

89. Cp. Singleton, *ad loc.:* "Francis, desiring to rise to Heaven 'from the lap' of Poverty, commanded his followers to strip his body, after his death, and let it lie for some time on the bare ground."

90. *Paradiso* 11.124–32.

91. Cp. Mark 1:38: "Ad hoc enim veni" (For this is why I have come). The moment is all the more poignant when we recall that Dominic would go on to found an order of great preachers. Not by coincidence, this canto again foregrounds the proper name as the construct of semiotic, etymological play (see vv. 67–70, 79–81); cp. earlier discussion of *Purgatorio* 30.

92. *Paradiso* 14.43–66. On the doctrine of the resurrected body, see, again, Bynum, *The Resurrection of the Body,* and the previous chapter.

93. *Paradiso* 14.61–64: "Tanto mi parver sùbiti e accorti/e l'uno e l'altro coro a dicer 'Amme!'/che ben mostrar disio d'i corpi morti:/forse non pur per lor, ma per le mamme,/per li padri e per li altri che fuor cari anzi che fosser sempiterne fiamme" (So sudden and eager both the one and the other chorus seemed to me in saying, "Amen," that truly they showed desire for their dead bodies—perhaps not only for themselves, but also for their mothers, for their fathers, and for the others who were dear before they became eternal flames).

94. *Paradiso* 14.97–108, and especially 97–102: "Come distinta da minori e maggi/lumi biancheggia tra ' poli del mondo/Galassia sì, che fa dubbiar ben saggi;/sì costellati facean nel profondo/Marte quei raggi il venerabil segno/che fan giunture di quadranti in tondo" (As, pricked out with greater and lesser lights, between the poles of the Universe, the Milky Way so gleams as to cause even the wise to question, so did those beams, thus constellated, make in the depth of Mars the venerable sign which joinings of quadrants make in a circle). For the Milky Way in John of Salisbury, see chapter 3. In *galassia,* Dante recognized the Greek word *gala,* "milk," thanks to Uguccione's *Magnae derivationes, s.v.;* see Paget Toynbee, "Dante's Latin Dictionary," 105. On *Galassia* here, see also Jeffrey Schnapp, *The Transfiguration of History,* 77–84.

95. Schnapp, *The Transfiguration of History.* For a more recent look at the Cacciaguida cantos, gender, and female citizenship in Florence, see Claire Honess, "Feminine Virtues and Florentine Vices." On linguistic registers in the Cacciaguida cantos, see Dino Cervigni, "I canti di Cacciaguida," and in part. p. 139, n. 1, for further bibliography.

96. *Paradiso* 15.97–102, 112–17.

97. *Paradiso* 15.115–17, 124, 133.

98. *Paradiso* 15.127–29: "Saria tenuta allor tal maraviglia/una Cianghella, un Lapo Saltarello,/qual or saria Cincinnato e Corniglia" (Then a Cianghella or a Lapo Salterello would have been as great a marvel as Cincinnatus and Cornelia would be now).

99. On *ovile* see earlier discussion of *Paradiso* 11.129.

100. At *Paradiso* 16.32–33, Cacciaguida responds to the pilgrim's inquiry into his *püerizia,* "con voce più dolce e suave,/ma non con questa moderna favella" (with a voice more sweet and gentle, but not in this our modern speech).

101. *Paradiso* 16.34–36: "Da quel dì che fu detto *'Ave'*/al parto in che mia madre, ch'è or santa,/s'allevïò di me ond'era grave" (From that day on which *Ave* was uttered, to the birth in which my mother, who now is sainted, was lightened of me with whom she had been burdened); cp. *Paradiso* 15.133. On the Virgin's womb *(ventre)* as the primal locus of human desire, cp. *Paradiso* 23.103–15.

102. *Paradiso* 16.49–57.

103. *Paradiso* 16.67–69: "Sempre la confusion de le persone/principio fu del mal de la cittade,/come del vostro il cibo che s'appone" (The intermingling of people was ever the beginning of harm to the city, as to you the food which is loaded on is to the body).

104. *Paradiso* 17.46–48: "Qual si partio Ipolito d'Atene/per la spietata e perfida noverca,/tal di Fiorenza partir ti convene" (As Hippolytus departed from Athens, by reason of his pitiless and perfidious stepmother, so from Florence must you depart).

105. *Paradiso* 17.55–60: "Tu lascerai ogne cosa diletta/più caramente; e questo è quello strale/che l'arco de lo essilio pria saetta./Tu proverai sì come sa di sale/lo pane altrui" (You shall leave everything beloved most dearly; and this is the arrow which the bow of exile shoots first. You shall come to know how salt is the taste of another's bread). We should recall here Dante's allusion to pre-exilic Florence as suckling at the mother's breast in *De vulgari* 1.6.3 ("quanquam Sarnum biberimus ante dentes").

106. *Paradiso* 17.130–32: "Ché se la voce tua sarà molesta/nel primo gusto, vital nodrimento/lascerà poi, quando sarà digesta" (For if at first taste your voice be grievous, yet shall it leave thereafter vital nourishment when digested).

107. See vv. 91 and 93; Wisdom 1:1: "Love justice, you that are the judges of the earth."

108. *Paradiso* 18.73–78: "E come augelli surti di rivera,/quasi congratulando a lor pasture,/fanno di sé or tonda or altra schiera, / sì dentro ai lumi sante creature/volitando cantavano, e faciensi/or D, or I, or L in sue figure" (And as birds,

risen from the shore, as if rejoicing together at their pasture, make of themselves now a round flock, now some other shape, so within the lights holy creatures were singing as they flew, and in their figures made of themselves now *D*, now *I*, now *L*). On the natural bases of language as a striking vibration of the air *(ictus)* by the vocal cords, we should recall that many ancient and medieval grammars began with a paragraph on the physical mechanics of speech, *De voce;* see, for instance, Heinrich Keil, ed., Priscian (vol. 2, p. 5); Probus (vol. 4, p. 47); Marius Victorinus (vol. 6, p. 4); Audax (vol. 7, p. 323). Cp. the speech of the imperial eagle, also a musical river flow, at *Paradiso* 20.16–30.

109. *Paradiso* 18.88–90: "Mostrarsi dunque in cinque volte sette/vocali e consonanti; e io notai/le parti sì, come mi parver dette" (They displayed themselves then, in five times seven vowels and consonants; and I took note of the parts as they appeared in utterance to me).

110. *Paradiso* 18.94–114. For a visualization of this semiotic process, see the diagrams in Singleton at 18.94.

111. *Paradiso* 19.7–12; *Paradiso* 20.16–30, and especially v. 21, where the source of the metaphorical brook is described as an elevated *ubertà* (from the Latin *uber, breast*); on *ubertà,* cp. *Paradiso* 23.130.

112. *Paradiso* 19.91–96.

113. *Paradiso* 21.19–24, 46–51.

114. *Paradiso* 21.115–20, 127–35.

115. *Paradiso* 22.1–6: "Oppresso di stupore, a la mia guida/mi volsi, come parvol che ricorre/sempre colà dove più si confida;/e quella, come madre che soccorre/sùbito al figlio pallido e anelo/con la sua voce, che 'l suol ben disporre,/mi disse . . ." (Overwhelmed with amazement, I turned to my guide, like a little child who always runs back to where it has most confidence; and she, like a mother who quickly comforts her pale and gasping son with her voice which is wont to reassure him, said to me . . .). Here again we note the figure of turning *(volgersi)*. Despite all the maternal imagery, Dante's text continues to assert the collapse of gender in Christian charity; at 22.52–60, Saint Benedict is an affectionate father.

116. *Paradiso* 23.1–21, and especially 1–10: "Come l'augello, intra l'amate fronde,/posato al nido de' suoi dolci nati/la notte che le cose ci nasconde,/che, per veder li aspetti disïati/e per trovar lo cibo onde li pasca,/in che gravi labor li sono aggrati,/previene il tempo in su aperta frasca,/e con ardente affetto il sole aspetta,/fiso guardando pur che l'alba nasca;/così la donna mïa stava eretta/e attenta" (As the bird, among the beloved leaves, having sat on the nest of her sweet brood through the night which hides things from us, who, in order to look upon their longed-for aspect and to find the food wherewith to feed them, wherein her heavy toils are pleasing to her, foreruns the time, upon the open bough, and with glowing

love awaits the sun, fixedly gazing for the dawn to break; so was my lady standing, erect and eager).

117. See above discussion and *Paradiso* 10.96; 11.25; 11.139. For the Muses as nurses, see *Purgatorio* 22.100–105.

118. *Paradiso* 23.55–60: "Se mo sonasser tutte quelle lingue/che Polimnïa con le suore fero/del latte lor dolcissimo più pingue,/per aiutarmi, al millesmo del vero/non si verria, cantando il santo riso/e quanto il santo aspetto facea mero" (Though all those tongues which Polyhymnia and her sisters made most rich with their sweetest milk should sound now to aid me, it would not come to a thousandth part of the truth, in singing the holy smile, and how it lit up the holy aspect).

119. *Paradiso* 23.121–24: "E come fantolin che 'nver' la mamma/tende le braccia poi che 'l latte prese,/per l'animo che 'nfin di fuor s'infiamma;/ciascun di quei candori in sù si stese" (And as an infant which, when it has taken the milk, stretches its arms toward its mother, its affection glowing forth, each of these splendors stretched upward with its peak); cp. v. 130, which describes the treasures of heaven as an *ubertà;* cp. *Paradiso* 20.21.

120. *Paradiso* 24.1–9: "O sodalizio eletto a la gran cena/del benedetto Agnello, il qual vi ciba/sì che la vostra voglia è sempre piena,/se per grazia di Dio questi preliba/di quel che cade de la vostra mensa,/prima che morte tempo li prescriba,/ponete mente a l'affezione immensa/e roratelo alquanto: voi bevete/sempre del fonte onde vien quel ch'ei pensa" (O Fellowship elect to the great supper of the blessed Lamb, who feeds you so that your desire is ever satisfied, since by the grace of God this man foretastes of that which falls from your table before death appoint his time to him, give heed to his immense longing and bedew him somewhat: you drink ever of the fountain whence flows that which he thinks). The passage is a patchwork of New Testament nutritional metaphors; cp. Apocalypse 19:9; John 1:29 and 6:35; Matthew 15:27; and see Singleton, *ad loc*. Here the pilgrim eats of the crumbs that fall from the table of the blessed; cp. *Convivio* 1.1.10.

121. On the pelican, see Psalm 101:7 and Singleton, *ad loc*. Popular belief associated the pelican with Christ *redentor,* for it was believed that the pelican brought its young back to life by nourishing them with blood drawn from its breast. Thus the image of Christ nurse is implicit. For the image of John at Jesus' breast, see John 13:23: "Erat ergo recumbens unus ex discipulis eius in sinu Iesu, quem diligebat Iesus" (Now one of his disciples, he whom Jesus loved, was reclining at Jesus' bosom). Jesus entrusts John with the care of Mary from the cross at John 19:26–27.

122. Dante alludes to both Apocalypse 1:8 ("'Ego sum A et Ω, principium et finis,' dicit Dominus Deus"; "I am the Alpha and Omega, the beginning and the end," says the Lord) at *Paradiso* 26.16–18, and John 1:1 ("In principio erat Verbum"; In the beginning was the Word) at *Paradiso* 26.43–45.

123. The pilgrim's encounter with John runs from verses 1 to 66; his encounter with Adam from 70 to 142. In between (vv. 67–69), the heavenly choir rejoices.

124. For all of John's authority, the Scripture most relevant to the theme of language and charity in this canto is Paul, 1 Corinthians 13–14. Indeed, for a Christian paradigm of individual development informed by charity, we might recall 1 Corinthians 13:11: "Cum essem parvulus, loquebar ut parvulus, sapiebam ut parvulus, cogitabam ut parvulus, quando factus sum vir, evacuavi quae erant parvuli" (When I was a child, I spoke as a child, I felt as a child, I thought as a child. Now that I have become a man, I have put away the things of a child). Cp. Augustine on his adolescent disdain for the simplicity of Scriptural language in *Confessions* 3.5; Dante Della Terza, "Tradition and Exegesis," 2; Miles, "Infancy, Parenting, and Nourishment," 359, 361–62.

125. In a passage where, again, language and charity merge in the Word. John 15:1–6: "Ego sum vitis vera et Pater meus agricola est, omnem palmitem in me non ferentem fructum tollet eum, et omnem qui fert fructum purgabit eum ut fructum plus adferat, iam vos mundi estis propter sermonem quem locutus sum vobis, manete in me et ego in vobis sicut palmes non potest ferre fructum a semet ipso nisi manserit in vite, sic nec vos nisi in me manseritis, ego sum vitis vos palmites qui manet in me et ego in eo hic fert fructum multum quia sine me nihil potestis facere, si quis in me non manserit mittetur foras sicut palmes et aruit et colligent eos et in ignem mittunt et ardent" (I am the true vine, and my Father is the vine-dresser. Every branch in me that bears no fruit he will take away; and every branch that bears fruit he will cleanse, that it may bear more fruit. You are already clean because of the word that I have spoken to you. Abide in me, and I in you. As the branch cannot alone bear fruit, unless it remains on the vine, so neither can you unless you abide in me. I am the vine, you are the branches. He who abides in me, and I in him, he bears much fruit; for without me you can do nothing. If anyone does not abide in me, he will be cast outside as the branch and wither; and they will gather them up and cast them into the fire, and they will burn." See Werner Ross, "Gott als Gärtner (zu *Par.* XXVI)."

126. Pertile, "L'albero che non esiste," 163, which cites Song of Songs 7:7–8: "Et erunt ubera tua sicut botri vinae."

127. At *De vulgari* 1.10.4, the infinite variety of Italian dialects is like rainfall off the Apennine ridge, which branches out in all directions to form countless rivers, streams, and rivulets.

128. See in part. *De vulgari* 1.8.1; 1.11.1; 1.14.1 ("humeros Apenini frondiferos"); 1.18.1.

129. *Paradiso* 26.137–38. See Horace, *Ars poetica,* vv. 60–63.

130. On the themes of language and love in *Paradiso* 26, Kevin Brownlee, "Language and Desire in *Paradiso* XXVI," is most insightful. In addition to the works mentioned above (Brownlee, "Language and Desire in *Paradiso* XXVI"; Franco Fido,

"Writing Like God—or Better?"; Peter S. Hawkins, "Virtuosity and Virtue"; Mazzotta, *Dante, Poet of the Desert;* Jeremy Tambling, *Dante and Difference*), I have consulted the following *lecturae:* Albino Zenatti, *Lectura Dantis;* Bruno Nardi, "Il linguaggio," *Dante e la cultura medievale,* pp. 148–75; André Pézard, "Adam joyeux"; Guido Barlozzini, *Lectura Dantis romana;* Eugenio Donadoni, *"Paradiso* XXVI"; Phillip Damon, "Adam on the Primal Language"; Giovanni Getto, *Lectura Dantis Scaligera;* Fernando Figurelli, "Il Canto XXVI"; Pier Vincenzo Mengaldo, "Appunti sul Canto XXVI del *Paradiso*"; Joseph Cremona, *Cambridge Readings in Dante's "Comedy";* Giorgio Santangelo, *Dante e la Sicilia,* 165–82.

131. The reading I am suggesting here is supported by the image of the stormy sea at *Paradiso* 27.145–48 (see below) and contradicts the standard reading espoused by Singleton and Sapegno, who interpret the verses in strict Neoplatonic terms, according to which the sea is dangerous, wrong love, and the shore is secure, right love. Thus they read: "Tratto m'hanno del mar de l'amor torto e m'han posto a la riva de l'amor diritto." This reading fails to recognize the Christian reversal of those standard Neoplatonic poles (as we saw in John of Salisbury) and ignores the celebration of language and charity as liquid flow which has been building throughout *Paradiso.* Thus I read: "Tratto m'hanno del mar de l'amor torto e m'han posto a la riva del mar de l'amor diritto." Indeed, I feel that my reading—more balanced in structure by implied repetition of the assonant phrase *del mar de l'amor*—constitutes the more obvious interpretation. In this context, we should recall *Inferno* 1.22–27.

132. *Paradiso* 26.89–90: "E poi mi rifece sicuro/un disio di parlare ond'ïo ardeva" (And then a desire to speak, wherewith I was burning, gave me assurance); cp. *Purgatorio* 21.103ff. and the above discussion.

133. See *Purgatorio* 27.45, 115–17 and above discussion.

134. *Paradiso* 26.92–93: "O padre antico/a cui ciascuna sposa è figlia e nuro" (O ancient father of whom every bride is daughter and daughter-in-law). On circumlocutions for Adam, cp. *Paradiso* 7.26, "quell'uom che non nacque," which still suggests a radical detachment from female corporeality; see Mengaldo at *De vulgari* 1.6.1; Bruno Nardi, "Il Canto XXVI," 29–30.

135. Adam's words precisely evoke the theme of nutrition and exile. *Paradiso* 26.115–17: "Or, figliuol mio, non il gustar del legno/fu per sé la cagion di tanto essilio,/ma solamente il trapassar del segno" (Now know, my son, that the tasting of the tree was not in itself the cause of so long an exile, but solely the overpassing of the bound); cp. *Inferno* 26.108–9: "Dov' Ercule segnò li suoi riguardi/acció che l'uom più oltre non si metta" (Where Hercules set up his markers, that man should not pass beyond).

136. *Paradiso* 26.139–42: "Nel monte che si leva più da l'onda,/fu'io, con vita pura e disonesta,/da la prim' ora a quella che seconda,/come 'l sol muta quadra, l'ora sesta" (On the mountain which rises highest from the sea I lived pure, then guilty,

from the first hour to that which follows, when the sun changes quadrant, next upon the sixth); cp. *Inferno* 26.139–42; Fido, "Writing Like God—or Better?," 256.

137. *Paradiso* 26.124–38: "La lingua ch'io parlai fu tutta spenta/innanzi che a l'ovra inconsummabile/fosse la gente di Nembròt attenta:/ché nullo effetto mai razïonabile,/per lo piacere uman che rinovella/seguendo il cielo, sempre fu durabile./Opera naturale è ch'uom favella;/ma così o così, natura lascia/poi fare a voi secondo che v'abbella./Prima ch'i' scendessi a l'infernale ambascia,/*I* s'appellava in terra il sommo bene/onde vien la letizia che mi fascia;/e *El* si chiamò poi: e ciò convene,/ché l'uso d'i mortali è come fronda/in ramo, che sen va e altra vene" (The tongue which I spoke was all extinct before the people of Nimrod attempted their unaccomplishable work; for never was any product of reason durable forever, because of human liking, which alters, following the heavens. That man should speak is nature's doing, but whether thus or thus, nature then leaves you to follow your own pleasure. Before I descended to the anguish of Hell the Supreme Good from whom comes the joy that swathes me was named *I* on earth; and later He was called *El:* and that must needs be, for the usage of mortals is as a leaf on a branch, which goes away and another comes).

138. On Babel, cp. *De vulgari* 1.7.4–8 and Mengaldo *ad loc.;* Maria Corti, *Il viaggio testuale;* Nardi, "Il linguaggio," 190–95.

139. *Paradiso* 26.133–35.

140. *Paradiso* 30.82–90: "Non è fantin che sì sùbito rua/col volto verso il latte, se si svegli/molto tardato da l'usanza sua,/come fec'io, per far migliori spegli/ancor de li occhi, chinandomi a l'onda/che si deriva perché vi s'immegli;/e sì come di lei bevve la gronda/de le palpebre mie, così mi parve/di sua lunghezza divenuta tonda" (No infant, on waking far after its hour, so suddenly rushes with face toward the milk, as then did I, to make yet better mirrors of my eyes, stooping to the wave which flows there that we may be bettered in it. And even as the eaves of my eyelids drank of it, so it seemed to me out of its length to have become round).

141. *Paradiso* 30.139–41: "La cieca cupidigia che v'ammalia/simili fatti v'ha al fantolino/che muor per fame e caccia via la balia" (The blind cupidity which bewitches you has made you like the little child who dies of hunger and drives away his nurse).

142. *Paradiso* 31.61–63: "Diffuso era per li occhi e per le gene/di benigna letizia, in atto pio/quale a tenero padre si convene" (His eyes and cheeks were suffused with benign gladness, his mien kindly such as befits a tender father). For a recent investigation into Bernard's role in Dante's poem, see Botterill, *Dante and the Mystical Tradition.*

143. *Paradiso* 33.1–39.

144. *Paradiso* 33.115–20.

145. See *Paradiso* 1.13–18 and above discussion.

BIBLIOGRAPHY

Abelson, Paul. *The Seven Liberal Arts.* New York: Teachers' College, Columbia University, 1906.

Acta sanctorum. Paris and Rome: V. Palmé, 1868.

Adelard of Bath. *De eodem et diverso.* Ed. H. E. E. Willner. Münster: Aschendorff, 1902.

Ageno, Franca B. "Gerundio." In *Enciclopedia dantesca,* appendix, 292–304.

Ahl, Diane Cole. *Benozzo Gozzoli.* New Haven: Yale University Press, 1996.

Alan of Lille. *Anticlaudianus.* Ed. R. Bossuat. Paris: J. Vrin, 1955.

———. *Anticlaudianus; Or The Good and Perfect Man.* Trans. J. J. Sheridan. Toronto: Pontifical Institute of Mediaeval Studies, 1973.

———. *De planctu naturae.* Ed. N. Häring. *Studi Medievali,* ser. 3, 19:2 (1978): 797–879.

———. *The Plaint of Nature.* Trans. J. J. Sheridan. Mediaeval Sources in Translation, vol. 26. Toronto: Pontifical Institute of Mediaeval Studies, 1980.

Alberti, Leon Battista. *I libri della famiglia.* 3d ed. Ed. R. Romano and A. Tenenti. Turin: Einaudi, 1969.

Alessio, Gian Carlo. "A Few Remarks on the *Volgare Illustre.*" *Dante Studies* 113 (1995): 57–67.

———. "La grammatica speculativa e Dante." *Letture classensi* 13 (1984): 69–88.

———. "I trattati grammaticali di Giovanni del Virgilio." *Italia medioevale e umanistica* 24 (1981): 159–212.

Alexander of Villedieu. *Das Doctrinale des Alexander de Villa-Dei.* Ed. D. Reichling. Monumenta Germaniae Paedagogica, vol. 12. Berlin: Hoffman, 1893. Reprint, New York: Garland, 1974.

Alighieri, Dante. *Convivio.* Ed. G. Busnelli and G. Vandelli. 2 vols. Florence: Le Monnier, 1954.

————. *Dante's Il Convivio:The Banquet.* Trans. R. H. Lansing. Garland Library of Medieval Literature, vol. 65, series B. New York: Garland, 1990.

————. *De vulgari eloquentia: Introduzione e Testo.* Ed. P. V. Mengaldo. Vulgares Eloquentes, vol. 3. Padua: Antenore, 1968.

————. *De vulgari eloquentia.* Ed. and trans. S. Botterill. Cambridge: Cambridge University Press, 1996.

————. *De vulgari eloquentia.* In *Opere minori,* vol. 2. Ed. and trans. P. V. Mengaldo, 3–237. Milan and Naples: Ricciardi, 1979.

————. *De vulgari eloquentia ridotto a miglior lezione e commentato.* Ed. and trans. A. Marigo. Florence: Felice Le Monnier, 1938.

————. *Dante in Hell: The "De vulgari eloquentia."* Ed. and trans. W. Welliver. L'interprete, vol. 21. Ravenna: Longo, 1981.

————. *De l'eloquence en langue vulgaire.* In *Oeuvres complètes.* Ed. and trans. A. Pézard. Paris: Bibliothèque de la Pléiade, 1965.

————. *La divina commedia.* Ed. N. Sapegno. 3 vols. Florence: La Nuova Italia, 1981–82.

————. *The Divine Comedy.* Ed. and trans. C. S. Singleton. 3 vols. Princeton: Princeton University Press, 1970.

————. *The Divine Comedy of Dante Alighieri: Inferno.* Ed. R. M. Durling and R. L. Martinez. Trans. Robert M. Durling. New York: Oxford University Press, 1996.

————. *Egloge.* In *Opere minori,* vol. 2. Ed. and trans. E. Cecchini, 645–89. Milan and Naples: Ricciardi, 1979.

————. *Epistolae.* Ed. G. Brugnoli and A. Frugoni. Milan and Naples: Ricciardi, 1979.

————. *The Letters of Dante.* 2d ed. Ed. P. Toynbee. Oxford: Clarendon Press, 1966.

————. *Questio de aqua et terra.* In *Opere minori,* vol. 2. Ed. and trans. Francesca Mazzoni, 691–880. Milan and Naples: Ricciardi, 1979.

————. *Vita Nuova.* Ed. E. Sanguineti and A. Berardinelli. Milan: Garzanti, 1977.

————. *La Vita Nuova.* Trans. B. Reynolds. New York: Penguin, 1969.

Anselm of Besate. *Anselm der Peripatetiker, Rhetorimachia.* Ed. E. Dümmler. Halle: H. Böhlau, 1872.

Argan, Giulio Carlo. *Storia dell'arte italiana.* 4 vols. Florence: Sansoni, 1968.

Aristotle. *Poetics.* Trans. K. A. Telford. Chicago: Gateway, 1961.

Armour, Peter. "Words and the Drama of Death in *Purgatorio* V." In *Word and Drama in Dante,* ed. John C. Barnes and Jennifer Petrie, 93–122. Dublin: Irish Academic Press, 1993.

Arrigo da Settimello. *Elegia.* Ed. G. Cremaschi. Orbis Christianus, vol. 1. Bergamo: Istituto italiano edizioni Atlas, 1949.

————. *Henrici Septimellensis Elegia sive De Miseria.* Ed. A. Marigo. Scriptores Latini Medii Aevi Italici, vol. 1. Padua: Draghi, 1926.

Arts libéraux et philosophie au moyen âge. Actes du Quatrième Congrès International de Philosophie Médiévale. Montreal and Paris: J.Vrin, 1969.

Ascoli, Albert Russell. "*Neminem ante nos:* History and Authority in the *De vulgari eloquentia.*" *Annali d'Italianistica* 8 (1990): 186–231.

Atkinson, Clarissa W. *The Oldest Vocation: Christian Motherhood in the Middle Ages.* Ithaca: Cornell University Press, 1991.

Auerbach, Erich. "*Sermo Humilis.*" In *Literary Language and Its Public in Late Latin Antiquity and in the Middle Ages,* trans. R. Mannheim, 25–66. New York: Pantheon Books, 1965. Originally *Literatursprache und Publikum in der lateinischen Spätantike und im Mittelalter.* Bern: Francke Verlag, 1958.

Augustine. *The City of God.* Trans. H. Bettenson. London: Penguin Books, 1984.

————. *The City of God against the Pagans.* Ed. and trans. E. M. Sanford and W. Green. Loeb Classical Library. Cambridge, Mass.: Harvard University Press; London: William Heinemann Ltd., 1965.

————. *Confessionum libri XIII.* Ed. L. Verheijen. Corpus christianorum, series latina, vol. 27. Turnhout: Brepols, 1981.

————. *The Confessions of St.Augustine.* Trans. R. Warner. New York: Mentor/New American Library, 1963.

————. *De doctrina christiana.* Turnhout: Brepols, 1982.

————. *On Christian Doctrine.* Trans. D. W. Robertson, Jr. New York and London: Macmillan/Collier, 1958.

Aulus Gellius. *Noctes Atticae.* Ed. and trans. J. C. Rolfe. Loeb Classical Library. Cambridge, Mass.: Harvard University Press; London: William Heinemann Ltd., 1948.

Aurelius Victor. *Origo gentis romanae.* Ed. G. Puccioni. Florence: Vallecchi, 1958.

Avalle, D'Arco Silvio. "L'ultimo viaggio di Ulisse." In *Modelli semiologici nella "Commedia" di Dante,* 33–63. Milan: Bompiani, 1975.

Aymard, August. *Ancienne peinture murale représentant les arts libéraux.* Paris: Victor Didron, 1850.

Ayrton, Michael. *Giovanni Pisano, Sculptor.* London: Thames and Hudson, 1969.

Baldelli, Ignazio. "Sulla teoria linguistica di Dante." *Cultura e Scuola* 13–14 (Jan.–June 1965): 705–13.

Baldwin, Charles Sears. *Medieval Rhetoric and Poetic to 1400.* Gloucester, Mass.: Peter Smith, 1959.

Ball, Robert. "Theological Semantics: Virgil's *Pietas* and Dante's *Pietà.*" *Stanford Italian Review* 2.1 (Spring 1981): 59–79.

Barański, Zygmunt G. "Dante and Medieval Poetics." In *Dante: Contemporary Perspectives,* ed. A. A. Iannucci, 3–22. Toronto: University of Toronto Press, 1997.

———. "Dante commentatore e commentato: Riflessioni sullo studio dell'*iter* ideologico di Dante." In *Dante nei commenti del Novecento,* 135–58. *Letture classensi,* vol. 23. Ravenna: Longo, 1994.

———. "Dante's (Anti-)Rhetoric: Notes on the Poetics of the *Commedia.*" In *Moving in Measure: Essays Presented to Brian Moloney,* ed. J. Bryce and D. Thompson, 1–14. Hull, England: Hull University Press, 1989.

———. "Dante's Biblical Linguistics." *Lectura dantis* 5 (1989): 105–43.

———. "'Significar *per verba*': Notes on Dante and Plurilingualism." *The Italianist* 6 (1986): 5–18.

———. *"Sole nuovo, luce nuova": Saggi sul rinnovamento culturale in Dante.* Turin: Scriptorium, 1996.

———. "'Sordellus . . . qui . . . patrium vulgare deseruit': A Note on *De vulgari eloquentia* I, 15, sections 2–6." In *The Cultural Heritage of the Italian Reinassance,* ed. C. E. J. Griffiths and R. Hastings, 19–45. Lewinston, N.Y.: Edwin Mellen Press, 1993.

Barchiesi, Alessandro. "Caieta." In *Enciclopedia virgiliana,* vol. 1.

———. "Palinuro e Caieta: Due 'epigrammi' virgiliani (*Aen.* V 870 sg.; VII 1–4)." *Maia* new series 31 (Jan.–April 1979): 3–11.

Barlozzini, Guido. *Lectura Dantis romana: Casa di Dante in Roma. L'11 marzo, 1956.* Turin: Società Editrice Internazionale, 1961.

Barolini, Teodolinda. "Arachne, Argus, and St. John: Transgressive Art in Dante and Ovid." *Mediaevalia* 13 (1987): 207–26.

———. "Dante's Heaven of the Sun as a Meditation on Narrative." *Lettere Italiane* 1 (1988): 3–36.

———. *Dante's Poets: Textuality and Truth in the "Comedy."* Princeton: Princeton University Press, 1984.

———. "Dante's Ulysses: Narrative and Transgression." In *Dante: Contemporary Perspectives,* ed. A. A. Iannucci, 113–32. Toronto: University of Toronto Press, 1997.

———. "Detheologizing Dante: For a 'New Formalism' in Dante Studies." *Quaderni d'Italianistica* 10, 1–2 (1989): 35–53.

———. *The Undivine Comedy: Detheologizing Dante.* Princeton: Princeton University Press, 1992.

Bartholomeus Angelicus. *De rerum proprietatibus*. Frankfurt: Richter, 1601. Reprint, Frankfurt: Minerva, 1964.

Bartolomeo di Bartoli da Bologna. *La canzone delle virtù e delle scienze*. Ed. L. Dorez. Bergamo: Istituto Italiano D'Arti Grafiche, 1904.

Battaglia, Salvatore. *Grande dizionario della lingua italiana*. Turin: UTET, 1961.

Battisti, Carlo, and Giovanni Alessio. *Dizionario etimologico italiano*. Florence: G. Barbèra, 1952.

Baudri de Bourgueil. *Les oeuvres poétiques de Baudri de Bourgueil*. Ed. Ph. Abrahams. Paris: Champion, 1926.

Baum, Richard. "Dante—fabbro del parlar materno." In *Dante Alighieri 1985*, ed. R. Baum and W. Hirdt, 65–88. Tübingen: Stauffenburg, 1985.

Baum, Richard, and Willi Hirdt, eds. *Dante Alighieri 1985*. Romanica et Comparatistica, vol. 4. Tübingen: Stauffenburg, 1985.

Behagel, Otto. "Lingua materna." *Zeitschrift für französische Sprache. Behrens Festschrift*. Supplementheft 13 (1929): 13–15.

Bell, Rudolph. *Holy Anorexia*. Chicago: University of Chicago Press, 1985.

Bellissima, G. "Sant'Agostino grammatico." In *Augustinus magister. Congrès International Augustinien, Paris, 21–24 septembre 1954*, 3 vols., 1:35–42. Paris: Études Augustiniennes, 1954–55.

Bernardus Silvestris. *Cosmographia*. Ed. P. Dronke. Leiden: Brill, 1978.

———. *The Cosmographia of Bernardus Silvestris*. Ed. W. Wetherbee. New York: Columbia University Press, 1973.

?Bernardus Silvestris. *The Commentary on Martianus Cappella's "De nuptiis Philologiae et Mercurii"Attributed to Bernardus Silvestris*. Ed. H. J. Westra. Toronto: Pontifical Institute of Mediaeval Studies, 1986.

Bibliotheca sanctorum. Rome: Città Nuova, 1968.

Biller, Peter, and Alastair J. Minnis, eds. *Medieval Theology and the Natural Body*. Rochester, N.Y.: York Medieval Press, 1997.

Bloch, R. Howard. *Etymologies and Genealogies*. Chicago: University of Chicago Press, 1983.

Boas, Henriette. *Aeneas's Arrival in Latium*. Amsterdam: N.V. Noord-Hollandsche Uitgeversmaatschappij, 1938.

Boethius. *The Consolation of Philosophy*. Trans. R. Green. Indianapolis: Bobbs-Merrill, 1962.

———. *Philosophiae Consolationis Libri Quinque*. Ed. K. Büchner. Heidelberg: C. Winter, 1960.

Boncompagno da Signa. *Rhetorica novissima*. Ed. A. Gaudenzi. Scripta anecdota glossatorum, vol. 2. Bibliotheca iuridica medii aevi, vol. 2. Bologna: Treves, 1892.

Bonner, Stanley F. *Education in Ancient Rome: From the Elder Cato to the Younger Pliny.* Berkeley: University of California Press, 1977.

Bonvesin da la Riva. *Vita scolastica. Quinque claves sapientiae.* Ed. A. Vidmanová-Schmidtová. Leipzig: Teubner, 1969.

Borst, Arno. *Der Turmbau von Babel: Geschichte der Meinungen über Ursprung und Vielfalt der Sprachen und Völker.* Vol. 2, 1–2. Stuttgart: Anton Hiersemann, 1958 and 1959.

Botterill, Steven. *Dante and the Mystical Tradition: Bernard of Clairvaux in the "Commedia."* Cambridge: Cambridge University Press, 1994.

Bowie, Malcolm. *Lacan.* Cambridge, Mass.: Harvard University Press, 1991.

Boyde, Patrick. *Dante Philomythes and Philosopher: Man in the Cosmos.* Cambridge: Cambridge University Press, 1981.

———. *Dante's Style in His Lyric Poetry.* Cambridge: Cambridge University Press, 1971.

Braidotti, Rosi. *Nomadic Subjects: Embodiment and Sexual Difference in Contemporary Feminist Theory.* New York: Columbia University Press, 1994.

Brehaut, Ernest. *An Encyclopedist of the Dark Ages: Isidore of Seville.* Columbia University Studies in History, Economics, and Public Law, vol. 48. New York: Columbia University Press, 1912.

Brown, Peter. *Augustine of Hippo.* Berkeley: University of California Press, 1967.

Brownlee, Kevin. "*Inferno* XXVI." *Lectura Dantis* 16/17 (Spring–Fall 1995): 388–401.

———. "Language and Desire in *Paradiso* XXVI." In *Lectura Dantis* 6 (Spring 1990): 46–59.

Brunetto Latini. *Li livres dou tresor.* Ed. F. J. Carmody. Modern Philology, vol. 22. Berkeley: University of California Press, 1948.

———. *La Rettorica.* Ed. F. Maggini. Florence: Le Monnier, 1968.

———. *Tesoretto.* In *Poeti del Duecento,* ed. Gianfranco Contini. Milan and Naples: Ricciardi, 1960.

Burge, Evan L., Richard Johnson, and William Harris Stahl. "Bibliographical Survey of the Seven Liberal Arts in Medieval and Renaissance Iconography." In *Martianus Capella and the Seven Liberal Arts,* vol. 1, appendix A. New York: Columbia University Press, 1971.

Burke, Kenneth. "Verbal Action in St. Augustine's *Confessions.*" In *The Rhetoric of Religion: Studies in Logology,* 43–171. 2d ed. Berkeley: University of California Press, 1970.

Bursill-Hall, Geoffrey L. "The Middle Ages." In *Historiography of Linguistics,* 179–230. Current Trends in Linguistics, vol. 13. The Hague: Mouton, 1975.

————. *Speculative Grammars of the Middle Ages: The Doctrine of the Partes Orationis of the Modistae.* The Hague: Mouton, 1971.

Butler, Judith. *Gender Trouble: Feminism and the Subversion of Identity.* London: Routledge, 1990.

Bynum, Caroline Walker. *Fragmentation and Redemption: Essays on Gender and the Human Body in Medieval Religion.* New York: Zone Books, 1992.

————. *Holy Feast, Holy Fast: The Religious Significance of Food to Medieval Women.* Berkeley: University of California Press, 1987.

————. *Jesus as Mother: Studies in the Spirituality of the High Middle Ages.* Berkeley: University of California Press, 1982.

————. *The Resurrection of the Body in Western Christianity, 200–1336.* New York: Columbia University Press, 1995.

Cambon, Glauco. "Dante and the Drama of Language." In *Dante's Craft: Studies in Language and Style,* 23–45. Minneapolis: University of Minnesota Press, 1969.

Capelli, Mario. "Il *Timeo* nell'opera di Dante." *Giornale dantesco* 2 (1895): 470–77.

Carli, Enzo. *Giovanni Pisano.* Pisa: Pacini, 1977.

Carugati, Giuliana. *Dalla menzogna al silenzio: La scrittura mistica della "Commedia" di Dante.* Bologna: Il Mulino, 1991.

Cassiodorus. *Introduction to Divine and Human Readings.* Trans. L. W. Jones. Columbia University Records of Civilisation, vol. 40. New York: Columbia University Press, 1946.

————. *Cassiodori Senatoris institutiones divinarum et saecularium litterarum.* Ed. R. A. B. Mynors. Oxford: Clarendon Press, 1937.

Castaldo, Dino. "L'etica del primiloquium di Adamo nel *De Vulgari Eloquentia.*" *Italica* 59, 1 (Spring 1982): 3–15.

Cervigni, Dino. "Beatrice's Act of Naming." *Lectura dantis* 8 (Spring 1991): 85–99.

————. "I canti di Cacciaguida: Significato della storia e poetica della lingua." In *Dante Alighieri 1985,* ed. R. Baum and W. Hirdt, 129–40. Tübingen: Stauffenburg, 1985.

Cestaro, Gary P. "*A la tetta de la madre s'apprende:* The Monstrous Nurse in Dante's Grammar of Selfhood." In *Monsters in the Italian Literary Imagination,* ed. Keala Jewell. Detroit: Wayne State University Press, 2001.

————. "Dante, Boncompagno da Signa, Eberhard the German and the Rhetoric of the Maternal Body." In *The Rhetoric Canon: Logic, Ethics, and Poetic Knowledge,* ed. B. Deen Schildgen, 175–97. Detroit: Wayne State University Press, 1997.

————. ". . . *quanquam Sarnum biberimus ante dentes* . . . : The Primal Scene of Suckling in Dante's *De vulgari eloquentia.*" *Dante Studies* 109 (1991): 119–47.

————. "The Whip and the Wet Nurse: Dante's *De vulgari eloquentia* and the

Psychology of Grammar in the Middle Ages." Ph.D. diss., Harvard University, 1990.

Chalcidius. *Timaeus a Calcidio translatus commentarioque instructus*. Ed. J. H. Waszink. Corpus Platonicum Medii Aevi, Plato latinus, vol. 4, ed. R. Klibansky. London: The Warburg Institute, 1962.

Charland, Thomas Marie. *Artes praedicandi*. Paris and Ottawa: J. Vrin and Institut d'études médiévales, 1936.

Cheles, Luciano. *Lo Studiolo di Urbino: Iconografia di un microcosmo principesco*. Modena: Panini, 1986.

Chenu, Marie Dominique. "Grammaire et théologie aux XIIe et XIIIe siècles." *Archives d'histoire doctrinale et littéraire du moyen âge* 10–11 (1935–36): 5–28.

Cicero. *Tusculanae Disputationes*. Ed. and trans. J. E. King. London: William Heinemann; New York: G. P. Putnam's Sons, 1927.

Clark, Donald Lemen. "The Iconography of the Seven Liberal Arts." *Stained Glass* 28 (1933): 3–17.

Clerval, Alexandre. *Les écoles de Chartres au moyen-âge du Ve au XVIe siècle*. Mémoires de la Société Archéologique d'Eure-et-Loir, vol. 11. Paris: A. Picard, 1895.

————. "L'enseignement des arts libéraux à Chartres et à Paris dans la première moitié du XIIe siècle, d'après l'*Heptateuchon* de Thierry de Chartres." In *Congrès Scientifique International des Catholiques tenu à Paris du 8 au 13 avril, 1888,* vol. 2. Paris: Bureaux des Annales de philosophie chrétienne, 1889.

Colish, Marcia L. "Eleventh-Century Grammar in the Thought of St. Anselm." In *Arts libéraux et philosophie au moyen âge, 785–95*. Montreal and Paris: J. Vrin, 1969.

————. *The Mirror of Language: A Study in the Medieval Theory of Knowledge*. New Haven: Yale University Press, 1968.

Collings, Stanley Tate. *The Interpretation of Virgil with Special Reference to Macrobius*. Oxford and London: B. H. Blackwell and Snipkin, Marshall & Co., 1909.

Comparetti, Domenico. *Vergil in the Middle Ages*. Trans. E. F. M. Benecke. London: Allen & Unwin Ltd., 1895. Reprint, Hamden, Conn.: Archon Books, 1966.

————. *Virgilio nel Medioevo*. Ed. and revised by G. Pasquali. Florence: La Nuova Italia, 1937.

Copeland, Rita. *Rhetoric Hermeneutics and Translation in the Middle Ages: Academic Traditions and Vernacular Texts*. Cambridge: Cambridge University Press, 1991.

Corpet, E.-F. "Portraits des arts libéraux d'après les écrivains du moyen âge." *Annales Archéologiques* 17 (1857): 89–103.

Corsi, Giuseppe. *Rimatori del trecento*. Turin: UTET, 1969.

Cortelazzo, Manlio, and Paolo Zolli. *Dizionario etimologico della lingua italiana*. Bologna: Zanichelli, 1983.

Corti, Maria. *Dante a un nuovo crocevia*. Florence: Sansoni, 1982.

———. *Il viaggio testuale: Le ideologie e le strutture semiotiche*. Turin: Einaudi, 1978.

Courcelle, Pierre. *La Consolation de la Philosophie dans la tradition littéraire*. Paris: Études Augustiniennes, 1967.

———. *Recherches sur les Confessions de saint Augustin*. Paris: De Boccard, 1950.

Cremona, Joseph. *Cambridge Readings in Dante's "Comedy."* Ed. K. Foster and P. Boyde. Cambridge: Cambridge University Press, 1981.

Crouse, Robert Darwin. "Honorius Augustodunensis: The Arts as 'via ad patriam.'" In *Arts libéraux et philosophie au moyen âge*, 531–39. Montreal and Paris: J. Vrin, 1969.

Curtius, Ernst Robert. *European Literature and the Latin Middle Ages*. Trans. W. R. Trask. Princeton: Princeton University Press, 1953.

D'Andeli, Henri. *The Battle of the Seven Arts*. Ed. and trans. L. J. Paetow. Memoirs of the University of California, vol. 4, n. 1. History, vol. 1, n. 1. Berkeley: University of California Press, 1914.

D'Alverny, Marie-Thérèse. "La sagesse et ses sept filles." In *Mélanges dédiés à la mémoire de Félix Grat*, vol. 1, 245–78. Paris: Pecquer-Grat, 1946.

Damon, Phillip. "Adam on the Primal Language: *Paradiso* 26.124." *Italica* 38 (1961): 60–62.

D'Ancona, Alessandro, ed. *In lode di Dante: Capitolo e sonetto di Antonio Pucci*. Pisa: Nistri, 1868.

D'Ancona, Paolo. "Le rappresentazioni allegoriche delle arti liberali nel medioevo e nel rinascimento." *L'Arte* 5 (1902): 137–55, 211–28, 269–89, 370–85.

D'Arras, Jean Le Teinturier. *Le mariage des sept arts*. Ed. A. Långfors. Paris: Champion, 1923.

Davis, Charles T. "Education in Dante's Florence." *Speculum* 40 (1965): 415–35.

De Lubac, Henri. "Saint Grégoire et la grammaire." *Recherches de Science Religieuse* 48, 1–2 (Jan.–June 1960): 185–226.

De Man, Paul. "The Rhetoric of Temporality." In *Blindness and Insight: Essays in the Rhetoric of Contemporary Criticism*, 187–228. 2d ed. Minneapolis: University of Minnesota Press, 1983.

De Nolhac, Pierre. "Manuscrits à Miniature de la Bibliothèque de Pétrarque." *Gazette Archéologique* 14 (1889): 25–32.

De Saussure, Ferdinand. *Course in General Linguistics*. Ed. C. Bally et al. Trans. W. Baskin. New York: McGraw-Hill, 1959.

Delhaye, Philippe. "'Grammatica' et 'Ethica' au XIIe siècle." *Recherches de théologie ancienne et médiévale* 25 (Jan.–June, 1958): 59–110.

Delisle, Léopold. "Les écoles d'Orléans au XII et au XIII siècles." *Annuaire-bulletin de la Société de l'histoire de France* 7 (1869): 1–16.

Della Terza, Dante. "Tradition and Exegesis: Semantics of Innovation and the Historical Context." *Modern Language Notes* 102 / 1 (Jan. 1987): 1–13.

―――. "An Unbridgeable Gap? Medieval Poetics and the Contemporary Dante Reader." *Medievalia et Humanistica,* new series 7 (1976): 65–76.

Derrida, Jacques. *Khôra.* Paris: Éditions Galilée, 1993.

―――. *Of Grammatology.* Trans. G. C. Spivak. Baltimore and London: Johns Hopkins University Press, 1974 and 1976.

Devoto, Giacomo. *Avviamento alla etimologia italiana: Dizionario etimologico.* Florence: Felice Le Monnier, 1968.

Di Capua, Francesco. *Insegnamenti retorici medievali e dottrine estetiche moderne nel "De Vulgari Eloquentia" di Dante.* Naples: Loffredo, 1945.

Donadoni, Eugenio. "*Paradiso* XXVI." In *Letture dantesche,* vol. 3. Ed. G. Getto, 525–48. Florence: Sansoni, 1961.

Donatus. *Donat et la tradition de l'enseignement grammatical: Étude et édition critique.* Ed. L. Holtz. Paris: Centre National de la Recherche Scientifique, 1981.

Douglas, Mary. *Purity and Danger: An Analysis of Concepts of Pollution and Taboo.* New York and Washington: Praeger, 1966.

D'Ovidio, Francesco. "Dante e la filosofia del linguaggio." In *Studi sulla Divina Commedia,* 486–508. Palermo: Sandron, 1901.

―――. "Sul trattato *De Vulgari Eloquentia.*" In *Versificazione romanza: Poetica e poesia medievale. Opere di Francesco D'Ovidio* 9.2. Naples: Guida, 1932.

Dragonetti, Roger. "La conception du langage poétique dans le *De vulgari eloquentia* de Dante." In *Aux Frontières du Langage Poétique.* Romanica Gandensia, vol. 9. Gent: Rijksuniversiteit te Gent, 1961.

DuCange, Charles, and G. A. L. Heschel. *Glossarium mediae et infimae latinitatis.* Graz: Akademische Druck- und Verlagsanstalt, 1954.

Dunchad. *Dunchad: Glossae in Martianum.* Ed. C. E. Lutz. Lancaster, Pa.: Lancaster Press, 1944.

Durling, Robert M., and Ronald L. Martinez. *Time and the Crystal: Studies in Dante's "Rime Petrose."* Berkeley: University of California Press, 1990.

Eberhard of Béthune. *Eberhardi Bethuniensis Graecismus.* Ed. I. Wrobel. Corpus grammaticorum medii aevi, vol. 1. Bratislava: Koebner, 1887.

Eco, Umberto. "Languages in Paradise." In *Serendipities: Language and Lunacy,* trans. William Weaver, 23–51. San Diego: Harcourt Brace, 1998.

―――. *The Search for the Perfect Language.* Oxford and Cambridge, Mass.: Blackwell Publishers Ltd., 1995.

Economou, George D. *The Goddess Natura in Medieval Literature.* Cambridge, Mass.: Harvard University Press, 1972.

Ellsperman, Gerard L. *The Attitude of the Early Christian Latin Writers Toward Pagan Literature and Learning.* Washington, D.C.: Catholic University of America Press, 1949.

Enciclopedia dantesca. 6 vols. Rome: Istituto della enciclopedia italiana, 1970–83.

Enciclopedia virgiliana. 5 vols. Rome: Istituto della enciclopedia italiana, 1984.

Eriugena, Johannes Scottus. *Iohannis Scotti Annotationes in Marcianum.* Ed. C. E. Lutz. Cambridge, Mass.: Mediaeval Academy of America, 1939.

Evans, G. R. "The Grammar of Predestination in the Ninth Century." *Journal of Theological Studies,* new series 33.1 (April 1982): 134–45.

Evans, M. W. "The Personification of the Arts from Martianus Cappella to the End of the Fourteenth Century." Ph.D. diss. University of London, 1970.

Ewert, A. "Dante's Theory of Language." *Modern Language Review* 35 (1940): 355–66.

Faidit, Uc, and Raimond Vidal. *Donats Proensals and Las Rasos de trobar.* Ed. J. H. Marshall. University of Durham Publications. London: Oxford University Press, 1969 and 1972.

Faral, Edmond, ed. *Les arts poétiques du XIIe et du XIIIe siècle: Recherches et documents sur la technique littéraire du moyen âge.* Paris: Champion, 1924. Reprint, Paris: Champion, 1971.

Ferguson, Margaret W. "Saint Augustine's Region of Unlikeliness: The Crossing of Exile and Language." *Georgia Review* 29 (1975): 842–64.

Fido, Franco. "Writing Like God—or Better?: Symmetries in Dante's 26th and 27th Cantos." *Italica* 63.3 (Autumn 1986): 250–64.

Fierville, Charles. *Une grammaire latine inédite du XIIIe siècle.* Paris: Imprimerie Nationale, 1886.

Figurelli, Fernando. "Il Canto XXVI." In *Nuove Letture Dantesche,* vol. 7, 127–49. Florence: Felice Le Monnier, 1969–75.

Filangieri di Candida, A. "Martianus Capella e le rappresentazioni delle arti liberali." *Flegrea* 2 (1900): 114–30, 213–29.

Fink, Bruce. *The Lacanian Subject: Between Language and Jouissance.* Princeton: Princeton University Press, 1995.

Fraenkel, Eduard. "Some Aspects of the Structure of *Aeneid* VII." *Journal of Roman Studies* 35 (1945): 1–14.

Freccero, John. "Dante e la tradizione del *Timeo.*" *Atti e memorie dell'accademia di scienze, lettere, ed arte di Modena* 4 (1962): 107–23.

———. *Dante: The Poetics of Conversion.* Ed. R. Jacoff. Cambridge, Mass.: Harvard University Press, 1986.

———, ed. *Dante: A Collection of Critical Essays.* Englewood Cliffs, N.J.: Prentice Hall, 1965.

Fredborg, Karin Margareta. "Universal Grammar According to Some 12th-Century Grammarians." In *Historiographia Linguistica,* vol. 7, no. 1/2. 69–84. Amsterdam: John Benjamins, 1980.

Freud, Sigmund. *The Case of the Wolf-Man (From the History of an Infantile Neurosis).* San Francisco: Arion Press, 1993.

————. *The Interpretation of Dreams.* Ed. and trans. J. Strachey. New York: Avon, 1965.

————. *Introductory Lectures on Psychoanalysis.* Ed. and trans. J. Strachey. New York and London: Norton/Liveright, 1977.

————. *Totem and Taboo.* Ed. and trans. A. A. Brill. New York: Vintage, 1918.

Fubini, Mario. "Canto XXVI." In *Letture dantesche,* 491–513. Florence: Sansoni, 1955.

————. "Ulisse." In *Enciclopedia dantesca,* vol. 5, 803–9. Rome: Istituto della enciclopedia italiana, 1970–83.

Fulgentius. *Fulgentius the Mythographer.* Ed. and trans. L. G. Whitbread. Columbus: Ohio State University Press, 1971.

————. *Opera.* Ed. R. Helm. Leipzig: Teubner, 1898. Revised by Jean Préaux. Bibliotheca scriptorum graecorum et romanorum teubneriana. Stuttgart: Teubner, 1970.

Gehl, Paul F. *A Moral Art: Grammar, Society, and Culture in Trecento Florence.* Ithaca: Cornell University Press, 1993.

Geoffrey of Vinsauf. *Instruction in the Method and Art of Speaking and Versifying.* Trans. R. P. Parr. Medieval Philosophical Texts in Translation, vol. 17. Milwaukee: Marquette University Press, 1968.

————. "The New Poetics." Trans. J. B. Kopp. In *Three Medieval Rhetorical Arts,* ed. J. J. Murphy. Berkeley: University of California Press, 1971.

————. *The Poetria Nova and Its Sources in Early Rhetorical Doctrine.* Trans. E. Gallo. The Hague: Mouton, 1971.

————. *The Poetria Nova of Geoffrey of Vinsauf.* Trans. M. F. Nims. Toronto: Pontifical Institute of Mediaeval Studies, 1967.

Gervais of Melkley. *Gervais von Melkley: Ars Poetica.* Ed. H.-J. Gräbener. Münster: Aschendorff, 1965.

Getto, Giovanni. *Lectura Dantis Scaligera.* Florence: Felice Le Monnier, 1966.

Girard, René. *Violence and the Sacred.* Trans. P. Gregory. Baltimore: Johns Hopkins University Press, 1977.

Giustiniani, Vito R. "Dante e la linguistica medievale e moderna." *Romanische Forschungen* 91.4 (1979): 399–410.

————. "Noterelle Gramatiche e Volgari." *Italica* 56 (Spring 1979): 369–76.

Godefroy, Frédéric. *Dictionnaire de l'ancienne langue française.* Paris: F. Vieweg, 1880–1902.

Godfrey de Breteuil. *Fons philosophiae.* Ed. M. A. Charma. Société des Antiquaires de Normandie. Mémoires, vol. 27:1, pt. 1. Caen, 1868.

———. *Fons philosophiae.* Ed. P. Michaud-Quantin. Analecta Mediaevalia Namurcensia, vol. 8. Namur: Editions Godenne, 1956.

———. *The Fountain of Philosophy.* Ed. and trans. E. A. Synan. Toronto: Pontifical Institute of Mediaeval Studies, 1972.

Grayson, Cecil. "'Nobilior est vulgaris': Latin and Vernacular in Dante's Thought." In *Centenary Essays on Dante by Members of the Oxford Dante Society, 54–76.* Oxford: Clarendon Press, 1965.

Greene, Thomas. *The Light in Troy: Imitation and Discovery in Renaissance Poetry.* New Haven: Yale University Press, 1982.

Gregory the Great. *Gregorii I Papae Registrum epistolarum.* Ed. P. Edwald and L. M. Hartmann. Monumenta Germaniae Historica, Epistolae 1–2. 1891–99. Reprint, Berlin: Weidmann, 1957.

Gregory, Tullio. *Anima mundi: La filosofia di Guglielmo di Conches e la scuola di Chartres.* Florence: Sansoni, 1955.

Gundissalinus, Dominicus. *De divisione philosophiae.* Ed. L. Baur. Beiträge zur Geschichte der Philosophie des Mittelalters, vol. 4. Münster: Aschendorff, 1903.

Guthmüller, Bodo. "'*Che par che Circe li avesse in pastura*' (*Purg.* XIV, 42). Mito di Circe e metamorfosi nella *Commedia*." In *Dante Mito e Poesia,* ed. M. Picone and T. Crivelli, 235–56. Florence: Cesati, 1999.

Hardison, O. B., Jr., ed. *Medieval Literary Criticism: Translations and Interpretations.* New York: Frederick Ungar, 1974.

Haring, Nicholas M. "The Liberal Arts in the Sermons of Garnier of Rochefort." *Medieval Studies* 30 (1968): 47–77.

Harrison, Robert Pogue. *The Body of Beatrice.* Baltimore: Johns Hopkins University Press, 1988.

———. *Forests: The Shadow of Civilization.* Chicago: University of Chicago Press, 1992.

Haskins, Charles Homer. "The Early *Artes Dictandi* in Italy." In *Studies in Medieval Culture,* 170–92. Oxford: Clarendon Press, 1929.

Hass, Louis. *The Renaissance Man and His Children: Childbirth and Early Childhood in Florence,* 1300–1600. New York: St. Martin's Press, 1998.

Hatzfield, Helmut A. "*Purgatorio* V." In *Letture dantesche,* vol. 2, 101–20. Florence: Felice Le Monnier, 1963.

Hawkes, Terence. *Stucturalism and Semiotics.* Berkeley: University of California Press, 1977.

Hawkins, Peter S. "Virtuosity and Virtue: Poetic Self-Reflection in the *Commedia*." *Dante Studies* 97 (1980): 1–18.

Henri d'Andeli. *The Battle of the Seven Arts.* Ed. and trans. L. J. Paetow. Memoirs of the University of California, vol. 4, 1. History, vol. 1, 1. Berkeley: University of California Press, 1914.

Heydenreich, Ludwig H. "Eine illustrierte Martianus Capella-Handschrift des Mittelalters und ihre Kopien im Zeitalter des Frühhumanismus." In *Kunstgeschichtliche Studien für Hans Kaufmann,* ed. W. Braunfels, 59–66. Berlin: Gebrüder Mann, 1956.

Hollander, Robert. *Allegory in Dante's "Commedia."* Princeton: Princeton University Press, 1969.

———. "Babytalk in Dante's *Commedia.*" *Mosaic* 8.4 (1975): 73–84.

Holtz, Louis. *Donat et la tradition de l'enseignement grammatical: Étude et édition critique.* Paris: Centre National de la Recherche Scientifique, 1981.

The Holy Bible. Translated from the Latin Vulgate. New York: C. Wildermann Co., 1911.

Homer. *The Odyssey.* Trans. R. Fitzgerald. Garden City, N.Y.: Doubleday & Company, 1961.

Honess, Claire. "Feminine Virtues and Florentine Vices: Citizenship and Morality in *Paradiso* XV–XVII." In *Dante and Governance,* ed. J. Woodhouse, 102–20. Oxford: Clarendon Press, 1997.

Horace. *Ars poetica.* In *Satires, Epistles and Ars poetica,* trans. H. Rushton Fairclough, 442–89. Loeb Classical Library. Cambridge, Mass.: Harvard University Press; London: William Heinemann Ltd., 1926.

Hugh of St. Victor. "Le *De Grammatica* de Hugues de Saint-Victor." Ed. J. LeClercq. *Archives d'histoire doctrinale et littéraire du moyen âge* 18 (1943): 263–322.

———. *De grammatica.* Ed. R. Baron. In *Hugonis de Sancto Victore opera propaedeutica.* Publications in Medieval Studies, University of Notre Dame, vol. 20. Notre Dame, Ind.: University of Notre Dame Press, 1966.

———. *Didascalicon de studio legendi: A Critical Text.* Ed. C. H. Buttimer. Studies in Medieval and Renaissance Latin, 10. Washington, D.C.: Catholic University of America Press, 1939.

———. *The Didascalicon of Hugh of St. Victor: A Medieval Guide to the Arts.* Trans. J. Taylor. New York: Columbia University Press, 1961.

Hunstman, Jeffrey F. "Grammar." In *The Seven Liberal Arts in the Middle Ages,* ed. D. L. Wagner, 58–95. Bloomington: Indiana University Press, 1983.

Hunt, Richard William. *The History of Grammar in the Middle Ages: Collected Papers.* Ed. G. L. Bursill-Hall. Amsterdam Studies in the Theory and History of Linguistic Science, series 3. Studies in the History of Linguistics, vol. 5. Amsterdam: John Benjamins, 1980.

Iannucci, Amilcare A., ed. *Dante: Contemporary Perspectives.* Toronto: University of Toronto Press, 1997.

Irvine, Martin. *The Making of Textual Culture: "Grammatica" and Literary Theory,* 350–1100. Cambridge: Cambridge University Press, 1994.

Isidore of Seville. *Etymologiarum sive originum libri XX.* Ed. W. M. Lindsay. 2 vols. Oxford: Clarendon Press, 1911.

Jacoff, Rachel. "'Our Bodies, Our Selves': The Body in the *Commedia.*" In *Sparks and Seeds: Medieval Literature and Its Afterlife. Essays in Honor of John Freccero,* ed. Dana E. Stewart and Alison Cornish, 119–37. Turnhout: Brepols, 2000.

————. "Transgression and Transcendence: Figures of Female Desire in Dante's *Commedia.*" *Romanic Review* 79.1 (Jan. 1988): 129–42.

Jacoff, Rachel, and Jeffrey T. Schnapp, eds. *The Poetry of Allusion: Virgil and Ovid in Dante's "Commedia."* Stanford: Stanford University Press, 1991.

Jacoff, Rachel, and William A. Stephany, eds. *Lectura Dantis Americana: Inferno II.* Philadelphia: University of Pennsylvania Press, 1989.

Jakobson, Roman. "Why *Mama* and *Papa*?" In *Selected Writings I: Phonological Studies,* 538–45. The Hague: Mouton, 1962.

Jean Le Teinturier D'Arras. *Le Mariage des Sept Arts.* Ed. A. Långfors. Paris: Champion, 1923.

Jernej (Zagreb), Josip. "Latino e lingue romanze nella concezione di Dante." In *Studien zu Dante: Festschrift für Rudolph Palgen zu seinem 75en Geburtstag,* ed. K. Lichem and H. J. Simon. Graz: Universitäts-Buchdruckerei Styria, 1971.

Jerome. *Lettres.* Ed. J. Labourt. 8 vols. Paris: Les Belles Lettres, 1949–63.

Johannes de Hauvilla. *Architrenius.* Ed. and trans. W. Wetherbee. Cambridge: Cambridge University Press, 1994.

John of Garland. *The Parisiana Poetria of John of Garland.* Ed. and trans. T. Lawler. New Haven: Yale University Press, 1974.

John of Salisbury. *Metalogicon.* Ed. C. C. J. Webb. Oxford: Clarendon Press, 1929.

————. *The Metalogicon of John of Salisbury: A Twelfth-Century Defense of the Verbal and Logical Arts of the Trivium.* Trans. D. D. McGarry. Berkeley: University of California Press, 1962.

————. *Policraticus.* Ed. C. C. J. Webb. Frankfurt: Minerva, 1965.

John Scotus Eriugena. *Iohannis Scotti Annotationes in Marcianum.* Ed. C. E. Lutz. Cambridge, Mass.: Mediaeval Academy of America, 1939.

Jones, Julian W., and Elizabeth F. Jones, eds. *The Commentary on the First Six Books of the Aeneid of Vergil Commonly Attributed to Bernardus Silvestris.* Lincoln and London: University of Nebraska Press, 1977.

Josephus, Flavius. *The Jewish War.* Trans. and introd. G. A. Williamson. Harmondsworth, Middlesex, Eng.; Baltimore, Md.: Penguin Books, 1959.

Kaster, Robert A. *Guardians of Language: The Grammarian and Society in Late Antiquity.* Berkeley: University of California Press, 1988.

Katzenellenbogen, Adolf. "The Representation of the Seven Liberal Arts." In *Twelfth-Century Europe and the Foundations of Modern Society,* ed. M. Clagett, G. Post, and R. Reynolds, 39–55. Madison: University of Wisconsin Press, 1961.

———. *The Sculptural Programs of Chartres Cathedral.* Baltimore: Johns Hopkins University Press, 1959.

Kay, Richard. "Priscian's Perversity: Natural Grammar and *Inferno* XV." *Studies in Medieval Culture* 4.2 (1974): 338–52.

Keil, Heinrich, ed. *Grammatici latini.* 8 vols. Leipzig: Teubner, 1857–80.

Kennedy, William J. "Irony, Allegoresis, and Allegory in Virgil, Ovid and Dante." *Arcadia* 7 (1972): 115–34.

King, Margot H. "*Grammatica Mystica:* A Study of Bede's Grammatical Curriculum." In *Saints, Scholars and Heroes,* ed. M. H. King and W. M. Stevens, 1:145–59. Collegeville, Minn.: Hill Monastic Manuscript Library, Saint John's Abbey and University, 1979.

Klapisch-Zuber, Christiane. *Women, Family, and Ritual in Renaissance Italy.* Trans. L. Cochrane. Chicago: University of Chicago Press, 1985.

Klein, Hans Wilhelm. *Latein und Volgare in Italien.* Munich: Hueber, 1957.

Klibansky, Raymond. *The Continuity of the Platonic Tradition During the Middle Ages.* London: The Warburg Institute, 1939. Reprint, Munich: Kraus International Publications, 1981.

Koechlin, Raymond. *Les ivoires gothiques français.* 2 vols. Paris: A. Picard, 1924.

Kristeva, Julia. *Desire in Language: A Semiotic Approach to Literature and Art.* Ed. L. S. Roudiez. Trans. T. Gora, A. Jardine, and L. S. Roudiez. New York: Columbia University Press, 1980.

———. *Étrangers à nous-mêmes.* Paris: Fayard, 1989.

———. *Interviews.* Ed. R. M. Guberman. New York: Columbia University Press, 1996.

———. "Noms de lieu." *Tel quel* 68 (Winter 1976): 40–56.

———. *Polylogue.* Paris: Seuil, 1977.

———. *Pouvoirs de l'horreur: Essai sur l'abjection.* Paris: Éditions du Seuil, 1980.

———. *Powers of Horror: An Essay on Abjection.* Trans. L. S. Roudiez. New York: Columbia University Press, 1982.

———. *La révolution du langage poétique.* Paris: Seuil, 1974.

———. *Revolution in Poetic Language.* Ed. L. S. Roudiez. Trans. M. Waller. New York: Columbia University Press, 1984.

———. *Strangers to Ourselves.* Trans. L. S. Roudiez. New York: Columbia University Press, 1991.

Künstle, Karl. *Ikonographie der christlichen Kunst,* vol. 1. Freiburg im Breisgau: Herder, 1928.

Lacan, Jacques. *Écrits.* Trans. A. Sheridan. New York: Norton, 1977.

———. *The Four Fundamental Concepts of Psychoanalysis.* Ed. J.-A. Miller. Trans. A. Sheridan. New York: Norton, 1981.

Laplanche, Jean, and J.-B. Pontalis. *The Language of Psychoanalysis.* New York: Norton, 1973.

Law, Vivien. *The Insular Latin Grammarians.* Studies in Celtic History, vol. 3. Woodbridge, Suffolk: Boydell Press, 1982.

Lechte, John. *Julia Kristeva.* London: Routledge, 1990.

LeClercq, Jacques. "Smaragde et la grammaire chrétienne." *Revue de Moyen Age Latin* 4.1 (Jan.–April 1948): 15–22.

Lehmann, Paul. *Die Parodie im Mittelalter.* 2d ed. Stuttgart: A. Hiersemann, 1963.

Leo, Ulrich. "The Unfinished *Convivio* and Dante's Rereading of the *Aeneid.*" *Mediaeval Studies* 13 (1951): 41–64.

Leonardi, Claudio. "I codici di Marziano Capella." *Aevum* 33 (1959): 433–89; 34 (1960): 1–99, 411–524.

Lo Piparo, Franco. "Sign and Grammar in Dante: A Non-Modistic Language Theory." In *The History of Linguistics in Italy,* ed. P. Ramat, H. J. Niederehe, and K. Koerner. Amsterdam Studies in the Theory and History of Linguistic Science, series 3. Studies in the History of Language Science, vol. 33. Amsterdam: John Benjamins, 1986.

Lombardo-Radice, Giuseppe. "Conobbe Dante il *Timeo* di Platone?" *Rassegna critica della letteratura italiana* 11 (1906): 241–46.

Lucan. *The Civil War.* Trans. J. D. Duff. London: W. Heinemman; New York: G. P. Putnam, 1928.

Lukacher, Ned. *Primal Scenes: Literature, Philosophy, Psychoanalysis.* Ithaca: Cornell University Press, 1986.

Lund-Mead, Carolynn. "Dante and Androgyny." In *Dante: Contemporary Perspectives,* ed. A. A. Iannucci, 195–213. Toronto: University of Toronto Press, 1997.

Lusignan, Serge. *Parler vulgairement: Les intellectuels et la langue française aux XIIIe et XIVe siècles.* 2d ed. Paris: J. Vrin, 1987.

Lutz, Cora E. "Remigius' Ideas on the Origins of the Seven Liberal Arts." *Medievalia et Humanistica* 10 (1956): 32–49.

Macrobius. *Commentarium in Somnium Scipionis.* Ed. F. Eyssenhardt. Leipzig: Teubner, 1868.

———. *Commentary on the Dream of Scipio.* Ed. and trans. W. H. Stahl. New York: Columbia University Press, 1952.

———. *Works.* Leipzig: B. G. Teubner, 1970.

Madec, Goulven. "*In te supra me:* Le sujet dans les *Confessions* de saint Augustin." *Revue de l'Institut Catholique de Paris* 28 (1988): 45–63.

Mâle, Emile. "Les arts libéraux dans la statuaire du moyen-âge." *Revue archéologique* 17 (1891): 334–46.

———. *The Gothic Image: Religious Art in France of the Thirteenth Century.* Trans. D. Nussey. New York: Harper Brothers, 1958.

Mari, Giovanni, ed. *I trattati medievali di ritmica latina.* Bologna: Forni, 1971 [reprint of Milan, 1899, edition].

Marrou, Henri Irénée. *A History of Education in Antiquity.* Trans. George Lamb. New York: New American Library, 1956.

———. *Saint Augustin et la fin de la culture antique.* Paris: De Boccard, 1949.

Martianus Capella. *De nuptiis Philologiae et Mercurii.* Ed. A. Dick. Leipzig: Teubner, 1925. Revised by J. Préaux. Stuttgart: Teubner, 1969.

———. *Martianus Capella and the Seven Liberal Arts.* Vol. 1: *The Quadrivium of Martianus Capella.* Ed., trans. and with commentary by E. L. Burge, R. Johnson, and W. H. Stahl. New York: Columbia University Press, 1971. Vol. 2: *The Marriage of Philology and Mercury.* New York: Columbia University Press, 1977.

Martin of Laon. *See* Dunchad.

Martina, Antonio. "Circe." In *Enciclopedia dantesca,* vol. 1, 19–21. Rome: Istituto della enciclopedia italiana, 1970–83.

Matthew of Vendôme. *The Art of the Versemaker.* Trans. R. P. Parr. Medieval Philosophical Texts in Translation, vol. 22. Milwaukee: Marquette University Press, 1981.

———. *The Art of Versification.* Trans. A. E. Galyon. Ames: Iowa State University Press, 1980.

———. "Matthew of Vendôme: Introductory Treatise on the Art of Poetry." Trans. E. Gallo. In *Proceedings of the American Philosophical Society,* vol. 118.1. Philadelphia: American Philosophical Society, 1974.

Matthews, Gareth B. *Thought's Ego in Augustine and Descartes.* Ithaca: Cornell University Press, 1992.

Mazzaro, Jerome. "Dante and the Image of the 'Madonna Allattante.'" *Dante Studies* 114 (1996): 95–111.

Mazzocco, Angelo. *Linguistic Theories in Dante and the Humanists. Studies of Language and Intellectual History in Late Medieval and Early Renaissance Italy.* Brill's Studies in Intellectual History, vol. 38. Leiden: Brill, 1993.

Mazzotta, Giuseppe. "Dante and the Virtues of Exile." *Poetics Today* 5.3 (1984): 645–66.

———. *Dante, Poet of the Desert: History and Allegory in the Divine Comedy.* Princeton: Princeton University Press, 1979.

———. *Dante's Vision and the Circle of Knowledge.* Princeton: Princeton University Press, 1993.

Meier, Gabriel. *Die sieben freien Künste im Mittelalter.* Einsiedeln and New York: Benziger, 1886–87.

Mengaldo, Pier Vincenzo. "Appunti sul Canto XXVI del *Paradiso.*" In *Linguistica e Retorica di Dante,* 223–46. Pisa: Nistri-Lischi, 1978.

———. "Gramatica." In *Enciclopedia dantesca,* vol. 3, 259–64. Rome: Istituto della enciclopedia italiana, 1970–83.

———. *Linguistica e retorica di Dante.* Pisa: Nistri-Lischi, 1978.

Merkelbach, Reinhold. "Aeneia Nutrix." *Rheinisches Museum für Philologie* 114.4 (1971): 349–51.

Miles, Margaret R. "Infancy, Parenting, and Nourishment in Augustine's *Confessions.*" *Journal of the American Academy of Religion* 50 (1980): 349–64.

———. "The Virgin's One Bare Breast: Female Nudity and Religious Meaning in Tuscan Early Renaissance Culture." In *The Female Body in Western Culture,* ed. S. Suleiman, 193–208. Cambridge, Mass.: Harvard University Press, 1986.

Minnis, Alastair J. *Medieval Theory of Authorship: Scholastic Literary Attitudes in the Later Middle Ages.* London: Scolar Press, 1984.

Minnis, Alastair J., and A. B. Scott, eds. *Medieval Literary Theory and Criticism c. 1100–c. 1375: The Commentary Tradition.* Oxford: Clarendon Press, 1991.

Mulchahey, M. Michèle. *"First the bow is bent in study . . .": Dominican Education Before 1350.* Studies and Texts, vol. 132. Toronto: Pontifical Institute of Mediaeval Studies, 1998.

Mulvey, Laura. *Visual and Other Pleasures.* Bloomington: Indiana University Press, 1989.

Muraro, Luisa. *L'ordine simbolico della madre.* Rome: Editori Riuniti, 1991.

Murphy, James J. *Rhetoric in the Middle Ages: A History of Rhetorical Theory from St. Augustine to the Renaissance.* Berkeley: University of California Press, 1974.

———. "The Teaching of Latin as a Second Language in the 12th Century." In *Historiographia Linguistica,* vol. 7, no. 1/2, 159–75. Amsterdam: John Benjamins, 1980.

Nardi, Bruno. "Il Canto XXVI." *L'Alighieri* 1 (1985): 24–32.

———. *Dante e la cultura medievale: Nuovi saggi di filosofia dantesca.* Bari: Laterza, 1942.

———. "Nomina sunt consequentia rerum." *Giornale Storico della Letteratura Italiana* 93 (1929): 101–5.

———. *Saggi di filosofia dantesca.* 2d ed. Florence: La Nuova Italia, 1967.

———. *Studi di filosofia medievale.* Rome: Edizioni di Storia e Letteratura, 1960.

Nicastro, Anthony. "Dante and the Latin Origin of the Romance Languages." In *From Dante to García Márquez,* ed. G. H. Bell-Villada, A. Gimenez, and G. Pistorius, 1–11. Williamstown, Mass.: Williams College, 1987.

Niermeyer, Jan Frederik. *Mediae latinitatis lexicon minus.* Leiden: Brill, 1976.

Norden, Eduard. *Die antike Kunstprosa,* vol 2. Leipzig: Teubner, 1898.

Norris, Christopher. *Deconstruction: Theory and Practice.* London: Methuen, 1982.

Nuove letture dantesche. 8 vols. Florence: Felice Le Monnier, 1951–72.

Oliver, Kelly. *Reading Kristeva: Unraveling the Double-bind.* Bloomington: Indiana University Press, 1993.

Oliver, Kelly, ed. *Ethics, Politics, and Difference in Julia Kristeva's Writing.* London: Routledge, 1993.

Ong, Walter J. "Latin Language Study as a Renaissance Puberty Rite." In *Rhetoric, Romance and Technology: Studies in the Interaction of Expression and Culture,* 113–41. Ithaca: Cornell University Press, 1971.

Orgel, Stephen. *The Philosophy of Images.* New York: Garland, 1979.

Le Origini: Testi latini, italiani, provenzali e franco-italiani. Ed. A. Viscardi et al. Milan: Ricciardi, 1956.

Origo, Iris. *The Merchant of Prato: Francesco di Marco Datini, 1335–1410.* New York: Knopf, 1957.

Ovid. *Metamorphoses.* 2 vols. Trans. F. J. Miller. London: W. Heinemann; New York: G. P. Putnam's Sons, 1929.

The Oxford English Dictionary. 2d ed. Oxford: Clarendon Press, 1989.

The Oxford Latin Dictionary. Oxford: Clarendon Press, 1968.

Padoan, Giorgio. "Ulisse *fandi fictor* e le vie della sapienza: Momenti di una tradizione da Virgilio a Dante." *Studi danteschi* 36 (1960): 21–61. Revised in *Il pio Enea. L'empio Ulisse: Tradizione classica e intendimento medievale in Dante.* Ravenna: Longo, 1977.

Paetow, Louis John. *The Arts Course at Medieval Universities with Special Reference to Grammar and Rhetoric.* University of Illinois University Studies, vol. 3, no. 7. Urbana-Champaign: University of Illinois Press, 1910.

Pagani, Ileana. *La teoria linguistica di Dante.* Nuovo Medioevo, vol. 26. Naples: Liguori, 1982.

Pagliaro, Antonino. "Il canto XXVI dell'*Inferno.*" In *Nuove letture dantesche,* vol. 3, 1–37. Florence: Felice Le Monnier, 1969–75.

———. "La dottrina linguistica di Dante." *Quaderni di Roma* 1.6 (Nov. 1947): 485–501.

———. "I 'primissima signa' nella dottrina linguistica di Dante." In *Nuovi saggi di critica semantica,* 215–38. Messina and Florence: D'Anna, 1956.

Panvini, Bruno. "Il latino e il volgare nel pensiero di Dante." *Siculorum Gymnasium* new series 19.1 (1966): 113–24.

Paratore, Ettore. "Caieta in Virgilio." *Atti della Accademia Pontaniana* new series 27 (1978): 313–21.

Passerin d'Entrèves, Alessandro. *Dante as a Political Thinker.* Oxford: Clarendon Press, 1952.

Patrologiae cursus completus; series latina. Ed. J.-P. Migne. 221 vols. Paris, 1844–64.

Paustian, P. Robert. "Dante's Conception of the Genetic Relationship of European Languages." *Neophilologus* 63 (1979): 173–78.

Pederson, Olaf. *The First Universities: Studium Generale and the Origins of University Education in Europe.* Cambridge: Cambridge University Press, 1998.

Peirone, Luigi. *Il "De Vulgari Eloquentia" e la linguistica moderna.* Genoa: Tilgher, 1975.

Pelikan, Jaroslav. *Eternal Feminines: Three Theological Allegories in Dante's "Paradiso."* New Brunswick, N.J.: Rutgers University Press, 1990.

Pertile, Lino. "L'albero che non esiste." In *Dante Mito e Poesia,* ed. M. Picone and T. Crivelli, 163–77. Florence: Cesati, 1999.

———. *"Così si fa la pelle bianca nera:* L'enigma di *Paradiso* XXVII, 136–38." *Lettere italiane* 43 (1991): 3–26.

———. "Dante e l'ingegno di Ulisse." *Stanford Italian Review* 1.1 (1979): 33–65.

———. "A Desire of Paradise and a Paradise of Desire: Dante and Mysticism." In *Dante: Contemporary Perspectives,* ed. A. A. Iannucci, 148–66. Toronto: University of Toronto Press, 1997.

———. "Paradiso: A Drama of Desire." *Word and Drama in Dante: Essays on the "Divina Commedia,"* ed. J. C. Barnes and J. Petrie, 143–80. Dublin: Irish Academic Press, 1993.

———. "'La punta del disio': Storia di una metafora dantesca." *Lectura Dantis* 7 (Fall 1990): 3–28.

Peter of Compostella. *De consolatione rationis.* Ed. P. B. Soto. Münster: Aschendorff, 1912.

Petrocchi, Giorgio. *La dottrina linguistica di Dante.* Messina: Editrice universitaria, 1958.

———. *Vita di Dante.* Bari: Laterza, 1983.

Pézard, André. "Adam joyeux: Dante, *Paradiso* XXVI.97–102." In *Mélanges . . . Roques,* 219–35. Paris: Champion, 1953.

———. *Dante sous la pluie de feu.* Paris: J. Vrin, 1950.

———. "Volgare e latino nella *Commedia." Letture Classensi,* vol. 2. Ravenna: Longo, 1969.

Picone, Michelangelo, and Tatiana Crivelli, eds. *Dante Mito e Poesia.* Florence: Cesati, 1999.

Pike, Joseph B. *Frivolities of Courtiers and Footprints of Philosophers.* Minneapolis: University of Minnesota Press, 1938.

Pinborg, Jan. *Die Entwicklung der Sprachtheorie im Mittelalter.* Münster: Aschendorff, 1967.

Pini, Virgilio. *Testi riguardanti la vita degli studenti a Bologna nel sec. XIII.* Bologna: Biblioteca di "Quadrivium," 1968.

Plato. *Timaeus.* In *Plato's Cosmology,* ed. and trans. F. M. Cornford. London: Routledge and Kegan Paul, 1937.

————. *Timaeus and Critias.* Ed. and trans. D. Lee. London: Penguin Books, 1965.

Pliny, the Elder. *Natural History.* Ed. and trans. H. Rackham. Cambridge, Mass.: Harvard University Press, 1938–63.

Plotinus. *The Six Enneads.* Trans. Stephen MacKenna and B. S. Page. Chicago: Encyclopedia Britannica, 1952.

La prosa del duecento. Ed. C. Segre and M. Marti. Milan and Naples: Ricciardi, 1959.

Quinones, Ricardo J. *Foundation Sacrifice in Dante's "Commedia."* University Park, Pa.: Pennsylvania State University Press, 1994.

Quintilian. *Institutio Oratoria.* Trans. H. E. Butler. Loeb Classical Library. Cambridge, Mass.: Harvard University Press; London: William Heinemann Ltd., 1980.

————. *Institutiones oratoriae libri duodecim.* Ed. M. Winterbottom. Oxford: Clarendon Press, 1970.

Rabanus Maurus. *De clericorum institutione.* Veröffentlichungen aus dem kirchenhistorischen Seminar München, vol. 5. Munich, 1901.

Rajna, Pio. "Le denominazioni *trivium* e *quadrivium.*" *Studi medievali* 1 (1928): 4–36.

————. *Il trattato "De Vulgari Eloquentia."* Florence: Le Monnier, 1896.

Remigius of Auxerre. *Remigii Autissiodorensis Commentum in Martianum Capellam.* Ed. C. E. Lutz. Leiden: Brill, 1965.

Reynold, Barbara. *Cambridge Italian Dictionary.* Cambridge: Cambridge University Press, 1962.

Reynolds, Susan. *Medieval Reading: Grammar, Rhetoric and the Classical Text.* Cambridge: Cambridge University Press, 1966.

Rheinfelder, Hans. "Lo efimero y lo impercedero en *De vulgari eloquentia.*" *Atlantida* 18 (1965): 700–717.

Rizzo, Stefano. "Il *De vulgari eloquentia* e l'unità del pensiero linguistico di Dante." *Dante Studies* 87 (1969): 69–88.

Robins, Robert Henry. *Ancient and Medieval Grammatical Theory in Europe.* London: Bell, 1951.

Rockinger, Ludwig. *Briefsteller und Formelbücher des elften bis vierzehnten Jahrhunderts.* Quellen und Erörterungen zur bayerischen und deutschen Geschichte, vol. 9. Munich: Franz, 1863.

Roddenwig, Marcella. "*Purgatorio* V nella esegesi antica e moderna." In *Dante Alighieri 1985,* ed. R. Baum and W. Hirdt, 31–47. Tübingen: Stauffenburg, 1985.

Ross, Werner. "Gott als Gärtner (zu *Par.* XXVI): Versuch einer Annäherung an Dantes Persönlichkeit." In *Dante Alighieri 1985,* ed. R. Baum and W. Hirdt, 49–62. Tübingen: Stauffenburg, 1985.

Rotta, Paolo. *La filosofia del linguaggio nella Patristica e nella Scolastica.* Turin: Fratelli Bocca, 1909.

Rowley, George. *Ambrogio Lorenzetti.* 2 vols. Princeton: Princeton University Press, 1958.

Sallis, John. *Chorology: On Beginning in Plato's "Timaeus."* Bloomington: Indiana University Press, 1999.

Salinari, Giambattista. "Il Canto V del *Purgatorio.*" In *Nuove letture dantesche,* vol. 3, 311–31. Florence: Felice Le Monnier, 1969–75.

Sandys, John Edwin. *A History of Classical Scholarship.* Vol. 1. Cambridge: Cambridge University Press, 1921.

Santangelo, Giorgio. *Dante e la Sicilia.* Palermo: Flaccovio, 1985.

Sapegno, Natalino, ed. *Poeti minori del trecento.* Milan and Naples: Ricciardi, 1952.

Scaglione, Aldo D. *Ars Grammatica: A Bibliographic Survey.* Janua linguarum series minor, vol. 77. The Hague: Mouton, 1970.

———. "Dante and the Ars Grammatica." In *The Divine Comedy and the Encylopedia of the Arts and Sciences,* ed. G. Di Scipio and A. Scaglione. Acta of the International Dante Symposium, 13–16 Nov. 1983, Hunter College, New York. Amsterdam: John Benjamins, 1988.

———. "Dante and the Rhetorical Theory of Sentence Structure." In *Medieval Eloquence: Studies in the Theory and Practice of Medieval Rhetoric,* ed. J. J. Murphy. Berkeley: University of California Press, 1978.

Schiaffini, Alfredo. *I temi del "De Vulgari Eloquentia."* Rome: Ateneo, 1949.

Schnapp, Jeffrey. "Dante's Sexual Solecisms: Gender and Genre in the *Commedia.*" *Romanic Review* 79.1 (Jan. 1988): 143–63.

———. *The Transfiguration of History at the Center of Dante's "Paradiso."* Princeton: Princeton University Press, 1986.

Scott, John A. *Dante magnanimo: Studi sulla Commedia.* Firenze: Olschki, 1977.

———. "*Inferno* XXVI: Dante's Ulysses." *Lettere italiane* 23 (1971): 145–86.

Sebastio, Leonardo. "Per una lettura del *De Vulgari Eloquentia.*" *L'Alighieri* 22.1 (Jan.–June 1981): 30–57.

Servius. *Servii Grammatici qui feruntur in Vergilii Carmina Commentarii.* 2 vols. Ed. G. Thilo and H. Hagen. Leipzig: Teubner, 1902–7.

Shahar, Shulamith. *Childhood in the Middle Ages.* London: Routledge, 1990.

Shapiro, Marianne. "Dante and the Grammarians." *Zeitschrift für Romanische Philologie* 105.5/6 (1989): 498–528.

————. *"De Vulgari Eloquentia": Dante's Book of Exile.* Lincoln: University of Nebraska Press, 1990.

————. "The Status of Irony." *Stanford Literature Review* 2.1 (Spring 1985): 5–26.

Shoaf, Richard Allen. *Dante, Chaucer and the Currency of the Word: Money, Images, and Reference in Late Medieval Poetry.* Norman, Okla.: Pilgrim Books, 1983.

Silverman, Kaja. *The Acoustic Mirror: The Female Voice in Psychoanalysis and Cinema.* Bloomington: Indiana University Press, 1988.

————. *The Subject of Semiotics.* New York and Oxford: Oxford University Press, 1983.

Silverstein, Theodore H. "Dante and Vergil the Mystic." *Harvard Studies and Notes in Philology and Literature* 14 (1932): 54–82.

————. "The Fabulous Cosmogony of Bernardus Silvestris." *Modern Philology* 46 (1948–49): 92–116.

Simone, Franco. "La 'Reductio Artium ad Sacram Scripturam' quale espressione dell'Umanesimo Medievale fino al secolo XII." *Convivium* new series 6 (1949): 887–927.

Simonelli, Maria Picchio. "Per l'esegesi e la critica testuale del *De Vulgari Eloquentia.*" *Romance Philology* 25.4 (May 1972): 390–400.

Singleton, Charles S. *Dante's "Commedia": Elements of Structure.* Cambridge, Mass.: Harvard University Press, 1954. Reprint, Baltimore: Johns Hopkins University Press, 1977.

————. "In exitu Israel de Aegypto." In *Dante: A Collection of Critical Essays,* ed. John Freccero, 102–21. Englewood Cliffs, N.J.: Prentice Hall, 1965.

————. *Journey to Beatrice.* Cambridge, Mass.: Harvard University Press, 1958. Reprint, Baltimore: Johns Hopkins University Press, 1977.

Smaragdus. *Liber in partibus Donati.* Ed. L. Holtz, B. Löfstedt, and A. Kibre. Turnholt: Brepols, 1986.

Spence, Sarah. *Texts and the Self in the Twelfth Century.* Cambridge: Cambridge University Press, 1997.

Spitzer, Leo. "Muttersprache und Muttererziehung." In *Essays in Historical Semantics,* 15–65. New York: S. F. Vanni, 1948. Originally in a shorter version in *Monatshefte für deutschen Unterricht* 36 (1944): 113–30.

————. "Speech and Language in *Inferno* XIII." In *Dante: A Collection of Critical Essays,* ed. John Freccero, 78–101. Englewood Cliffs, N.J.: Prentice Hall, 1965.

————. "La 'tipologia ideale' nel *De Vulgari Eloquentia* di Dante." In *Studi italiani,* ed. C. Scarpati, 191–212. Milan: Vita e pensiero, 1976.

Statius. *Silvae. Thebaid. Achilleid.* Trans. J. H. Mozley. 2 vols. Cambridge, Mass.: Harvard University Press; London: William Heinemann Ltd., 1928.

Stengel, Edmund. *Die beiden ältesten provenzalischen Grammatiken.* Marburg: Elwert, 1878.

Stock, Brian. *Augustine the Reader: Meditation, Self-Knowledge, and the Ethics of Interpretation.* Cambridge, Mass.: Harvard University Press, Belknap Press, 1996.

————. *Myth and Science in the Twelfth Century.* Princeton: Princeton University Press, 1972.

Strecker, Karl, ed. *Moralisch-Satirische Gedichte.* Heidelberg: C. Winter, 1929.

Suleiman, Susan, ed. *The Female Body in Western Culture: Contemporary Perspectives.* Cambridge, Mass.: Harvard University Press, 1986.

Sutter, Carl. *Aus Leben und Schriften des Magisters Boncompagno.* Freiburg and Leipzig: Mohr, 1894.

Tambling, Jeremy. *Dante and Difference: Writing in the "Commedia."* Cambridge: Cambridge University Press, 1988.

Terracini, Benvenuto. "Natura ed origine del linguaggio umano nel *De Vulgari Eloquentia.*" In *Pagine e appunti di linguistica storica,* 237–46. Florence: Le Monnier, 1957.

Théodulph of Orléans. *De septem liberalibus artibus in quadam pictura depictis.* Monumenta Germaniae Historica. Poetae Latini Aevi Carolini, vol. 1, poem 46. Ed. E. Dümmler. Berlin, 1881.

Thesaurus linguae latinae. Leipzig: Teubner, 1900–.

Thompson, David. *Dante's Epic Journeys.* Baltimore: Johns Hopkins University Press, 1974.

Thorndike, Lynn. *A History of Magic and Experimental Science.* 8 vols. New York: Macmillan, 1923–58.

Thurot, Charles. *Notices et extraits de divers manuscrits latins pour servir à l'histoire des doctrines grammaticales au moyen âge.* Notices et extraits des manuscrits de la Bibliothèque Nationale, vol. 22, part 2. Paris, 1869. Reprint, Frankfurt: Minerva, 1964.

Tiberi Claudi Donati Interpretationes Vergilianae. 2 vols. Ed. H. Georges. Leipzig: Teubner, 1906.

Tilton, Katharine. "Bibliography of the *De vulgari eloquentia.*" *Italica* 11.4 (Dec. 1934): 117–21.

The Tongue of the Fathers: Gender and Ideology in Twelfth-Century Latin. Ed. D. Townsend and A. Taylor. Philadelphia: University of Pennsylvania Press, 1998.

Toynbee, Paget. "Dante's Latin Dictionary (the *Magnae derivationes* of Uguccione da Pisa)." In *Dante Studies and Researches,* 97–114. New York: E. P. Dutton, 1902.

————. "Dante's Obligations to the *Magnae derivationes* of Uguccione da Pisa." *Romania* 26 (1897): 537–54.

Trovato, Mario. "The Semantic Value of *Ingegno* and Dante's Ulysses in the Light of the *Metalogicon*." *Modern Philology* 84.3 (1987): 258–66.

Uguccione da Pisa. *Die "Magnae Derivationes" des Uguccione da Pisa*. Ed. C. Riessner. Temi e testi, vol. 11. Rome: Edizioni di Storia e Letteratura, 1965.

Valla, Lorenzo. *L'arte della grammatica*. Ed. P. Casciano. Milan: Mondadori, 1990.

Van Marle, Raimond. *Iconographie de l'art profane au moyen-âge et à la renaissance*, vol. 2. The Hague: Mouton, 1932.

Van Winden, J. C. M. *Calcidius on Matter, His Doctrine and Sources: A Chapter in the History of Platonism*. Leiden: Brill, 1959.

Vance, Eugene. "Augustine's *Confessions* and the Grammar of Selfhood." *Genre* 6.1 (March 1973): 1–27.

———. "Augustine's *Confessions* and the Poetics of the Law." *Modern Language Notes* 93 (1978): 618–34.

———. *Mervelous Signals: Poetics and Sign Theory in the Middle Ages*. Lincoln: University of Nebraska Press, 1986.

Venturi, Adolfo. "Galleria nazionale delle stampe in Roma: Il libro dei disegni di Giusto." *Le gallerie nazionali italiane. Notizie e Documenti* 5 (1902), 391–92. Rome: Ministero della pubblica istruzione.

———. "Galleria nazionale e gabinetto delle stampe in Roma: Il libro di Giusto per la cappella degli Eremitani in Padova." *Le gallerie nazionali italiane. Notizie e Documenti* 4 (1899), 345–76. Rome: Ministero della pubblica istruzione.

Verdier, Phillipe. "L'iconographie des arts libéraux dans l'art du moyen age jusqu'à la fin du quinzième siècle." In *Arts Libéraux et Philosophie au Moyen-Age*, 305–55.

Vinay, Gustavo. "Ricerche sul *De Vulgari Eloquentia*." *Giornale Storico Della Letteratura Italiana* 136 (1959): 236–74, 367–88.

———. "La teoria linguistica del *De Vulgari Eloquentia*." *Cultura e Scuola* 5 (1962): 30–42.

Vincent of Beauvais. *Speculum doctrinale*. Graz-Austria: Akademische Druck- und Verlagsanstalt, 1965.

Viollet-Le-Duc, E.-E. "Arts (libéraux)." In *Dictionnaire raisonné de l'architecture française du XIe au XVIe siècle*, vol. 2. Paris: B. Bance, 1859.

Virgil. *Aeneid*. 2 vols. Ed. and trans. H. Rushton Fairclough. Cambridge, Mass.: Harvard University Press; London: William Heinemann Ltd., 1916–18. Reprint, 1986.

Virgil. *The Aeneid*. Trans. Robert Fitzgerald. New York: Random House, 1981.

Von Böck, M. *Die sieben freien Künste im 11. Jahrhundert*. Donauwörth: C. Veith, 1847.

Von Richthofen, Erich. "Traces of Servius in Dante." *Dante Studies* 92 (1974): 117–28.

Von Schlosser, Julius. "Beiträge zur Kunstgeschichte aus den Schriftquellen des frühen Mittelalters." In *Sitzungsberichte der Wiener Akademie der Wissenschaften philosophische-historische Klasse* 123.2 (1890): 1–186.

———. "Giustos Fresken in Padua und die Vorläufer der Stanza della Segnatura." *Jahrbuch der kunsthistorischen Sammlungen des allerhöchsten Kaiserhauses* 17 (1896): 13–100.

Wartburg, Walther von. *Französisches etymologisches Wörterbuch.* Bonn: F. Klopp, 1929; Tübingen: Mohr, 1950; Basel: Zbinden, 1957.

Webb, C. C. J. *John of Salisbury.* London: Methuen, 1932.

Weiss, R. "Links Between the *Convivio* and the *De Vulgari Eloquentia.*" *Modern Language Review* 37 (1942): 156–68.

Wetherbee, Winthrop. *Platonism and Poetry in the Twelfth Century: The Literary Influence of the School of Chartres.* Princeton: Princeton University Press, 1972.

Witt, Ronald G. "Boncompagno and the Defense of Rhetoric." *The Journal of Medieval and Renaissance Studies* 16.1 (Spring 1986): 1–31.

Wittkower, Rudolf. "'Grammatica' from Martianus Capella to Hogarth." *Journal of the Warburg and Courtald Institute* 2 (1938): 82–84.

Wood, Charles T. "The Doctor's Dilemma: Sin, Salvation, and the Menstrual Cycle." *Speculum* 56.4 (1981): 710–27.

Woodhouse, John, ed. *Dante and Governance.* Oxford: Clarendon Press, 1997.

Yalom, Marilyn. *A History of the Breast.* New York: Knopf, 1997.

Zenatti, Albino. *Lectura Dantis ("Paradiso" XXVI).* Florence: Orsanmichele, 1904.

Ziolkowski, Jan. *Alan of Lille's Grammar of Sex: The Meaning of Grammar to a Twelfth-Century Intellectual.* Speculum Anniversary Monographs, vol. 10. Cambridge, Mass.: Medieval Academy of America, 1985.

Zumthor, Paul. *Babel ou l'inachèvement.* Paris: Éditions du Seuil, 1997.

INDEX